Faith and Reason in Continental and Japanese Philosophy

Also available from Bloomsbury

Chinese and Buddhist Philosophy in Early Twentieth-Century German Thought,
by Eric S. Nelson
Comparative Philosophy without Borders,
edited by Arindam Chakrabarti and Ralph Weber
Wisdom and Philosophy: Contemporary and Comparative Approaches,
edited by Hans-Georg Moeller and Andrew Whitehead
The Bloomsbury Research Handbook of Contemporary Japanese Philosophy,
edited by Michiko Yusa

Faith and Reason in Continental and Japanese Philosophy

Reading Tanabe Hajime and William Desmond

Takeshi Morisato

BLOOMSBURY ACADEMIC
LONDON • NEW YORK • OXFORD • NEW DELHI • SYDNEY

BLOOMSBURY ACADEMIC
Bloomsbury Publishing Plc
50 Bedford Square, London, WC1B 3DP, UK
1385 Broadway, New York, NY 10018, USA

BLOOMSBURY, BLOOMSBURY ACADEMIC and the Diana logo are trademarks
of Bloomsbury Publishing Plc

First published in Great Britain 2019
This paperback edition published in 2021

Copyright © Takeshi Morisato 2019

Takeshi Morisato has asserted his right under the Copyright, Designs and
Patents Act, 1988, to be identified as Author of this work.

For legal purposes the Acknowledgments on pp. xii–xiv constitute an extension
of this copyright page.

Cover design by Maria Rajka
Cover image: Calligraphy (sumi in and brush on paper), Japanese School © Davis
Museum and Cultural Center, Wellesley College, MA, USA / Bequest of Merrill
Millar Lake (Class of 1936) / Bridgeman Images

All rights reserved. No part of this publication may be reproduced or transmitted
in any form or by any means, electronic or mechanical, including photocopying,
recording, or any information storage or retrieval system, without prior
permission in writing from the publishers.

Bloomsbury Publishing Plc does not have any control over, or responsibility for,
any third-party websites referred to or in this book. All internet addresses
given in this book were correct at the time of going to press. The author
and publisher regret any inconvenience caused if addresses have
changed or sites have ceased to exist, but can accept no
responsibility for any such changes.

A catalogue record for this book is available from the British Library.

A catalog record for this book is available from the Library of Congress.

ISBN: HB: 978-1-3500-9251-8
PB: 978-1-3502-1794-2
ePDF: 978-1-3500-9252-5
eBook: 978-1-3500-9253-2

Typeset by Integra Software Services Pvt. Ltd.

To find out more about our authors and books visit www.bloomsbury.com and
sign up for our newsletters.

To Katrijne Merrigan

Contents

Foreword	viii
Acknowledgments	xii
List of Abbreviations	xv
Introduction	1

Part 1 Methodological Reflections on Comparative Philosophy: Through the Works of Desmond and Tanabe

1	The Metaxological Methodology of Comparative Philosophy	15
2	The Metanoetic Methodology in the Contemporary Comparative Philosophy of Tanabe Hajime	37

Part 2 The Fundamental Problems of the Philosophy of Religion: Thinking through Rational Universalism

3	Kant and the Problems of Religion: Practical Reason and Rational Faith	61
4	Hegel and the Problem of the Philosophy of Religion: Dynamic Reason and Its Sublation of Faith	71

Part 3 Metaxology and the Problems of the Philosophy of Religion

5	Metaxological Fidelity to the Absolute and the Singular: From the Hyperboles of Being to the Agapeic Origin	87
6	The Metaxological Absolute and Its Interrelation with the Singular	113

Part 4 Metanoetics and the Problems of the Philosophy of Religion

7	Tanabe Hajime and Buddhism for the Philosophy of Religion	137
8	Tanabe Hajime and the Problems of the Philosophy of Religion	149

Conclusion	181
Notes	192
Bibliography	254
Index	265

Foreword

It is a pleasure to offer praise for the work of Takeshi Morisato. This book is a first-rate contribution to a number of philosophical areas: comparative philosophy; the philosophy of religion; the thought of thinkers like Kant, Hegel, and Tanabe Hajime and the Kyoto School; the dialogue of metanoetic and metaxological thinking. I am happy to speak warmly of its excellences as a scholarly and philosophical investigation. It displays close attention to primary texts and an impressive array of significant commentators, yet it seeks a distinctive path with its own philosophical attractions. The writing is well structured, engaging, and ambitious for illumination with regard to perplexing questions. It is not simply exposition and commentary but also a reflection on the questions themselves in a spirit of independent thinking.

While Takeshi's work is concerned with an exploration in comparative philosophy, he importantly focuses on the thought of the Japanese philosopher Tanabe Hajime, a significant figure in the Kyoto school, but who is not as well known in the West as Nishida Kitarō and Nishitani Keiji. His research on Tanabe's idea of philosophy as metanoetics, as well as his translation into English of a significant number of texts of Tanabe, offers some redress for the relative neglect of Tanabe in the English-speaking world. Takeshi is an important contributor to the East–West dialogue, not least because of his native Japanese and excellent English, but also because of his knowledge of both the Western tradition of philosophy and the Japanese. The interest shown to his work in Europe, the United States, and Japan is a sign that he has hit upon a very fertile area of study in comparative philosophy. One looks forward to a future of excellent work from him as a philosopher and scholar. From this book, it is evident that he has much to offer, not only in the field of comparative philosophy.

My own interest in Tanabe was occasioned by a contingent discovery of his *Philosophy as Metanoetics*. I came upon the book in a bookstore by chance and my experience was not altogether unlike the experience of Nietzsche on picking up Schopenhauer: I felt I had to read this book. I was taken by the view being presented and the courageous honesty of the writer about whom I then knew nothing. In fact, I bought two copies of the book, in order to give a gift to a friend who I now suspect was not as entranced as I was. I would not want to compare Tanabe to either Schopenhauer or Nietzsche, given that in Tanabe I was drawn to his vision of philosophy as metanoetics, and given that what this portends is in quite a different register to either of these other thinkers. I saw here a convergence with my own sense of the need of philosophy to pass through its own death in one form and to be reborn again in a form posthumous to the first life of thought. Confronting the so-called end of metaphysics, confronting the increasing colonization of all knowledge with determinate forms of scientific cognition, confronting the pervasive contemporary skepticism about philosophy as metaphysics, I had proposed in *Being and the Between* a form of metaphysical thinking as second born: born-again in the dimension of the overdeterminate, beyond determinate, and self-determining cognition. This would be metaphysical mindfulness in a second dimension, so to say, a mindfulness I associated with metaxological philosophy, as a post-dialectic rethinking of the constant and recurrent perplexities of metaphysics. This same metaxology as a second birth would also enter into a new porosity between philosophy and religion, and indeed with the poetic or the artistic. I felt I had found a companion in my quest who perhaps had also traveled some of the ways that lay before philosophy. With this work of Takeshi Morisato I can see much better that this realization of mine was not off the mark. His work has delivered an impressive confirming gift of the powers of philosophy as metanoetics and as metaxological as companioning ventures in thought beyond the forms of determinate and self-determining cognition.

The use Tanabe makes of metanoetics calls up the suggestion for thought of the Christian injunction: *metanoeite* (μετανοεῖτε). This is Christ's first word when he assumes his public ministry. But the "meta" of *metanoeite* can be understood in more than one simple univocal sense. It has been often translated as "repent," but the invocation of the "meta," and moreover, in connection with "noesis" invites us to pursue a new mindfulness that is to be "meta," as well as a new mindfulness of this "meta." Furthermore, this "meta" might be seen in the double sense of its Greek meaning as either being "above" or "in the midst." This doubleness, as I have thought through the "meta," has metaxological significance: we are in the between, in the midst of what is, but in the midst thus there is something of the "above" that we have to seek, or acknowledged that it comes to us. The tense togetherness of the "in-the-midst" and the "above" calls forth metaxological thought concerning the panorama of the given between as well as the invitation of what still is "more," more even than the prodigious "too-muchness" of the given "more" of the finite creation. Metaxology is a metanoetics in this sense, and Takeshi Morisato undoubtedly voices important reflections on this matter.

This book will be a great addition to engagement with the Kyoto school, and the articulation of the space between that school and significant ways of thinking in the West. Tanabe is a relatively neglected member of that school, perhaps because of his more overt willingness to engage with the Christian way of being. In addition, the willingness to invoke possibilities of thought suggestive of openness to Christian sources seemed to me a worthy thing. It is my impression that the Western engagement with the Kyoto school is mediated much more often through the eyes of a Heidegger or a Nietzsche, with the result that a more generous openness to Christian sources of metaphysical mindfulness is generally eschewed, if not silenced outright. Tanabe struck me as standing for an exception to that, and my suspicion is that just because of what I take to be his more sympathetic orientation to Christianity he has received less attention by Western thinkers who often are in flight from Western thought that, let us be honest, is hugely shaped by the legacy of Christianity, even when that fugue thought is itself anti-Christian.

I am struck also by Tanabe's engagement with the modern master of dialectical philosophy, Hegel, a companion, even if a contested companion, in my own efforts to think metaxologically. I have contested the view that Hegel is the last great Christian philosopher (suggested by Karl Löwith, for instance, a scholar who had his time in Japan). To the contrary, I think Hegel is in the philosophical business of creating a counterfeit double of God. The Hegelians who still are pious are affronted by this view. The Hegelians who are impious are indifferent to it. In the very recent past of Continental philosophy, any kind word about Hegel's philosophical enterprise was rarely heard. Tanabe is not a pious Hegelian nor an impious one, and yet he engages Hegel with great seriousness, and is to be honored for doing so with philosophical genuineness. In relation to Hegel's dialectic I have wondered if what he means by absolute dialectic does quite what I want to do with metaxology. My first intuitions of convergences and divergences are in many ways confirmed by the present work.

In a way, we are joined by our questioning the nature of dialectical philosophy and the desire to open up what I would call trans-dialectical thinking. Tanabe seems very much shaped by a response to the antinomies of Kant, and by a seeking beyond antinomic reason. And although one sees the hand of Hegel, there is a desire to go beyond him too. Absolute critique puts me in the mind of Hegel's advocacy of what in the *Phenomenology of Spirit* he calls "self-accomplishing skepticism" (*sich vollbringende Skeptizismus*). If reason turns against reason, at a certain extreme there is a reversal and transformation that takes place. This current work has renewed perplexities that continue to haunt one. I want to mention a few for which this book has offered light. There is criticism of Hegel as reverting to a logic of identity and Tanabe will speak of absolute mediation, but does the accent fall on a reformed sense of reciprocal mediation? How trans-dialectical is this? How crucial is the role of the other as other in all this? There is an impressive treatment of a certain asymmetry in the relation of absolute nothing and the finite beings. But if one wants to speak of a mutuality of mediation(s), does this go far enough in safeguarding the asymmetrical otherness of nothingness or God? Or does it turn back to an immanently holistic logic—even if not the logic of identity—a logic of immanent mutual determination? Is there enough of the "trans" in this? Hegel is tilted to the immanence of such a mutual or reciprocal determination, but in the end to the compromise of the "trans." All honor to Tanabe in stressing what seems to be the very strong priority of other-power, a stress I take to overlap with the metaxological sense of intermediation. Sometimes I wonder if Tanabe is somewhere between Hegelian dialectic and metaxology, rather than being coincident with the former or the latter. But then one has to recall how Takeshi connects agapeic generosity and the great compassion, and underscores so well the issue of the singular as singular.

Takeshi's work is impressive in the extensive range of its concerns, and in the intensive understanding of key concepts in a plurality of significant thinkers, not least among them Kant, Hegel, and Kierkegaard. His suggestions for comparative philosophy seem well-directed and thought-out. I have always believed that a metaxological philosophy would be a natural fit for scholars and thinkers involved in comparative philosophy. I had waited for someone else to pursue the possibility rather than take up the challenge myself. Takeshi Morisato has done us signal service on that score. The mutual engagement of philosophy and religion, whether metanoetically or metaxologically understood, is a strong excellence of this work. This is a book seeking a space beyond the epoch of default atheism, and seeking the promise of thought, again whether metanoetically or metaxologically, in conversation with religion as perhaps philosophy's most intimate other. This is a tale of passage in the between. We find fruitful soil for the nurturing of the philosophical possibilities of the between.

I take Tanabe as a remarkable cultivator of original insights in that vineyard. My own voice finds its other and comes back to itself renewed and extended fruitfully. Flight from the West meets again some echo of the West in its Japanese other, but this meeting in the between goes the other way also, as metaxology and metanoetics offer the space for a companioning togetherness of different philosophers. Companions in philosophy can be with each other, allowing the otherness of each, being in relation without freezing into dualistic opposition, or seeking a unity that would include one from the side of the other or vice versa. The between remains open but just because of that it remains full with the reserved promise of genuine communication.

This work is Takeshi Morisato's philosophical debut: it is a splendid arrival, giving promise of more still to come, and now to be warmly welcomed.

William Desmond
David Cook Chair in Philosophy, Villanova University, USA
Thomas A.F. Kelly Visiting Chair in Philosophy, Maynooth University, Ireland
Professor of Philosophy Emeritus, Institute of Philosophy, KU Leuven, Belgium

Acknowledgments

The final version of this text was prepared in Brussels. There is a striking similarity between the composition of my book and the structure of this city. If you walk for more than fifteen minutes in the capital of Europe, you will be amazed by its lack of uniformity, or what I would like to describe as its "exuberant chaos," which generates a beautiful diversity everywhere. While one street can greet you with a beautiful scene that could turn an everyday pedestrian into the protagonist of an epic poem, the next street seems to be eternally under (de)construction, with an unspeakable stench justifying Baudelaire's famous hatred of this town. Yes, the weather is terrible here and it is certainly not as beautiful as Paris. But if I go up and down from Gare Centrale to Flagey on my way to the Université libre de Bruxelles (ULB), I pass the Magritte Museum, the Royal Palace, a major bank headquarters that looks like an inverted beehive, and my beloved district, Matongé. My multicultural neighbors in this African quarter cannot be any more different from the multinational office workers at the European Parliament, just a few streets away. Flagey is a public space that is not particularly monumental or photogenic but somehow its lack of pretentiousness touches the hearts of the Bruxelloises.

I commute to the university by Bus 71 (which passes all of these places like the slowest roller coaster in the world). What I really like about my ride is that I always hear so many different languages being spoken among the passengers and this never seems to cause anyone to stare. In many other parts of the world, they would be immediately regarded as "foreigners." What Rebecca Solnit beautifully said in *Wanderlust* about the most European city of the United States, San Francisco, is also true of this most European city of Europe:

> Every building, every storefront, seemed to open onto a different world, compressing all the variety of human life into a jumble of possibilities made all the richer by the conjunctions. Just as a bookshelf can jam together Japanese poetry, Mexican history, and Russian novels, so the buildings of my city contained Zen centers, Pentecostal churches, tattoo parlors, produce stores, burrito places, movie palaces, dim sum shops. Even the most ordinary things struck me with wonder, and the people on the street offered a thousand glimpses of lives like and utterly unlike mine.[1]

This is an academic book in philosophy and it tackles central questions in the philosophy of religion. Of course, the coherence is of the essence in a project such as this. But, mind you, it is a comparative project that refers to Irish and Japanese thinkers. It deals with both methodology and philosophical questions, in combination with various types of poetry and literary expressions that highlight the creativity of the conjunction. If you are used to a Western style of philosophizing in one specific school of thought, or are much more familiar with Zen or Buddhist traditions than European critical engagement with philosophical methods, then this book might be as shocking to you as Brussels is to many visitors. This open togetherness of multiple voices, however, is the reality of the extraordinary ways in which we live our lives in Europe. The ways of philosophically thinking about our existence, too, should be truthful to the ways of our living. I hope this book will live up to the promise of an *intimate* cosmopolitan life that many of us are enjoying today, and will help us feel at home in the midst of a cultural diversity where comparative thinking emerges.

Many have helped me pave the passages in this book with philosophical rigor and literary playfulness. I would especially like to thank Katrijne Merrigan. Without her personal support throughout my doctoral research and post-doctoral uncertainties, I would have never been able to finish any of this. She is the one who taught me to appreciate what is in front of us every day. To her, this book is dedicated with love, and I hope she will help me write the next one.

My mother and brother in Tokyo have played a significant role in my life as a philosopher. When we suddenly lost our father in 2008, we could not imagine how we were going to organize our lives without him. Our perseverance as a family over the last decade has been the foundation for my growth as a thinker and human being. I would like to thank them for being there for me no matter how far away we were from each other.

I would like to thank my extended family in Turnhout, Belgium. Over the past years, Dr. Terrence Merrigan and Mevrouw Claire Vervliet have provided me with shelter and an infinite amount of gluten-free bread and great meat loaf, in addition to their boundless hospitality and kindness. I can't wait to put this book on one of the many shelves in Dr. Merrigan's massive library.

Among my friends, a special thanks must go to Cody Staton, Hugh and Eleonora Desmond, Pierre Bonneels, Rocky Esteraich, and Matthew Edelman.

Cody's dedication to philosophy and appreciation of multicultural culinary experiences have been a great inspiration to me. We talked so much about ideas, ramen noodles, food, football, relationships, and many other things (with or without Belgian beer) in the streets of Brussels and beyond. Our friendship and his editorial skills have been one of the key ingredients of this book, and I hope we will continue our quest in comparative philosophy for years to come.

Hugh and Eleonora are true friends who came to check on me many times, especially when I had locked myself up in my room, and worked on my doctoral project for days on end, like a madman in Leuven. Their diligence as academics and commitment as parents to their three boys have been inspirational to me. They have always included me into their lives, and together we have shared many great stories. Our philosophical discussions and day-to-day conversations about life always made me smile and helped me stay sane during my life abroad.

I would like to thank Pierre Bonneels for his inexhaustible patience and perfect detachment filled with compassion. His tenacity as an academic has allowed me to unleash my creative madness at our workplace. We have made a lot of progress together at the ULB, which might only be measurable in history. We can count this publication as one of the great achievements accomplished by team Japan at ULB-EASt.

Since the beginning of my philosophic studies at the University of Nebraska at Kearney, Rocky has been my best and most philosophical friend for more than fifteen years. It has been a pleasure to see that a fellow philosophy major can become a medical doctor. But even more so, it has always been a great encouragement to me to hear him say, "Philosophy is much more important than you think, Takeshi." I hope I will get to see this book on the top shelf of the library at his office.

Matthew Edelman taught me that John Coltrane could be the sixth proof for the existence of God. He is the only person in this digitized world who still writes me hand-written letters to tell me what is going on in his life, and I have no doubt that he will be reading this book in hardcover. I hope he accepts my writing as a part of our never-ending crusade for clarity.

To the European Network of Japanese Philosophy (ENOJP) members: European academia has not been an easy place to work on comparative and Japanese philosophy. When I started my doctoral project in 2012, I could not openly say, with full confidence, to other philosophers that there is such a thing as Japanese philosophy. After working with them as a team for more than five years, we have created annual conferences that charge no registration fees, an affordable peer-reviewed multilingual journal, and a publishing house that brings forth mostly creative philosophical books. They are a living testimony to the fact that we can change the world if we work together with passion and selflessness.

My researcher status at the Research Centre for East Asian Studies (EASt) and the Centre Interdisciplinaire d'Etude des Religions et de la Laïcité (CIERL) at the ULB is funded by the Actions de Recherche Concertée (ARC) Project, GENEsYs. Without this generous financial and tactical support, it would have taken much longer to publish this book. Many thanks to all the academic members and administrative staff who have made this project possible and have welcomed me as a team member at the ULB. Special thanks to my project supervisor and great Francophone philosopher, Baudouin Decharneux.

Last but not the least, I would like to thank William Desmond, an academic and a philosopher, whose scholarly achievements have made the content of this book possible. But, more importantly, I am deeply grateful for his Socratic character as a human being. It was only through his agapeic service that I was able to find my path in comparative philosophy, and our countless conversations about philosophy, literature, and all things related to life and being (often at Café Universum in Leuven) have been and will always be a vital source for my thinking. I hope you will receive this text as both a homage to the grand between and a token of my appreciation for our friendship in philosophy.

List of Abbreviations

Languages

Ch.   Chinese
Jpn. Japanese
Skt. Sanskrit

Works by William Desmond

AA	*Art and the Absolute: A Study of Hegel's Aesthetics*, 1986.
DDO	*Desire, Dialectic and Otherness: An Essay on Origins*, 1987; 2014.
DMA	"Dream Monologues of Autonomy," 1988.
PO	*Philosophy and Its Others: Ways of Being and Mind*, 1990.
BHD	*Beyond Hegel and Dialectic: Speculation, Cult, and Comedy*, 1992.
BB	*Being and the Between*, 1995.
PU	*Perplexity and Ultimacy: Metaphysical Thoughts from the Middle*, 1995.
HT	"Hyperbolic Thoughts: On Creation and Nothing," 1999.
BR	"On the Betrayals of Reverence," 2000; 2001.
AOO	*Art, Origins, Otherness: Between Philosophy and Art*, 2003.
ITST	*Is There a Sabbath for Thought?: Between Religion and Philosophy*, 2005.
BBCIT	*Being Between: Conditions of Irish Thought*, 2008.
GB	*God and the Between*, 2008.
AWASN	"Are We All Scholastics Now?: On Analytic, Dialectical and Post-Dialectical Thinking," 2011.
WDR	*The Willliam Desmond Reader*, 2012.
ISB	*The Intimate Strangeness of Being: Metaphysics after Dialectic*, 2012.
IU	*The Intimate Universal: The Hidden Porosity among Religion, Art, Philosophy, and Politics*, 2016.

Works by Tanabe Hajime

THZ	*Tanabe Hajime Zenshū*, 1963–1964.
PM	*Philosophy as Metanoetics*, 1946.
ELP	*Existence, Love and Practice*, 1947.
DC	*The Dialectic of Christianity*, 1948.

Introduction

The question of faith and reason in contemporary philosophy and a methodological preamble to comparative questioning

Augustine once spoke to his reason, "I desire to know God and the soul."[1] This "two-fold question of philosophy" constantly resurfaces in the history of philosophy.[2] The profound desire for the knowledge of the ultimate, and of our own "self" in relation to it, has driven humanity to think about the relation of faith and reason over generations. The founding motivation of this book is rooted in this desire, and it strives to voice its answer in the age-old question of the absolute—and of our relation to it—in the field of contemporary comparative philosophy of religion. It will reconsider the profound dissatisfactions with the ways in which our intellectual forefathers, namely, Kant and Hegel, had formulated their answer(s) to the question regarding faith and reason. From there, it will search for an alternative approach regarding the decisive answer to the very question in reference to the philosophical works of Tanabe Hajime (田辺元) (1885–1962) and William Desmond (1951–).

Most philosophers by now would already have a few procedural questions on the peculiarities of this project. Why comparative philosophy? Why do we start with Kantian and Hegelian philosophies of religion? Why do we look at the works of Tanabe and Desmond? From what standpoint do we question the relation of faith and reason and provide our answer(s) to it? In later chapters, I will develop the answers that Tanabe and Desmond provide to these probing questions. But unless preliminary responses to these questions are given, the initial set-up of the central question will suffer from a crowd of ambiguities and suspicions. So, by way of introduction, I will give my brief responses to these questions, set forth the central issue that this book aims toward, and provide short summaries of eight chapters that constitute this project as a whole.[3]

Why comparative philosophy?

My working definition of the term "comparative philosophy" in this section is a widely shared one: "a comparative examination of thinkers or ideas from two distinct intellectual traditions and one of them is from outside the western canon of philosophy."[4] The majority of Western philosophers question the actual significance or possibility of this approach within philosophy. This may initially sound strange to many of us who are familiar with the world outside academia.[5] The rapid growth in the mobility of transportation in the last century testifies to the undeniable fact of globalization. In the contemporary historical milieu, it seems obvious that we need to engage in some forms of the intercultural dialogue, or else the peaceful organization of our lives in modern times will be impossible. This is especially true for those living in places that have received a considerable number of immigrants and resident aliens. Nevertheless, there are several reasons that make it difficult to demonstrate the necessity of this field of comparative philosophy. First, comparative philosophy does not fall into the conventional categories that classify philosophical works in general. These are (1) historical categories (e.g., ancient, medieval, renaissance, modern, etc.), (2) topical categories (e.g., metaphysics, ethics, aesthetics, philosophy of science, philosophy of mind, etc.), and (3) the established schools of thought following the intellectual legacies of classical thinkers (e.g., Plato, Aristotle, Augustine, Aquinas, Descartes, Kant, Hegel, Nietzsche, etc.). Notice how (1) and (3) consist mostly of Western thinkers, and consequently, there is no need for the second to incorporate the works of those who fall outside the other categories.

As a result, "non-Western" thinkers are often awkwardly grouped according to geographical or linguistic categories (e.g., Eastern, Asian, Indian, Chinese, Korean, Japanese, Māori, African philosophy, etc.).[6] Comparative philosophy brings some of these non-Western thinkers into a dialogue with major figures from the conventional lineage of Western philosophy (i.e., 1 and 3) and thereby tries to shed light on the specific issues (i.e., 2) from allegedly wider angles. But this effort not only gives further trouble to the librarians (who must somehow scientifically categorize these books into a specific shelf) but also sounds superfluous to those who think that there are awfully a lot of thinkers in the West such that we do not need any more thinkers to our reading list.[7] The familiar milieu of philosophy traditionally engages in the common intellectual languages of Greek, Latin, German, French, and English. Clearly, the works written in languages that fall outside the Western canon compound the problem. When the significance of studying philosophy is emphasized only in relation to the works of Western thinkers, the voice of a comparative philosopher—expressing the heterogeneous mixture of familiar and foreign tunes—sounds like white noise to most of us in the West.

The weakness of comparative philosophy lies in that it looks into an intellectual tradition that has not been incorporated into the conventional lineage of another, and thereby generates ambivalent reactions in those who belong to the latter. But this weakness can be a strong asset for the general practice of philosophy. The discipline of philosophy is characterized by its inherent drive to question the foundation of its meaning. It carries a critical requirement to discern its limit in relation to what is other to itself. This long line of self-criticisms has repeatedly (re-)defined the significance of philosophy throughout history. This is the reason why there are so many different ways of doing philosophy. Thus, to be truthful to the practice of philosophy, our intellectual endeavor demands a dynamic process of self-examination—a process that could seriously undermine the fixed notion of what we have thought represents philosophy. I am not saying that by studying Western philosophy, our minds will somehow automatically recoil from questioning the ways in which our intellectual forefathers have tried to answer the important philosophical questions. Not at all! But I am saying that by looking into the intellectual works of a tradition that is foreign to our familiar boundary, we can become more attentive to the foundation(s) in which each of them is considered to be "philosophical" or "intellectual" in the first place. In the same way that the heterogeneous mixture of foreign and familiar tunes in the last century reminds us of the primordial sense of music (e.g., Jazz), a thoughtful approach to comparative philosophy should provoke our attentiveness to the primordial desire for philosophizing. The effort to construct a meaningful dialogue between two intellectual traditions can, therefore, facilitate our reflections on the depth of human thinking and its relation to religious faith.

Starting with Kant and Hegel

The Kantian and Hegelian formulations of the relationship between faith and reason are not only relevant to those who study their works, nor are they significant only in their historical contexts, but also indicative of the serious problems that we can find in the current (mis-)understandings of religious faith in the West. The rampant process of secularization in many European countries, and the widely shared notion that religion is something inherently against the autonomy of each free citizen, points us back to the ways in which Kant tries to clarify the distinction between philosophy and religion, as well as the ways in which Hegel explains the secondary status of religion in relation to the primacy of philosophy. As many postmodern thinkers were suspicious of the legitimacy of Kant's moral religion and Hegel's dialectical concept of religion, the death of God that leads to the death of religion is already at work in the Kantian and Hegelian notions of God, religion, and philosophy. This point will be further clarified in relation to the central question that this book will investigate. But it suffices to say here that Kant's and Hegel's philosophies of religion serve as a springboard from which we can dive into an inquiry concerning the nature of religion and its relation to philosophy.

Reading Tanabe and Desmond

Regarding the selection of Tanabe and Desmond as the main source of this project, I would like, first, to give a short biography of each thinker and then explain why the selection of these two philosophers is suitable for the purpose of this book. Tanabe was one of the founding members of the most influential Japanese schools of thought, the "Kyoto School" (*Kyōto-gakuha*, 京都学派). After teaching "Introduction to Science" courses at Tōhoku Imperial University (later Tohoku University) for several years, he finished his dissertation on the philosophy of mathematics and received his Ph.D. from the Imperial University of Kyoto (later Kyoto University) at the age of thirty-three in 1918. The most renowned Japanese philosopher, Nishida Kitarō (西田 幾多郎) (1870–1945), was directing the philosophy department in Kyoto at the time, and he invited Tanabe to act as his future successor in 1919. Between 1922 and 1924, Tanabe received a government grant to go overseas. In those years, he studied under Alois Riehl in Berlin, and Edmund Husserl, Martin Heidegger, and Oscar Becker in Freiburg.[8] From the time he returned to Japan in 1924, he continued to produce a great number of articles and voluminous monographs till his retirement in 1945. For the remaining seventeen years till his death in 1962, his abnormal rate of literary output did not show any sign of what we usually associate with the term "retirement." The relatively isolated residence in Kita-Karuizawa after the Second World War gave him the ascetic lifestyle necessary for bringing out his mature thoughts on metaphysics and the philosophy of religion. One of his later works published in the beginning of this period, *Philosophy as Metanoetics* (1946), is fully translated into English, Korean, Italian, and Spanish. But with regard to the fifteen volumes of *The Complete Works of Tanabe Hajime* (i.e., *Tanabe Hajime Zenshū*), that text occupies only half of a single volume.[9] Given that this translation roughly consists of 300 pages, the rate of Tanabe's productivity is quite exceptional. Although his life and thought are relatively unknown to most philosophers in the West, he is considered to be one of the most important thinkers in the East.[10]

William Desmond is an Irish philosopher and a distinguished scholar in the field of metaphysics and philosophy of religion. After finishing his MA in philosophy at the National University of Ireland Cork (later University College Cork) in 1974, he moved to the United States and finished his Ph.D. at Pennsylvania State University in 1978. His dissertation has been published twice as a monograph entitled *Desire, Dialectic and Otherness: An Essay on Origins* in 1987 and 2014. He began his publication of scholarly articles in the midst of his doctoral years in 1976, and since then, he has published seventeen books and more than 100 articles. His forty years of philosophical output almost equal the rate and quantity of publications that Tanabe had achieved in the course of forty-four years (1918–62). Desmond's scholarly achievement is most celebrated in the field of Hegel and German Idealism, yet the topics that he challenges in many of his other articles, book chapters, and newspaper columns show a remarkably wide range of his philosophical interests. The fact that he has written on Shakespeare, Solovĕv, and Chinese philosophy in some of them demonstrates how comprehensive his coverage of the history of philosophy has been, and how dynamic the process of his thinking in relation to the areas of philosophy that are relatively underdeveloped. What distinguished him as a philosopher in his own right, however, are his monumental contributions to metaphysics, namely, his philosophy of "metaxology."[11] He develops metaxology in a trilogy that unfolds this comprehensive framework of thinking in relation to metaphysics, ethics, and philosophy of religion: *Being and the Between* (1995), *Ethics and the Between* (2001), and *God and the Between* (2008). These works are supplemented by a series of works, which are themselves self-standing: *Art, Origins, Otherness, Philosophy and Its Others, Perplexity and Ultimacy, Is There a Sabbath for Thought?, The Intimate Strangeness of Being*, etc. Although his life and thought are relatively unknown to most thinkers in the East, he is one of the important thinkers in the twentieth to twenty-first centuries of the West.[12]

There are at least four reasons why I will consult the works of Tanabe and Desmond to revisit the age-old question concerning the relation between faith and reason in the works of modern thinkers. First, there are significant similarities in their philosophical developments. Tanabe initially worked on Kantian philosophy (including Kant and neo-Kantian schools) in a somewhat sympathetic manner to their method of philosophy. Yet, from early on, he managed to speak from the systematic viewpoint, where he clearly found some limitation in the Kantian framework of thinking. Especially for answering the questions in metaphysics, ethics, and philosophy of religion that he wanted to answer decisively, he differentiates what he thinks that Kant should say from what Kant actually says in his texts. In that regard, Tanabe aims to articulate his own thought through his reading of Kant. Through great encouragement from his notable students and colleagues (e.g., Miki Kiyoshi, Tosaka Jun, and Nishitani Keiji), he came to work on dialectic as a "concrete theory of the historical world."[13] This initially marks the transition in Tanabe's focus from Kant to Hegel. But his priority continued to be oriented toward the *Sache selbst*.[14] He realized that he was unable to articulate the truly concrete form of dialectic through the works of Hegel; accordingly, he began constructing what would later distinguish him as an originator of "Tanabean Philosophy," namely, the "absolute dialectic," or the "logic of species," as it is also called. It takes Tanabe roughly fifteen years to fully work out the satisfactory form of dialectical thinking, but clearly his engagement with Kantian and Hegelian philosophy in his early and middle period served as the way for the establishment of his own metaphysics and philosophy of religion.[15]

Unlike the radical transformation taken in the course of Tanabe's philosophical development, Desmond is much more consistent with regard to the standpoint from which he develops his philosophy. This standpoint is both regulative and constitutive of his ways of thinking. It is that from which, in which, and according to which he examines, elucidates, and unfolds the strengths and weaknesses of various philosophical standpoints in the history of philosophy. Essential to his effort of "thinking in the 'metaxu' or the 'between,'" Desmond strives to bring light to the multiplicities of interrelated philosophical ideas, and hence, he calls this method of thinking the "metaxology." Even though he does not fully spell out these ideas in his earlier works, there is already something metaxological about the ways in which he delivers his ideas in the first work, *Desire, Dialectic and Otherness*. The most accessible point of reference to navigate through Desmond's thinking concerns his distinction between the so-called "fourfold sense of being." From there, we can approach the systematic terms with more ease, which will help us grasp the kernel of his metaxological thinking (e.g., agapeic origin, hermeneutic of generosity, posthumous thinking, and hyperboles of being, etc.). All of these philosophical concepts belong to the trilogy.

Among the twenty-two titles of Desmond's monographs and edited volumes, four monographs are dedicated to his critical investigations of Hegel's dialectic, while at least three others provide chapters that elucidate the fundamental problems of Kant and German Idealism.[16] The trilogy itself also elaborates significantly on his interpretation of Western philosophical systems, which are all characterized by a tendency toward the univocal, the equivocal, and the dialectical sense of thinking. In this sense, Desmond's comprehensive analysis of these forms of thinking as a way to formulate his own thought shows its great indebtedness to his continuous engagements with the works of Kant and Hegel. Given that this text starts with its dissatisfaction with the ways in which Kant and Hegel conceptualize religion, it will be of great benefit to my overall efforts to work off the basis of Tanabe and Desmond, as they assume their critical stance toward the problem of metaphysics and the theories of religion from the perspective of Kantian and Hegelian philosophy.

Second, both Tanabe and Desmond provide original contributions to the discussion concerning reason's capacity to recognize its constitutive relation to the mysterious richness of faith beyond, and in the midst of, its autonomy. I will discuss these relations in more detail in due course. But the fact that both Tanabe and Desmond are not only great critics of previous thinkers but also self-standing thinkers who can present their own takes on the significance of religion, and its relation to philosophy, indicates at least two important factors for producing a critical monograph in philosophy. The first is this: the fact that they are philosophers in their own right can testify to the need that we should generate scholarly literature that sheds light on their works. Nobody has extensively talked about Tanabe and Desmond in the field of comparative philosophy. If this work can clearly outline their systematic thinking, it can be a welcoming addition to those who wish to understand the works of Tanabe Hajime and William Desmond. Although this may represent a piece of successful scholarship on philosophy at any respected standard of academia, it could still fail to be a philosophical text. What is required in this project, and this is the second factor, is not only to fulfill its scholarly function of elucidating the key elements of others' thoughts on the philosophy of religion but also to find its own voice through the comparative examination of the others and further to contribute to the pre-existing discussion on the question of faith and reason. Alexander Solzhenitsyn is absolutely right when he said,

> If we wait for history to present us with freedom and other precious gifts, we risk waiting in vain. History is us—and there is no alternative but to shoulder the burden of what we so passionately desire and bear it out of the depths.[17]

To really know the history of philosophy, then, is to know that the "history is us." So long as we write on philosophical questions, we must try the best we can to live up to this task of intellectual participation. This drive to be faithful to the spirit of philosophy is remarkably prominent in the works of both Tanabe and Desmond. This brings the strength of a comparative approach to these thinkers to the fore. By bringing an original thinker into dialogue with another, the examiner is pushed to find the self-critical stance from which he comes not only to demonstrate his understanding of these interlocutors but also, through his communicative relation to them, articulate his own self-critical thought and enter the very discussion of philosophy. This book will attempt to take on this common characteristic of a philosophical text, that is, to dare to ask the question that it cares and dare to find its own answer through its relative position to the other original thinkers that have done the same.[18] There is something in the works of Tanabe and Desmond that could liberate us from the heavy burden of historical scholarship or grant us a philosophic release to speak from a systematic (rather than a solely historical) point of view.

Third, the comprehensive frameworks in which these thinkers unfold their philosophical reflections can ease the initial shock and challenge of comparative thinking. The level of difficulty with regard to comparative philosophy typically increases as the distance between two thinkers increases. This distance can be measured at least in terms of history, culture, philosophical themes, and available scholarship. Take, for instance, the following sets of two thinkers: (1) Ōmori Shōzō (大森荘蔵) (1921–97) and Wittgenstein (1889–1951), and (2) Dōgen (道元) (1200–53) and Wittgenstein. For those who are familiar with the basic notions that these thinkers propose, it strikes us that the former is much easier to carry out than the latter. This is especially the case if we were concerned with the philosophy of language. This is because the historical and cultural distance between the two thinkers in the former is much closer than that of the latter. If we are aware that Ōmori had acknowledged Wittgenstein's influence on his own works, it seems quite unlikely that we face any great obstacles for launching this investigation. Moreover, this contemporary Japanese philosopher has written a monograph specifically on the philosophy of language in 1971, while there is still debate as to whether or not it would be appropriate to say that there is a "philosophy of language" in the works of Dōgen. In terms of philosophical themes, then, we can still hold the same verdict: it is much easier to work on the comparative examination of the first set of thinkers rather than the second.[19]

Now the distance between Tanabe and Desmond is much more similar to (1) than to (2). The strength of this pair, then, is that Western readers could easily enter into a dialogue between them without finding themselves constantly distracted by foreign terms or overwhelmed by the unfamiliar historical and cultural background. The fact that there is no prior scholarship on the Tanabe–Desmond connection might cause some worry.[20] As we have seen previously, both Tanabe and Desmond have extensively worked on the history of Western philosophy. The former, moreover, comes to incorporate some of the key elements from the Eastern intellectual tradition of Mahāyāna Buddhism into his philosophical discussions, while the latter's framework of thinking, which attempts to uncover the underlying themes in the entire history of Western philosophy, calls for our attentiveness to the energy of our self-transcendence. In other words, granted that the self can come to be fully itself when it finds itself in its communicative relation to the other, the system of metaxological thinking neither confines itself into a closed whole of self-thinking thought nor draws a monolithic boundary through which it distinguishes the Western intellectual tradition over here and the Eastern intellectual tradition over there. It requires a kind of "intimate strangeness"—a certain distancing that allows the other to speak for itself, but in its intimate communicative relativity to the other, in turn, it finds its own voice to speak for itself. Tanabe's practice of (comparative) philosophy and Desmond's self-transcending performance of metaxology, in this sense, are kindred spirits. The initial closeness between the thinkers can help us bypass the technical requirement for bridging their historical and cultural distance from each other, while the closeness of their thematic distance will further enable us to enter into their open dialogue—the constructive dialogue that can illuminate the deeper resonance in their distinct ways of philosophizing.

Fourth, the strong existential dimension that counterbalances the theoretical discussions of religious faith enables both Tanabe and Desmond to keep the intermediating relationship between philosophy and religion. Bret Davis argues that the excellence of Nishida's philosophical exposition of Zen lies in its faithfulness to the dual directionality of the preposition "of" in his "philosophy *of* religion."[21] According to Davis, the Western philosophical tradition has often fallen victim to the limited vision of the either/or: viz., either that philosophy uncritically presupposes a set of religious precepts in its foundation (i.e., religious philosophy) or in a manner of Enlightenment rationalism, the self-sufficient self-criticism of reason alone can "recognize the divinity of a [religious] teaching promulgated to us."[22] The "of" in the former emphasizes the superiority of religion to philosophy, while the "of" in the latter gives philosophy the independent status through which it alone can sentence the rational verdict on religious beliefs. Philosophy either serves as a handmaiden of religion or lords over the authority of religion as a rational judge.

The problems that we find in the Kantian and the Hegelian philosophy of religion are the various ways in which they try to hold on to the second horn, signaling the superiority of philosophy over religion. What is presupposed in this either/or is highly problematic: viz., the determinate rationality is granted to the side of philosophy, while religion is understood to consist of indeterminate beliefs and irrational practices (e.g., meditation, prayer, worship, etc.), such that the latter needs to be filtered through the determinate rationality of the former. Davis claims that "Nishidian philosophy" preserves both the continuity and discontinuity of philosophy and religion and thereby demonstrates its faithfulness to their interplay.[23] This attempt to recuperate the open mediation of philosophy and religion, which is key to our solution to the problems in Kant's and Hegel's philosophy of religion, is what Nishida's successor, Tanabe, existentially takes on as the task of metanoetic awareness, and Desmond, as that of metaxological mindfulness.[24] The works of these thinkers are, therefore, indispensable for contemporary philosophical discussions regarding the relationship between religion and philosophy.

A contemporary comparative standpoint

Finally, the question concerning the standpoint of this volume is not a determinate question to which I can give a determinate answer. Since it requires more than a paragraph to convey its dynamic movement, I must beg readers some patience. However, I would like to give its preview *via negativa*: a standpoint for comparative philosophy that can neither offer a mere static point from which one can juxtapose two thinkers from two different intellectual traditions in an external relation to each other nor can it suppose an Archimedean point from which one can observe each of their thoughts and their interrelation to each other from the outside. We are born into a certain tradition and, therein, come to form our own thought in our internal relation to it. We are in the midst of this process of forming and reforming our intellectual traditions; our confrontation with the strange other does not allow us to step completely outside of that process.[25] The complication of this internal process is multiplied in our modernity, for some of us are born in the West, yet extensively educated in the East, while others have enjoyed the opposite. But what we will see as an important task of comparative thinking is that when we look to the East from the West and find something foreign to our Western ways of thinking, we learn to give the space, where the other can speak for itself even in the midst of our process of forming our own tradition, and in doing so, we come to reformulate our tradition anew in its relation to the other. Since the same structure of intermediation is required among the Eastern thinkers in relation to the Western intellectual tradition, they can find their voices expressed in relation to the West. This book, therefore, will aim to achieve this two-way communication of comparative philosophy. Should this be successful, this text will claim that both Eastern and Western readers will be able to find that their traditions are expressed anew in their communicative relation to the other.

The main philosophical question

The central issue that this present volume deals with echoes the central problem that Kierkegaard finds in the Kantian and Hegelian configuration(s) of religious faith. Both Kant and Hegel interpreted the religious doctrines of the Judeo-Christian tradition in accordance with each of their own systematic conceptions of ethics. Kierkegaard seems to think that these interpretations ultimately risk the reduction of the relationship between the divine absolute and human individuals to the immanent universality of human/societal self-relation—the self-relation that is solely grounded in the autonomy of human reason.[26] This radical commitment to reason's autonomy in the works of Kant and Hegel foreshadows two crucial problems: (1) an eclipse of divine transcendence, and (2) an extirpation of the single individual in its relation to the rational universal as the immanent absolute.[27]

What concerns Kierkegaard in this twofold critique is that the systematic accounts of the divine-human relation in Kant and Hegel are faithful neither to the sense of the divine absolute worshipped in the Judeo-Christian tradition nor to the possibility of each human's relation to such an absolute in his irreducible singularity. Now some may argue in relation to the first that they are not interested in salvaging the Judeo-Christian God. But what is problematic here in the eclipse of divine transcendence is not only the Western problem of the "death of God" or "Godlessness" but also the one-way communication between philosophy and religion. As we have seen earlier, when a thinker reduces the "inter" of the interrelation between religion and philosophy to the one-sided either/or, she or he tends to think either that philosophy presupposes the mindless precepts of religious faith in its foundation or that philosophy serves as a reasonable judge that can validate the rationality of some of these precepts. In this case, what is dead is not only the sense of the divine absolute in the Western religious tradition but the authority of religion as what is other to philosophy. This is a crucial problem even for those who strive to give a philosophical account of their religious faiths in the Eastern traditions.

The second half of Kierkegaard's critique should be of great concern for all of us. If there is no divine absolute that is other to the immanent self-relation of human autonomy, there will be no other way for each of us as a finite individual to relate ourselves to the infinite universal but to negate the singularity of our finite existence. This further contains the following problematic implications: (a) the self-negating self-transcendence of the singular to the universal is ultimately a one-way movement, (b) while the worth of the finite singular cannot be granted to the singular. In addition to the reduction of religion to philosophy, we now face the reduction of each human being to the rational whole of humanity. If we say that Kant and Hegel are not guilty of (1), which is to say that we can preserve the sense of divine transcendence apart from the self- and intermediations of the finite individuals, then two problematic implications (a and b) of (2) will remain in relation to their understanding of religion. Whether the absolute is what is other to the self-relation of humanity or not, the relation of the absolute and the singular must be reconsidered.

We will see more in detail how these problems are inherent in the ways in which both Kant and Hegel unfold their understanding of the finite-infinite, particular-universal, and human-divine relations. Given these problems, we will ask the following questions: How can we conceive of the continuity between philosophy and religion without reducing their interrelation into a domination of one over the other? Could there be a sense of the absolute that is other to the self-organizing whole of human autonomy? Could a relation between the individual and the absolute beyond the rational universal be other than a heteronomous subordination of mind to the mindless precepts of faith? How could we account for the finite singular for the singular without disregarding its relativity to the divine absolute? How can we think of the absolute that can grant the worth and existence of the particular for the particular without compromising its status as the absolute? How can this absolute let the particular be for itself without ultimately reducing this particularity to and for itself? These are the contemporary reformulations of Augustine's twofold question of philosophy, which will drive us to investigate the nature of the absolute, the universal, the particular, and their relations to each other. This book will seek to answer these questions in and through the works of Tanabe and Desmond.

Structure of the work

We will explore the answers to these questions through the following eight chapters in four parts. In Part One, Chapters 1 and 2 will outline methodological reflections on comparative philosophy through the relevant ideas found in the works of Desmond and Tanabe. Instead of adopting a method that is foreign to their philosophical programs, I will seek to establish the very possibility of comparative thinking in the foundations of their respective systems. The "pre-established harmonies"[28] that sound through these examinations will be the methodological ground for my comparative examinations of these contemporary thinkers. In Part Two, Chapters 3 and 4 will investigate the Kantian and Hegelian frameworks of philosophy of religion. In these sections, we will witness the legitimacy of Kierkegaard's discontent and, on the basis of this existential malaise, the emergence of the fundamental problems of the philosophy of religion. In Part Three, Chapters 5 and 6 will explore Desmond's metaxological effort to elucidate how our proper understanding of the significance of the single individual leads to our understanding of the infinite absolute as divine transcendence. The intimate strangeness of the singular in relation to the ultimate shows a remarkable passage to recuperate the robust sense of divine transcendence without problematically conceptualizing the divine-human relation in dualistic terms. In Part Four, Chapters 7 and 8 will explore Tanabe's reconfiguration of human autonomy with its inherent openness to the divine absolute in reference to the Mahāyāna tradition (especially Pure Land/Shin Buddhism). In this part, we will discuss the general difficulty of treating Buddhism in the field of philosophy of religion and further investigate the noteworthy ways in which Tanabe brings various notions in Mahāyāna Buddhism (along with those of the Judeo-Christian tradition) to the fore in his mature works on the philosophy of religion. In the closing section, the astonishing consonance of metaxology and metanoetics will be amplified as a contemporary comparative response to the fundamental problems of the philosophy of religion.

Part One

Methodological Reflections on Comparative Philosophy: Through the Works of Desmond and Tanabe

1

The Metaxological Methodology of Comparative Philosophy

A preliminary reflection

The number of academic works published on the general methods of comparative philosophy is much fewer in comparison with those published in many other subfields of philosophy. The scarcity of scholarship alone calls for methodological reflections at the overture of any works on comparative philosophy today.[1] But what stimulates one to develop a method of philosophy also accounts for the motivations in which one's inquiry is practiced, which is to say that the investigation into a method of thinking necessarily entails philosophical self-reflection. For this reason, the establishment of a philosophical method has never been a simple task in the history of philosophy. As Hegel famously observes in the preface to *Phenomenology of Spirit*, many thinkers have been tempted to lay out what he calls "a lifeless universal"[2]—viz., a descriptive statement of what a philosophical method will aim to achieve, while failing to abide by the dynamic processes in which the significance of the very method becomes manifest. This should remind us of the old adage "one cannot learn to swim unless one jumps into the water." What is peculiar to reflections on ways of doing philosophy is that each of us must find ourselves always already immersed in the activity of thinking. If we give a comprehensive description of a method to which the process of our thinking ultimately belongs, then the ways in which we describe it should not be exempted from that very process. Rather, through our intense self-reflection, our viewpoint should account for the fact that the description of a philosophy presupposes the dynamic praxis of philosophizing.

A lack of insightful self-narrative in any methodological reflection leads to a failure to demonstrate the significance of the philosophical method. In the context of comparative philosophy, this failure to think internally about the possible ways of relating one way of thinking to another often runs a serious risk—i.e., the risk of conjecturing an abstract standpoint from which we can externally examine these thoughts and their relations to each other. Contrariwise, a comparative philosopher must always remain attentive to the reciprocal relationship between the method and its description. This means that she must internally navigate through two distinct paths of philosophical thinking and then examine if she can reach a comprehensive method that reflects what is at work in both of them. This is to conduct immanent critiques on the ways in which two thinkers conceive of the relationship between each of their philosophies and the other. Without doing this comparative examination, we will not be able to account for the proper relationship between them. Our discovery of the common ground in which two distinct paths of thinking can cross and crisscross each other will be the result of our self-reflections in and through their works. This chapter will follow through with this task of self-critique in its search for the standpoint from which we can compare Tanabe's metanoesis and Desmond's metaxology.

This search for the method of comparative philosophy will be conducted from two different angles. First, I will investigate the possibility of comparative philosophy through Desmond's metaxological way of thinking. Desmond's comprehensive (and flexible) framework of thinking, originating from his engagement with the entire history of Western philosophy, should serve as the suitable starting point and the appropriate preparation for our future explorations into the less familiar waters of non-Western thought. Second, I will examine how the absolute dialectic in Tanabe's metanoesis can help us understand the relationship between one framework of thinking and another. Neither Desmond nor Tanabe explicitly talks about the method of comparative philosophy. However, the process of their philosophical thinking opens the door to investigating such comparative methods of philosophy. In this second approach, I will also point out *en passant* some of the notable consonance between Tanabe and Desmond. After explicating the possibility of comparative philosophy from these two perspectives, we will be able to discover the common ground in which we can approach their works and therein demonstrate the proper method of comparative philosophy in accord with what is at work in the works of these thinkers.

Metaxology in the context of comparative philosophy

Desmond's original contributions to the areas of metaphysics, ethics, aesthetics, and philosophy of religion originate from his extensive reflections on fundamental philosophical problems rooted in the history of Western philosophy. Most of his works, however, do not make any substantive claim regarding the nature of comparative philosophy, nor do they explicitly incorporate the works of non-Western thinkers into the development of his own conceptual framework. In contrast, a more obvious place to look for comparative methodologies would be the Anglo-American pragmatist and process tradition. Robert W. Smid, for instance, cites William Earnest Hockings, Filmer S.C. Northrop, David Hall, Roger Ames, and Robert C. Neville as the leading philosophers who have made notable contributions to the development of comparative philosophy in recent years.[3] The extent of their contributions is noticeably different from one thinker to the other. But Smid indicates that they are bound by a common thread: they explicitly discuss the importance of incorporating non-Western thought to develop a genuine world philosophy and/or that they actually engaged in the projects that attempt to realize this incorporation. However fruitful the outcome of these efforts has been, that domain of philosophy is not a suitable environment that would allow us to engage the works of Desmond as a basis for thinking comparatively. It is very likely that Desmond's philosophy could be considered too "Eurocentric" from that perspective.[4]

Nevertheless, the fact that a thinker has worked extensively on the philosophical leitmotifs developed in the Western intellectual tradition is not a sufficient reason to disqualify his works as possible contributions to discussions concerning the methods of comparative philosophy.[5] For sure, we can characterize Desmond's thought as originating in the history of Western thought, and one may even argue that his philosophy owes much to a specific culture of Ireland.[6] This judgment not only neglects the fact that comparative philosophy requires a constructive dialogue between multiple distinct intellectual frameworks, but also follows the problematic logic by which non-Western thought have been marginalized from the main discourses of philosophy in Western academia for ages. As much as we ought to be open to the possibility of finding a source of inspiration, and insight into the works of non-Western thinkers, we should never forget the possibility of finding another source of great insight right under our noses in the works of Western thinkers. Without maintaining this double openness to two distinct intellectual traditions, we will fail to practice comparative philosophy in the genuine sense of the word, let alone to generate an effective method for it.

Note also that the practice of philosophy ultimately requires an answer to a raised question. What is important is not only to chase the letters of a great thinker but also to think about the question that these letters are addressing.[7] Since the systematic viewpoints that the letters signify are not exhaustible by the letters, every reader of a philosophic work can think with the philosopher, see through the viewpoints that these letters signify, and even when we cannot find any explicit treatment of a specific question that we would like to answer on the surface of these works, we can still strive to find out if there is any way to answer the question through the proposed viewpoints. This stance of "thinking with," or what I would like to call "intellectual companionship," will be taken in relation to the texts of Desmond, and it will enable us to describe how he would answer the question concerning the method of comparative philosophy.

Metaxology for the context of comparative philosophy

The framework of metaxological thinking, despite its lack of explicit reference to non-Western philosophy, is comprehensive in that it offers insight into the ways of practicing comparative philosophy. One of its characteristics is an effort to make sense of the intermediations between identity and difference, unity and multiplicity, self and other, etc. Its dynamic process of accounting for their interrelations is highly relevant for our understanding of the proper relationship between multiple frameworks of thinking in comparative philosophy. Put differently, metaxological metaphysics tries to make sense of the different ways of being in its communicative relation to the different ways of thinking about being and vice versa; hence, the relation between two ways of philosophical thinking apropos of given reality naturally falls within the scope of its analysis.[8] To prove this point, I will roughly take the following three steps: (1) I will introduce the "fourfold sense of being," (2) demonstrate its metaxological grounding, and (3) expose its implications to the current methodological discussions on the critical comparison between two distinct intellectual traditions.

The first step: A summary of the metaxological fourfold

The "fourfold way" of understanding being, according to Desmond, is practiced in the univocal, the equivocal, the dialectical, and the metaxological sense.[9] These quadruple layers of metaphysical thinking represent major trends in the Western history of philosophy. The univocal sense emphasizes the unity of mind and being. It strives to demonstrate the intelligibility of reality through the recognition of an immediate togetherness between the structure of consciousness and that of being. The best example of univocal thinking can be found in our mathematical reasoning, where the rigid self-identity of a natural number is firmly defined as that which equals nothing but itself.[10] The application of this univocal thinking to our understanding of reality can be traced back to its first appearance in the fragments of Parmenides. Yet the most prominent manifestation of it occurs in the notion of *mathesis unviersalis*, envisioned by modern philosophers like Descartes and Leibniz.[11] The second, equivocal sense calls for our attunement to the "unmediated difference between mind and being."[12] It constantly urges us to re-evaluate our confidence in their immediate sameness and to question seriously the intrinsic value of their togetherness. Heraclitus' infinite flux and Nietzsche's transvaluation of all values are the prime examples of the call. We are called to attune ourselves to that which is other to the self-identity of univocal thinking.

The dialectical sense configures the "mediated conjunction of mind and being."[13] It intermediates the formal unity of the univocal with the concrete multiplicity of the equivocal. Desmond argues that "at least in modern philosophy, [this mediation] is primarily self-mediation, [and] hence the side of the same tends to be privileged in this conjunction."[14] The dialectical sense thus recognizes the interplay of univocity and equivocity, specifically in terms of unity's self-determination. This means that unity takes multiplicity as an indispensable moment for its development into the concrete unity of multiplicity. This is neither a simple affirmation of unity in the univocal sense nor an obstinate rejection of it in the equivocal sense, but a complex reconfiguration of their porous relativity that comprises the concrete totality of multiplicities. What is distinct in this dialectical way of thinking about being is that the sameness is ultimately crowned as that which blooms into the totality of difference, whereby the latter is never given for itself, but always for the former to mediate with itself. The concrete unity of multiplicity constitutes the immanent whole in this manner of metaphysical thinking.

Similar to the dialectical sense, the metaxological shows its faithfulness to the "mediated community of mind and being."[15] It recognizes the interplay between unity and multiplicity and tries to make sense of this interrelation. In contrast with dialectical thinking, however,

> [the metaxological sense] calls attention to a pluralized mediation, beyond closed self—mediation from the side of the same, and hospitable to the mediation of the other, or transcendent, out of its own otherness. It puts the emphasis on an intermediation, not a self-mediation, however dialectically qualified. ... [T]he *inter* is shaped plurally by different mediations of mind and being, same and other, mediations not subsumable into one total self-mediation.[16]

From the viewpoint of metaxology, the dialectical mediation is seen to be ultimately one-sided, for it undermines the status of otherness to the secondary position in relation to the totalizing unity of sameness. Contrariwise, the metaxological awareness remains attentive to the plurality of mediations in the self, the other, and their communicative relation to each other. It is mindful of the fact that the self can fully mediate with itself in its porous relativity to the other, while this intermediation does not deprive the other of its original status of being—that it is given to be for itself. Metaxology, in this sense, refrains from seizing otherness for the determination of the self as it is seen in dialectical thinking. But it proposes to give the space in which the self can let the other be for the other, and thereby each of them can enter into its open communication with the other.

This "giving of the space" does not mean that the self produces the space in which its intermediation with the other takes place within the more comprehensive framework of its self-determining process.[17] (This is precisely what the dialectical understanding of being tries to demonstrate.) Rather, it indicates the openness of the self to the very space as that which is prior to and foundational for its self-mediations. This primal space is not reducible to the immanent totality of self-determining unity but allows the plurality of self- and intermediations both for the self and the other.[18] Desmond calls this hyperbolic space, which is both transcendent to and immanent in the plurality of mediations, the "between" (*metaxu*). In making sense of this space or the between, being is always seen as an unmerited gift for all that is—if it is anything at all—to be. It is given both to the self and the other. It is given to each of them to be for itself, and given to both of them to be for each other. Hence, the proper relation between self and other, sameness and difference, or unity and multiplicity must reflect their intermediations that account both for their irreducible difference from and indispensable relativity with each other. This irresistible intimation and liberating distancing demonstrate the metaxological mindfulness that shows its fidelity to the "intimate strangeness" of being.

The second step: The metaxological grounding of the fourfold

The awareness of this "intimate strangeness" saves us from the temptation to master the middle space (i.e., the between) of mind and being through ourselves alone. It enables us to break away from their one-way communication in the dialectical sense and further releases us into their open community. It constitutes a kind of community, where mind and being are in an intimate rapport with each other. This community is open because mind knows that the plurivocal (inter-)mediation of being is not dictated entirely by the self-mediation of mind. The metaxological sense of being, in other words, always pays attention to the *doubleness* of the mediations between self and other: the self is mediating itself through its intermediation with the other, as the other is mediating itself through its intermediation with the self. The mediations are neither subsumable to nor identical with the other. Nor are they together subsumable into one more inclusive dialectic/speculative self-mediation of the Hegelian type. The metaxological mind lets being be, lets being fully realize itself in its relativity to mind, and through this compassionate mindfulness toward being, comes to understand the full significance both of itself and of what is other to itself. The metaxological mind that remains aware that being is neither reducible nor entirely subsumable to its own self-mediation appropriately articulates the self- and intermediations of mind and being as the plurivocal community enabled in, and manifested through, the hyperbolic space of the between.

The metaxological configuration of being and mind, moreover, is attentive to their multilayered community or what Desmond calls their "communivocity."[19] Its relation to the previous threefold of being, in this sense, is neither a simple negation nor dialectical sublation, but a comprehensive acknowledgment of their legitimacy and limitations. The univocal simply denies the equivocal and vice versa. The dialectical recognizes the mutual implication of these two but fails to work out their fuller intermediation by contracting the openness of their two-way communication into one-sided self-determining monologue. Instead, the metaxological configuration claims to recognize the full significance of all three by taking into account the primordial togetherness of mind and being (i.e., the univocal), their profound difference through which each of them comes to insist on its singularity (i.e., the equivocal), and the open mediation of sameness and difference in which the possibility of collapsing their intermediation into the self-determining sameness (i.e., the dialectical) is granted. All three senses are different ways of being—being that comes out of and takes place in the mysterious richness of the middle space—and the different ways of "minding" that are called for the various manifestations of dynamic being in the very space of given reality.

What the metaxological sense denies, then, is the claim to ultimacy made by any of these three voices at the cost of the other. Each of them has some legitimacy in its way of understanding the given reality, but to reduce these different senses into either one of them is to blind oneself to the ontological matrix of reality, namely, the ultimate plurivocity of being. The fourfold understanding of being in the metaxological sense refuses to think of being only in terms of its own self-mediation, or favor one way of understanding over the other but serves instead as a patient companion to the communicative relations in which being can fully realize itself.[20] Thus, the quadruple ways of "being" and "being mindful" in the metaxological sense demonstrate the full significance of the univocal, the equivocal, and the dialectical sense of being by showing both their indispensable importance and undeniable limitations for understanding the plurivocity of being.

Before the third step: The problem of the division between the West and the non-West

What implications can we draw from the metaxological fourfold in relation to the current methodological discussions concerning the critical comparison of Western and non-Western philosophy? Many scholars in the field of comparative and intercultural philosophy have argued that philosophy has been *univocally* Western.[21] They claim that the majority of the thinkers in the history of philosophy have emphasized the Western origin of philosophy, while (whether intentionally or unintentionally) marginalizing other forms of human thinking that originated from different historical and cultural roots. Despite different understandings of philosophy as such, they generally hold that the ultimate legitimacy of philosophy belongs to the intellectual tradition of the West. Perhaps this explains the dearth of discussions regarding the relevance of other intellectual traditions until the end of nineteenth century.

Now this criticism could take much more complicated forms once we try to clarify what counts as the "Western" history of thought and to what degree one is responsible for the long-lasting negligence of the non-Western thought in the West. Some feminists and philosophers of race would argue that it belongs to a group of privileged white European males, while some comparative philosophers, along with a few specialists of the comparative religions, attribute the dismissal of non-Western thought to the (allegedly) rigid self-identity of the Judeo-Christian faith.[22] As we can see, the list of victims that are marginalized from the formation of the "history of ideas" goes longer, depending on how we group the victimizers.[23] The process of persecuting a certain thinker and measuring a degree to which she or he is responsible for the marginalization also suffers from great complications.[24]

The thinkers who have incorporated non-Western thought into the formation of their own thinking (e.g., Hegel, Schopenhauer, and Nietzsche), moreover, have received mixed reviews. For instance, Schopenhauer's articulation of Indian philosophy seems misguided according to anyone with a basic knowledge of its tradition.[25] The same goes for Hegel in relation to Chinese philosophy. Some may argue that in view of what was available at the time, their efforts to understand non-Western modes of philosophy were not at all shabby. We may even go so far as to say that their works contributed to the growth of comparative philosophy in the years to follow. Others may still seriously take issue with the ways in which they approached Indian and Chinese philosophy. At any rate, it can easily take the length of a monograph to give a comprehensive taxonomy of the Western history of thought in relation to non-Western philosophy, what has been marginalized from it, and the degree to which a certain thinker is responsible for the discriminatory development of so-called "intellectual history." It will certainly be a much more complicated process to generate an argument that satisfactorily qualifies an appropriate path of conceiving the division between Western and non-Western philosophy.

A survey of contemporary Western philosophy

The possible ways of demarcating the division between Western and non-Western thought do not discount the fact that most comparative theorists maintain their basic agreement: viz., philosophy has been *univocally* Western. Their responses have by and large sought the possible integration or interrelation between what is univocally claimed to be the *philosophia perennis* and what is other to this univocity, just as much as about the differences between the two approaches to philosophy. This means that the problem of comparative philosophy—i.e., the philosophical problem of comparing two systems of thinking rooted in different cultural and intellectual contexts—ultimately lies in the question of how we can work out the relationship between universality and particularity, univocity and equivocity, unity and multiplicity, and sameness and difference. Looking at the Western/non-Western division from this systematic perspective, we should be able to give a reasonable account of their intermediation, as well as coming to terms with the exclusive univocity of the former. In that regard, I will, first, refer to some arguments that clearly set forth the univocity of Western philosophy in contemporary contexts. Second, I provide metaxological analyses of the reasons why the univocal presentation of philosophy might have come about in the contemporary West (or Europe); and finally, I explore the possible ways in which we can practice the Western and non-Western intermediations.

The trailblazer of intercultural philosophy in Germany, Ram Adhar Mall, argues that the term *philosophia perennis* was originally used by Agostino Steuco (1497–1548) to indicate the fundamental truths belonging to all humanity beyond their cultural and racial differences, but "in spite of this liberal attitude, philosophers have not stopped claiming to have located *philosophia perennis* in a particular race, culture or philosophical convention."[26] Mall further names four modern thinkers who are guilty of this crime (namely, Hegel, Husserl, Heidegger, and Gadamar), while he pardons Jaspers among some others.[27] What Mall finds faulty in the works of these philosophers is that they end up privileging philosophy that originates from a particular cultural background, as well as their (somewhat naïve) arrogance toward other intellectual traditions.

Take, for instance, Mall's issue with Husserl. In his *Vienna Lecture*, Husserl elaborates on the form of Europe—namely, the spiritual backbone that runs through all European nations as the common "consciousness of homeland."[28] He argues that it runs through other historico-cultural spheres like the "Indian historical sphere [*die indische Geschichtlichkeit*]," but these forms of consciousness are quite foreign to each other.[29] He further articulates:

> There is something unique [in Europe] that is recognized in us by all other human groups, too, something that, quite apart from all considerations of utility, becomes a motive for them to Europeanize themselves even in their unbroken

will to spiritual self-preservation; whereas we, if we understand ourselves properly, would never Indianize ourselves, for example. I mean that we feel (and in spite of all obscurity this feeling is probably legitimate) that an entelechy is inborn in our European civilization which holds sway throughout all the changing shapes of Europe and accords to them the sense of a development toward an ideal shape of life and being as an eternal pole.[30]

The particular kinship that runs through European nations seems to be equal with the other that runs through the diversity of linguistic, ethnic, political communities in India. Since the intellectual, cultural, and spiritual development of such consciousness in India receives great benefit from internally grasping that of the other in Europe, it seems quite logical to consider the possibility of their reciprocal relationship, namely, that European consciousness can enjoy further development and prosperity through internally recognizing what is at work in the intellectual unity (if there is any) of diverse traditions in India. Instead, Husserl ends up attributing the single destiny of human development (especially of philosophy) to his idea of Europe, and thus tacitly denies the possibility that any of the other forms of intersubjective consciousness (e.g., India, China, Korea, Japan, etc.) can reach this destiny or that there could be the plurality of ends that are at work in different forms of the "we" in the world. This tendency to univocalize the end toward which all historico-cultural spheres strive and to attribute this end to a single sphere above all else, according to Mall, is the common problem that runs through other influential thinkers such as Hegel, Heidegger, and Gadamar.

To that end, Steven Burik investigates the possibility of comparative philosophy in the works of Heidegger and Derrida. Burik rightly points out that Heidegger is a "very Eurocentric thinker" in his earlier works, and "even in some of his later work, there are instances where we can apparently read this Eurocentric inclination."[31] This is evident from the fact that Heidegger predicates "philosophy" only to the Occidental-European tradition, and then even favors German language that shows its strong affinity with Greek over English or French, which he considers contaminated by linguistic adulteries with Latin, especially for the purpose of philosophical thinking.[32] As both Mall and Burik rightly state, this one-sided attitude in the works of Heidegger, which reduces the ground and the end of philosophy to a single cultural milieu, is highly problematic for understanding the significance and possibility of comparative thinking. Burik, therefore, tries to save Heidegger from this negative image by referring to at least three positive points. First, Heidegger's deconstruction of Western metaphysics hints at the importance of comparative philosophy, notably in reference to its consequential notion of "the other way of thinking," or the "other commencement (*Anfang*)."[33] Second, his (imaginary) conversation with the Japanese scholar demonstrates the exemplary attitude of openness necessary for the praxis of intercultural dialogues.[34] Third, "The End of Philosophy and the Task of Thinking" denounces the Eurocentric stance that *Time and Being* has taken and "looks to other cultures for ways of thinking that can assist him in his efforts of preparing the other way of thinking."[35]

Burik is certainly right to indicate that the notion of the "other *Anfang*" can open a door for a Heideggerian investigation into non-Western intellectual traditions and serve as a possible ground for the further intercultural dialogues.[36] It is also true that

Heidegger's conversation with the Japanese scholar text marks its overture to the rich growth of comparative philosophy from his phenomenological standpoint. Given these two elements in the works of Heidegger, it is not a coincidence that many comparative thinkers today have worked intensely on his thought and followed through the implication of the other commencement. But it is still questionable whether we can place emphasis on these aspects of Heidegger's works and if we can really cancel all the other negative elements that he sets against the possibility of comparative philosophy.

Burik refers to another passage from Heidegger's Spiegel Interview to settle this suspicion: "Who knows one day in Russia or in China ancient ways of thinking come to the fore that can help us in our struggle against metaphysics."[37] But Burik's paragraph, which elaborates on the significance of Heidegger's text (and immediately follows the quote), resurrects the very suspicion we must avoid.

> The working title [i.e., "The End of Philosophy and the Task of Thinking"] explicitly refers to the end of philosophy, which Heidegger has by then come to see as something profoundly Western. With this Heidegger's statement that neither India nor China has philosophy comes to stand in a different light. Heidegger wishes to express the idea that philosophy is but one way of thinking (i.e., the Western one that has been characterized before by terms as ontotheology, metaphysics, logic, and reason) and that there may be greater "thinkers" in other parts of the world than there are philosophers in the West. Thinking is much more than just philosophy.[38]

The division between philosophy and thinking is clever. Philosophy is the Western intellectual endeavor and thinking signifies a more comprehensive category that applies both to Western and non-Western intellectual traditions. But if the other way of thinking (with which the ancient way of thinking had allegedly much more rapport with "Being") could belong to non-Western intellectual tradition, would Heidegger be willing to call it thinking, but not "philosophy" in any sense of the word? The whole point of privileging ancient Greek thought is precisely to acknowledge that it has the primal rapport with Being. And Heidegger seems to think that this is the foundation of the Western (and only) philosophical tradition. But if this ancient way of thinking belongs to any "other way(s) of thinking" than that of ancient Greek, then can we preserve the sense of philosophy only to the Western intellectual tradition?

I also think that Heidegger, and any of his followers, would probably like to consider this alternative passage of human thinking as the true foundation of philosophy. If this were the case, then Heidegger would have to admit that either philosophy could apply both to Western and non-Western thinking or that philosophy really belongs to the Western tradition but somehow exempts the ancient Greeks and/or modern Germans like Hölderlin, Rilke, and himself.[39] If we maintain that Heidegger divides philosophy and thinking as Burik indicates above, the latter option seems to follow through and leaves us with an awkward conclusion. But if the title of philosophy can be transferred to non-Western intellectual traditions originating outside ancient Greece, as Burik suggests through his references to Daoism in the rest of his book, we have to give up the division between philosophy exclusively as the Western activity of thinking and thinking as the activity that belongs also to the other intellectual traditions in the rest of the world. Or else, we cannot conceive of the possibility of comparative examinations of Heideggerian phenomenology and non-Western thought as being philosophical at all. Perhaps after all, Mall is right in saying that Jaspers is much more attuned to the history of world philosophy because his notion of "axial age" marks the plurality of the philosophical beginnings in Greek, Persia, India, and China, whereas for Heidegger, the "ancient way of thinking" very much seems to single out the Greeks.[40]

From the circle of Francophone thinkers, Derrida may deserve to be mentioned as an important figure from the past century. To begin with a conclusion (as a tribute to his later literary style), he is a puzzling case. His deconstruction of Western metaphysics, critiques of the major religions based on Abrahamic faith, and the notion of otherness emerging from such deconstructive approach seem logically to direct him toward the non-Western intellectual and religious traditions. But as Burik points out,

> Derrida does not further explore the consequences of these ideas for other ways of thinking, and neither does he ever incorporate other ways of thinking into his own critique of western metaphysics. So in a very surprising fashion, … he leaves out any serious approach to other cultures and ways of thinking which might show him some possible forms of nonlogocentric thinking.[41]

This does not mean that nobody can use Derrida's notion of alterity as the foundation for seeking the possibility of comparative philosophy (although this constructive dialogue with non-Western thought might suffer from further deconstruction in the end).[42] Certainly, the same goes for Heidegger's notion of the other *Anfang*. But this scarcity of reference to non-Western philosophy—along with a problematic statement that the term "religion" should never be used for non-Christianity—does say something about the postmodern boldness to reconsider the interdependence of philosophy with the other domains of intellectual discourses—the boldness with which Derrida is often credited in the West. To borrow Davis' expression,

> [T]he post-modern philosophy in the west, when it confronts non-western tradition, unexpectedly becomes conservative and ironically shows its tendency to become even Eurocentric. They seem to think as if to deconstruct western tradition and to provide a concrete option to it were completely different matters.[43]

Is Derrida's silence over the intercultural dialogues and the possibility of comparative philosophy like Plato's silence on the most crucial derivative of the term "*pharmakon*" (i.e., scapegoat)?[44] Or was Derrida just not interested in looking beyond the confine of the intellectual and cultural tradition of which he remained always critical? I cannot answer these questions with absolute confidence or demonstrate any direct reference to the indicative passages in Derrida's texts. But it suffices to say that even an eccentric thinker like Derrida seems to stall in the process of deconstruction and remains within the confine of Western philosophy in the end.

The short summaries of Eurocentric tendencies in Husserl, Heidegger, and Derrida are exemplary of what comparative theorists often find problematic in the works of the influential figures in contemporary Western philosophy. As I stated earlier, there could be different ways of defining Western and non-Western philosophy. Even Heidegger's definition of the West differs from that of Husserl's or Derrida's. But most comparative thinkers would agree that these thinkers are significant figures of the twentieth century and also that they share the propensity to privilege their own particular tradition over against others. This is not to eliminate the possibility of conducting comparative philosophy through the systematic frameworks of thinking that they left us but to demonstrate that there is still a strong tendency toward the reservation of philosophy only as the Western activity of thinking. Then why does the history of Western philosophy, even with its radical shift toward alterity in postmodernity, still suffer from the very tendency to univocalize philosophy on its own terms and fail to extend the parameter of its intellectual activity beyond itself? How can we save Western philosophy from the self-thinking logicism that it has condemned so vehemently in recent years and help it transcend to what is other to the self-circling philosophy? Here, the metaxological analysis can help shed some light on these questions. It can lead us to the ways in which we can conceive the possible development of Western philosophy in its interrelation with non-Western philosophy.

Metaxological analysis of Western philosophy I: Modern univocity

Metaxology elucidates how the univocal understanding of being shapes multiple discourses of human thinking. These discourses manifest themselves in the areas of mathematics, logic, science, metaphysics, aesthetics, ethics, and the philosophy of religion. This grand narrative takes place in reference to an enormously large group of significant thinkers in the history of Western philosophy, extending from Parmenides to Paul Weiss. So what we will see here covers only a few aspects of this comprehensive analysis of univocal thinking, especially those that are relevant to our current discussion on the general tendency to close the circuit of philosophical discourse within the Western tradition.

In metaxology, the univocal sense of being represents "diverse ways of privileging the notion of unity."[45] According to Desmond, all of us begin with our "immediate immersion" in the rich givenness of being and thereby enjoy our primordial rapport with the ontological plentitude in our purely aesthetic presence. In this state of "metaphysical Eden," there is no clear division between mind and being.[46] Instead, we experience the "agapeic astonishment"[47] over the givenness of *to be*, astonishment that there is anything at all rather than nothing. This rapturous mode of our primordial relation to being is intimate in the sense that it is both prior to and foundational for our determinate knowing of its quiddity. The division between self and being, which is the condition for the possibility of determinate knowledge, comes forth in our understanding of reality once "the self, as thinking about being, is set over against being as the other"[48] and thereby "being, beings, the world present themselves as enigmas, as ambiguous"[49] or sometimes even as the "hostile" other to the self. In face of this ineluctable equivocity in the ways of being, Desmond argues, "we develop our own rational univocity to take away or mitigate the seeming threat of enigmatic being."[50]

The fall from the metaphysical Eden is the division of mind and being from their primordial togetherness. In face of this division, the univocal mind initially vacillates between two forms: aesthetic and dianoetic univocity. The aesthetic univocity perceives reality as an aggregate of univocal atoms (i.e., the sense data) and presupposes that these data are received with certain "uniformity" (to borrow Mill's expression) in the sense of the knowing subject.[51] The dianoetic univocity presupposes a process of "idealization" in a broad sense of the term. It exercises "abstraction from the reality of aesthetic univocity"[52] and conceives "corresponding 'objects' at the ideal level."[53] These abstracted objects are often conceived as the ideas or categories in the history of philosophy. Then, this movement from the first unity, through its division, to the second unities shows the oscillating development into empiricism and rationalism in context of modern philosophy. The univocal mind further sways between these two because neither a mere aggregate of sense data in the former nor the abstracted categories in the latter alone are capable of accounting for their unity with being. The mind that tries to be faithful to the univocal understanding of being must reject this equivocal indetermination between two kinds of univocity. Hence, it strives to conceive of a higher unity, that is, the "transcendental univocity," to bring itself at peace with the totalizing unity of aesthetic and dianoetic univocity.

It is important to note here that this univocalizing process in modern context inherits the framework of Cartesian metaphysics, namely, the radical division between mind and being to the point of their disjunction. It presupposes the dualism between the mindful knower, on the one hand, and being as the mindless matter, on the other. In this framework of thinking, the primary sense of unity shifts from the first community of mind and being (where mind is overwhelmed with the richness of being yet still much more in rapport with being's plentitude in its otherness) to the univocal mind of thinking subject that strives to eradicate the ambiguity of being as the mindless other. The sense of the "between," in this sense, suffers from a reduction from the open community of mind and being to the constructed unity that the thinking subject categorially frames—or more bluntly put, rationally generates for—the dead objects in meaningless *res extensa*. The univocal mind comes to emphasize the "irreducible unity" of the subject by presupposing Cartesian dualism and, therefore, tries to mitigate the equivocal oscillation between aesthetic and dianoetic univocity as an intelligible mediator.

This also means that the higher unity of subject tends to demote the hyperbolic space of the communivocity between mind and being to their contracted unity mediated mostly from the side of mind.[54] Desmond further critiques this aspect of the transcendental univocity by saying that:

> The between rather becomes the self as the medium of intelligibility, medium in no passive sense, but medium as the mediating power, the privileged determiner of the intelligibility of being. The self becomes the ultimate source of the determinate

intelligibility of the between; the self is the between. The other tends to be defined derivatively, relative to the constitutive or constructing power of the mediating self. There is a subordination of the other in the determination of being, its meaning and intelligibility.[55]

The thinking subject in modern philosophy comes to conceive of itself as the only source of determinate intelligibility both for itself and being: accordingly, it thinks of itself as the sole constituent of the transcendental unity of itself and object. Stated otherwise, the modern subject comes to be conscious of itself as the self-thinking substance that accounts for the determinate intelligibility of all being through mediating itself with being as the other. The self in modernity, thus, privileges itself as the ground of unifying intelligibility and intelligible unity of all things.

This determination of reality through the self-mediation of the subject (i.e., transcendental idealism) suffers from several intricately intermingled flaws. First, we detect its forgetfulness of the first communivocity in the between, where being is given to be for itself in its plenitude. This means that intelligibility belongs not only to mind but also to being prior to the mind's making of it. Second, in addition to and because of this forgetfulness, the transcendental univocity in modern form presupposes the Cartesian dualism, wherein being is preconceived as the meaningless thereness rather than the hyperbolic richness just mentioned. Since the forgetfulness of the initial astonishment over the givenness of being is further aggravated through the acceptance of the Cartesian framework of thinking, mind in modernity is tempted to look nowhere but in itself as the source of unifying intelligibility. Third, given that reason in the transcendental univocity claims itself to be that which formatively grants the intelligibility of being, it cannot dodge the following criticism: transcendental univocal reasoning fails to do justice to the concrete richness of the aesthetic happening, which is given prior to mind's understanding of it. This criticism further wins its support if we pay attention to the following fact: when the mindful self loses the sight of being as having its own integrity in its otherness prior to their division, it loses the sight of itself—viz., "the self as it exists in the happening of the between, where it lives and dies and tries to determine its destiny and relation to others."[56] In this self's self-loss owing to its overconfidence of itself as the only source of unifying intelligibility, Desmond detects the postmodern "*recoil* back to the happening of the between as existentially lived and historically shaped."[57] The abovementioned postmodern thinkers, for instance, emphasize the phenomenal sphere of reality by calling for our attunement to the historical, natural, cultural, or linguistic milieu of which the categorial formalism of transcendental reasoning is both oblivious and derivative. This "recoil back" to the concrete ambiguity of given being is evident in Husserl's emphasis on "life world," Heidegger's suspicion of logocentrism in the history of Western metaphysics, and Derrida's insistence on *différance*. The deconstruction of modern reason's unifying intelligibility, as Desmond acutely puts, marks our recent realization that the univocal understanding of being ultimately fails to account for the "lived equivocities of existence, or history, or language."[58]

Consider the implication of univocal reasoning in relation to our discussion on the methodologies of comparative philosophy. It should be clear from Desmond's analysis that the univocal thinking cannot conceive of the ultimate plurality of philosophical discourses on being. The univocal understanding of being provides us with one systematic form of human thinking. Since it serves as the sole basis of calibrating being's unifying intelligibility, moreover, it comes to dictate the sense of being through its universal form. In relation to this univocal thinking, then, there could be one and only way of understanding reality, and hence, only one sense of being. If we take this to be the only way in which we can make sense of given reality, then it is impossible for us to think about a meaningful dialogue between two different types of philosophical discourses on being. What is other to the transcendental univocal understanding of reality is neither determinately intelligible nor philosophical nor even said to *be* from the viewpoint of totalizing univocity. This metaphysical understanding, according to Desmond, characterizes the basic philosophical tendency shared among the major thinkers in Western modernity (Descartes, Leibniz, and Kant, to name a few). If this is the case, then their systematic thinking, no matter how different they might be from each other, would equally try to reserve the predicate "philosophy" to their own form(s) of thinking and greatly limit us from considering the possibility of intercultural or comparative philosophy.

Another problematic aspect of the univocal thinking lies in the one-sided mediation of self and other. We have seen in Desmond's reflections that the thinking subject in modern philosophy tends to privilege itself as the only source of determinate intelligibility, and because of that, it thinks itself to be the sole constituent of the unity between itself and object. The self, in this sense, becomes the "privileged determiner of the intelligibility" of what is other to itself. This mediation of self and other in the univocal thinking, along with its propensity to singularize the way of philosophizing, follows again the same logic of univocalization that significantly limits us from conceiving the interrelation between one intellectual tradition and another. Recall Husserl's passage as the prime example of this one-sided mediation: "something unique [in the notion of Europe] becomes a motive for [all other human groups] to Europeanize themselves ... ; whereas, we, if we understand ourselves properly, would never Indianize ourselves, for example." If "Occidental-European" philosophy becomes the self as the mediating power and privileged determiner of intelligibility in any forms of human thinking, then only Western philosophy can determine the intelligibility of non-Western thought. In this univocal framework of thinking, non-Western intellectual traditions must Westernize itself to become intelligible, while the Western intellectual tradition alone has the key to turn the meaningless thereness of non-Western philosophies into the intelligible unity of world philosophy (if the former wishes to do so). But again, what we have in the end of this intermediation between Western and non-Western intellectual traditions is the Westernization of the whole intellectual world. The world philosophy, as the unity of the Western and the non-Western, will be just another way of saying that there is only Western philosophy, since to Westernize essentially means to give the unifying intelligibility or determinate identity of philosophy to any given forms of human thinking. Husserl's formulation of intermediation between Europe and non-Europe is spoken in relation to the entire sphere of human civilizations. But if we limit his argument to the realm of various intellectual traditions, what he would say about their intermediation should essentially echo Heidegger's point: the Western intellectual tradition alone is worthy of the name "philosophy." Thus, the logic of transcendental univocity in the end of univocal thinking has significantly slowed (if not completely incapacitated) its search for another source of intelligibility beyond itself.

Metaxological analysis II: Equivocal postmoderns

Why, then, do these thinkers from postmodernity still make their claims on the privileged status of Western philosophy over against non-Western intellectual traditions? As we have seen earlier, their criticisms concerning reason's confidence in its capacity to achieve the ideal unity of subject and object clearly show their deconstructive stance toward transcendental univocity. Their different emphases on the concrete richness of equivocal phenomena in its irreducible otherness to the unifying intelligibility of modern subject clearly show their break from the univocal understanding of being. This marks their movement back to the existentially lived and historically shaped reality, whether it is practiced under the name of existentialism, phenomenology, or deconstructionism. How do they come to betray their allegiance to the equivocity of concrete phenomena through univocalizing the sense of philosophy within what they think as their own intellectual tradition(s)? Desmond's analysis of the postmodern metaphysical "recoil" suggests an answer to this question.

Desmond, first, detects the "significant residues of the idealistic absolutization of some version of self-mediation" in the historic, existential, or linguistic concretizations of transcendental univocity—concretizations that we clearly see in the works of Husserl, Heidegger, and Derrida.[59] He further articulates:

> [The ambiguous legacy of the absolutization of self-mediation] haunts even poeticized or grammatological deconstructions of this absolutization. At the outset, the doubleness of the between is reduced to the self-mediating power of the self as a unity; now the doubleness is dissolved by that same power, but as turned into an equivocal negating or deconstructive power. The mind of finesse, beyond the univocal mind of geometry or transcendental science, still remains elusive. The finesse of the deconstruction of the transcendental ego into the equivocities of language is itself ambiguous. It is not marked by the requisite metaphysical finesse.[60]

The self-mediation of transcendental univocity attempts to eradicate the equivocal distance between mind and being—i.e., the constitutive equivocity that is inherent in the space of the between, where each of mind and being is always given both to be for itself and to be with the other. The mindful subject tries to recover its initially experienced communivocity only through its self-mediation, as it mistakes itself as the sole ground of unifying intelligibility. The self-deconstruction of the subject goes directly against the possibility of its unifying self-mediation as the determiner of intelligible reality. Desmond points out that this self-deconstructive movement also gives the same subject, except this time, the subject that serves as the negative medium through which it denies the possibility of the integral togetherness between itself and other. Instead of the self-mediating unity of self and other, it gives their self-mediating disunity.[61] Univocal thinking thinks itself as the only source of the unity between mind and being, while the self-deconstructive mind in the equivocal thinking thinks itself as the only source of disunity between mind and being. In both cases, the mind seems to mistake itself as the mediating determiner (i.e., the between or the inter) of the interrelation (or lack thereof) between mind and being. Each of them equally mistakes itself as the foundation of togetherness or difference between self and other.[62]

The postmodern recoil to the concrete richness of what is other to mind can certainly motivate us to rethink the one-sided self-mediation of mind and being pertaining to the transcendental univocity. It can wake us up to the irreducible otherness of being to self-mediating unity of our mind. I am not denying this possibility, as I am fully aware that many of the works by postmodern thinkers, like Heidegger and Derrida, show some openness to what is other to their thinking. The trajectory of their intellectual movement seems to point toward the recovery of our original attunement to the profound togetherness of mind and being in their ineradicable difference. But if the postmodern response to the contracted togetherness of mind and being is to emphasize their difference only through the medium of mind's self-disunity or various forms of irrationalism, then it cannot retrace the passage of metaphysical thinking to this original community of itself and other. Rather, it makes the same mistake of privileging itself as the mediating ground for the (negative) relation between itself and other. In this case, the deconstruction of univocal thinking is still entangled with the problematic propensity to favor the self as the maker of its interrelation with the other. This infection with the equivocal "legacy of the absolutization of self-mediation" in the works of the postmodern thinkers can explain their negative comments toward non-Western intellectual traditions. Unless the self-deconstructive self-mediation of self and other in their form(s) of thinking becomes free from its tendency to privilege the self, it cannot transcend itself or intermediate itself with other in its genuine openness to the latter in its irreducible otherness. Comparative philosophy as the open communication or constructive dialogue between what one thinks as one's form of thinking and what is other to it requires more than the postmodern self-deconstruction of univocal thinking.

If comparative philosophy is to envisage the compossibility of diverse intellectual traditions, it needs something more than the deconstructive flattening of mind's self-unifying intelligibility in favor of the equivocal alterity of concrete being. The equivocity between mind and being or self and other (as the consequence of such self-deconstructive thinking) can certainly enable us to accept the plurality of intellectual traditions. But for us to recognize these traditions as voicing something intelligible and worthy of their mutual attention in their distinct ways, we must subscribe to the idea of sameness as much as that of difference. That is precisely because the term "intellectual" or "philosophical" must be applicable to both of them, while this application does not deprive them of their differences from each other. Thus, we have to find the *finessed* intermediation between totalizing univocity and complete equivocity for the comparative examination of two diverse intellectual traditions.

Metaxological analysis III: The dialectic

The dialectical and the metaxological sense of being deal with this question of the proper intermediation between univocity and equivocity. The dialectical sense, especially in Hegel's formulation in modernity, acknowledges the dualistic division between abstract univocity of mind and unmediated equivocity of being. But it also realizes that the relation of two opposing terms should not be seen as the sharp division in which each of them could subsist apart from the other. Rather, it conceives of their profound togetherness through the logic of dialectical self-determination. What is problematic in this way of formulating the interrelation between self and other is the way in which it assimilates the equivocal ways of being into the totalizing unity of self-determining mind. Desmond succinctly explains this dialectical interrelation of self and other with Hegel's famous scheme: i.e., universal, particular, and singular:

> The first universal is an abstract universal; as indefinite, it needs the definiteness of determinate particularity. But this particularity comes to be seen by Hegel as the universal's own *self-particularization*. And so the universal *comes back to itself* in what Hegel calls the [singular], which is the concrete universal. ... There is finally the concrete universality of the whole, which is the One that mediates with itself in and through its own otherness.[63]

Unlike the univocal mind that confines itself in its abstract unity, the dialectical mind moves beyond itself and concretizes itself in and through the otherness of being. In other words, it shows the movement from the "abstract unity, through difference, to unity mediated through differences" as the inclusive self-determination of intelligible unity in multiplicity.[64] At the outset, this logic that concretizes unifying intelligibility in the various forms of being seems to contribute to our practice of comparative philosophy, especially in comparison with the univocal thinking. The dialectical sense sets forth a philosophical thinking that reaches beyond the confines of what it initially thinks as its unified form of thinking. In view of the initial exigency of concrete integrity in its own unity, the mind drives itself to reach out to what is other to itself. This seems to correspond well with the fact that Hegel was one of the few thinkers in the nineteenth century who paid attention to various forms of non-Western thought, specifically for his exposition of the concept of the world history and religion.

However, the problem that Desmond points out in the logic of dialectical self-determination enables us to understand why Hegel's intermediation of Western and non-Western philosophy would be highly problematic for the method of comparative philosophy. Desmond's analysis of Hegel's dialectical thinking basically demonstrates that "the initially abstract universal reaches out to the particular, sees its otherness as its own self-alienation, and then finally comes back to itself as the concrete universal that includes the otherness of particular."[65] This is what Hegel means by the absolute or the concrete universal. The problem in this logic is that the difference or otherness of the particular occupies the secondary position to the absolute status of the mediated unity or sameness of the universal in the end of dialectical process.[66] We will discuss this more in detail in relation to Hegel's texts on religion in Chapter 4, Part Two. But if the self extends its hand to the other as its self-othering, as Hegel maintains, then the other is not seen to be given for itself, but ultimately for the self's self-mediating self-completion as the absolute whole. If all the differences of what is other to self are dialectically assimilated into such self-mediating totality, the dialectical logic shows the self's dialectical instrumentalization of alterity in its own self as the higher, more complex, and the most comprehensive unity. To wit, what is other becomes a means for the self to mediate with itself.

This risk of the self's "dialectical instrumentalizing" of finite other also anticipates the following problem: any self can claim to be the agent of the absolute whole, and thereby attempts to advance the instrumentalizing process allegedly for the sake of the whole.[67] The combination of the first and the second problem culminates in Hegel's intermediation of Western and non-Western philosophy in his *Lectures on the Philosophy of History*. According to Hegel, the self-determining development of the absolute spirit constitutes history as rational progress of (human) reason. The dialectical relation of the universal (i.e., eternity) and the particular (i.e., each age) follows the same pattern of the dialectical progress: the eternity that stands apart from each age is indeterminate and abstract; hence, for it to achieve the concrete status of true eternity, it must mediate with itself in and through all the particular ages. This means that the true eternity is the absolute whole of all the ages (i.e., the concrete universality of time), and consequently, each age always serves as the means for the self-realization of the absolute whole. This dialectical instrumentalization of time for the constitution of history enables Hegel to draw the infamous conclusion that his present age (i.e., modern Germany) is the consummate age in which the absolute whole of rational history realizes itself.[68] The complex intermediation of Western and non-Western intellectual traditions in Hegel's dialectical conception of history, in this sense, illustrates the asymmetrical relationship in which non-Western philosophy (i.e., the other) serves as the means for Western philosophy (i.e., the self) to affirm and manifest itself as the consummate form of human thinking.

The logic of self-determination can be used to favor any particular tradition over against the others regardless of Hegel's emphasis that the self-determining development of spirit must always move from the East to the West. For instance, the same propensity to dialectical instrumentalization has certainly infected some Japanese philosophers in the 1930s, and this led to the infamous discussion of the "overcoming of modernity," where these thinkers, in one way or another, defended the self-determination of Japanese philosophy in and through Western philosophy, thereby problematically supplying intellectual support to the government war-propagandas.[69] This historical fact alone shows that nothing in the self-determining logic of dialectical thinking can ground Hegel's claim that the historical development of the spirit must move westward. In the worst-case scenario, it can even aid anyone from any corner of the world outside the western hemisphere to subordinate the Western intellectual tradition for the self-completing self-determination of his or her own tradition. The dialectical understanding of being, since it fails to think what is genuinely other to itself or bring the other into its relativity as it privileges its own self-determination, carries within itself a tendency to privilege a single intellectual tradition as the consummate form of human thinking; and in this sense, it always anticipates various forms of "centrism" as Euro-centrism, Asia-centrism, Sinocentrism, Japonism, etc. Thus, the dialectical framework of thinking cannot provide the ground for a mutual understanding and meaningful dialogue between Western and non-Western thought.

Metaxological alternative: The way of the *Metaxu*

The metaxological understanding of being remains attentive to the constitutive doubleness in the mediations between self and other. Desmond describes this doubleness in two senses: (1) the double mediation of mind and being, and (2) the double mediation of mind and being within mindful existence.[70] With regard to the first, he argues that "each being is a center of self-mediation and hence is for itself; each being is defined in a network of intermediating relations with what is other to itself."[71] These mediations can by no means be singularized into a totalizing self-determination seen in the dialectical sense.[72] But they are multiplied and redoubled as they are seen in light of their original givenness. To see this original givenness as well as the openness between the mediations of mind and being, Desmond points us toward the second doubleness, that is, the "inward otherness" of the "to be" in our mindful self.[73] Our mind never gives itself to be, but is always already given to be before determining itself to be what it is or before intermediating itself with what is other to itself. The otherness of being in our mindful self keeps us aware of the givenness of our being and shows us the limitation of our self-mediation in relation to being as what is other to ourselves. While being attentive to the double sense of the doubleness between mind and being, metaxology remains faithful to the fact that everything, including our being, our mindfulness, and what is other to ourselves, is all given to be prior to their self- and intermediations.

Desmond calls this metaphysical attentiveness to the openness of the mediation between self and other "agapeic mindfulness."[74] This mindfulness comes to realize that the valueless thereness of being, calibrated through the determinate knowing of our mind in face of its ineluctable separation from being, demonstrates the mind's forgetfulness of its primal position, wherein what is other to it is equally given to be for itself. In other words, the agapeic mind realizes that being as what is other to itself is marked with ontological richness that exceeds its self-mediation, the richness that enables even mind to exist before coming to know itself. We have seen that the univocal and dialectical understanding (especially in modern formulations) try to overcome the neutral thereness of being through the unifying intelligibility of mind, whereas the equivocal sense emphasizes ambiguity of being as incommensurable with such abstract unity of univocal thinking or self-determining totality of dialectical thinking. These three senses have failed to give a comprehensive framework in which we can work out the proper intermediation of mind and being, because they fail to pay attention to the ontological surplus of "that it is" given *both* to mind *and* being.

Being is never given to us as the meaningless *thereness* or given only for us to fill it with meanings through our unifying intelligibility. But by being aware of the inner otherness of "that it is"—the otherness saturated with value exceeding our determinate knowing—we become aware that the same elemental energy of existence, gratuitously given prior to our self-mediation, also sustains the existence of other beings in reality.[75] We come to know that what is other to us is never exhaustively mediated by our self-mediation, and that our movement toward the other, sustained by the common ground of "that it is," calls for our genuine transcendence to the other in its irreducible otherness. Desmond describes this metaxological self-transcendence to the intimate otherness of being as follows:

> Metaxological metaphysics goes towards the other, out of the double mediation of thought, but lets the thinking of the other be guided by an agapeic mindfulness that goes towards the other as other, not on a mediating detour that recoils back on itself, once having appropriated the other. Agapeic mind is an exemplification of communicative being; it is a being mindfully there for the other as other, and not for the self itself. It goes towards the other, it delivers itself over to the other; and this making itself available for the other is its communication of itself to the other. It communicates itself not out of lack merely, but out of an excess or surplus, out of a generosity of being that gives to the other for the other.
>
> Agapeic mindfulness, as communicative thinking of the other, is an intermediation which, in going towards the other, gives itself to the other as other, and does not think about what it gets from what it gives .... Its generosity of transcendence is a giving for nothing, nothing beyond the goodness of the giving itself. Agapeic mind gives its understanding over to the position of the other from its otherness, seeks to see the other from within the intimacy of its own integrity of being. ... There is compassion in this knowing, an undergoing with the other, not a standing above in the mode of mastery or mediation.[76]

Unlike the dialectical self-transcendence in which the self appropriates the other as its self-othering, the framework of metaxological intermediation bears in mind that the self is not privileged over against other. There is no subsumptive re-articulation of otherness in terms of self-determination. Rather, what we see here is the self's compassionate knowing of the other as the other. This is what Desmond calls the "hermeneutic of generosity,"[77] a kind of compassionate thinking that "prepares the ways for the other to come to [its] self-manifestation"[78] or self-articulation for itself. The self that recognizes the intimate strangeness of "that it is" within itself recognizes that the same ontological energy that exceeds its mastery is somehow also at work in the other. Through this realization that the ontological ground of self and other is both transcendent to, and immanent in, both of them, the self can humble itself before the other and communicatively share its equal position of givenness with the other.

The third step: Concluding the metaxological contributions to the method of comparative philosophy

The metaxological self, therefore, knows the crucial importance of letting the other be for the other and letting the other speak for itself. This framework of thinking thinks what is genuinely other to itself and brings the other into its relativity, as it gives the space for the self-articulation of the other: hence, it can recognize the plurivocal compossibility of self and other in their intermediations.[79] The methodological contribution of metaxology to comparative philosophy lies precisely in this configuration of the interrelation between self and other. We have seen that the general tendency to privilege a single form of human thinking (i.e., Western philosophy) over against the others (i.e., non-Western philosophy) roughly originates in our age-old tendency to uphold the logic of univocal thinking. The notable thinkers in postmodernity, such as Husserl, Heidegger, and Derrida, have seriously questioned the legitimacy of this form of thinking and further called for our attunement to the equivocity of the historically lived reality. Yet their critical attitude still suffered from the root of the same problem as the univocal, namely, its adherence to the "absolutization of self-mediation." As a result, even these thinkers could not help but hesitate to celebrate the alterity of other intellectual traditions when they confronted the real possibility of intercultural, interreligious, and interphilosophical dialogues beyond the confines of what they thought of as the only form(s) of philosophical thinking.

Contrary to the problematic absolutization of self-mediation, the metaxological thinking encourages self to transcend itself and reach what is other to itself. In this movement, the self is called to acknowledge the equal status of the other to its own and give the space in which the other can speak for itself in its otherness. This framework of thinking grounds and foreshadows the open communication between Western and non-Western philosophy. Western philosophy, insofar as its members are willing to cultivate their metaxological mindfulness, can bring itself to the position of non-Western philosophy and seek to understand from within the integrity of non-Western thinking. Husserl is right. Non-Western philosophers can benefit from Westernizing themselves in their engagement with Western way(s) of thinking.[80] But he is wrong to think that the members of Western civilization would not benefit from this compassionate understanding of what is other to their own intellectual tradition(s). Desmond's framework of thinking, that is, agapeic mindfulness, clearly shows that Western philosophy can also non-Westernize itself and strive to think within the frameworks of the traditions that are foreign to its own.[81] It grounds the possibility of the two-way communication between Western and non-Western philosophy, or more precisely, the plurivocal compossibility of various intellectual traditions, wherein each of them can reach out to communicate with other through their compassionate understanding.[82] Thus, metaxology as a comprehensive method of intermediating univocity of total identity and equivocity of radical difference can serve as the metaphysical condition *sine qua non* for the possibility of our comparative thinking.[83]

2

The Metanoetic Methodology in the Contemporary Comparative Philosophy of Tanabe Hajime

The historical background and the significance of *Tetsugaku* (哲学) in modern Japan[1]

The Kyoto school thinkers are the pioneers in the field of comparative philosophy. This has become increasingly evident as the number of the specialists in the field of comparative and Japanese philosophy grew over the last few decades. It may seem a matter of course to most of the Western scholars in philosophy that an Eastern thinker or a group of non-Western thinkers would end up engaging in critical introductions of their own intellectual traditions in relation to the philosophical leitmotifs developed in the West. But this seemingly natural movement toward the incorporation of their non-Western intellectual tradition in their engagement with Western philosophy was as challenging for the Kyoto school thinkers as for the contemporary Western thinkers to engage in comparative philosophy.[2] To make this point clear, I will briefly introduce the history of modern Japan and then evaluate the significance of the Kyoto school thinkers' contributions to the field of comparative philosophy.

The islands of Japan went through a peculiar historical development. Indeed, many of its particular historical episodes would sound quite strange to those who are familiar only with the history of Western civilization. What especially interests us in this context, however, is the transition from the strong politico-cultural isolation that the feudal military regime of Tokugawa Shogunate (1603–1867) enforced over the whole country for the entire modern period. The Japanese diplomatic policy under this regime, generally known as *Sakoku* (鎖国), prohibited any foreigners to enter the country roughly between 1639 and 1854. During this period, the government kept only commercial relations with China (from Ming to Quing dynasty) and the Dutch East India Company (*Vereenigde Oostindische Compagnie*); hence, except a limited access to the Dutch texts on medicine and science, most Japanese people were totally kept apart from any Western influence. Think of the wealth of the intellectual legacies that we have inherited from this historical period in the West. The works of Descartes, Hume, Rousseau, Kant, Fichte, Schelling, and Hegel, just to name a few major thinkers, had never made it to the Japanese soil, let alone all the philosophical texts that predate the works of these famous philosophers.

Think, in turn, how astonishing and overwhelming it was for the Japanese to open their boarders, travel abroad, and face the Western intellectual tradition for the first time in the middle of the nineteenth century.[3] The father of modern Japanese philosophy, Nishi Amane (西周) (1829–1897), was one of the few Japanese intellectuals who was able to go abroad (i.e., the Netherlands) under the government order for the first time in 1862. And he experienced a full exposure to the Western civilization for two years. After the return to his native land in 1865, Nishi dedicated his life to introduce comprehensively the Western intellectual tradition, including the law, economics, military science, philosophy, psychology, aesthetics, and literature, to his fellow countrymen. His famous text *Hyakuichi Shinron* (百一新論), originally delivered as a lecture right before the fall of Tokugawa regime in 1867, coined the first translation of the term "philosophy" as *tetsugaku* (哲学).[4]

We cannot afford going into the detailed genealogy of the term *tetsugaku* in the history of modern "Japanese philosophy" (*nihon tetsugaku*, 日本哲学) from the end of the nineteenth to the beginning of the twentieth century. But it is worth noting that Nishi predominantly used the term to indicate Western philosophy, which he learned and conceived as a complete and self-enclosed system of thinking that would leave no room for indeterminate uncertainty in the end of its process.[5] This definition, then, led to a division between "philosophy" (*tetsugaku*) as a self-enclosed system of thinking originating from the Western intellectual tradition and "thinking" (*shisō*, 思想) as that which signifies the broadest sense of human thinking. Notice how we find here the same problematic division that we saw in Heidegger's notion of philosophy and thinking. Naturally, this distinction foreshadowed the same problematic consequences in Japanese intellectual history: viz., it has encouraged many Japanese scholars in the field of Western philosophy to hold that the term "philosophy" applies only to the Western intellectual tradition, while it has discouraged many of those who investigate the Japanese intellectual history from applying the term "philosophy" (*tetsugaku*) or "Japanese philosophy" (*nihon tetsugaku*) to the intellectual texts predating the birth of the term *tetsugaku*, in the mid-nineteenth century.[6]

The historical background of the Japanese intellectual tradition in the dawn of the twentieth century just inherited this limited notion of philosophy.[7] Hence it was not entirely hospitable to those pursuing the possibility of comparative philosophy. In this historical context, then, one of the major contributions that the Kyoto school thinkers had provided was that they managed to establish their own methods of philosophical inquiry—an inquiry that enabled their intellectual tradition to engage in a meaningful dialogue with Western philosophy. Nishida was undoubtedly the first major figure that took on, and successfully accomplished, this task of comparative thinking especially with his maiden work, *An Inquiry into the Good* (1911). Tanabe critically followed Nishida's footsteps as he laid out his understanding of the works of his intellectual forefathers in the tradition of Japanese Buddhism in relation to his reflections on the ideas developed in the Western intellectual tradition. I will explore, in the following, how Tanabe's philosophical works demonstrate his remarkable effort to expand the notion of philosophy beyond the self-enclosed system of modern thought that Japanese intellectuals have inherited from the West in the nineteenth century and then show how his grounding of metanoetics marks an establishment of contemporary comparative philosophy of religion in Japan.

Tanabe's contributions to the method of comparative philosophy

The discussions on the method of comparative philosophy became much more vibrant among the Japanese intellectuals posterior to Tanabe's philosophical career.[8] Unlike these thinkers, Tanabe did not really leave any explicit remark on the method that he presumed in his examination of all the philosophical texts both from the Eastern and the Western intellectual traditions. Nor did he explicitly take any issue with the general sentiments shared among Japanese intellectuals that the term "philosophy" only applies to the Western intellectual works. But his treatment of Japanese thinkers often looks as though it assumed the *de facto* equality between the Eastern and the Western intellectual tradition.[9] This may give many of us an impression that Tanabe did not give any thought to the possibility of comparative thinking but simply moved with the conviction that it was possible. With this conviction, he kept incorporating the works of the Eastern thinkers to his discussions on the various philosophical topics that he found in the works of the Western thinkers. This practical approach to the method of comparative thinking may satisfy Mall and other theorists who hold that comparative philosophy represents a sort of a regulative ideal or a kind of existential "attitude" that we both adopt and aim at through extending our intellectual interests beyond the confine of our conventional lineage of philosophical thinking.[10] But this would not only overlook the constitutive aspect of the method that Tanabe presumes in his path to comparative thinking but also fail to make any contribution to our current discussion on the method of comparative philosophy. As it was the case with the works of Desmond, therefore, we must unfold Tanabe's methodology from the systematic viewpoint that his texts are signifying to us.

On Tanabe as a comparative/world philosopher

Even though Tanabe does not explicitly discuss how to interrelate Eastern and Western philosophy, he gives various passages through which we can think how he should be conceiving the relationship between two historical frameworks of thinking. Also, as I have mentioned earlier, his philosophy shows its serious commitment to the Western philosophy prior to and in the midst of its critical introduction of Eastern philosophy. Hence, his standpoint as a whole does not completely break away from either the Western or the Eastern philosophical tradition.[11] Rather, it occupies the middle position through which he can think through and beyond the confines of the particular intellectual traditions.[12] In this regard, the whole picture of the process through which Tanabe develops his own philosophy will serve as the great example that reflects his conception of comparative thinking.

The fact that Tanabe thought himself belonging to the Western intellectual tradition as much as to the Eastern intellectual tradition also plays an important role for our exposition of his methodology of comparative philosophy. Most notably, Tanabe does not conceive of contemporary philosophy as comprising a rigid division in which Western intellectual tradition stays over here in the West and the Eastern intellectual tradition lurks over there in the East. But he seems to think that our intellectual framework, whether it initially belongs to the East or the West, can undergo its dynamic development into a kind of world philosophy that takes every tradition as its integral parts. This notion of the historico-intellectual development of philosophy, comprising its movement from the West-East disjunction to the West-East community, enables us to situate Tanabe's philosophy in relation to the history of (world) philosophy.[13] This process of proving the significance of Tanabe as a contemporary (world) philosopher will enable us to examine the interrelation of what he thinks as the conventional lineage of philosophy in the West and his framework of thinking that redefines the border of such intellectual tradition.

The relation of "Tanabe Philosophy" and the history of philosophy

To think about the relationship between two historical frameworks of thinking, consider the relationship between the works of a contemporary philosopher (from the twentieth to the twenty-first century) and the history of philosophy. When we visualize this, we are immediately tempted to draw a somewhat linear depiction of the progress of intellectual history. If we take up a certain issue that contemporary intellectuals find in the works of modern philosophers and show how the former solve some of these problems, then we seem to witness a linear progress of ideas in the history of philosophy. Tanabe takes issue with some of the key formulations in the works of modern philosophers. If we can demonstrate that he solves some of these problems, why not we label him as a contemporary philosopher? This tentative labeling of Tanabe as a philosopher in our present age, however, encounters a few serious issues.

One of the most pressing problems is the very possibility of using the term "philosophy" in the epoch that we sometimes call "postmodernity." If we can sum up modern philosophy as reason's endeavor to account for our comprehension of reality as what it is, that is, to demonstrate systematically the togetherness of subject and object, contemporary thinkers are much more skeptical of reason's ability to follow through with this project. So, many of them would argue that the intellectual movements of the modern thinkers in their original formulations are fundamentally flawed and that anyone claiming to make a progress within these frameworks is oblivious of the fundamental problem. This shows the reason why there seems to be a general consensus of radical skepticism, which discounts any fixed notion of philosophy, among some of the contemporary philosophers. This consensus is particularly vocal when the notion of philosophy is voiced in accordance with the works of the modern thinkers.

Hence, the contemporary thinkers tend to remain skeptical of anyone insinuating the systematic completion of these philosophical projects—whether this system would be represented in the form of reason's self-critique in the manner of Kantian criticisms or dynamic self-knowing of the absolute spirit in that of Hegelian dialectic. Postmodern thinkers are the ones that take a fundamental issue with any uncritical inheritance of the rational projects handed down from thinkers such as Kant and Hegel. They move us to break away from the foundations of systematic thinking from modern philosophy and hold fast to the praxis of constant doubt.

We can sympathize with the contemporary general attitude of radical skepticism to the extent that we should take issue with the foundation of modern philosophy. This seems to coincide with the general spirit of the Kyoto school philosophy as well. However, we will soon face another problem: what is assumed in the contemporary propensity to doubt any fixed notion of what counts as philosophy is that the sense of philosophy is exhausted in the modern frameworks of thinking (especially originating from the German Idealism). This is precisely what we saw in Desmond's analysis of the "ambiguous legacies of the univocal thinking" in the works of many postmodern thinkers.[14] So, many of the contemporary thinkers who are driven by the deconstructive spirit naturally end up declaring the crisis of philosophy, the crisis in which philosophy can no longer systematically account for the ground in which it can ask any of the philosophical questions that it has faced in the course of human history.[15]

But in order for the intellectual works in our present age to be seen as a form of philosophy, we must not only acknowledge the breakdown of modern philosophy but also make our breakthrough to the sense of philosophy that is not exhausted in the process of the breakdown.[16] This means that we would have to constitute a kind of philosophy that requires an overhaul of the set of terms calibrated in the framework of modern philosophy. This is the very sense in which Tanabe characterizes his later philosophy of religion (i.e., metanoetics) as "a philosophy that is not a philosophy":

> Such is the non-philosophical philosophy that is reborn out of the denial of philosophy as I had previously understood it. I call it a philosophy that is not a philosophy because, on the one hand, it has arisen from the vestiges of a philosophy I had cast away in despair, and on the other, it maintains the purpose of functioning as a reflection on what is ultimate and as a radical self-awareness, which are the goals proper to philosophy.[17]

Thus, the progress from modern to contemporary philosophy, especially in relation to the works of Tanabe, can neither be a linear progress from what is worse to what is better within the same framework of thinking nor a mere negation of what has been given as philosophy but a critical reconfiguration of the ways in which we can think about any philosophical issues in the first place. That is to say, contemporary philosophy must overcome the framework of modern philosophy and in its process of overcoming, establish a renewed sense of philosophy.

Tanabe gives a brief description of what his process of overcoming must look like in his essay entitled "The Logic of Species and the World-Scheme"[18]:

> If there are two things that mutually negate each other and if one negates the other as that which cannot be established at the same time with the other, then this relationship of the two does not signify one's overcoming of the other but only a simple negation. For one to surpass the other, one would have to affirm what confronts it (i.e., the other) as one denies the other and thereby enable the other to live as one embraces the other within oneself. Accordingly, one's overcoming of the other must imply that as the self is being negated by the other, it, in turn, transforms the other's negation into the medium for the affirmation of the self.[19]

So for the contemporary thinker to offer a comprehensive form of human thinking beyond the limitation of modern philosophy, he must not fall into the "simple negation" of what he finds problematic in the past framework of thinking. But as he negates the validity of the latter, he must trace back the source of human thinking—the inexhaustible source that enables the expressions even of his intellectual forefathers—and then through this negative relation to the form of thinking in the previous age, he makes his first leap from the barren shore of radical skepticism.

From the philosophy of history to the history of philosophy: A Rankean alternative to Hegelian concept of history as progress

The constitution of contemporary philosophy beyond the framework of modern philosophy is quite consistent with what Tanabe lays out through his interpretation of Ranke's philosophy of history in his essay "Eternity, History and Act."[20] Tanabe argues that Ranke goes against the Hegelian philosophy of history and puts an end to the general rationalism dominating our understanding of history since the time of Enlightenment.

> [Ranke] criticizes that Hegelian idea of rational progress has a tendency to relativize each age of history simply as a moment for the development of the next age, reduce it to the status of the means for the end of the whole, and keep it from having an absolute meaning that is peculiar to it. So, [Ranke] claims that each age in history, as it remains to be particular, must possess the absolute meaning that is peculiar to it and be directly connected to eternity. This certainly captures the essential nature of history, establishes the standpoint for grasping individuality that characterizes history and rejects the relativism that rationalistic universalism has claimed since the time of Enlightenment.[21]

The rational theory of history, seen especially in light of Hegel's philosophy, considers the whole of human progress as the foundation of what counts as history and thereby it comprises a teleological view of the development in which each age serves as a particular means for the self-determining whole of the universal humanity (i.e., the absolute self-knowing of the spirit and/or the state).

Contrary to this picture of history, Ranke paints the communal picture of world history where the particular (i.e., each age) has access to the absolute (i.e., eternity) without instrumentalizing the other particular age for determining itself to be the absolute. Put differently, a particular age relates to the other in the way that an autonomous and individual subject would relate to the other with its respect of the other for the other.[22] Tanabe further reads into Ranke's philosophy of history in the following passage:

> Each age that is truly in touch with divine eternity does not remain as a mere single individual but since it has to be the single individual in divine universality, there is no longer the struggle [among the particular ages] for the power. But rather there must govern peace and harmony in which each age respects the individuality of the other and acknowledges the dignity of the other for the other. Also, since one age necessarily undergoes its transition to another, as each of them maintains its absolute and independent status, the new age should be able to hold its superiority to the old one in terms of order not through the mechanical relations of power, but by transcending this relation. This means that we can avoid simply placing the individual ages in parallel relation to each other, but place them in order of succession. Here we find the characteristics of the relations among ages. We will be able to find the path to acquire the concept of development, which consistently maintains the absolute status of each age as the relative relation of the ages that follow each other, without including the propensity to instrumentalize each of them for the ultimate purpose in the concept of progress.[23]

History as the rational progress of humanity allows one particular age to subordinate the other for its rise to the status of the absolute, and thereby, the interrelation of the ages in the mechanics of power—as if it were driven by the will to power— is degenerated into the state of epochal warfare. This is clearly the case for what we have seen in Hegel's self-determining concept of world history.[24] But Ranke's picture of history, according to Tanabe, regards the communal relations among different ages as the plurivocal expressions of world history. Here we find a stark difference between the history of progress that affirms the worth and value of one age at the cost of all the previous ones and history as the plurivocal development that affirms the worth and value of each age for itself.[25]

If we apply Ranke's logic of world history to the history of ideas, then we can shed some light on our discussion on the development of contemporary philosophy. When we see the problem in the foundation of modern philosophy, we are inevitably led to search for a new philosophy that can overcome the problem. But if this transition from the old to the new follows the footstep of the dialectical progress seen in the rational theory of history, we will face two possible outcomes: (1) we realize that the basis on which we make the philosophical advancement from the old to the new is still dictated by the logic of the old and (2) the self-determining logic behind the teleological progress will tend to degenerate the relationship between one framework of thinking and another into the state of intellectual warfare—i.e., the constant struggle through which the strongest must dominate for its self-realization. Notice how both of these implications are conducive to the contemporary mood of radical skepticism. On the one hand, if the new philosophy that is critical of the foundation of the old is fundamentally operative on the same ground as that of the old, then it must undermine its own activity as a legitimate form of thinking. But, on the other hand, if the new philosophy is to instrumentalize the old for its self-realization through the mechanics of power, then the driving force for the self-determining reason, that is, the will to power, becomes the fundamental guideline of philosophizing. If we remain faithful to our assessment of the serious problem in the framework of modern philosophy, we must turn away from any advancement of philosophy within the same framework. If we force the progress of philosophy with the brute force of the will to power, nothing will stop us from stepping into the quagmire of the intellectual world war, the war of everyone against everyone. It is a matter of course that many of our contemporary thinkers have become reluctant (or even hostile) to endorse any positive notion of philosophy.

What is important in Tanabe's reflection on the Rankean philosophy of history is that he clearly takes a passage beyond his rejection of the teleological "progress" of history, viz., the breakthrough to another kind of historical development. Each age, according to Tanabe, does not exist as the means for the other but "one age must have an intermediating relation in which it affirms the previous age while at the same time denying it."[26] He further articulates that

> the relation of an individual age … to another must not be the external relation in which one age is exchanged with another or one dies out and another takes its place. But the extinction of one becomes the medium for the generation of the other; accordingly, the former as the necessary moment for the existence of the latter must itself be preserved inside the latter as it dies. This mediatory nature of development alone constitutes the history.[27]

Tanabe's understanding of history, therefore, acknowledges not only that one age must die out and thereby give room for the next but also at the same time the next age must intermediate with the previous one in such a way that the former would both negate and preserve the latter.[28]

This double structure of affirmation/negation in the transitory relation of two ages may sound quite similar to the dialectical progress of history in Hegel (the dialectical progress that we have previously deemed as unsuitable for grounding the open communication between Eastern and Western philosophy). For one age to realize itself, according to Hegel, one must use the other and realize itself in and through the other. One negates the other, but through this negation one would be able to truly affirm oneself. But notice how unlike Hegel's violent structure of self-determining progress, Tanabe's conception of history (*à la* Ranke) clearly grants that each age has the absolute and eternal value for itself and "so long as it exerts its subjective energy to realize and represent this value, it establishes the relation pertaining to the transition (*tenkan*, 転換) of ages."[29] This *tenkan* (i.e., transition, transformation, conversion) of time, which brings us back to the abovementioned concept of overcoming, is not a domination of one over the other, but what Tanabe articulates as the "metanoetic intermediation," or the "absolute dialectic," of the two ages. We will discuss the structure of *tenkan* in relation to the structure of Tanabe's absolute dialectic or metanoetic intermediation much more in detail later. But it is clear at this point that if there can be a transformative change (*tenkan*) from modern to contemporary philosophy, or more precisely if Tanabe's thinking is to overcome the shortcomings of modern philosophical thinking and to constitute a renewed sense of its own philosophy, the framework of the new must not only negate the validity of the old. Rather, the present must trace back the source of human thinking—the inexhaustible source that equally enables the expressions both of the past and of the present—and therefore the present will preserve the past insofar as it recognizes the basis on which the past formulation of philosophy was established in the first place while denying it, insofar as the present formulation remains more faithful to the source of human thinking.[30] This transformative intermediation of modern and contemporary philosophy, according to Tanabe, follows the logic of absolute dialectic.

A negation of modern philosophy in the Western intellectual tradition: Tanabe's internal struggle with Kant and Hegel

We have seen that Tanabe essentially echoes Ranke's idea of history and also that the formal concept of the relationship between two historical ages is applicable to the formulation of the proper relationship between two historical frameworks of thinking. Tanabe's systematic viewpoint further suggests that the transformative interrelation of two frameworks of thinking in the history of philosophy follows the logic of "absolute dialectic." Now to unfold the proper method of comparative thinking that is at work in Tanabe's philosophy, we must investigate how this notion of "absolute dialectic" constitutes the historico-intellectual rise of his contemporary thought out of its engagement with modern philosophy of the Western intellectual tradition. I will conduct this investigation through the following three steps: First, I will briefly define the sense of modern philosophy pertaining to the Western intellectual tradition. Second, I will explore the way in which Tanabe's struggle with such philosophy from the past (both historically and intellectually) led him to formulate the notion of absolute dialectic in the present. Finally, I will elucidate the senses in which absolute dialectic can be said to overcome the limitation of modern philosophy. In this section, I will discuss the first two of these steps and pave the road to our understanding of Tanabe's absolute dialectic.

There are various ways in which we can characterize the so-called "modern philosophy." But I think the philosophies of Kant and Hegel play a tremendously significant role for demarcating its boundary. Think, for instance, how Nietzsche and Kierkegaard are both considered to be postmodern existentialists despite the fact that their authorial intents along with their philosophical conclusions are completely different from each other. What brings them together as the thinkers of postmodernity in one sense, therefore, is their profound dissatisfaction with Kantian and Hegelian configurations of the ultimate truth—the truth concerning the relationship between faith and reason as well as reason and reality.[31] These thinkers realize that both Kantian and Hegelian philosophies are unfaithful to the source of truth, i.e., the creative power behind our understanding of reality and our existence.[32] Thus, they urge us to break off from the modern framework of thinking. Our reflections on the transformative transition of time from the past to the present also help us place Kant and Hegel as the progress theorists who relativize one age for the determination of the other in the sense of rationalistic universalism. In relation to the metaxological elucidation on the method of comparative philosophy, we have also seen that their formulations of metaphysics (or the univocal and the dialectical understanding of being) are unfit for grounding our comparative thinking. So, in light of these discussions, we can group Kant and Hegel as the representatives of modern philosophy, and then apropos of our reflections on the transformation (*tenkan*) of a framework of human thinking in one age to another, we can examine Tanabe's struggles with Kant and Hegel as his first step toward the overcoming of modern philosophy.

Tanabe published two monographs outlining his extensive reflections on the works of Kant and Hegel, namely, *Kant's Theory of Teleology* (1924)[33] and *Hegel's Philosophy and Dialectic* (1932).[34] The first text strives to give a coherent theory of teleology by elucidating the dialectical relationship among the three kinds of purposiveness in the *Critique of the Power of Judgment* (i.e., formal, internal, and self-aware purposiveness).[35] The second text tries to give solutions to two demands: (1) Tanabe's discontent with Cohen's theory of the "infinitesmal" as the key term for achieving the subject-object unity within the framework of Kantian Criticisms and (2) the historical confrontation with the "swelling billows of the Proletarian World Revolution"[36] in the late 1920s in Japan. What interests us are not the details of these arguments but the significance of Tanabe's critical engagement with Kant and Hegel in relation to the development of his own thought. So, I would like to draw our attention to the second preface to the text of *KTT*. This text was published twice in 1924 and 1948. The second edition was accompanied with the essay entitled "Hegel's Philosophy and Absolute Dialectic" and the additional preface was inserted to give a brief description of their significance in relation to the author's philosophical development.[37] This small segment of writing could help us unfold the significance of Tanabe's earlier works on Kant and Hegel in relation to his later works representing his distinct philosophy.

By looking back his earlier struggle with Kant and Hegel, mature Tanabe plainly states, "When I reflect on the passage in which my own thinking has taken, each of these essays marks a certain decisive step for its development."[38] In the following passage, he gives the full account of the critical engagement with Kant:

> After producing the text of *KTT*, it served as the turning-point (*tenki*, 転機) of my philosophical interest, which moved from the viewpoint of critique to the investigation of the world-view; and from mathematico-physical nature to the history of human society. In this process of transition, it is undeniable that I was trying to proceed to post-Kantian German idealism instead of staying within the Kantian critical position …. As I sought for the theory of the world-view, moreover, I could not move on to Hegel's theory, which develops the unique dialectic for the same demand of unifying the subject and the object …. Then I was capable of doing nothing but rationalizing Kant's teleology through Cohen's theory, which

I used to consult solely for supporting my own interpretation. Even though the limit of my personal capability left me in this position and I had no other choice but to rely on Cohen's understanding of Kant, I could not help but be aware of my discontent with this limited framework of thinking. ... Ultimately this text stops at the demarcation of the turning point (*tenki*) in which I tried to move from critique to speculative thinking, and hence, it belongs to the stage in which I did not touch upon dialectic as the theory of the historical world.[39]

Tanabe's following confrontation with Hegel, driven by his discontent with the Kantian framework of thinking, seems to mark his advancement toward the "dialectic as the theory of the historical world." However, the ways in which the text of *HPD* approaches Hegel's works prevent us from easily finding this advancement. Tanabe compiled a series of his essays on Hegel, published between 1927 and 1931, into the monograph in reverse order of their appearance because (he argues) his philosophical position had somewhat shifted in the course of these years.[40] What these essays essentially demonstrate is that Tanabe is trying to develop an absolutely concrete theory of the historical world through the framework of Hegelian dialectic. Hence, as the focus of the *HPD* shifts from his attempt to understand Hegel's dialectic to the exposition of what dialectic should be, Tanabe seems to become increasingly frustrated with Hegel's systematic framework wherein he cannot freely spell out what he thinks as the most concrete form of dialectical thinking.[41] Thus, Tanabe confesses, "Two years after having started to write this text, I faced a deadlock, where I was no longer capable of continuing my writing and finally had no choice but to stop."[42] If his preface to the second edition of the *KTT* ended there, he might have joined the circle of those who gave up all hope for any positive advancement of philosophy in the present age.

But listen carefully to the way in which Tanabe calls the movement from Kantian critique to the "dialectic as the theory of the historical world" a turning point (*tenki*) in his thinking. If we take our previous reflection on the transition (*tenkan*) of time, as well as of the conversion (*tenkan*) of one framework of thinking to another, this turning (*Kehre*) within the history of Tanabe's philosophical works could suggest two possibilities: (1) the continuous progress from Kantian rational universalism to Hegelian dialectical universalism or (2) the transformative development from the framework of modern philosophy (i.e., both Kant and Hegel) to a kind of dialectical thinking that serves as the legitimate theory of the historical world. If Tanabe only intended the first sense of transition, then he has already given his conclusion to the end of this advancement: viz., the philosophical deadlock that resulted in the discontinuation of his writing. In *Philosophy as Metanoetics*, Tanabe describes what this philosophical despair looks like.[43] But after three and half years of silence, he took up his pen in hand again and continued the work that later distinguished him as the originator of "Tanabean philosophy."[44] As if he were resurrected from the complete destitution from having worked within the framework of modern philosophy, Tanabe writes down another paragraph in the end of the second preface to the *KTT*. This paragraph opens with the following line: "The idea of absolute dialectic is still my position today."[45] Given that Tanabe associates the progress of humanity as based on the logic of rational universalism with Hegel and takes the Rankean alternative as the passage beyond it, the "transition to the dialectic as the theory of historical world" could also point us to the second possibility: viz., the transformative development from the modern rationalistic framework of thinking to another sense of philosophy that overcomes the former. Thus, Tanabe goes through the transition not only from the Kantian to the Hegelian framework of thinking but also from both of their rational universalisms to his own framework of thinking based on absolute nothingness, that is, the absolute dialectic, in the course of his lifetime.

The transformation of thought: Beyond universal rationalism

It is difficult to define where exactly the transition from the Kantian and the Hegelian framework of thinking to the metanoetic framework of the absolute dialectic occurs in the entire corpus of Tanabe. If I have to choose one in this transition that is most visible, I would nominate *Philosophy as Metanoetics* (where the Mahāyāna concept of nothingness is clearly named as the ultimate source of reality), while yet others must be included as a significant point of departure in Tanabe's oeuvre. Indeed, there are moments that spark novel views in the earlier texts, whose shape and color look almost identical to the beauty and valor of thought developed in the later texts.[46] The most difficult yet the most important work to categorize in relation to this concept of transition is the collection of thirteen essays, which distinguished Tanabe as an original philosopher in his own right, that is, *The Logic of Species*. The massive text of over 1200 pages, written in the course of fifteen years (1932–1946), continuously addresses the relation between genus, species, and individual. The text strives to show how each of these categories engages in dialectical relation to the other. This distinction is compared to the state, the racial/ethnic group, and the single individual, while later he uses these categories for demonstrating the intermediating relation of religion, philosophy, and politics/science. If we examine the different ways in which Tanabe formulates the triadic unity of these terms, we will likely encounter many problems. However, the most important issue that cuts through many of them, which is indeed the most relevant problem for our present discussion, is the fact that the absolute dialectic in *The Logic of Species* transitions from a nonreligious tone—one that makes it difficult for us to distinguish it from the contracted framework of Hegelian dialectic—to the truly absolute and most concrete dialectic that Tanabe develops more clearly in his later philosophy of religion.[47]

Let me elaborate on this difficulty of differentiating Tanabe's philosophy from modern rational universalism with a textual example. In "A Clarification of the Meaning of the Logic of Species," Tanabe writes that "to interpret the world as the self-determination of the absolute nothingness is in fact to place the standpoint that overcomes the dialectic over the dialectic."[48] Coupled with his constant criticisms of Hegelian dialectic throughout *The Logic of Species*, this statement clearly insinuates that the absolute dialectic in the logic of species (i.e., the metanoetic intermediation of genus, species, and the individual) must indicate a passage beyond the dialectical (mis-)conception of history as a rational progress.[49] However, we should also notice how, from the outset, Tanabe's use of the term "self-determination of the absolute" alarmingly resonates with that of Hegel. In fact, there are moments in Tanabe's language concerning the genus-species-individual intermediations that sound essentially the same as Hegel's self-determining universalism.[50] Some of these lines could be a result of Tanabe's inability to move beyond the bounds of Kantian and Hegelian philosophy, whereas the others could be a result of our inability to detect the key differences between Tanabe's philosophical thinking, incorporating the Eastern concept of absolute nothingness, before and after its transformation. In the next section, therefore, I will emphasize some of the key elements of the absolute dialectic and elucidate how it can be thought to overcome the limitation of Hegelian dialectic. This will enable us to conceptualize the interrelation between modern philosophy of rational universalism that pertains to the history of Western philosophy and Tanabe's contemporary comparative philosophy and to unfold Tanabe's method of comparative philosophy.

The four elements of absolute dialectic

There are four senses in which we could argue that Tanabe's dialectic overcomes the limitation of rational universalism especially in the form of Hegelian dialectic. First, Tanabe argues that the absolute dialectic must provide an alternative to Hegel's formulation of the mediation between the universal (i.e., rational) and the particular (i.e., irrational). Tanabe stresses that the logic of absolute mediation

> does not try to deny the irrationality in the content of life, but it rather takes irrational immediacy as its negative moment. It certainly rejects the abstract rationalism that abstracts the content of direct experience and regards the parts that can be deduced from its logic alone as the content of philosophy, but it also rejects the pan-methodological and ultimate rationalism, which stands between abstract rationalism and totalistic rationalism, takes intuition as its task for speculation, and tries to resolve its content to the development of the concept through an infinite rationalizing process. ... The dialectical logic of absolute mediation does not rationalize the irrational, but while maintaining the irrational as the irrational, it mediates and develops the corresponding (*sō-soku-teki* 相即的) unification of the rational and the irrational.[51]

Hegel's panlogistic rationalism can account for the irrational only as the particularized moment in the process of the mind's ultimate self-knowing as the rational universal. If the irrational status of the particular can have its significance as the irrational only in reference to the infinite rationalizing process of the universal, can it really be irrational? Can it really be resistant to the development of dialectical reasoning? Can anything in the framework of Hegelian dialectic escape its rationalizing process and truly address itself as the irrational? In his development of the logic of species, Tanabe frequently criticizes Hegelian dialectic for being incapable of taking into account the contradictory division of the particular and the universal.⁵² What he offers as the alternative to the dialectical incorporation of the irrational into the rational whole of the Hegel's self-determining concept is the logic of absolute mediation.⁵³ Tanabe's absolute dialectic neither places the ultimate emphasis on the rational universal nor affirms the significance of the irrational merely in relation to the self-determining rational whole. However, by setting forth the notion of species as the irrational substratum of the particular and placing the focal point of the dialectical intermediations on absolute nothingness, Tanabe offers a way to account for the irrationality of the particular in its interrelation with the rationality of the universal—yet without reducing this intermediation to the closed circuit of rational self-determination.⁵⁴ There is an intermediation of two opposites through the absolute that is irreducible to either one of these terms.

Second, as we will see more in detail later, the self-determination of nothingness in absolute dialectic radically differs from that of the absolute spirit in Hegel because the sense of the absolute communicated through the former radically differs from that through the latter. The absolute spirit in Hegel (as Desmond often acutely points out) is a kind of a gnostic god: out of its initial indeterminacy, it creates the world as the particularized moment of itself and uses this other for the fuller realization of itself.⁵⁵ This god of the consummate whole comes to be in the end of its self-mediating progress (wherever or whenever this end would be) and reveals itself as an "erotic" universal that grants the worth and the being of the particular ultimately for itself. The ultimate in Tanabe's absolute dialectic, however, is inspired by the "nothingness" of Mahāyāna Buddhism. It comprises the intermediation of the universal (i.e., genus), particular (i.e., species), and the individual such that it always already enables the individual to be for itself as the singular, to be with the others in species, and to freely concretize genus through its intermediation with species.⁵⁶ Since it ultimately accounts for the inter (i.e., *aida* (間) or the *between*) of the intermediations among genus, species, and individual, Tanabe's absolute cannot be reduced to any one of these terms, but appears only in their interrelations.⁵⁷ It is neither the irrational of the particular nor the rational of the universal, nor even the dynamic exigency of the indeterminate universal that needs its self-othering irrationality for determining itself as the rational whole. Rather, out of its eternal fullness the absolute nothingness always gives the worth and the being of the individual, species, and genus in their porous relativity to each other, not for itself, but for their self- and intermediations.⁵⁸ Tanabe further states that the universality of genus can achieve its concrete manifestation only through various self- and intermediations among species and individuals. In the same manner, the absolute achieves its concrete manifestation through the triadic intermediations of these terms. But this absolute always remains empty of any selfish desire to affirm itself in and through any of these terms. Tanabe's absolute nothingness, unlike Hegel's absolute spirit, determines itself to be infinitely "self-negating love"⁵⁹ that enables self- and intermediations of all others ultimately for themselves.⁶⁰

Third, for us to see the self-determination of absolute nothingness as a selfless granting of the worth and the being of our existence ultimately for us, we must reconfigure our understanding of the universal-particular-individual relations. That is to say, we have to cultivate our hearts-and-minds to see that our being, whether as an individual or species, is ultimately enabled, but enabled to be free by the great compassion of absolute nothingness. This recalibration of the relevant terms in the ways of our being-in-the-world (i.e., genus, species, and individual) requires a conversion (*tenkan*) of our hearts-and-minds (*kokoro*, 心) from the logic of self-determination, haunted by the great thirst of the will to power, to the self-less intermediation of hearts-and-minds, saturated with the overflowing spirit of great-negation-qua-great-compassion (*daihi-soku-daihi*, 大非即大悲).[61] Tanabe calls this transition between two ways of philosophizing the "metanoetic conversion" and claims that it has enabled him to think beyond the deadlock to which his previous ways of thinking led him. Since we have to let go of our inherent desire to subjugate all the others to determine ourselves and claim our status as the absolute beyond the others, the absolute dialectic asks for our penitent confessions (*zange*, 懺悔) of our sinful will to power and constant "practice of love."[62] Without this act of true generosity that dedicates the self for the other, we can neither repent our will to power nor escape its self-obsession. "Without metanoetics," as Tanabe clearly states, "there cannot be any act of nothingness."[63] Thus through the metanoetic conversion of our hearts-and-minds, we enter the open community of genus, species, and individual beyond the self-determining circle of Hegelian dialectic.

Finally, the structure of absolute mediation in Tanabe's metanoetics constitutes world history as a plurivocal community of different ages. With regard to the intermediation between the divine and the worldly, Tanabe describes the divine way down as "*gensō* (還相)" and the world's way up as "*ōsō* (往相)" in accord with his understanding of *gensō-ekō* (還相回向) and *ōsō-ekō* (往相回向) in the teachings of Pure Land and Shin Buddhism.[64] He further articulates,

> The movement from what is immanent to what is transcendent is made possible when the latter intermediates and transforms the self to the former and pulls up the former into itself; hence, the upward movement of *ōsō* must always correspond with downward movement of *gensō*. There is no one-way path from the immanent to the transcendent.[65]

This two-way intermediation of the divine and the worldly as *ōsō-qua-gensō* (往相即還相) also echoes the two-way intermediation of time and eternity. Tanabe writes:

> [E]ternity as absolute nothingness can realize and manifest itself only through the medium of time that takes the negative opposition of the past and the future as a moment of its establishment. If time needs eternity as the ground of its constitution as the self-negating unity and can only be established as the internalization of eternal transcendence, then eternity … must be that which affirms and restores time by retuning to time (*gensō-suru*, 還相する) as it assimilates the latter into itself in the manner of absolute negation. In this sense, we can say that time goes toward eternity and eternity returns to time. Eternity is mediated through the self-negation of time and through its absolute negation, it returns to time as the transcendent ground that realizes time in its immanent unity. Outside this mediating realization of time, there could be no eternity as absolute nothingness.[66]

The most important point concerning the intermediation of time and eternity for the constitution of history in the absolute dialectic is that each point of time as the relative has its access to eternity as the absolute. Whether each point of time is new or old, it has an equal opportunity to manifest the ideal of absolute nothingness through the self-negating practice of love. Only in this manner can it achieve its own unified existence as a particular age and the integrity of its own meaning. To do so, each age must go through a metanoetic conversion of its hearts-and-minds and constantly engage in the selfless act of great compassion. Only in this sense, Tanabe argues that,

> each age has the absolute status in connection with the divine, each age, whether it is new or old, must independently exert its subjective energy and only so long as it realizes and represents the truly absolute and eternal value, it establishes the relation pertaining to the transition (*tenkan*) of ages.[67]

This transformative transition between two ages in the context of the absolute dialectic indicates that one age comes to realize its connection with the eternal presence of absolute nothingness through its developmental intermediation with the other. This interrelation among the ages does not signify the self-determining progress of rational history where the latest age claims itself to testify to the absolute, thereby signaling the end of historical progress. But by recognizing the common roots in the eternal source of history, the present age can enter an open dialogue with the previous age. Insofar as one age is aware of the basis on which all the ages are established, it can learn from the mistakes of the past and, without falling into the same pitfalls, fulfill the sense of time by making further advancement on its realization of absolute nothingness (*zettai-mu no genjō*, 絶対無の現成). Thus, Tanabe's absolute dialectic shows the transition of two ages as the metanoetic conversion of the ways in which time relates to eternity and constitutes history as an open community of different ages.

The method of comparative thinking at work in Tanabe's philosophy

As we have seen above, Tanabe's theory of the historical world (i.e., absolute dialectic) abandons the notion of rational progress and recognizes the kind of the historical development that allows the open community of various ages. The movement from one age to another in this (Rankean) theory of history signifies the transformative advancement that grants the equal significance of each particular age in its capacity to realize its eternal significance yet simultaneously indicates its advancement such that it can better itself for the fuller realization of such ideal. This conception of history is perfectly in line with our discussion on the history of philosophy—an intellectual history that constitutes a transformative advancement from one framework of thinking to another. I have argued that the intellectual development in recent history of philosophy must signify this transformative advancement that grants the equal significance of each particular framework of thinking in its potential capacity to articulate what is true about the given historical reality yet indicates a historical advancement of one over the other in the sense that the new can fundamentally overcome the shortcomings of the old. The advancement of the history, according to Tanabe, is transformation of one age into another and follows the logic of absolute dialectic. This logic, which integrates the Buddhist notion of absolute nothingness, signals the historico-intellectual advancement of Tanabe's philosophy beyond the confines of modern philosophy of the West.

Then what implications on the method of comparative philosophy can we draw from the historico-intellectual significance of Tanabe's philosophy? We have seen that modern thinkers from the West tended to hold the notion of philosophy as a self-enclosed system of determinate thinking, and because of that, even many of the Japanese thinkers in the mid-nineteenth century had acknowledged such rationalistic framework of thinking as the distinct characteristics of the Western (and only) philosophy. As a result, they were strongly tempted to construe the purely disjunctive or the one-sided relation between two distinct intellectual traditions for their conception of the world intellectual history. As our earlier discussion shows, the variations of the modern form(s) of thinking (that we find in the works of Kant and Hegel) are not suitable for the foundation of comparative thinking, as it tends to privilege a particular intellectual tradition as the sole determiner of the philosophical discourse. The significance of Tanabe's philosophy for the method of comparative philosophy, then, lies in its process and the grounding metaphysical supposition through which it overcomes the limited notion of philosophy conceived in modern rationalistic framework of Western thought.

The most important metaphysical supposition through which Tanabe brings forth the wider notion of philosophy is what we have seen as the application of his concept of world history to the concept of the history of world philosophy. When the notion of "transition" (*tenkan*) in absolute dialectic is applied to the history of philosophy, the interrelation of two historical frameworks of thinking can be seen not as the sublationary progress of self-determining thinking but as a transformative advancement that allows the open community of various frameworks of thinking in the world history. From this viewpoint, Western philosophy does not need to simply reject or dialectically supersede non-Western intellectual traditions for affirming itself to be the sole determiner of the world philosophy. Rather, by basing its philosophical foundation on the self-negating compassion of absolute nothingness, it can let any intellectual tradition—no matter how irrational or foreign it might sound to its own at first—speak for itself and thereby enter into an open dialogue in which it can patiently listen to the wisdom of the other and integrate this wisdom for overcoming its own limitation.

This view of the open community of various intellectual traditions is also consistent with the way in which Tanabe grounds the specific differences of cultural traditions (i.e., species) in absolute dialectic. As I have shown in the previous section, Tanabe sets the notion of species as the irrational substratum of the particular and then places the focal point of the intermediations among the single individual, the particular (i.e., species), and the universal (i.e., genus) on the notion of absolute nothingness. In this case, since the absolute is infinitely self-negating compassion irreducible to any of the relevant terms, we can account for the irrationality of the particular in its interrelation with the rationality of the universal without reducing their intermediation into the self-enclosed self-determination of the universal rationality as the absolute. In other words, the self-negating absolute in Tanabe's absolute dialectic can set a specific intellectual tradition to freely determine its own rationality through its intermediation with the other particular traditions while also letting a single individual freely constitute the particular intellectual tradition with other single individuals. Since none of the intermediating terms can claim itself to be the absolute but the self-negating absolute lets each of them be for itself and intermediate freely with the other, the determination of the universal rationality through the intermediations of the particular intellectual traditions neither downgrades the significance of their particular differences for their universal togetherness nor runs the risk of crowning one tradition as the privileged mediator of such self-determining universal. This means the differences of the particulars are kept open and constitute the universal intellectual world as the plurivocal community of various philosophical traditions. Thus, as the notion of the dialectical "transition" allows Tanabe to conceive of the history as an open community of historical ages, his absolute dialectic allows him to ground the conception of the intellectual history as an open community of various frameworks of thinking. Because of this constitutive presupposition concerning the history of philosophy, Tanabe can freely transcend the specific confines of various intellectual traditions, listen to each of them with patience, and integrate them into the wider framework of thinking in his own works.[68]

The process through which Tanabe reaches the later standpoint of absolute dialectic shows a certain characteristic conductive to the practice of comparative thinking. For instance, Tanabe carries out his earlier engagement with Kant and Hegel not to reject the validity of their original project (i.e., to comprehend the given historical world as what it is) but shows his patient effort to complete this task as comprehensively and coherently as possible through their systematic viewpoints. In this sense, his struggle with the works of the modern thinkers was never external or dismissive from the beginning but always internal and consistently intimate. Accordingly, the overcoming of their limitations in his later works should be seen as the transformation (*tenkan*) of his way of thinking or the conversion (*tenkan*) of his standpoint from the self-enclosed framework of self-determining thinking to a kind of thinking that finds its foundation in the self-negating compassion of absolute nothingness. This foundation of Tanabe's later philosophy will eventually allow him to integrate multiple intellectual traditions for answering the philosophical question—the question that moved him to think through the modern frameworks of the Western philosophy in the first place. What is particularly interesting here, moreover, is that prior to his arrival at this standpoint, Tanabe was already practicing the kind of compassionate thinking—thinking that is marked with the selfless effort to allow each thinker, each framework of thinking, and each intellectual tradition to speak for the best of itself. The principle of charity (to borrow Augustine's expression) was already present in Tanabe's early engagement with the works of the modern thinkers, and because of that, he was able to fully adopt the principle of self-negating compassion as the foundation of his mature philosophical thinking.

Tanabe's later adaptation of absolute nothingness as the foundation of absolute dialectic also demonstrates his existential stance conducive to the practice of comparative philosophy. At a glance, some might wonder that Tanabe's metaphysical worldview just ends up favoring his own intellectual tradition by inserting the Buddhist notion of the divine absolute into its systematic framework. But notice how Tanabe clearly argues that the realization of absolute nothingness (as the constitutive ground for our proper understanding of the historical world) requires our constant practice of metanoesis. This means that we must continuously engage in our penitent confessions (*zange*) over our natural propensity to follow the logic of self-determination. The truth is that all of us want to prove in one way or another that our specific intellectual tradition carries the universal validity or the infinite worth that we give to the name "philosophy." In this sense, when we face the world history that constitutes the multiplicity of various intellectual traditions, we are tempted either to eliminate what is other to our own as a worthless cluster of irrationalism or try to make sense of them through our own tradition as the privileged mediator of the world philosophy. In either case, the logic of self-determination fuels our desire to reduce the polyvocal community of various intellectual traditions ultimately into the single voice, namely our own that naturally seems to make most sense to us.

Absolute dialectic, however, shows that the world is different from what our self-determining thinking projects precisely because it moves us to give up such self-centered manner of thinking. It moves us to give up recreating the world in image of ourselves but follow, in humility, the self-negating logic of great compassion that enables the world to be in many different ways. What we can find in Tanabe's mature standpoint, therefore, is not a simple adaptation of an Eastern concept under the same elocution of self-glorifying self-determining thinking. Rather, it signals a transformation of such intellectual arrogance or egoity into the spiritual humility that enables him to exercise the compassionate thinking. It thinks of what is other to itself for the other and tries to make sense of the other in terms of the other as much as possible. By following the self-negating logic of absolute dialectic, Tanabe becomes capable of listening to the interlocutions of various intellectual traditions as the equal partners in the open stage of the world philosophy. This compassionate thinking, fully embraced as metanoesis in later works of Tanabe, makes possible the comparative examination of the Eastern and the Western intellectual tradition without committing injustice to either one of them.

On the comparative examination of Desmond and Tanabe

In overture to the methodological reflections on the comparative examination of Tanabe and Desmond, I have argued that we cannot hold an abstract standpoint from which we externally compare one intellectual tradition with another. This is especially the case when we find ourselves belonging to either one of these traditions. Nor can we attempt to describe a method of (comparative) philosophy from such a monolithic standpoint since a method of our thinking is often already at work in our description of it. I have also argued that if we find ourselves being much more at home in the Western intellectual tradition, we should think about the possibility of comparative philosophy not only through the works of the thinkers working in the field of non-Western philosophy but also through the works of those engaging in the philosophical questions within our own intellectual tradition in the West. Even if the latter might suffer from the contemporary criticisms of "Eurocentrism" or "Occidentalism," we should never cease to think of the implications that their systematic thinking can provide for the possibility of a meaningful dialogue between what they think as their form(s) of thinking and what are others to it. With all fairness to the spirit of comparative philosophy, therefore, I have proposed to think through the works both of Desmond and Tanabe and then lay out their contributions to the method of comparative philosophy.

As my expositions of the key elements in the works of Desmond and Tanabe show, whether we think through the framework of the former or the latter, we can come to a similar understanding of how we should practice any comparative examination of the multiple frameworks of thinking. Metaxology indicates that the full realization of self requires its genuine transcendence to what is other to itself as the intermediation of the self and the other must constitute their two-way communications. Agapeic mindfulness that remains faithful to this communicative interrelation of two relevant terms, as we have seen above, both grounds and anticipates the plurivocal compossiblity of various intellectual traditions. Similarly, Tanabe's absolute dialectic holds the structure of intellectual history to consist of the open community of various frameworks of thinking. Through the metanoetic notion of "transition" (*tenkan*), the Japanese philosopher strongly suggests that Western philosophy can base itself on the self-negating compassion of absolute nothingness and thereby enter into an open dialogue in which it can patiently listen to what is other to itself and integrate the wisdom of the other to overcome its own limitation.

What these thinkers require for the proper intermediation of multiple frameworks of thinking, or in this context, the comparative examination of one intellectual tradition with another, then, is a kind of intellectual selflessness. This selflessness is expressed in such terms as "humility," "patience," "generosity," and "compassion." I would like to beg this sort of patience from my readers at this point too since I cannot help but repeating the crucial passage of the metaxological thinking:

> Agapeic mindfulness gives its understanding over to the position of the other from its otherness, seeks to see the other from within the intimacy of its own integrity of being. ... There is compassion in this knowing, an undergone with the other, not a standing above in the mode of mastery or mediation.[69]

It is about putting oneself in the shoes of the other, listening to the other by letting the other speak for the other, and then thinking from the perspective of the other. In the same spiritual manner, Tanabe explains that our realization of absolute nothingness requires our constant practice of metanoesis (*zange*) and demands us (as much as he demands himself) to be selfless and compassionate in the manner of the divine absolute. This is to say, the practice of metanoetic philosophy makes an effort to allow each intellectual tradition (i.e., species) or each work of an individual thinker in the whole history of philosophy to speak for the best of itself.

Thus, whether we begin our exploration for the methodology of comparative philosophy from the metaxological or the metanoetic standpoint, we reach the same conclusion: that is, we must practice a certain "tolerance of otherness" in our examination of multiple frameworks of thinking and thereby we must let each of them speak for itself in its communicative relation to the other. I certainly admit that there is something quite intuitive and ordinary about this practice. After all, don't we, students of philosophy, always let each thinker speaker for herself and end up either agreeing or disagreeing with her point? If we put it in this way, I agree that it sounds quite ordinary. But I would like us to ask ourselves again the difficulty of the ordinary practice of the philosophical study. How many of the thinkers in the history of philosophy have failed to listen to the others with judicious fairness or sufficient level of compassion? How many thinkers have impatiently ventriloquized their own voices through the others? How many postmodern thinkers have failed to confront the voice of the otherness beyond their loud voice of the "other!"—the voice that seems to be humming and resounding only within the confine of their own intellectual tradition? It is easy to say that we tolerate the otherness in our critical effort to understand ourselves but actually to do it well and reach out to listen to what is other to our own framework of thinking is tremendously difficult.

This "tolerance of otherness," furthermore, is not a passive observance of the exotic terms that add nothing valuable to the significance of one's intellectual tradition. As Desmond elegantly puts,

> Tolerance ... is not defined as a neutral indifference or disinterest; it is a heightened interest, which nevertheless is noninterfering. It is an *inter-esse*, a being between, that is potentially agapeic. It is a willingness to allow the thing in its otherness manifest itself without interference by our abstract mediations.[70]

The tolerance in this passage is spoken in terms of "aesthetics tolerance" as "an ontological respect for the thing in the thereness of its otherness."[71] But what I am suggesting here through the initial explorations of metaxology and metanoetics is the intellectual inclusion of what is other to one's intellectual tradition. It is about cultivating a generous mind marked with the true respect for the foreign intellectual tradition in the thereness of its otherness. The mind that is filled with the spirit of generosity can open itself beyond the confine of its own intellectual tradition and bring itself and other into a larger togetherness of human thinking. The methodology of comparative philosophy that we can propose through our examinations of metaxology and metanoetics, therefore, is to abide by this intellectual openness to and active reception of these frameworks of thinking. Thus, in relation to the fundamental questions for the philosophy of religion, I will look at each of their takes on the problems, patiently think through the ways in which they have worked out their solutions, and, with utmost respect to their ways of philosophizing, strive to voice my answers to the questions.[72]

Part Two

The Fundamental Problems of the Philosophy of Religion: Thinking through Rational Universalism

3

Kant and the Problems of Religion: Practical Reason and Rational Faith

Prelude

In this chapter and the one to follow, I will set forth the central problems of the philosophy of religion in reference to the works of Kant and Hegel. As I have briefly discussed in the Introduction, these issues essentially echo Kierkegaard's dissatisfaction with the Kantian and the Hegelian accounts of religion. Given that Tanabe and Desmond share the same critical stance with the Danish thinker, the critiques of universal rationalism in the works of Kant and Hegel will provide for us a common ground from which we can approach their responses.[1] This would enable us to look for solutions to the problems of the philosophy of religion through our critical engagement with the works of Tanabe and Desmond. However, if we were to enumerate the ways in which each of these contemporary thinkers interpret the works of their intellectual forefathers, and to then investigate whether or not each of their interpretations are well founded in the classical texts, it would take too much space. What is worse, this would commit insignificant repetitions. What is philosophically needed here, then, is not so much as to show how exactly Tanabe and Desmond understand the works of Kant and Hegel, but to see how they respond to the problems that are inherent in the Kantian and the Hegelian views of religion.[2] Thus, to set the stage for further investigations into the significance of metaxology and metanoetics in the field of philosophy of religion, I will exhibit, in the following, the fundamental problems of the philosophy of religion through the direct engagements with the works of Kant and Hegel.

Kierkegaardian discontent: Five charges against Kant and Hegel

Recall the Kierkegaardian concerns with the Kantian and the Hegelian concept of religion. The Danish thinker suggests (especially via Johannes de Silentio) that there are five interrelated issues with their notions of religion:

1. Their accounts of religion tend to reduce the divine-human relation to the immanent universality of human/societal self-relation that is based solely on the autonomy of reason.

The primacy of human autonomy, then, anticipates the second and the third problem:

2. It ultimately rejects the robust sense of divine transcendence.
3. It requires the extirpation of the single individual in its relation to the rational universal as the immanent absolute.

These problems implicitly hold that the authority of religion as what is other to philosophy must be compromised in relation to the superiority of the latter. Then the third problem further anticipates or at least implies the following two problems:

4. The self-negating self-transcendence of the finite individual to the infinite universal is a one-way movement.
5. The worth of the finite individual cannot be granted for itself, but always in relation to the universal.

The ways in which Kant and Hegel formulate the continuous relationship between philosophy (i.e., reason) and religion (i.e., faith) are quite different. Hence, the ways in which we will detect these problems in their systematic accounts of religion will also reflect these differences. But if we are to think only within the frameworks that these thinkers have provided for us through their texts, then we will equally be faced with the tremendous difficulty of avoiding any of these principal problems for the philosophy of religion. Thus, we will see how the German thinkers conceptualize religion through their systematic formulations of the relevant metaphysical terms (e.g., finite-infinite, contingent-necessary, natural-rational, particular-universal, human-divine, etc.) and further investigate how and to what extent their philosophical doctrines of religion are guilty of these charges.

Kant's ethics: A summary

Kant's understanding of religion problematically presupposes the unmediated tension between the immanent *telos* of the ethical and the "higher" *telos* of (Judeo-Christian) faith. This dualistic outlook on the relationship between faith and reason, as well as philosophy and religion, never gets resolved, even when Kant suggests their strong continuity through his doctrine of moral theology. In order to elucidate this point, we will examine in the following what it means to be ethical and religious for Kant, and to expose serious problems in the Kantian formulation of the relationship between faith and reason.

In the Kantian framework of *Moralität*, the empirical, contingent, and sensible aspect of human existence counts as the particular, while the universal pertains to the rational, self-determining, and supersensible aspect of humanity.[3] What makes each of us particular as a single individual are the sensible characteristics of our existence in this world, as well as the empirical conditions in which our actions are externally determined (i.e., pathological inclinations). Yet each of us is also endowed with reason, and because of that, we are capable of representing an objective principle of morality to ourselves as a command of reason. In other words, we can free ourselves from the mechanistic causality of the external world by conforming ourselves to the moral law as rational beings.[4] This moral law is universal because it is not relative to our contingent and subjective conditions in which we exist and determine our actions in this world as phenomenal beings, but necessary and binding for all of us as intellectual beings. Kant calls this necessity of determining our dispositions purely from respect for the moral law "duty" and formulates this command of practical reason in terms of the categorical imperative. The categorical imperative, as Desmond rightly characterizes, is the way for us to lift ourselves to the level of the rational universal.[5] In rising above the particularity of his sensible existence, a human being can give the universal law of morality to himself by conforming his maxim to the law, and by doing so for its own sake, he manifests his infinite value of humanity as an end in itself.[6]

The categorical imperative requires us to act in such a way that we always treat humanity, whether for ourselves or for others, as an end in itself, but never as means.[7] What is inherent in this command, Kant explains, is "the concept of autonomy of every rational being," where each human being regards himself as giving universal law to himself and determining himself as end in itself.[8] This leads to the ideality of "a kingdom of ends," namely, "the systematic union of various rational beings" made possible by the commonality of each person giving moral laws to themselves.[9] Morality, which requires the self-determination of each single individual to bring himself to be one with the universal moral laws, enables one to participate in this kingdom as a law-giving "sovereign,"[10] and to thereby hold respect for the dignity of his human nature as a rational being, which is derived from the autonomy of reason. By giving the moral law to ourselves, we can rise above the particularity of our sensible existence, become autonomous law-giving members of the universal ethical community, and obtain the dignity of humanity as rational beings. This process of exercising autonomy of our will in accordance with the moral command of pure practical reason is, for Kant, the only way for us to become ethical and unconditionally good as members of the universal kingdom of ends.

From morality to rational faith

How, then, does this conception of the ethical constitute Kant's theory of religion? Kant thinks that morality is based solely on the conception of human autonomy—namely, conforming our will to the laws that we give ourselves through our practical reason. Because of this, the idea of divine transcendence is unnecessary for us to recognize our moral obligations or to find ourselves responsible for attaining our moral worth.[11] But the practical task of pure reason, he further argues, posits the idea of the highest good (i.e., *summum bonum*) as the necessary a priori object of our will and the final end of our moral endeavors.[12] This idea consists of two elements: (1) the complete conformity of a will to the moral law, which posits the immortality of soul for the endless progress to our moral perfection as rational beings, and (2) happiness proportioned to this moral achievement. We cannot prove the necessary connection of these two for three reasons: first, experience tells us otherwise[13]; second, the moral law tells us to determine our dispositions independently of sensible nature[14]; and third, a human being, as a finite rational being, is not the cause of the world or of nature itself.[15] In short, there is nothing in the process of ethical self-determination in conformity with the universal moral law that grounds the necessity of the connection between our morality and proportioned happiness, nor can we bring our happiness in harmony with our practical lawgiving by our own powers as finite intellectual beings.

But Kant further explains that the moral law requires us to "strive to promote the highest good"[16] in this world, and just because of that, we have to think that it is (somehow) possible. And to think this possibility of the exact correspondence between morality and happiness, we have to posit "a supreme cause of nature having a causality in keeping with the moral disposition"[17]—that is, the divine absolute that can unite these two elements of the highest good, as both an omnipotent and morally perfect being. Thus, Kant argues that "it is morally necessary to assume the existence of God."[18] He indicates that this postulation of the idea of the divine calls for the "pure rational belief"[19] because we cannot know the objective reality of this idea, but we have to think that it is possible as the condition for the possibility of the highest good. We can also describe this belief in the "future" possibility of *summum bonum* to be rational because, according to Kant, the practical postulate of God is derived solely from our reason.

Questions concerning practical reason and rational faith

Now Kant's formulation of the relationship between morality and rational faith calls for a few questions. First, we immediately detect an unmediated tension between the infinite value of humanity as an end in itself and the final end of the morality postulated beyond the conduct of a morally good life. This anticipates two interrelated questions: (1) Which is the ultimate end of a moral life: the highest good or the good will? Furthermore, (2) does morality precede faith or the other way around?[20] To answer these questions, then, we must examine the nature of the rational faith that we ought to have in Kant's divine absolute as a practical postulate. What kind of God is this? And how is it related to human autonomy as the source of our dignity and moral worth? These questions are extremely important for understanding the Kantian formulation of the relationship between practical reason and rational faith.

The practical postulation of the existence of God means that a human being is essentially "driven to believe in the cooperation or the management of a moral ruler of the world"[21] as the condition for the possibility of the highest good. But Kant also thinks that this "opens up before him the abyss of a mystery regarding what God may do."[22] If the highest good is the ultimate end to which all of our moral actions are to be directed, we have to consider the divine attributes and the conditions by which the divine will would grant us the fulfillment of our moral destiny as the *summum bonum*. But these are the mysteries extending beyond the limits of our reason. And what is most important, as Kant repeatedly emphasizes, is that the idea of God rises out of our awareness of moral laws and of reason's need to assume a power capable of procuring the highest good for the final destiny of our moral endeavors; yet, this idea itself by no means serves as the foundation of morality, but strictly the other way around.[23] That is to say, morality based on the autonomy of reason must precede faith (and hence the latter is always rational) because "morality alone gives us a determinate concept of God as a holy legislator of moral laws,"[24] and his "holiness is the absolute or the unlimited moral perfection of the will."[25] Without morality, we cannot think of God, nor practice religion through our determinate concept of God.

If God's existence as the ruler of ethical community is the foundation of our moral laws, and the ethical laws are proceeding from his will, Kant argues that these laws would cease to be moral "for the duty commensurate to them would not be a free virtue but an externally enforceable legal duty."[26] Because he has difficulty in penetrating the question regarding how rational beings could be "created to use their powers freely,"[27] Kant cannot think of the constitutive relation of God to human autonomy without conceiving it as a great threat to the latter, where reason can give itself the universal moral law and each rational being freely complies to the self-given moral principles. For this reason, Kant is almost "ecstatic" in defending the supremacy of reason's morality over the mystery of the divine will.

> [I]t is also necessary that God's will should not be made the principle of rational morality; for in this way we could never be sure what God had in mind for the world. How can I know by reason and speculation what God's will is, and what it consists in? Without morality to help me here, I would be on a slippery path, surrounded by mountains which afford me no prospect. How much danger I would be in of having my foot slip, or, because no clear horizon ever meets my eyes, of wandering lost in a labyrinth![28]

Here Kant confronts a great problem, in my view: he cannot rid himself of the notion of the divine absolute, particularly because practical reason needs to think the *summum bonum* as being possible. Moreover, practical reason commands that we ought to promote this idea as far as possible (regardless of the fact that we cannot know its objective reality).[29] That is to say, Kant wants to have God as the condition for the possibility of the highest good, while keeping the supremacy of moral autonomy uncompromised. Because of this, he holds that the practical postulate of God serves only as a regulative ideal in relation to our practice of morality and thereby shows that it is neither indispensable for the determination of our will in accordance with the moral law nor constitutive of the infinite (moral) value of humanity as an end in itself.[30] Thus, for Kant, morality has to precede faith; the infinite value of humanity as an end in itself is the true *telos* of our moral life; and the *summum bonum*, which is only posited ideally, can only be believed within the confines of our reason during our continuous labors toward moral autonomy.

How, then, does this regulative idea of God play its role in relation to the formulation of the relationship between faith and reason? Kant argues that "religion is the recognition of all our duties as divine commands"[31] and maintains that

God can be thought of as the supreme lawgiver of an ethical community, with respect to whom all true duties, hence also the ethical, must be represented as at the same time his commands; consequently, he must also be one who knows the heart, in order to penetrate to the most intimate parts of the dispositions of each and everyone and, as must be in every community, give to each according to the worth of his actions.[32]

God, in this sense, is presented as the moral judge who gives moral laws to rational beings and distributes the reward proportioned to the labor of virtue (hopefully after this life).[33] But as we have seen, Kant wants to have the autonomy of moral reason as both necessary and sufficient for determining one's moral worth and the divine ideal as that which is derived from morality. If this is the case, then it follows that rational beings are giving themselves the same laws as those of this divine lawgiver (otherwise they would not be observed as the moral laws). Since God's relation to the moral principles cannot be constitutive, but only regulative, this supreme ruler can only give the commands that are identical with the ones that rational beings are giving to themselves as the universal commands of their practical reason. On this basis, the divine authority, according to the Kantian formulation of moral religion, is the same as the authority of practical reason; that is, the divine commands given in the ethical community are identical with the moral laws given by our practical reason. As a result, there is an essential identity between religious faith and moral reason in Kant's philosophy of religion.[34]

Problems in Kant's theory of religion

If an ethical task is the task of true religion as Kant maintains, it is logical to think that "[our moral actions] are constantly in the service of God; and it is absolutely impossible to serve [God] more intimately in some other way"[35] than to fulfill our moral obligations. What Kant provides in his account of moral religion, in this sense, is the strong continuity between (rational) faith and (practical) reason. Closer examination of his concept of the divine absolute as the practical postulate, however, along with his take on the uncompromising supremacy of moral autonomy, demonstrates that there is no essential difference between what rational faith holds as the highest commands from those of practical reason in ethics. Kant claims that true religion recognizes the moral laws as divine commands, but the term "divinity" here has neither conceptual nor practical bearing on the fact that these laws are merely moral commands given in accordance with the autonomy of practical reason. This essential identity between religion and morality brings us to the five fundamental problems that we have seen since the beginning of this chapter.

With regard to the first problem, Kant's moral religion clearly has a strong tendency to define the divine-human relation in terms of the immanent self-relation of rational beings—the self-relation based solely on the autonomy of practical reason. Consider the following question: If God gives the moral laws and humans give themselves the same laws in accordance with their practical reason, why do we have to posit God as the moral legislator of these laws at all? This God does not have any constitutive influence on the significance of our moral worth as an end in itself; rather, we merely think of this legislator as a regulative ideal for enabling the possibility of the highest good. The basis of this postulation is again our practical reason, while the unconditional good is our moral goodness, which we attain through determining our will in consonance with practical reason. It is no wonder, then, that Kant claims that we are the "the sole author of all our actions"[36] determining our unconditional moral worth. What constitutes ourselves as members of the ethical community (i.e., *Reich*) is our own freedom to determine our will according to the form of our reason. This is precisely the reason why Kant insists that no deity can be the creator of the moral laws. If so, why cannot we not just say that our autonomy is the condition for the possibility of our infinite value as an end in itself, and that our reason is the highest authority? Insofar as the primacy of autonomy is the source of our moral dignity, nothing can prevent us from dispensing with the divine absolute (and religion), and thereby claiming ourselves as the highest rational beings that, in turn, grant ourselves the infinite worth of morality.[37] Kant's arguments for the supposed continuity between philosophical reason and religious faith end up reducing the latter to the former.

Kant remains somewhat equivocal in relation to the second problem. On the one hand, he clearly indicates that we do not need any notion of divinity, either to recognize for religious purposes or to account for our moral obligations. In that vein, he further specifies that the notion of the divine absolute can only be derivative of the moral concept. In this sense, Kant clearly rejects the robust sense of the divine transcendence that is both irreducible to and constitutive of the human/societal self-relations. But, on the other hand, he also argues that our reason must contemplate the importance of the highest good, which seems to exceed the end and the capacity of our moral self-determination; and thereby, the necessity of postulating the ideal of God suggests that reason and moral existence, just as much as defining themselves as the highest authority of their own worth, cannot help but recognize the metaphysical "beyond" pointing toward the higher authority to which their freedom might be accountable.[38] Kant's doctrine of moral religion, in this manner, consistently suffers from the unresolved tension between the primacy of human autonomy and the necessity of postulating the idea of God as the moral legislator. This split between the immanent universality of human autonomy and the metaphysical vision of what is other to it could lead us to face the necessity of rethinking the possibility of faith in divine authority without conflating it with the human authority of reason. But by calling the divine absolute as a regulative ideal of reason, Kant refrains from dealing with this problem and ultimately holds on to the supremacy of human autonomy. Consequently, his postulated divinity only comprises an empty echo of practical reason and affords him the methodical reduction of religion to moral philosophy.[39]

The process through which each human individual achieves the infinite value of his moral existence signals the presence of the third problem. In relation to the continuity between practical reason and rational faith, Kant presupposes a sharp division between the contingent particularity of our sensible existence (i.e., "empirical character") and the necessary universality of our moral existence (i.e., "intelligible character"). In order for a single individual to be religious (which is essentially to be ethical), he must strive to free himself from the mechanistic causality of the external world by conforming himself to the universal form of reason (i.e., moral law). This means that the process of ethical/religious self-determination for a critical moralist requires his negation of the empirical character for the ultimate affirmation of the intelligible character.[40] But what distinguishes us from each other as single individuals is the fact that we are bound by the principle of individuation in the spatio-temporal realm of nature, while our subordination to this principle prevents us from becoming moral and free. So, the movement from the sensible character that suffers from the causal limitation of the phenomenal world to the intelligible character that promises the moral freedom in the realm of noumena implicitly points toward the ultimate dismissal of our existence as a single individual in nature. This disjunctive division between the causal reality of the phenomenal world and the noumenal ideality of moral freedom in relation to each of our existence as a human being causes great concern: that is, a human subject cannot be thought to maintain its status as a single individual when he succeeds in making his maxim in conformity with the universal moral law while also entering the kingdom of ends.

The third problem further anticipates the fourth and the fifth problem of the philosophy of religion in Kant's theory of ethics. Kant insists on the notion of individual self-legislation as the primary foundation for the constitution of the universal moral community. This means that the finite individual must comprise the infinite universality of the rational community by negating its sensible individuality. In this case, the kingdom of ends is merely the result of autonomous moral subjects individually completing their self-legislations. This clearly shows the one-way development from the finite particular to the infinite universal, and thereby the worth of the finite individual is granted always in reference to the rational universality of the moral law. However, as Desmond rightly points out in *EB*, the "*pluralizing* of self-legislation create serious difficulties to holding on to the notion of *self*-legislation as the primary model of moral freedom."[41] Stated otherwise, once we envision the multiplicity of self-mediating moral subjects, we must think about the nature of the intermediation between these subjects apropos of the constitution of their community, as well as the interrelation of the whole of such a community with each of its self-mediating members.

As we have seen above, Kant initially claims that God is the moral ruler of the *Reich* (hence, we traditionally translate this term as *king*dom), and therefore, he seems to present a picture in which the divine absolute rules over the community of the moral subjects as the king. But since what constitutes this community are our individual self-legislations, as the autonomous moral "sovereigns," while the notion of the divine is merely a practical postulate derivative of our reason, the title of the "infinite absolute" goes to the immanent universality of the ethical community—the community constituted through our dutiful compliance of our will to the unified form of practical reason. But this constitution of the universal ethical community is problematic, since the self-legislation of the individual, which marks the movement toward the attainment of the "intelligible character," supposedly annuls the individuality of its "empirical character" as the single individual. If this is the case, how could these individuals constitute the *plurality* of morally autonomous subjects into and within the universal ethical community? If the principle of individuation lies in the spatio-temporal representation of phenomenal objects, it would have to be impossible for us to understand the multiplicity of the rational beings. This is precisely what Kant says about the application of categories to the rational and noumenal objects in the third paralogism.[42]

The only way in which we can account for the finite particularity of rational beings in the infinite universality of their ethical community, then, is to think about the constitutive relationship between the infinite whole of the moral community and the moral subjects as its finite parts, as well as to conceptualize the ways in which the intermediations of the finite parts constitute the whole. Yet, to do this, Kant must rethink the relationships between his relevant metaphysical terms (e.g., the finite-infinite, the sensible-rational, the phenomenal-noumenal, the particular-universal, etc.), and carefully examine the horizontal and vertical intermediations in relation to the ethical community of humanity as rational beings. The one-way movement from the finite individual to the infinite universal in Kant's formulation of morality and rational theology, thus, uncritically assumes that the autonomous self-constitution of the moral subject alone can somehow constitute the community of such self-constitutions. This "somehow," however, only highlights the impossibility of understanding the relationship between the finite moral subject and the infinite moral community by means of the notion of individual self-legislation.

The difficulty of conceiving of any plurality in relation to the infinite worth of humanity as the end in itself immediately leads to the difficulty of granting any worth to the finite individual as the finite. The single individual, in other words, must always shed his individual particularity to be in line with the universal form of practical reason, yet Kant does not give a sufficient explanation for the possibility of this plurality in relation to the rational universal. Unless we critically reconsider the ways in which we can ground the individuality of the rational subjects who are in conformity with the universal form of practical reason, there is no way for us to avoid the fifth problem of philosophy of religion in the Kantian rational theology.

Beyond Kant's moral religion

I have shown that Kant's accounts of morality and his moral doctrines of religion have tremendous difficulties in avoiding the five fundamental problems of the philosophy of religion. If our fulfillment of the ethical duties is the true and only service of the divine absolute, and further, if our autonomy is the sole basis of ethical value and (immanent) *telos* of our moral life, then any specific religious doctrine—whether it pertains to the Judeo-Christian tradition in the West or to the Mahāyāna Buddhist tradition in the East—could not offer anything more important to our moral endeavors. In this sense, the strong continuity between philosophy and religion in Kant's formulation ultimately reduces the human-divine relation to the immanent universality of human self-relation. This absolutization of the moral universal as the sole motive for the reduction of religion to philosophy also makes it impossible to conceive of the worth of the human individual without negating his singularity for the determination of the ethical universal.

Kant paints a picture of the ethical community as that in which rational beings can autonomously give themselves the moral law and constitute the unity of their multiplicities. But there is nowhere in Kant's oeuvre that sufficiently supports this condition of possibly grounding the particularity of human individuals in relation to their intelligible character(s). Despite the language of "community" or "rational beings" in Kant's elaborations on the ethical universal, his doctrine of moral religion cannot account for the irreducible singularity of the human individual in its relativity to the ethical universal, let alone the relation of the single individual to the divine absolute beyond such rational universal.

Within the bounds of moral religion, neither the notion of divine absolute nor the authority of religion can be given as that which is irreducible to the immanent *telos* of human self-determination to be ethical and universal. Nor can we make sense of the divine-human relationship, where the divine can account for the irreducible singularity of a human existence for the singular and ground the community of such singular as the plurality of rational beings, and where the human singular can relate himself to the divine absolute beyond the intersubjective constitution of the ethical community. Unless we can account for these possibilities in the relationship between the human and the divine, any philosophical account of religion will only amount to a systematic reduction of religion to ethical reasoning. So, to give a genuine philosophical account of religious faith as something more than what philosophical reason can dream of, we must go beyond the boundary of practical reason.

Kant might be right in saying that, if we venture beyond the boundaries of his critical reason and presume to continue our flight beyond them, we only "fall into whirlpools and turbulent waters [of confusions], plunging ourselves into a bottomless abyss where we are wholly swallowed up."[43] But he has already pushed us into the depth of the metaphysical question when he equivocally asks us to think about the *Reich* or to recognize the necessity of postulating the divine absolute. We have seen that this postulated divinity is an empty echo of practical reason and that we supposedly need nothing beyond ourselves to live up to the absolute worth of moral freedom. We have also seen that there is no way for Kant to account for the plurality of rational beings in the realm of the intelligible or for the constitution of such plurality merely through the individual model of self-legislations. Nonetheless, Kant still requires us to think through the necessity of these ideas. These equivocal requirements in Kantian ethics constantly point us beyond the limits of practical reason and push us into the depths of the metaphysical question concerning our faith in the absolute beyond ourselves. Unless we learn to swim to a shore where we can ground the constitutive relation of divinity to humanity beyond the universal command of practical reason, we will, therefore, never make sense of faith or religion as signifying anything more than the determinate concepts of moral reasoning.[44]

4

Hegel and the Problem of the Philosophy of Religion: Dynamic Reason and Its Sublation of Faith

To see how the fundamental problems of the philosophy of religion are also inherent in Hegel's concept of religion, I will carry out the following three investigations in this section: First, I will examine how Hegel criticizes Kant's moral religion in his early theological works. Second, I will elucidate Hegel's systematic responses to the problems that he works out in *Lectures on the Philosophy of Religion*. Third, we will see whether or not Hegel's philosophical conception of religion, allegedly dissolving the problems of Kantian rational theology, ultimately falls victim to the same problems of the philosophy of religion.

Early Hegel and his criticism of morality and moral religion

The young Hegel finds two explicit problems in Kant's theory of religion. First, he sees an irresolvable tension between the autonomy of practical reason and the heteronomy of faith. He thinks that one's respect for the moral law in Kantian ethics is aroused insofar as the law is self-given and its objectivity is derived solely from the form of practical reason. However, Hegel adds that Christianity, as a positive religion, "proclaims that the moral law is something outside us and something given,"[1] and "if it is given, then virtue becomes an art of a very complicated kind in contrast with an uncorrupted moral sense which is in a position to decide any issue on the spot because it dares to make its decisions for itself."[2] Hegel, in this sense, clearly takes issue with Kant for conflating the moral laws with the divine and for then holding the primacy of practical reason in conjunction with God as the moral legislator. If we give the laws to ourselves, then we do not need God beyond us. But if these laws are given, then the status of our autonomy has to be reformulated in its relative position to their originating source. As the previous chapter shows, Kant wants to have it both ways by making the divine commandments mere repetitions of our self-given moral laws. Hegel, however, argues that either morality based on the autonomy of our reason is the sole basis in which we can give ourselves the moral laws or we find the divine absolute as the giver of the moral laws outside of our reason.

Second, Hegel criticizes Kant's reduction of the divine commandments to moral obligations. Duty, according to the dialectical metaphysician, accommodates the dualistic division between reason and inclination, where the universal does not only claim its necessity as the objective form of reason but also remains as something alien to the particularity of subjective inclinations. And thanks to this object/subject split (*Entzweiung*), reason always excludes inclination and inclination is always dominated by reason. In having our whole existence constantly divided within itself, we can never be at home with ourselves, and therefore, moral laws as the commands of practical reason carry the dictatorial sense of "ought" or "duty." But, as Hegel believes, what Jesus is trying to get at through his exposition of the divine commandments is that these laws should not be observed as moral obligations, but practiced out of "love," through which we fulfill the laws by mediating the internal conflict between reason and inclination and exceed the previous sense of moral obligations.[3]

Hegel's responses to the problems of the Kantian philosophy of religion

Hegel's solutions to these problems can be found in his later work, *Lectures on the Philosophy of Religion*. The concept of religion is the seed of the absolute spirit, whose development is constitutive of the doctrines of all religions in the world. This initially abstract concept sprouts its particular stems in the course of human history as various forms of determinate religion and reaches its final form in Christianity.[4] This fruit of human religious thinking is the consummate religion, where the absolute spirit reveals itself in its final concreteness and manifests its rich content as the "determinate rational knowledge of itself."[5] In this systematic unfolding of the history of religion as the manifestation of the absolute knowing of divine consciousness, Hegel discusses the particular as that which is finite, natural, contingent, and untrue; and the universal as that which is infinite, rational, self-subsisting, and true. The relation of these contradictory terms is initially discussed in their dualistic opposition and then intermediated with one another in their reference to the self-determining process of that which is infinite, rational, and absolutely universal. There are three layers to this dialectical intermediation: (1) between the finitude of all contingent existence in/of nature and the infinite divine being, (2) between the natural and spiritual being within human existence, and (3) between the whole of human existence as a finite spirit and God as infinite spirit.

First, Hegel explains that finite objects have the characteristic of "perishing"[6] and this leads us to think of the division between the world and God.[7] He thinks "this distinction relies upon the most universal categories within our mind,"[8] and therefore, the self-destructive contingency of the world is seen as the finite particular, and the self-subsisting necessity of the divine being as the infinite universal. Then, Hegel shows that this dyadic opposition is nonsensical, since the infinite is reduced to "one particular in addition to which finite is the other," while the finite, which is placed over against the infinite, comes to have "an equal dignity of subsistence and independence" to that of the infinite.⁹ Instead, we have to see each of these terms as being what it is in virtue of not being the other and each is only what it is insofar as the other (i.e., what it is not) is.¹⁰ In order for the infinite to be truly positive, what is negative (i.e., the finite) must be negated for its own affirmation. In facing this division, therefore, one must move from an initially immediate affirmation of the abstract infinite through its negative (i.e., the finite) to the true affirmation of the infinite as that which mediates with itself in and through the finite.¹¹ As we have seen previously in relation to Desmond's exposition of dialectical thinking, this gives the circle of the self-mediation of the infinite in and through the finite and demonstrates the inclusive self-determination of the infinite wherein the opposition between the finite and the infinite is held together as difference. This structure of dialectical thinking dissolves the first antithesis by demonstrating the finite world as the means for the infinite divinity to mediate with itself.

Second, the inherent truth of humanity for Hegel is its essential rationality, and this implicit characteristic as rational being must unfold itself through differentiating its immediate status of natural being as an other to itself. On the basis of this self-surpassing characteristic of human self-consciousness, there is the split (*Entzweiung*) between the particularity of our natural being and the universality of our rationality.¹² This is the split that we see in Kant's formulation of moral duty and pathological inclinations. Hegel argues that this split does not remain as a stark ontological distinction, but rather is held as an internal difference through the infinite power of unifying self-consciousness. The rational comes out of the natural as what is implicit therein, while the natural is recognized as such insofar as there is rationality in us. This development of the universal out of the particular follows the dialectical structure of self-determination.¹³ In the immediate state of humanity as the natural, human rationality is still indeterminate and abstract, and this original state of human rationality as abstract universal needs to bring itself forth by recognizing its natural being as the self-particularized expression of itself. This means that human reason does not only recognize itself as natural being but also "embodies" itself as natural being and posits the rational/natural cleavage in itself.

This indicates the difference between the static distinction of the universal and the particular in Kantian duty and what the young Hegel would call an incarnation of the moral laws as the "work of love." For Kant, the "ought" of moral duty stems from the dualistic universal/particular opposition and implies a constant internal conflict between reason and desire, whereas the young Hegel's love indicates the higher stage of life in which the universal and the particular are harmonized with each other.¹⁴ This is "a specific modification of life"¹⁵ through which we can fulfill the moral laws by bringing our inclination in union with our reason and concretizing them. We are the sensible manifestation of the moral laws and our act, practiced through the (w)holistic interrelations between reason and desire, requires no opposition within ourselves.¹⁶ In light of this particular determination of the universal as embodied reason, humanity as spirit comes back to itself as the concrete universal and stands above the previously indeterminate universal (of the moral laws). Thus, by moving from its initially abstract form of implicit rationality, through the determinate particularity of its natural being, to the manifestation of its infinite power of unity as the concrete rational being, humanity will come to recognize the infinite power of reason in itself and place the internal antithesis only as the ideal moments of its self-determination. The constant civil war between the rational and the sensible in ourselves is now reconciled and integrated into the unifying process of our self-determining self-consciousness.[17]

Finally, there is the antithesis between our self-contradictory finite existence as a whole and the infinitude of what is at home with itself—i.e., the divine absolute.[18] Our self-surpassing desire to be harmonious with ourselves drives us to elevate ourselves to the infinite activity of divine consciousness.[19] Yet we are burdened with the internal antithesis, and what we hope to attain through religious thinking cannot be attained within the framework of our existence as finite subjective spirit(s). This lack of correspondence between the human and divine consciousness is the most extreme antithesis where the particular as finite spirit and the universal as the infinite spirit are placed over against each other.[20] The dialectical development of divine consciousness further intermediates this gap in three moments. First, God is seen as the abstract universal, consisting only of his pure self-relation and devoid of any particular determination. Second, the divine spirit creates the finite world (including nature and humanity as finite spirit[s]) and this is the divine act of positing what is other to itself as being apart from itself.[21] Third, through recognizing what is separated from itself as what it distinguished from itself in its act of self-particularization, the initially abstract universal comes back to itself in concrete form; and here, the divine spirit is seen to restore what is other to itself as the transitional moment in the process of its self-determination.[22] The completion of this dialectical circuit brings about the absolute spirit realizing itself through the finite particular and having the determinate knowledge of itself as the absolute truth. The finite creation as a whole and humanity as a part of it are grasped as the means for the universal self-realization of God as absolute spirit.[23]

Hegel's conception of the divine-human relationship: A seeming success vis-à-vis Kant

The second intermediation of human rationality and natural being directly deals with the problems of Kantian ethics as it appropriates the internal antithesis of human existence. In relation to this intermediation, Hegel seems to give a more concrete picture of the human being as the embodied rationality and thereby provides the foundation in which we can account for the ethical community of humans as the plurality of self-mediating rational beings. Also, the dialectical interrelation of the universal and the particular seems to account for the givenness of the moral law (i.e., initial indeterminacy of human rationality) as it articulates the relation of the divine absolute to the ethical intermediation of a human subject as that which is irreducible to the self-determinations of the latter. As the third antithesis of the divine and the human indicates, our self-surpassing desire to elevate ourselves to the infinitude of divine consciousness cannot be fulfilled through our internal intermediation alone, because the need for this mediation is itself the mark of our finitude. Hegel argues that this human finitude, separating us from the divine unity, calls for the necessity of our "religious reconciliation" with God, and this reconciliation seems to come from the side of divine infinite; for the finitude of human existence is conceived as the particularized expression of the divine consciousness in the process of its dialectical self-determination. This means that the initially indeterminate divine consciousness (i.e., abstract universal) manifests itself as human self-consciousness (i.e., the particular) and constitutively expresses itself in humanity while fully mediating with itself as the absolute self-consciousness (i.e., the concrete universal).[24]

Thus, if we follow what Hegel says about the relationship between humanity and divinity, and the particular and the universal, it really seems that the self-determination of the divine consciousness constitutively grounds the ethical intermediation of humanity and also that the dialectical interrelation of the particular and the universal in terms of the universal's self-determination (as the absolute) fully accounts for one's relation to divinity as the irreducible singular. To wit, there could be some credibility to the conclusion that Hegel draws, whereby he accounts for the interrelationship between the ethical self-mediation of humanity and the religious self-mediation of divinity without collapsing the latter into the former. Or at least Hegel's dynamic reason seems to be able to grasp the divine-human relationship beyond the abstract universality of practical reason. Insofar as the concrete universality of self-determining divine self-consciousness (i.e., the divine absolute) is clearly distinguished from the self-determining human self-consciousness(es), we seem to be able to say that Hegel's concept of religion is not guilty of the systematic reduction of religion to philosophy and, hence, successfully avoids its subsequent problems.

Two ways to go wrong

There are two serious reasons why his formulation of the constitutive relationship between divine and human self-determination must be re-examined. First, Hegel formulates the relation of the infinite creator to finite creation in such a way that human finite existence can be affirmed insofar as it serves to mediate with itself for the sake of the infinite divine. As we have seen previously, the universal as initially indeterminate infinite must first alienate itself as the finite particular and bring itself forth by negating what is other to itself as the transitional moment of its self-particularization. Put differently, God, in his initial indeterminacy, sees finite creation only as the self-particularized expression of itself and needs this finite other for its becoming the self-determining absolute.[25] Because of this "dialectical need"[26] to mediate with itself in and through the particular and seeing the particular as its own self-alienation, Hegel's divinity cannot be the self-same God who, out of his inexhaustible richness, gratuitously creates what is other to Himself for the other and affirms the existence of the other for the other.[27] The particularity of the finite other is instrumentalized for the final emphasis on the concrete universal as the divine absolute and its status of being particular for itself is "extirpated" as it is seen in relation to the universal's self-determination.²⁸ In this dialectical framework, each of our relations to the absolute will cost us our particularity as a means for the self-concretizing self-affirmation of the universal, while our existence as a single individual will ultimately be "swallowed up" (to use Desmond's expression) in the universal's self-affirmation as the absolute.²⁹ This problem clearly demonstrates that Hegel's account of the divine-human relationship falls victim to the charges of (3) and (5) that we saw in the fundamental problems of the philosophy of religion.

Second, Hegel tends to blur any strong ontological break between the human and divine self-determination. This equivocity in the foundation of Hegel's philosophy of religion ultimately falls victim to (1), (2), and (4) of the five fundamental problems. Let me elaborate further on this point in the following.

The basis on which the humanity-divinity divide is posited is the conflict of reason and desire in humanity. But as the second dialectical mediation (concerning the division between the rational and the natural in human existence) shows, humanity is explicated as capable of overcoming this finitude through self-surpassing unity of self-consciousness and seeing its naturalness as the finite expression of its infinite rationality. Hence, God as infinite other to human finitude, in Hegel's account, does not actually come into the picture, whereby humanity overcomes its own limitation. What is problematic is that self-infinitization of the finite human subject does not need the self-particularization of the infinite divine subject as the other to itself. This means that, since finite humanity already possesses the infinite power of unity in itself, God as infinite subject might be considered nothing but a projection of humanity as infinite spirit. This conflation of human autonomy to divine self-determination can be seen in two ways: (1) the sublation of the sensible object and the rational subject in terms of the intersubjective self-consciousness and (2) the elevation of the natural will to the universal rational will in terms of the social self-determination.

In Hegel's seminal work, *Phenomenology of Spirit*, the division between the sensible object and the rational subject is held by the self-differentiating unity of the self-consciousness—the "I." Hegel explains:

> Consciousness … has a double object: one is the immediate object, that of sense-certainty and perception, which however for self-consciousness has the character of a negative, and the second, viz. itself, which is the true essence, and is present in the first instance only as opposed to the first object. In this sphere, self-consciousness exhibits itself as the movement in which this antithesis is removed, and the identity of itself with itself becomes explicit for it.³⁰

The sensible object as that which self-consciousness distinguished from itself is granted its substantial existence as a living being (rather than a mere amalgamation of sense data or appearance), and this creates another distinction between the pure undifferentiated self-consciousness, which tautologically relates itself to itself, and the sphere of life that can exist independently of self-consciousness.³¹ In this division, the former can recognize itself as the maker of the very distinction between itself and the other (or else it is not being conscious of itself), and as being this unity of the difference, it realizes itself as "a living self-consciousness."³²

This concrete self-consciousness, always mediating with itself in and through the other, can come to recognize itself as existing for the other self-consciousness in the process of its self-determination. According to this insight, Hegel remarks,

> We already have before us the Notion of Spirit. What still lies ahead for consciousness is the experience of what Spirit is—this absolute substance which is the unity of the difference independent self-consciousnesses which, in their opposition, enjoy perfect freedom and independence: "I" that is "We" and "We" that is "I."[33]

Stated otherwise, the reconciliation of our naturalness (i.e., life) and rationality (i.e., abstract self-consciousness) implies the necessary interrelation of one human subject to another, and this dialectical intersubjective relation gives the idea of God, through which we can be at home with ourselves. Hegel's detailed account of human self-consciousness, therefore, illustrates the emergence of human rationality from the standpoint of self-consciousness in each individual to that of the rationality of humanity as a whole. This indicates that the development of each self-consciousness and of its interrelation with other self-consciousness(es) does not need the notion of spirit as the ontologically enabling ground of their possibility (hence ontologically superior to their self-determinations), but it represents the mere consequence of exercising one's endowed capacity to become a living self-consciousness, as well as to recognize the inherent necessity of its interrelations with the others in society.

Also if the notion of spirit is a social self (i.e., We) that is inclusive of many self-determining human subjects (i.e., the I), the divine subject in the divine-human intermediation is no longer ontologically transcendent to the finitude of human existence as such. The elevation of a finite human subject to the infinitude of the "divine" subject is discussed as the way in which each single individual is incorporated (and/or incorporates itself) into the social whole. Hence, the finitude of the human subject is seen only as the self-particularization of the universal totality of such human subjects in the process of their social self-determination. This point is elaborated in the context of the dialectical elevation of the natural will of single individuals to the universal rational will of the state in Hegel's mature work—*Philosophy of Right*. This ethical determination of human autonomy as the dialectical development of the absolute idea comes in three moments: (1) family, (2) civil society, and (3) the state. Family is the natural immediacy of ethical spirit, whereby a single individual has its particular self-consciousness within the unity of family members and recognizes its essential inseparability from the others for its self-determination. In civil society, the particular interests of the single individuals are mediated through the "formal universality"[34] of rational measures (e.g., private contracts, and official agreements, etc.), and these individuals determine themselves as the "links in this chain of social connections."[35]

The formal determination of freedom in civil society is still subjective in the sense that the protection of private property and the security of personal freedom are its highest priorities. Hence, this subjective form of ethical spirit needs to constitute itself as objectified spirit—i.e., the state.[36] Hegel argues as follows:

> The state is the actuality of concrete freedom. But concrete freedom consists in this that, personal individuality and its particular interests not only achieve their complete development and gain explicit recognition for their right (as they do in the sphere of the family and civil society) but … they also pass over of their own accord into the interest of the universal, and, … they know and will the universal; they even recognize it as their own substantive spirit; they take it as their end and aim and are active in its pursuit. The result is that … individuals … do not live as private persons for their own ends alone, but in the very act of willing these they will the universal in the light of the universal, and their activity is consciously aimed at none but the universal end.[37]

The state is the universal will willing itself in self-differentiated togetherness of family and the civil society, and thereby the will of a single individual in its natural immediacy comes to have ethical validity as it takes part in this social self's absolute self-willing. In light of this state as rational determination of human freedom, Hegel explains that "spirit, which, sundering itself into the two ideal spheres of its concept, family and civil society, enters upon its finite phase, but it does so only in order to rise above its ideality and become explicit as infinite actual spirit."[38] Thus, the finitude of each human autonomy is taken up to the state in the process of the latter's dialectical self-determination, and this self-determining rationality of the social self is the ultimate destiny of each single individual to live the universal life of ethics (*Sittlichkeit*).

At the end of *Lectures on the Philosophy of Religion*, Hegel similarly explains that this rational determination of freedom is the result of the reconciliation between humanity and divinity. He argues that a human subject who is reconciled with God comes to have "infinite value in virtue of his vocation"[39] to properly exercise his freedom in the world and this calling to determine his freedom is "made effective in the community."[40] Where can we find this religious community in which the determination of human autonomy is absolutely in consonance with the self-determination of the divine subject? He writes:

> It is in the organization of the state that the divine has broken through (*eingeschlagen*) into the sphere of actuality; the latter is permeated by the former, and the worldly realm is now justified in and for itself, for its foundation is the divine will, the law of right and freedom. The true reconciliation, whereby the divine realizes itself in the domain of actuality, consists in the ethical and juridical life of the state. … The institutions of ethical life are divine institutions.[41]

If the ethical life is enabled by the self-determination of the state, and the reconciliation of the worldly and divine—resulting from the humanity-divinity reconciliation—is essentially ethical life, then this rational totality of the social self would have to be God, whose self-determination brings forth our ethical life.[42] What is required of each finite human subject is his rational obedience to the state as the universal and absolute spirit.[43]

The Hegelian reduction of the divine to the human self-consciousness

Once we comparatively examine the second dialectical mediation (concerning the internal division of humanity) and the third mediation (concerning the divinity-humanity division) and analyze how Hegel deals with them in various texts, the legitimacy of the basis in which the antithesis between humanity and divinity is posited becomes highly questionable. On the one hand, the human subject is presented as capable of overcoming the basis in which there is the humanity-divinity opposition. The split in human existence can be mediated through the self-surpassing unity of self-consciousness; accordingly, the antithesis between humanity and divinity becomes an unnecessary problem, and thereby the latter looks more like a simple projection of the former. On the other hand, if we grant that there is a division between the finite and the infinite subject and the elevation of the former requires the self-determining process of the latter, then the distance between them is the distance between individual human beings and the rational totality of the social whole constituted by such individuals. Since, in this case, Hegel's God is not ontologically transcendent to human existence as a whole, what he means by "divine" in posing the human-God antithesis is bound up with the rational totality of the state.[44] Then the state as the social self becomes the new God that determines itself in and through individual human subjects.[45] In both cases, Hegel's divine absolute no longer carries the stature of being transcendent to self-determining human self-consciousness but becomes a self-manifestation of humanity, either individually or collectively, as infinite Spirit.[46]

If Hegel's absolute is either our self-determining self-consciousness or the interrelation of finite self-consciousness(es) in form of the state, we are left with the same question of conflating the divine-human relation of the religious to the human self-relation of the ethical. Granted that Hegel goes beyond Kant's dualism and deals with the complicated issue of the constitutive relationship between divine authority and human autonomy, one could still ask if Hegel is guilty of projecting the self-differentiating unity of humanity's self-determining self-consciousness onto itself as the divine absolute. No matter how majestic and sophisticated this projection is, the originating source of humanity's self-determination is nothing but our own self-determining reason. Divine freedom here is also created in the image of our human autonomy. Then what's the meaning of the constitutive relations of divinity and humanity at all? This seems to signal that the divine absolute in Hegel's formulation is an empty echo of (self-determining) human reason.

Absolute supremacy of dialectical reason and its problems for religion

But what would it be like for Hegel (and those of us who walk along his philosophical path) to think of the absolute beyond the concrete universal? There are two reasons why Hegel cannot think this possibility: (1) the secondary status of religion as representation (*Vorstellung*) to that of his speculative thinking (*Denken*) and (2) his absolute commitment to this dialectical framework of thinking where the religious concept (*Begriff*) can come to its fruition. For Hegel, religion is characterized as two modes of immediate knowledge of God's existence: religious feeling (*Gefühl*) and representation.[47] The feeling of this immediate certainty (i.e., faith) is subjectively particular and indeterminate; hence it cannot justify its content on its own account.[48] The religious representation objectively determines what this subjective feeling is about through imagistic thinking and/or nonsensible reflection. So, for instance, the story provided in the Scripture is symbolic of something other than its literal meaning and/or is interpreted to carry within it some dualistic opposition through our nonsensible reflections. That is to say, the determinate characteristics of the religious content in the *Vorstellung* (e.g., finite, infinite, universal, particular, etc.) are framed in the one-sided category of understanding (*Verstand*), where each of these terms is abstractly conceived of as standing apart from its opposite.[49] A historical faith pertaining to any particular tradition, then, can register as either or both of these precepts of religious representation. Hence, Hegel would think that his speculative thinking is needed to ultimately account for the dialectical interrelation of these opposites and acquire a concept of the determinate, rational content of the religious representation.[50] His philosophy, in this sense, is the supreme judge that gives the rational verdict on any content of religious teachings, and no faith can provide anything more than what the self-determining reason articulates.

If Hegel's philosophy is the highest "service of God" (*Gottesdienst*) to which every religious representation is subordinated and his speculative thinking is the ultimate ground in which the divine absolute realizes itself in and through the finite particular, then his commitment to the dialectical framework of thinking is unconditional, and his answer to any question concerning religion (or philosophy) would have to be made in accordance with its logic of self-determination.[51] Consequently, to contemplate the possibility of the divine absolute beyond the concrete universal is to acknowledge certain religious representations or teachings to be capable of conveying something more than his dialectical thinking can penetrate.[52] This thinking beyond dialectical thinking, which strives to look beyond the whole of human self-determining thinking, must sound utterly impossible for Hegel.

If we patiently reflect on Hegel's philosophy, however, his religious language (i.e., God, reconciliation, etc.) does not prevent us from recognizing his incredibly elaborate apotheosis of our self-determining mind (*Geist*). This dialectical elevation of humanity to the absolute status of divinity clearly entails the fundamental problems of the philosophy of religion. It is guilty of reducing the divine-human relation to the immanent universality of human-societal self-relation. This reduction of the religious community between humanity and divinity to the ethical community of humans rejects any sense of divine transcendence irreducible to the human self-organization of the highest ethical community (i.e., the state). The dialectical structure of this human self-organization entails the problematic extirpation of the single individual in its relation to the concrete universal as the immanent absolute.[53] As I have shown in reference to Hegel's texts, his notion of the universal always carries the "dialectical need" to mediate itself with what is other to itself as its own self-particularization. In this case, even though the universal seems to constitutively ground the existence of the particular (whether it is seen in relation to the internal division of humanity or the alleged antithesis of divinity and creation), the particular carries only the instrumental significance as the means for the universal's self-determining self-mediation. The final emphasis on the (concrete) universal in its self-determining process, therefore, makes it impossible to account for the particular as the particular within the framework of dialectical thinking. The worth of the finite individual, in this sense, can never be granted for itself but always seen in relation to the dialectical self-determination of the absolute spirit in Hegel's concept of religion.

The lack of a clear ontological distinction between the self-determining self-consciousness of humanity and that of divinity in Hegel's philosophy of religion also marks the problematic one-way movement between the human relative and the divine absolute. The internal antithesis of human existence, which is the basis for recognizing the finitude of human existence and posing the human-divine antithesis in the first place, can be mediated through the self-surpassing unity of self-consciousness. This self-overcoming of human finitude accentuates the ascent from the realm of the human finite to that of the divine infinite more than its allegedly indispensable other, that is, the descent from the divine to the human. Hegel's account of the self-surpassing unity of self-consciousness also gives a more sophisticated form once the distance between humanity and divinity is grasped as the distance between individual human beings and the rational totality of the social whole. But even in this case, what we can find is the dialectical process in which human individuals constitute their ethical community as the immanent absolute. The self-elevating apotheosis of humanity as the absolute spirit does not leave any room for the religious community of humans and the divine as something irreducible to the self-determining self-mediation of humanity. What we have in the end of Hegel's dialectical thinking is the one-way self-constitution of the ethical community as the divine absolute. Thus, Hegel's philosophy of religion falls victim to all of the five charges pertaining to the fundamental problems of the philosophy of religion.

Concluding remarks

Although Kant and Hegel are far from agreeing on what they can deem possible by "reason," they essentially argue in consonance that the precepts of faith in the Judeo-Christian tradition are fundamentally consistent with their systematic configurations of rational ethics. Nevertheless, their elaborate expositions of the continuity between religion and philosophy are far from showing their constitutive relationship with each other, for they problematically end up favoring the autonomy of human reason over the heteronomy of religious faith. For these thinkers, religion consists of indeterminate beliefs and irrational practices that need to be mediated through the determinate rationality of philosophical thinking. As a result, their configurations of the relationship between faith and reason ultimately equivocate what it means to be religious with what (each of them thinks) it means to be ethical. This is exactly what

Kierkegaard's de Silentio rightly anticipates. If the ethical entirely equals the divine absolute, he laments,

> It is proper to say that every duty is essentially duty to God, but if no more can be said than this, then it is also said that I actually have no duty to God. The duty becomes duty by being traced back to God, but in the duty itself I do not enter into relation to God. ... The whole existence of the human race rounds itself off as a perfect, self-contained sphere, and then the ethical is that which limits and fills at one and the same time. God comes to be an invisible vanishing point, an impotent thought; his power is only in the ethical, which fills all of existence.[54]

I have shown that the systematic reduction of religion to philosophy, accompanied by the absolutization of human autonomy to the level of the unconditioned or the absolute, reveals the five fundamental problems of the philosophy of religion in the works of Kant and Hegel. If reason's universal as the ethical represents the divine absolute as these thinkers maintain, then any historical faith in divinity as that which is irreducible to the autonomy of human reason becomes impossible.[55] What also becomes impossible, as Johannes' malaise with rational ethics points out, is the core constituent of religious practices, namely, the relation of the single individual to the divine absolute in the midst of, and beyond, his intersubjective self-organization of the ethical community with the other individuals. Think of a prayer given by a religious devotee in solitude, a cry for a divine help in the midst of one's persecution by the collective, a confession of one's inequity not absolvable by the state authority, or the profound experience of joy in the midst of religious awakening—experience excessive to the determinate expressions of any human language. All of these "religious experiences" or "practices of faith" will have to be either dismissed or exhaustibly superseded by the ultimate rationality of philosophical thinking. For a framework of thinking that cannot account for the worth of the individual as the individual, but always takes it as being secondary to the immanent whole of the human-societal self-relation, the "personal" or "intimate" relation of each singular to the divine absolute both in the midst of and beyond the self-organization of humanity as a (rational) whole is impossible.

But this conclusion of the death of religion, deriving from our critical engagement with the works of Kant and Hegel, does not exterminate the legitimacy of the fundamental questions pertaining to the philosophy of religion. On the contrary, our disorientation in our attempt to answer the twofold question of philosophy (*à la* Augustine) within the framework(s) of rational universalism can wake us up to the most important question: Could there be a sense of the absolute that is other to the self-organizing whole of human autonomy?

What we have seen in Part Two is that to give a reasonable account of religion as that which is irreducible to the confines of philosophical reason is impossible so long as we remain faithful to the Kantian or Hegelian understanding of religion. This only means, however, that there is the unresolved "perplexity over ultimacy" toward which our philosophical thinking cannot help but tending. Our awareness of the philosophical enigma, in other words, can always push us further than the determinate cognitions of religion in the works of Kant and Hegel.[56] This profound "disturbance" at the heart of our reasoning can make us realize that we still need to search for the possibility of the faith-reason continuity without disintegrating it into the domination of one over the other, the possibility of a relationship between the single individual and the divine absolute beyond the rational universal, the possibility of this relation as something more than a heteronomous subordination of mind to the mindless precepts of faith, and the possibility of accounting for the finite singular as the singular without disregarding its relativity to the divine absolute beyond human self-determining self-organization as the rational universal. Our response to the metaphysical perplexity just mentioned is for each of us to search for these possibilities. This response essentially requires us to look beyond the boundaries of the Kantian and Hegelian philosophies of religion, and this task of philosophical thinking is precisely what Tanabe and Desmond have embarked upon in their works. In facing the questions of ultimacy left unanswered in the end of Kant's moral theology and Hegel's dialectical concept of religion, therefore, this philosophical investigation will proceed to its critical engagement with metaxology and metanoetics.

Part Three

Metaxology and the Problems of the Philosophy of Religion

5

Metaxological Fidelity to the Absolute and the Singular: From the Hyperboles of Being to the Agapeic Origin

The inseparable problems of the singular and the absolute

The eclipse of divine transcendence and the "extirpation" of the singular for the determination of the rational universal are not two separate problems. As the lack of our proper understanding of the divine absolute (as that which is irreducible to our ethical self-determination) entails the problematic subordination of the singular to the universal in immanence, the lack of our proper understanding of the ethical self- and intermediations in relation to the human singulars foreshadows our counterfeit apotheosis of ourselves as the rational universal. Stated more theologically, without seeking a proper understanding of God, we will fail to understand who we are; and at the same time, without having the proper understanding of ourselves as a part of creation, we cannot properly seek to know God. Desmond's metaxological metaphysics consistently shows its intellectual fidelity to this double relativity between the infinite absolute and the finite relative. It strives to capture both of these terms simultaneously in their proper relation to each other.

There is something seriously difficult about this metaphysical effort to grasp the absolute-relative porosity, since our mind almost always works discursively. In many occasions, it even proceeds from one determinate proposition through another to a fixed conclusion. What is required of a metaphysician to think about the interrelation between origin and creation, however, is to see the "way up" of the creation to the origin and the "way down" of the latter to the former at the same time. What metaxology precisely offers us are the various ways in which we can practice this double attentiveness—attentiveness necessary for approaching the twofold question of philosophy, that is, God and soul. In other words, metaxological thinking points us to the ways in which we can cross and crisscross the passages between our ethical mediations (i.e., "selving" in Desmond's terms) in the finite particular and the divine absolute as irreducibly other to such ethical selving. In these passages, we can find *both* the underlying problems of modern philosophy that have resulted in the loss of religion *and* the way out of the very "Godlessness" to the possibilities of religious faith. Metaxology, in this sense, shows how the breakdown of the absolute confidence of reason in modern philosophy can turn into reason's breakthrough to the question of ultimacy discussed at the end of Part Two.

In Part Three, therefore, I will examine some of the ways in which Desmond diagnoses the underlying metaphysical problems in the modern philosophies of religion and then investigate the passages where he demonstrates how metaxology moves from the finite relative to the infinite absolute and vice versa. In paying attention to the variety of ways in which we can move from being to God, we will see how the metaxological configuration of the divine absolute can recuperate the robust sense of divine transcendence and simultaneously account for the finite singular as the singular without constraining this account to the contracted framework of dualistic thinking.[1] This double attentiveness to God and creation beyond dualism in metaxology will provide us the ground from which we can articulate Desmond's response to the fundamental problems of the philosophy of religion.

The problem of rational universalism: A metaxological analysis

In the brief exposition of metaxological metaphysics in Chapter 1, I elucidated Desmond's analysis of transcendental univocity (Kant) and dialectical thinking (Hegel). Since this metaphysical analysis of the univocal and the dialectical sense of being touches on the core problems of Kantian and the Hegelian philosophies of religion, I would like to highlight some key points that will prepare our exploration of the metaxological philosophy of religion. First, Desmond emphasizes that our ontological status in its original position is mysteriously marked with the hyperbolic givenness. This is what he calls "hyperboles of being."[2] We have seen earlier that, in this original state of our existence, we simply enjoy our primordial rapport with the ontological plentitude in our purely aesthetic presence. Yet, our fall from the rapturous immersion in the rich givenness of being dissipates our "agapeic astonishment" over the givenness of our "to be." Then, as we lose our attentiveness to the foundation of our existence, we are pushed to face being as the enigmatic other to our mind. Consequently, many of the best minds in the history of humanity have tried to come up with a number of different ways to "take away or mitigate the seeming threat of enigmatic being."[3] Transcendental univocity as espoused by Kant and dialectical thinking as conceptualized by Hegel are the prime examples of these philosophical efforts to make sense of the togetherness between mind and being beyond their initial separation.

According to Desmond, both transcendental univocity and dialectical thinking suffer from at least three interrelated problems: First, they remain forgetful of the primal communivocity between mind and being prior to their "thetic" separation; second, they problematically inherit the Cartesian metaphysical framework—that is, the dualism between mindful self and mindless other; and third, unifying consciousness of the mindful self generates the rational unity between itself and the other. We can spot a few significant differences between the ways in which Kant and Hegel strive to account for the unity between the structure of consciousness and that of being. The dialectical sense in Hegel's formulation recognizes porosity between them. It also pays closer attention to the concrete richness of aesthetic happening. Nevertheless, the logic of dialectical self-determination sees no value in the finite other in its otherness (hence it adopts the default position of being as Cartesian *res extensa*) and assimilates inherent equivocity of being into the totalizing unity of self-determining mind. As a result, just like the transcendentally univocal reason, the dialectical mind ultimately determines itself to be the privileged determiner of both intelligibility and ontological worth of the finite happening. In this sense, neither Kantian univocity nor Hegelian dialectic succeeds in recuperating the primal communivocity of being and mind where both of these terms are given to be for themselves in their communicative openness to each other. These determinate and self-determining forms of reason, however, problematically hold the one-sided unity of itself and being. These unities are one-sided exactly in the sense that they are always mediated from the side of reason.

This mind's incapacity to reach out to being as having its own inherent value or impotence to open itself to what is other to itself foreshadows its inability to conceive of the divine absolute as something more than *its* postulated ideality or *itself* as the sublationary infinitude of self-thinking thought. As we have seen earlier, in the context of metaphysics, a mindful self loses sight of itself when it loses the sight of being as having its own integrity in its otherness. What it also loses in this metaphysical self-loss is the primal position in which it is given to be, that is to say, its relativity to the metaphysical origin from which its mindful existence is derived. With regard to this loss of self in the death of God, I cannot help but repeat the same theological point: without having the proper understanding of ourselves as a part of creation, we cannot properly seek to know God.

In order for us to account for the concrete singularity of the mindful self, then, we must *both* reach out to being in its irreducible otherness *and* open ourselves to the divine absolute beyond ourselves. This is precisely what metaxology aims to accomplish in the space between philosophy and religion, as well as through the trilogy of the between.[4] What is required for a metaxological philosopher of religion to go beyond the limits of rational universalism, therefore, is to account for the singularity of finite being as the singular and conceive of the divine absolute as irreducible to our determinate or self-determining unity of mind. This would entail the recuperation of the primal communivocity between mind and being and also require a metaxological thinker to regain his mind's capacity to listen to the undeniable intimacy, as well as the ambiguous openness, between his mindful self and what is other to himself. We will see in the following how metaxological philosophy of religion accomplishes these two tasks through the genuine transcendence of mind to being and of the finite being to infinite origin—the tasks that Kant and Hegel were unable to accomplish.

The hyperboles of being in the between

To break through the confines of rational universalism is to go beyond the constrained unity of mind and being, a "constructed" unity mediated mostly from the side of mind. In order to achieve this "breakthrough," Desmond suggests that we have to pay attention to the "hyperboles of being," namely, to look for the transfinite signs of transcendence both hidden and shown within immanent finitude.[5] As the etymology of the term "hyperbolic" indicates, *hyper-ballein* points to the primal status of (our) being as thrownness—being *thrown above* the abyss of nothingness—and also as givenness—given beyond the determinate exchange of finite goods that we can conceptualize through the determinate economy of distributive goods.[6] Beings are witnessed in this primal awareness as being suspended above the "not to be" with the marvelous truth of their original "given to be" (i.e., *passio essendi*). This truth of being as a gift is beyond any self-determining efforts to be (i.e., *conatus essendi*). The opening of otherness in ourselves as mindful beings breaks down the constructed mind-being unity—which transcendental and dialectical reason compel us to hold dear—and breaks us open to the primal community of mind and being beyond our mind. This means that metaxology does not announce the complete death of reason, like so many of the post-Hegelian philosophers advocate. On the contrary, it recalibrates the proper relation of mind and being in reference to their hyperbolic origin. This rather marks a resurrection of mind that remains attentive to the otherness of given being, the givenness of itself as the mindful being, and their profound communivocity in their primordial mode of *passio essendi*. Desmond calls this renewed sense of reason that remains attentive to the irreducible otherness of being the "intimate universal" beyond the "homogeneous universal"[7] of the univocal or dialectical reasoning. This is the passage that moves beyond the contracted mind-being unity of the rational universal to their metaxological community as the intimate universal—or, as Desmond puts it, the agapeic "universalism as mindful of the richness of singularity as of the manifold togetherness; a non-totalizing universalism, not closed to otherness; a non-reductive universalism not emptying of singularity."[8]

What we need to keep in our mind in relation to such renewed sense of philosophical mindfulness or agapeic universalism is that our mind's transcendence to being as other to itself also marks our undeniable relativity to the divine absolute. Desmond articulates as follows:

> Being thrown by the hyperbolic is being in the throes of an undergoing which is an overgoing, an abovegoing in receiving, or being received by, the *huper*. The hyperbolic is not a hypertrophy of will to power, but a poverty in extreme porosity that is filled full with richness from the superior other.[9]

This means that the transcendence of the divine absolute is communicated through the immanent life in the between; and to see this point, we have to look for the infinite reserve of divinity in our finite immanence or something more than immanence (or what we can comprehend in any immanent terms) in our immanence itself. The questions that we should subsequently ask then are the following: What are the hyperboles of being? How do these transfinite signs of the divine infinite show in the finite reality of our being? How do they move us toward the transcendence of the absolute original beyond ourselves as the originated relatives in immanence? Desmond provides four kinds of hyperboles as the general guidelines for tracing the metaxological interplay of the finite and the infinite, the relative and the absolute, and the originated and the original. These four ways to reach the absolute from the relative are (1) the "idiocy of being," (2) the "aesthetics of happening," (3) the "erotics of selving," and (4) the "agapeics of community."[10] In the rest of this chapter, I will elucidate these essential movements pertaining to these four hyperboles of being and demonstrate how they indicate metaxological ways toward the divine absolute.

The idiot self and posthumous mind

The first hyperbole, which has the highest relevance to the philosophy of religion, has something to do with the singular status of finite being. We have seen that Kantian philosophy has a tremendous difficulty in conceiving the inherent ontological value in the sensible particularity of each being. Given that he adopts the duality between the rational and irrational, universal and particular, and necessary and contingent in the foundation of his critical thinking, Kant finds the principle of individuation only in spatio-temporal determinations; and because of this, he regards the concept of plurality as that which is applicable only to the phenomenal objects in the domain of our experience. In this sense, his third Paralogism concludes that we cannot apply any categories to what is purely necessary, rational, and universal. However, we have also seen that this monolithic dualism renders an awkward ambiguity in his discussion of the plurality of intelligible characters in the kingdom of ends. His notion of the ethical community as the *Reich* simply calls for a different way to account for the multiplicity of intelligible subjects.

Contra Kant, Hegel demonstrates his speculative openness to the equivocity of historical being. His systematic thinking is dynamic in the sense that it sees the mutual implication of two opposing terms and strives to account for the embodiment of the intelligible character in each human subject. What is problematic in Hegel's dialectical logic of self-determination is that each single individual is always "*world-historically redeemed* as preparing a more thoroughgoing victory for reason in history."[11] In this dictum of world-historical universalism, the value of the finite particular is ultimately reduced to a transitory moment necessary for the concrete self-manifestation of the infinite universal. Johannes de Silentio hits the mark:

> The single individual has his ethical task continually to express himself in the universal and annul his singularity in order to become the universal. [But] as soon as the single individual asserts himself in his singularity before the universal, he sins, and only by acknowledging this can he be reconciled again with the universal.[12]

The finite singular is an embodied rationality in Hegel's dialectic, and thus, it overcomes Kant's incapacity to conceptualize the plurality of intelligible beings. However, the singular in Hegel's formulation still needs to recognize itself as a transitory moment for the further self-determination of the infinite universal in history. In this case, we cannot account for the inherent ontological value of the singular for the singular, but it must be radically relativized with the universal for the latter's self-completing self-concretization as the absolute. Whether this absolute self-knowledge of the infinite spirit takes place in a philosopher's self-consciousness or concretized as the intersubjective self-determination of human self-consciousnesses in the objectified form of the state has little relevance here. The central problem is that Hegel argues that the particular indeterminacy (or a determinable lack) needs to be overcome by the self-determining infinite. As a result, the dialectical model of the interrelation between the finite and the infinite shows the instrumentalization of the finite for the infinite to determine itself and grants the ultimate ontological value only to the concrete universal in the end of its self-determining process.

Now Desmond's metaxology raises the following questions to Kant's and Hegel's treatment of the singular: Are these accounts of the singular really truthful to the nature of the singular? Is there not something in the singular that resists its complete subordination to the conceptual clarification of the rational universal? Can the rational universal, either in the Kantian or the Hegelian formulation, exhaustibly negate the singular in order to claim itself as the absolute? I have asked if there is any absolute that exceeds reason's universal. Metaxology leads us to think if there is something "more" in the finite that escapes the conceptual clarifications of reason's universal—the "more" that signals its ontological excess beyond mere indeterminacy and, thus, escapes the dialectical instrumentalization.

In consonance with Kierkegaard's de Silentio, I seriously doubt that either Kant or Hegel could affirm the single individual before the universal.[13] Unlike these philosophers, however, the singular status of a thinker is extremely important for Desmond. In the process of explaining the metaxological sense of being, he frequently stresses his ecstatic "yes" to the singularity of his mindful existence and shows the signs of the transfinite (i.e., the "hyperboles" of being) in the immanence of his finite existence. He names this positive value the "idiocy of the singular" and articulates our awakening to this value as "posthumous thinking."[14] These are important points for understanding metaxological philosophy of religion not only because they mark Desmond's clear departure from the Kantian and the Hegelian framework of thinking but also because, in them, we can find the passages to the divine absolute beyond the immanent absolute of the German philosophers. Let me explain these notions in reference to the works of Desmond in the following.

The idiocy of the singular has to do with the *onc*eness of our finite existence as a *this*. This uniqueness of our existence as a single individual in the course of history is counterintuitive to our general practice of academic philosophy. The general tendency of our philosophical writing is to hold the objective standard applicable to all people at all times regardless of their diverse socio-economic, historical, and cultural backgrounds. Just as a stone released in mid-air must fall to the ground, a well-constructed paper in philosophy must bring forth a conclusion that falls rightly with the constant force of universal validity. Perhaps it is more telling to use the administrative expression so familiar to our scholarship in Europe today: our monograph or article must be qualified as a "*scientific* publication."[15] This might be an oversimplified version of what is actually going on in the field of philosophy. But consider how the writings of Kant and Hegel have the same thrust toward the universal validity or rigorousness of scientific objectivity. The German language can allow them to speak in the passive voice much more than English can. But still, they seem to speak much more frequently in passive voice than most contemporary philosophical texts in German do. They hardly ever talk about themselves as single individuals, and their status as individual human beings recedes far back behind their massive systems of universal thought.[16] A prominent scholar of Hegel, George di Giovanni, talks about the "protagonist" of the *Phenomenology of Spirit* and never refers to it as the historical Hegel. I find this to be an accurate interpretation, since Hegel clearly intends that the protagonist of his texts is not himself in his concrete individuality, but the world-historical reason or spirit. The underlying drive toward the establishment of philosophy as a systematic science seems to blind Hegel and others from paying attention to the ineradicable significance of the single individual.

A distinct characteristic in Desmond's writings is that he often talks about the undeniable status of himself as a singular *this* behind the systematic expression of his thought. For instance, *Perplexity and Ultimacy* provides a series of personal reflections on the author's youth in Cork, Ireland; his natural aptitude for science and philosophy; along with a great love of poetry. He talks about the shock of moving to the United States to study continental philosophy, his work and personal encounters in Inchydoney, etc. This volume, saturated with references to the historical Desmond, is written as a companion volume to *Being and the Between*. Even in more systematic works like the trilogy and other principal works, we can come to know his affectionate tie to his family members, admiration for his friends, the love of his country and language, his upbringing in Irish Catholicism, his passion for long-distance running, etc., in much more poetic expressions.[17] From the midst of things in the transient universe, Desmond reminds us that *this* single individual is the author of the works on metaxology.

In contrast to the public neutrality of philosophical language, these poetic references to the singular status of a thinker can be read as an invitation to our "private" reflections on the deepest reserve of what is more than the indeterminate particularity in each of our own existence.[18] I am tempted to go on with my own rhapsodies on the uniqueness of my individual life here. But because an academic text on the philosophy of religion is probably not an appropriate place to do this, and also because it requires me to write in my native language (i.e., Japanese), I will refer to one of the best examples that Desmond gives in relation to the poetic thinker par excellence, Plato, and his philosophical admiration of Socrates.

> [Plato] presents Socrates as a particular human thinker. Socrates explicitly says in the *Apology* (32a) that to survive as a philosopher it was necessary for him to live as an idiot (*idioteuein*). He would have been dead earlier if he had not lived as an idiot. ... Socrates does not give us systematic science or a world historical account in exoneration of his philosophy, his life. We are given an apology for an *individual life*. Though that life involved the search for the universal, the life itself was the mindful existing of a *this*. Only a this can apologize; a universal does not apologize, nor does it live the inviolable inwardness of an ethical life. ...
>
> Socrates' death makes us reconsider the enigma of his life as philosophical. We begin to sense that there was something ineradicably Once about this life. Death

revealed to us, to Plato, the Once of this life, in confronting us with this Never: once Socrates was but now never more. ... Can we imagine Plato howling: Why should a rat, a horse, a dog have life, and Socrates no life at all? Will Socrates ever again? The answer is: Never, never never! Hegel will say this: No, no, no! Socrates will always come again. But he will not come as this Socrates but as universal thought. But Plato knew: that is not Socrates. It is Socrates as a *this* that concerns us: it is Socrates as a this that apologizes for philosophy; it is not the universal using Socrates as an instrument that apologizes; it is not the Socratic spirit. Socrates says: I, I, I and the I is ineradicably singular, irreplaceable. There was only one Socrates, one and one only, even though this unique singular claims to speak on behalf of the universal.[19]

The nature of the singular signifies the unrepeatable once-never that we cannot exhaustively explain through the conceptual clarification of the rational universal.[20] We occasionally experience this rude awakening—awakening to the inexhaustible enigma of the singular—when we lose someone we love so dear or face a near-death experience that shocks us to the core of our existence.[21] In these occasions of life, the singular communicates something that the Kantian or the Hegelian framework of thinking cannot fully conceptualize. The singular can be "not to be" at all, but somehow—regardless of the fact that it could be "not to be"—it is. The mere presence of the contingent singular astonishes us with the marvel of its presence.[22] Thus, the ontologically rich status of the singular can seriously challenge the confidence of universal reason that sees mere indeterminacy in the singular—a challenge of the singular that opens our mind to something more than what we can make sense of in terms of the rational universal. Desmond calls this thinking "posthumous thinking"—that is, a contemplation from the side of the "never" that faces the ontological wealth of the once "to be."[23] Beyond the indeterminate particularity and the determinate rationality, the singular can communicate to us the enigmatic source from which our spatio-temporal haecceity as the finite singular is derived.

The thinking from the side of never is not a glimpse of pessimistic fatalism or a cheap death wish that fixates on an adrenaline rush. It is an intense awareness of our life as given to be beyond any categorical reason. Desmond provides the best example of this posthumous thinking as the image of prisoners from *The Idiot*. This image based on Dostoyevsky's life shows its serious bearing on our understanding of life's significance in relation to a single individual. Let me retrace the story to ruminate on this point. A group of convicts who are sentenced to death for their crime against the state wake up to the sudden announcement in the early morning that they will be put to death that afternoon. Each of them is made to wear special white clothes for the execution and then put in groups of three to face the firing squad. Then, "when the priest moved down the row and held up the cross to their lips, they unanimously—including such confirmed atheists ... —kissed it."[24] The first three are tied to the poles with their eyes covered, while the felon in the next group makes the final steps to the abyss of his "never." What would the world look like in face of the precipice of nihility in the last minutes of his life? Dostoyevsky continues as follows:

He said that those five minutes seemed to him an infinite length of time, an immense richness; it seemed to him that during those five minutes he would live so many lives that there was no point in thinking about the last moment yet, so he divided up the time that still remained for him to live: two minutes to say goodbye to his companions; two minutes for *inward meditation* for the last time, and then look around him for the last time. He remembered perfectly having fulfilled these dispositions just as he had calculated. He was going to die at twenty-seven full of health and vigor. ... After saying good-by to his companions, came the two minutes he had set aside for thinking about himself; he knew in advance what he was going to think about: he wished to focus his attention firmly, and as rapidly and clearly as possible, on what was going to happen: now he existed and was alive, but in three minutes' time he would be *something*, someone or something—but who? And where? He thought he would be able to determine all this in those two minutes! Not far away there was a church, and the top of it, with its gilded roof, was sparkling in the bright sunlight. He remembered looking at that roof with awful persistence, and at the beams of light that sparkled from it; he could not tear himself away from them; it seemed to him that they were his new nature, those beams, that in three minutes' time he would somehow fuse with them ...[25]

When the dead man walks to the scaffolding, he cherishes everything that he can behold through his heightened senses and embraces every second of his remaining existence with utmost intensity. As he comes to know that the uniqueness of his life is about to be exterminated, he experiences the mysterious communivocity of mind and being in the infinite richness of the "to be" in the ray of sunshine. (Why do I think of Plato's cave?) This is where the terrible declaration of an imperial mercy grants the prisoners their lives—the same life to be lived and enjoyed in deadly Siberia.[26]

Imagine the intensity of the reflection that each of these prisoners has to go through. How starkly different the feel of the same life in prison has become after this! The language of the rational universal in Kant and Hegel claims to explain clearly the significance of the singular as that which ought to be negated for the sake of the universal. But their existential return to each of their "to be" as a *this* brings the prisoners to the edge of their rationality through the abyss of their "not to be."[27] Here, each of them, or at least one of them, finds within his finite immanence something more than indeterminate particularity of valueless thereness that simply needs to be negated for the rational universal. Although one might disagree with this point, let me ask this question again: What goes through the prisoner's mind when he is forced to wear the clothes signaling him to be another indefinite particular that needs to be negated by the state? On the day of his death, the prisoner could find the hyperintelligible value given to his existence as a single individual and show his attentiveness to its ineradicable uniqueness by communicating with others and communing with the glory of creation. What he saw in his "inner meditation" was not only himself as the singular in the colorless garment of the state execution, but in the face of death, he catches the glimpse of the source from which the uniqueness of his once is given to be.

These prisoners are like us (ὁμοίους ἡμῖν).[28] We go through the daily routines of eating breakfast, washing our faces, putting our clothes on, and fulfilling our social functions as if our lives will go on forever, undisturbed. But who among us can guarantee that we will live another day? Who can bear the thought that the "I" that each of us takes for granted every morning will drop dead like a rock this afternoon? Are we just like another nameless "I" that passed before us? How can we make sense of the full significance of ourselves as individuals in the face of our seemingly senseless death? These are hard questions. Just as one of the prisoners, Nikolay Grigoriyev, does not regain his sanity after facing his mock execution, these questions can risk mental breakdown, precisely because they test us to the limit of our reason without any guarantee of a safe return.[29] Many of us are not ready to deal with the terrible truth about the finitude of our existence. But in our recoil from the monstrous truth that our days are numbered, some of us are led to rethink the ineradicable significance of the singular and even find something more than indeterminate particularity in each of our existence.[30]

As one of those who have asked the hard questions, Desmond argues that "the 'once' of irreplaceable singularity gives a shimmer of transcendence"[31] in the deepest interior of our existence as the finite singular. The term "transcendence" here does not mean exterior otherness or divine aloofness to our determinate being, but rather radical intimacy at the core of our immanent finitude, yet simultaneously signaling the ontological "more" that exceeds what we can grasp in immanent terms. Desmond describes this "beyond" of the singular as "an *inward* otherness, more intimate to inwardness than all its own self-possessions."[32] He further articulates,

> This sense of inward idiocy makes us defend, not only the radical singularity of self beyond all objectification and reduction, but also the opening of the self within itself to its own inexhaustible dimension of depth. The "monad" of self is infinitely rich in itself. The reserves of self cannot be exhausted by any finite possibility; there is a certain infinite promise at work here that transcends all logics of determinacy.[33]

This metaphysical realization of the transfinite "more/superior" in our finite "interior" points us to the intimate source of our "to be" beyond ourselves. This is precisely the passage, and the porous relativity, between the singular and the absolute before the rationalistic universal. In this way, our posthumous thinking of ourselves as being the singular *once* from the side of *never* releases us beyond the bounds of rational universalism and cultivates our mindfulness of the divine otherness in our irreducible singularity.

The metaphysics of creation and the aesthetic happenings: The transnatural show of the divine absolute in nature

Metaxology unfolds the passages toward the divine absolute not only through the idiocy of the singular in each of human existence but also in every fiber of creation. This pertains to the second hyperbole, that is, the "aesthetics of happening." It points to the fact that there are some occasions in which the rich givenness of the "to be" is communicated in our encounter with everything, if it is anything at all, in nature. Our beholding of the shimmer of the divine absolute in the finite must also be characterized with our poetic finesse—a kind of nonscientific mindfulness that lets go of the dualistic division between mind and being. In this metaphysical awareness, we let being be and noninsistently let it speak to us for itself (just as the way in which Augustine speaks about creation in *Confessions*).[34] With this mode of mindfulness, we witness the enigmatic showing of the infinite absolute in the thereness of finite particulars in creation.

This attentiveness to the ambiguous sign of the divine in the finite not only affords us our release from the dualistic framework of thinking—the thinking that problematically assumes the distinction between the ontologically worthy subject, on the one hand, and the worthless object, on the other—but also leads us to engage in our festive celebrations of the ontological plentitude in the thereness of finite beings beyond our individual or societal self-mediations. It should be described as the feast of the ontological richness in the created particularity. It is hardly the mind's constructive understanding of (otherwise meaningless) being, but it is the sheer enjoyment of our communicative interrelation with being. This elementary rapport with the worth of being is both felt and affirmed for the being in its otherness to our mind beyond dualism. This is extremely difficult to understand. Nor is it easy to conceptualize it clearly. That is precisely because it gives the primal communivocity of mind and being in their irreducible plentitude to each other prior to and beyond our determinate understanding of it. In this (re-)turning to the primal position of the rich togetherness between being and mind in their overdeterminate otherness to each other, however, Desmond finds the "plurivocal ways" of being that guide us toward God. These metaphysical passages, according to the metaxological metaphysician, will allow us to access the true God beyond the "Godlessness" of Kantian univocity or the Hegelian dialectic.

Beyond transcendental univocity and dialectic, the metaxological understanding of reality stresses the way back to the primal communivocity of mind and being through the notion of creation, that is, the radical granting of existence that serves as the overdeterminate grounding of the determinate beings and of their self- and intermediations. In relation to the particular, the metaxological metaphysician frequently draws our attention to the different notes of "coming to be" and "becoming."

> For A to become B, there must be more than complete determinacy to A; it must be open to further determination, hence "indeterminate," as yet open with respect to that further determination, B; hence becoming something is a dynamic transformation of this antecedent indeterminacy ... into a subsequent determination B .... But—and this is the point—*this* process of determining the indeterminate in a becoming is not the more original determining. Something more original is reserved relative to becoming, while being communicated in the coming to be at all of becoming, just as finite happening. There is a more original overdeterminacy that first grounds *coming to be* and not just becoming. *Coming to*

be and becoming are not to be identified. For becoming already grants the givenness of determinate beings and happenings, whereas coming to be is just about the original arising in being of such beings and happenings.³⁵

If I use a metaphysical term from the classical tradition, we can describe this process of becoming as the way in which every finite being goes through the determining development of its potency to actuality (e.g., an acorn to an oak tree).³⁶ Desmond is saying that *this* determining process from potency to actuality itself is marked with ontological givenness prior to the process of determinate actualization. Note also that he is not talking about the multiple determining factors that ground this single movement from an acorn to an oak tree (water, soil, the sun, weather, season, etc.). The whole series of potency to actuality in relation to all finite happenings (as much as each part of the series) is enabled by something other than the series of these determinations. That is to say, all spheres of finite happenings are accompanied with the hyperbolic note of the "coming to be."³⁷ The radical origination of the determinate becoming that we detect in the finite process of becoming, thus, points us to the infinite originator beyond the finitude of determinate processes as becoming.

To listen to the metaphysical note of the radical origination (i.e., creation), we must maintain the vigilance of posthumous thinking. In *BB*, Desmond describes the overdeterminate origination of *coming to be* as the "that it is" of the singular and shows how this enigma of its being vis-à-vis nothing exceeds our determinate understanding of "what it is"—the understanding made always in reference to the process of *becoming*.

> There is shown something in the singular that is not reducible to univocal predicates nor dialectical universal or concepts, that is not a mere equivocation in relation to determination, that is not exhausted by being an instance of a universal nor dissoluble into a system of universals. This is so because the singular exhibits a *thatness* that is the show of excess. There is a *that it is* whose givenness of being exceeds its determination as a kind of being. This *that it is* does not make it to be that kind of being; it is that it should be so at all, not that it is thus and thus. Its very being there as singular is given, a gift; ... [the univocal predicates and dialectical universals] do not supply either the how or the why as to the *that it is* of the singular being.³⁸

Given that the "*[finite particular] is and it is not nothing*,"³⁹ neither univocal nor dialectical thinking can make sense of why or how this must be the case. Our mind can only understand what kind of thing it is, and often it makes this judgment in relation to the process of its becoming. But this determinate understanding is always already derivative of the first possiblizing givenness of its "to be." Hence, we cannot know why the world is and how it is given to be in the first place, but only that it is there, even though it could be "not to be" there at all.

This is exactly why we tend to take the existence of the world for granted and engage in determinate understanding of its various whatness to satisfy our determinate curiosities. We almost always wake up in the morning and go about doing the business of an ordinary life. We take care of this and that on the list of our to-dos and live another day. I doubt that many of my readers sprung up from their beds this morning and celebrated another day of their being-in-the-world with sheer joy. Yet, what we forget in our posture of taking the thereness of the world, and our existence therein, for granted, Desmond argues, is the fact that all of this is actually granted in the first place.[40] All of what we see in *this* moment could have been "not to be" but somehow it is; and we cannot explain why this is the case, but only know that it exists prior to our determinate knowing of any of it. Our vigilance to the hyperbolic givenness in the thereness of nature and ourselves can wake us up to the extraordinary presence of overdeterminate divinity in the midst of the ordinary scene of given reality—the between in which we are unknowingly invited to freely exercise our determinate knowing. In this manner, metaxological mindfulness recognizes the hyperintelligible strangeness of the divine transcendence in each part of finite creation in immanence.[41]

To appreciate the aesthetic appearance of the divine absolute in finite happenings, we are called to practice a kind of intellectual expedition to the outskirts of philosophical language. To see what is shown in this unfamiliar terrain requires our mindfulness of the singular and of its source as exceeding our determinate minding, precisely because it deals with the "radical origination of the new; its giving to be of the 'never before' into unique 'once.'"[42] The poetic language in this respect has the feel for the singular in its unique form and shows its capacity to capture the "glimpses"[43] of creation as the divine *poiesis*.[44] Desmond gives many examples of these appearances of the divine transcendence in the ordinary objects of our life.

> The agapeics of the divine arrive unobtrusively in the most hidden elemental things: a mustard seed, a smile, a song, a glint of sun, a drink of pure water, a child holding one's hand, the comfort of fire on a bitter day, the uninsistent aid of an agapeic servant. The agapeics of the good communicate almost nothing and yet without them life loses its charge of worthiness, becoming loveless and unloved. Like the simplicity of the broken bread in which the risen Christ was recognized, there is no world-historical fanfare that prepares for us an overpowering spectacle. There is just the elemental and unfathomable mystery of the sweetness of the "to be" as gift of God. Overdeterminate providence provides the bread and wine of consecrated time.[45]

"It is the gloriously common, the ordinary," that Desmond finds in

> a glass of wine on an oak table; a shine of sunlight through a shutter; a blossom on a bush swaying; a squall of sudden rain; a crow cawing on a twilight tree; a girl giggling behind hiding hands; a saucy rogue winking; the last sigh of a man dying; the bawl of a baby born.[46]

But how ordinary are these things? How do we get from the "glint of sun" or the "squall of rain" to the divine absolute? It is indeed as mysterious and ordinary as C.S. Lewis' conversion: a critical atheist comes to be convinced of God's existence when he was "going up the Headington Hill on the top of a bus."[47] I do not know how to describe this realization of the hyperboles without repeating what Desmond says. I am not capable of writing poetic verses to describe the extraordinary breaches of the divine "beyond" in the ordinary immanence. What I can do, however, is to give some space to the poetic passages where the divine solicitation is best felt. To this end, I would like to recall a scene from *The First Circle*.

Solzhenitsyn beautifully describes the divine show of creation in the chapter entitled "Sawing Wood."[48] The protagonist, Nerzin, is a state prisoner of the Soviet Union, and he is forced to work with his knowledge of engineering for the formidable tyrant, Stalin. Despite his tragic circumstances, he enjoys the daily routine of splitting wood. This work is necessary for sustaining the fire in their kitchen and also undoubtedly serves as the source of life for the rest of prisoners in the brutal winter. Out in the field of Russia, Nerzin and his friend, Sologdin, volunteer to do this work every morning. The rhythm of the simple labor puts them in a great mood. But most importantly, they work for the life of others, and there is something rewarding in this service beyond their instrumental servility to the state. They know that the work that they do is good for them, for they sustain their lives by the fire in the kitchen, but more than that, they know that they are working for the good of others, a kind of work that kindles the heart of human spirit. There is some inexplicable (and yet natural) liberation in this labor. Their sweat comes forth from their bodies like sap, steam comes out of their body under blue sky, and their white breath spreads like leaves in the bright morning. After the good work is done, the workers look up and see the frost on barbwires shining like the glory of heaven. The hostile fence that keeps them in the degraded position of "serviceable disposability" communicates with the mysterious goodness of "to be" beyond the confines of human understanding. Dostoyevsky is right: "Beauty will save the world."[49] It saves the humans in the midst of their sufferings in the world. Rilke is right: some beauties can convince us that "we must change our lives."[50] The divine breach to the ordinary can happen in the desolate field of Russian winter. There is no reason that this cannot happen to the rest of us anywhere else in the world.[51]

The idiocy of the singular and the aesthetics of the happening in the transfinitude of creation demonstrate the intimate signs of the divine transcendence in immanence. Kantian and Hegelian philosophies of religion have a tendency to regard (either consistently or initially) the singular as the indeterminate particular in its oppositional relation to reason's universality: consequently, the significance of the singular (whether it is in relation to human subjects or natural objects) is always understood in its subordinated position to that of the universal. However, unlike these metaphysical formulations, metaxological metaphysics recognizes the overdeterminate absolute in the inner depth of the finite. This enigmatic presence of the divine origin in the sensible particular precedes, exceeds, and radically grounds the boundaries of our determinate thinking. Desmond, in this manner, strives to think of the singular as the singular and, in the process of doing so, comes to see the ways in which the singular communicates the infinite significance of the absolute beyond the limits of our reason. Thus, metaxology pays attention to the fact that the significance of the singular is irreducible to the language of the rational universal and further that this singular as an irreducible *this* points to the divine origin from which its inconvertible oneness is derived.

The inner opening to the divine transcendence: The infinite restlessness in the erotics of selving

The third hyperbole, the "erotics of selving," demonstrates how the complex processes of our ethical determination from its lack to fullness is "incarnating a primal porosity to what exceeds our own determination and self-determining."[52] To grasp the essential movement of the human (self-)becoming in metaxology, it is important to recall the doubleness of the mediations between self and other: viz., the self is mediating itself through its intermediation with the other as the other is mediating itself through its intermediation with the self. This metaxological intermediation was spoken in relation to the communivocity of mind and being. In context of the philosophy of religion, this also refers to the interrelation of the relative self and the absolute other. Desmond explains this divine-human intermediation as the "heteroarchic relation," where the infinite absolute enables the finite relative to be and to be free. Because of this "agapeic release" of the relative self for the relative, the self is charged with a "double metaxological process of self-becoming and becoming-other."[53] We will see more about this "heteroarchic" intermediation between humanity and divinity in the next chapter. But note here how the ethical determination of the self is always already charged with its double orientation toward both itself and what is other to itself. This means that the finite individual, in order for him to fully determine himself, must determine himself in relation to what is other to himself. And this other is not only the finite other in immanence but also the infinite other that we come to face as the inner otherness or the infinite transcendence that ultimately grounds our autonomous self- and (heteroarchic) intermediations in immanence. The metaxological doubleness in the process of selving, therefore, calls for our attention to the inner otherness of the divine absolute that is both transcendent to and immanent in the process of our ethical self- and intermediations.

How do we come to realize this "inward source of [our] transcending—strange otherness in innerness itself, not susceptible to complete self-mediation"?[54] Desmond draws our attention to the "infinite restlessness" that we cannot avoid feeling in one's process of coming to oneself, namely, the restlessness from facing the endless process of satisfying one's determinate desires. The Irish philosopher refers to this erotic self-development from one's lack toward fullness as "desire's distention."[55] He explains thus:

[It] is a voracious seeking of this and that as good. In that distention, our coming to some completion is lost in the very energy of going towards all of these goods. I love this and that, and soon it is less the love that counts, but that I am caught in a spiral of rush, in which I no sooner have this than then I want that. I see, I own, I crow, I sink back into indifference, inquietude stirs afresh, I seek again, but now this other and that other, and always I self-surpassing towards things takes over as a flight from self that is most a flight when it is most in search of itself as the empty voraciousness that must be satiated. Satiation of self secretes now boredom, now disgust with self, and hates itself in the very puffery of its supreme self-seeking.[56]

Nobody but we, the residents of the contemporary capitalist societies, are more surrounded by the madness of this distention. We have a determinate want of something finite and we go out to satisfy it. Sometimes we do think that this would lead to some kind of self-fulfillment. A usual result of this satisfaction, however, is just a momentary pause before feeling again the need to scratch the next itch. Augustine is right: when our mind is distended to the indefinite series of finite desires, we become the "land of want."[57] The rate in which we plunge ourselves into this empty voraciousness is unprecedented in the history of humanity, too. Every day, we see a number of advertisements or new cellphones, computers, cars, or whatever we are running low on in our kitchens, bathrooms, bedrooms, etc. The fashion industry no longer has seasonal collections, but to meet everyone's desire to look good or different or whatever, it has relentlessly maximized our accessibility to its new products (by continuously risking the lives of the workers in developing countries). Every grocery shop in the industrialized world seems to have every kind of produce from everywhere at all times. Our intellectual desire, too, is no exception to this madness. After all, we are only one "click away" from buying another book on Amazon.com.[58]

Whether one's determinate desires pertain to one's body or mind, what is insane about this process of self-surpassing self-determination from our lack toward fullness is not only that it is endless but also that we are supremely dissatisfied with ourselves even when we satisfy all of these desires.[59] Regardless of the fact that we have started this process of satisfying ourselves ultimately for finding some kind of our self-fulfillment or "happiness" (to borrow Aristotle's term), we seem to have lost the sight of ourselves. In continuously supplying the satisfactions of our wants, we now find ourselves most empty of any substance or value. There are so many great lines that sing the poverty of our existence—spiritual destitution resulting from enslaving ourselves to the indefinite distention of our desires. Yet none speaks better than Shakespeare's Hamlet: "Your worm is your only emperor for diet: We fat all creatures else to fat us, and we fat ourselves for maggots; Your fat king and your lean beggar is but variable service—two dishes, but to one table. That's the end."[60]

But isn't there another kind of hunger that lingers after the end of eating? Are we not hungry for something that exceeds our finite satisfactions of our determinate hungers? If the physical sustenance of our bodily existence is the sole purpose of our life, it should perfectly make sense that we do nothing more than eating and that nobody should be able even to question if his eating is really the end of his life. But humans are the only creatures that are attached to the indigestible anxiety in the garden of the dead and driven to question the whole point of their living.[61] The end of the mere sustenance of life is nothing but to be eaten by the worms—worms that would never ask the metaphysical question of "to be or not to be." When we are disturbed by the fate of our finitude, our food turns into ashes and then we begin to realize that we are absolutely starving for the meaning of our lives.

Is this not also true about the food for our thought? We have been told to study various subjects and to learn what they can offer us as the truths of the world in which we live. But not many of us are told to ask continuously why we should study these things in the first place. It is undeniable that many academic disciplines (including philosophy) can bring us useful knowledge for whatever use that we can find in our contemporary societies. Some of them could bring us a couple of degrees that help us find some decent jobs. But if this were the only point of learning, they would bring us nothing but more food on the table.[62] Why should we even eat if it all comes to nothing? There is also a deeper metaphysical problem in our general habit of using our minds to satisfy determinate intellectual desires. This (ab)use of reason is classically termed "curiosity." Desmond describes,

> One is curious about this, that, or the other. Curiosity is not vague, though it may be itchy, that is, greedily extend itself to everything coming within its purview. It is with curiosity that definite questions arise about particular beings and processes, definite questions that seek determinate answers.[63]

The results of determinate knowing, like food, never seem to satisfy our deeper intellectual desire that drove us to ask the two-fold question of philosophy or what Desmond calls "metaphysical astonishment" as the underling motivation of any philosophizing.[64] Why is there anything at all rather than nothing? Why is there anything to be known? What is the point of learning about all these things when all comes to nothing? Why do I exist? What is the purpose of life? Even though we keep scratching our intellectual itch, no determinate knowledge of anything in the world can heal our soul bleeding with these questions. We continue to buy more books, download more articles, and claim that we are wiser. But all we read are "Words, words, words." All knowledge turns into ashes, and we, the children of postmodernity, stay malnourished with the words that signify nothing about the point of our "to be."[65]

This infinite restlessness felt in the endless process of satisfying our determinate desires, Desmond argues, is not entirely negative. The fact that we are not completely satisfied with the very process of scratching the surface of our existence shows that there is a deeper sense of lack that we cannot alleviate with any set of determinate objects or knowledge.

> In transcending desire, we suffer not just the opening of any lack but the upsurge of infinite lack. The notion of infinite lack makes little sense in terms of finitely determinable entities. ... It is beyond univocal determination. It seems *hyperbolic*. It refers to the impotence of the finite to quell our extraordinary transcending. Defined in an interplay between our desire and the goods it seeks, infinite lack opens up in the disjunction between seeking and sought, though no determinate name can be given to what is being sought.[66]

What opens up in the "dynamic interplay of desire and finite goods," therefore, is the hyperbolic presence of the infinite transcendence in our finite existence—that is to say, our existence is marked with the infinitely self-surpassing desire tending toward something more than what we can supply in the realm of our finite existence. In this sense, when the finite self busies itself with its determinate desires and continues to turn away from the infinite other, it can be attacked by the awareness of the infinite lack. In relation to this overwhelming sense of absolute want, however,

Our doubleness comes back: finite and infinite, but infinite restlessness emerging in and beyond our finitude, thrusting for something more; and infinite restlessness teaches us our finitude in a deeper sense, since we come to despair if we get no further than finite goods. The infinite restlessness throws us back upon finitude in a way that opens up the possibility of another sense of the infinite, an infinite not at all defined by the mediation of finitude and infinity in our self-mediation: an appearance of the infinite into the middle and in a relation of superiority relative to our infinite restlessness. The doubleness, properly interiorized, pushes us towards the double vision that blindly sees beyond death, by itself being touched by death. The other of which it is blindly prescient is above it. It comes from the height of transcendence as other.[67]

The infinite restless in the endless process of our determinate desiring/satisfying not only ends with our despair in finitude but also points to the fact that this "erotic process of selving" from our determinate lack to determinate fullness presupposes the enigmatic presence of the infinite transcendence in ourselves. The infinite transcendence is there as something that our hearts and minds ultimately desire but not there because it cannot be there in the same sense as any determinate object is said to be in the realm of the finite. The "prescience" of the infinite cannot mean another determinate knowledge that can satisfy us at the level of curiosity either.[68] But prior to any of our determinate knowing or "coming to ourselves in determinate character," we are always already in touch with the infinite transcendence; and because of this mysterious interrelation with the infinite in and through ourselves, there can be any sense of our moving toward it as something that we have not yet achieved.[69]

The presence of the infinite transcendence, in this manner, is first felt through the overdeterminate sense of our lack that we cannot alleviate through ourselves, and then, in face of this lack, we are woken up to the infinite transcendence as the inner source of our infinitely transcending desire. This divine solicitation in the deepest foundation of our (self-)becoming calls us to recognize that we cannot rest the weight of our infinite love on finite goods in immanence. We must go beyond ourselves and seek to desire infinite transcendence as the ultimate good beyond ourselves.

According to Desmond, there are different ways in which the finite self can exercise its transcending power and deal with the infinite restlessness. First, it can give a series of "equivocal transcending" where it plunges itself to the "vehemence of unchecked desire."[70] In this mode of transcending, the self strives to feed any desire that it fancies and prevents itself from recognizing the infinite source of its transcending power. The best literary example of this equivocal transcending is found in *The Picture of Dorian Grey*. The young and innocent Dorian follows what Lord Henry advocates as the "New Hedonism."[71] In this philosophy of pleasure, one is expected to follow whatever one desires with no prudence or moral judgment. There is only one principle that makes sense to those who live the life of pleasures: "the only way to get rid of a temptation is to yield to it."[72] The most alarming end of this immanent ecstasy is naturally found in the last image of Dorian: that is, the complete deformation of the self where nothing but his material possessions can define his identity.[73] This is the slavery of our soul to finite goods, which carves "a monster more complicated and more furious than Typhon"[74] out of a human soul in its equivocal transcending.

Second, the self can strive to harness the transcending energy for itself and overcome the infinite lack in terms of its self-transcending. Desmond calls this "erotic transcending" and describes the circular movement in which the self goes beyond itself toward the other and comes back to itself as it overcomes the other. In this mode of self-transcending, the self initially recognizes the source of its transcending power as other to itself. Yet it sees this other only as its self-alienation: hence, the self comes to assimilate this otherness (originating from the self) as the means for its self-completing self-mediation in immanence. As we have seen in relation to Hegel's dialectical self-determination, this erotic mode of self-transcending cannot genuinely transcend itself toward the infinite transcendence as the superior other to itself.[75] Rather, it ends up absolutizing itself as the concrete manifestation of such infinity in immanence. This logic of self-determination is a refusal to recognize the implication of infinite restlessness, for the otherness of the lack is something more than what the self can overcome through itself.

Finally, in agapeic transcending, the self is fully aware that what its heart and mind desire (i.e., the infinite) is beyond the reach of what it can provide through itself in immanence. This awareness, however, anticipates its further realization that the infinite desire is minted into its finite framework of existence. Hence, the self not only despairs in finitude but also, through its infinite restlessness, finds in itself its openness to the inexhaustible source of its transcending desire beyond itself.[76] Stated succinctly, the self comes to realize the infinite transcendence as the constitutive ground of its self-transcending existence. This agapeic mode of transcending is significantly different from the previous two because it gives up the idea that it can satisfy what it really wants through itself alone and undergoes a transformation in which the self fully takes into account the implication of the infinite restlessness—viz., it opens itself up to the "height of (intimate) transcendence" as other to itself and genuinely transcends to this infinite other without reappropriating this alterity as the means for determining itself as the infinite absolute in immanence.[77] Without falling victim to the self-circling logic of self-determining self-mediation, the self maintains its awareness that its transcending power is ultimately given from the infinite as other to itself. With gratitude and humility, the knight of agapeic transcending leaps beyond itself to the other as the other.

What we see in this mode of agapeic transcending is the self that shows its fidelity to the source of its transcending power, the self that goes beyond itself toward the other and gives itself to the other for the other without constraining the energy of its transcending back to itself. It recognizes that its infinitely transcending power comes from the infinite source beyond itself and also that it must let go of itself to go beyond itself, for only the infinite transcendence can satisfy its infinite desire in immanence. Here we find the self that remains faithful both to itself (as a metaxological being marked with the double orientation toward infinite and finite) and to the infinite transcendence as the ultimate ground of its existence. The agapeic self is fully attentive to its finitude in that it knows itself as being incapable of bringing its infinitely restless heart to rest and strongly aware of its porosity to the infinite in that it sees the origin of its infinitely transcending power beyond itself.

The fruits of this agapeic transcending are the various forms of agapeic communities or the metaxological communivocities of self and other in all levels of our given reality. The self that transcends toward infinite transcendence transcends also toward other finite beings in immanence, and this community of the finite selves is sustained by the infinite/intimate source of their transcending. We will turn to this communicative interrelation of self and other, which is woven into the fabric of all existence, as the fourth hyperbole.

The primordial givenness of being: The agapeics of community and the *Compassio Essendi*

The last hyperbole, the "agapeics of community," has to do with the ways in which the double orientation of human existence manifests itself in various forms of communicative relations between self and other. We have seen that a human being is marked with a continuous interplay of self-mediation and intermediation. This metaxological doubleness in human selving is best explained in Desmond's account of the interrelation between *passio essendi* and *conatus essendi*. The *passio essendi* points to the primal givenness of all beings. In relation to the mindful existence of a human self, this refers to the "passion of being,"[78] that is, the primal receptivity of the "to be" that the self cannot exhaustively explain through any of its determinate or self-determining thinking. What is felt as the received in the side of the self is the "surplus immediacy" and "inner otherness" of its "to be" that precedes, exceeds, and grounds its determinate or self-determining "effort to be." The *conatus essendi*, in turn, refers to this "effort to be" as the derivative of its first givenness, a givenness implicating the otherness of the giver. It represents our endowed capacity to be and to be free for ourselves. These two terms, *passio* and *conatus essendi*, according to Desmond, are not mutually exclusive. As the etymology of the Latin term *co-natus* (i.e., "coming to birth with"[79]) indicates, the self's "endeavor to be" always presupposes the givenness of the "to be" regardless of its awareness of itself as a gift.

Now, a process of (self-)becoming in a finite being faces two possible directions in which it can navigate its *conatus essendi*: it can *either* grow impatient to, and subsequently become more and more negligent of, its prior givenness apropos of the other *or* come to be "awakened to the porosity between itself and the divine, an awakening that exceeds the power of [its] self-determination."[80] I have shown that the equivocal and erotic transcending, on the one hand, takes the first path. The self, in this case, gives the primacy to the *conatus essendi* and fails to recognize its prior *passio essendi*. It cannot acknowledge its openness to the infinite source of its transcending power as other to itself. Agapeic transcending, on the other hand, takes the second path. The self in this mode of transcending goes through a transformation from the self that strives to fulfill its infinite desire through itself to the self that sees in itself its openness to the otherness of infinite transcendence. The second self genuinely transcends to the infinite other without contracting the energy of its transcending back to itself. This agapeic self navigates its *conatus essendi* in its relativity to the primacy of the *passio essendi*. This "porosity to what transcends us," Desmond further articulates,

> makes us potentially liable to attack from hostile others, human or nonhuman; but it also constitutes the promise of our community beyond hostility with others. ... This is not just a matter of judging how things stand with our own endeavor to be; it is a matter of a fidelity to the patience of our own being, and that of the suffering others. One might perhaps here speak of a kind of *compassio essendi*, a compassion of being, in which both strong and weak can participate. And perhaps this *compassio essendi* communicates a sign of what a more divine love might be for mortal creatures.[81]

With its intense awareness of the primacy of the *passio essendi* before the *conatus essendi*, the self comes to realize that the unmerited gift of the "to be" is given both to itself and what is other to itself prior to their self- and intermediations. Also, in maintaining its porosity to the surplus generosity of infinite transcendence, the finite self comes to realize that it can fully determine itself only if it participates in this divine generosity by transcending itself and thereby dedicating itself to the other for the other. Stated otherwise, the vertical transcendence of the finite self to the infinite other constitutes the community of what Desmond calls "agapeic service" among the finite selves, the community of compassionate beings that incarnates the infinite/inexhaustible/divine love that gives everything to the other for the other. This community of agapeic service as the concrete manifestation of the divine *(com)passio essendi* both grounds the possibility of our determinate or self-determining *conatus essendi* and gives the hyperbolic sign of divine transcendence in immanence.

How can we find this "agapeics of community" in the midst of our free self- and intermediations? How does it constitutively ground our "endeavor to be"? I would like to reflect on a few examples in the following in order to provide a preliminary response to these questions.[82]

The best way to visualize the priority of the *passio essendi* toward the *conatus essendi* is to think about what Rowan Williams (*pace* Dostoyevsky) discusses as a "dependent freedom" or "a liberty that *depends* on otherness."[83] Williams explains that "[this freedom] is generated by what is other to the mind or self or will; it is through response to—including contradiction of—what is given that we develop as subjects."[84] This notion is extremely helpful for understanding the "agapeics of community," and so let us follow the example that Williams provides to evince this notion: "it is one sense true that we can say what we like; in another sense, manifestly not true, since we are performing linguistically within a world in which we have to make ourselves recognizable to other speakers as they are to us."[85] One's freedom to express one's feelings, thought, will, and desire—that is, to express oneself freely—depends on the patience of the other that lets the one speak and speak for oneself. Thus, the self's freedom in his process of linguistic communications presupposes its relation to the other and this community between self and other is excessive to the self's freedom or total control.

Allow me to ruminate on this point with my personal reflection as a single individual. At the age of twenty, I moved from Japan to the United States and barely spoke English. But I intensely learned from my teachers and friends how to construct sentences properly and to pronounce certain words correctly (and even to deviate from some grammatical rules to comply with the colloquial expressions of the land) solely for the purpose of communicating what I felt, thought, willed, and desired. What comes to my mind in relation to this language acquisition is that my current ability and freedom to express my thoughts and feelings in English is heavily dependent on this prior learning, along with my numerous interactions with other speakers in the course of the last fourteen years. Unless most of these others taught me the truth about their language and the truth about the world and themselves through it, I would not be able to describe any of my thoughts or feelings in it, let alone write a book on the philosophy of religion like this. I also need to emphasize that my friends and teachers taught me in such a way that I would be able to make their language my own. They did not teach me with their own definitions of the words, nor did they try to take advantage of me through teaching less than what I needed to know for my independence. They taught me to the fullest so that I would become as free and adept in the language as they were, and some of them even tried to make me become better and freer than they were.[86]

What is also astonishing is that the same relation between learning and the learned goes for native speakers: unless they had someone like their parents, teachers, siblings, and friends who taught them the language for their sake, they could not have taught me any of the truths about the language, the world, and themselves through their words.[87] The transmission of linguistic freedom, in this manner, presupposes the communicative relation in which the knowledgeable passes its knowledge and freedom to the ignorant and unfree.[88] For this exchange of the language capacity to take place, both parties must be participating in the prior community of the free speakers who have patiently received and given their knowledge of the language to others.[89] This means that nobody gives himself his capacity to speak his language, but his fluency or literacy is the endowed freedom that requires the *compassio essendi* of those who speak the truth about the world and themselves. The interlocutors who forget this prior givenness of their ability to express themselves often forget that their freedom is given. Consequently, it is not difficult for them to neglect the fact that they would need other interlocutors (and certainly a set of grammatical rules inherited from other speakers) for adequately communicating their thoughts or feelings.[90] In this example of linguistic communication, we witness how free *conatus essendi* of a single individual presupposes the prior *compassio essendi* of other single individuals. Without those who remain attentive to the givenness of their freedom in their giving of the freedom to the other, the single individual can never acquire his freedom, for what gives him the freedom in speaking the language is his communicative relation to the other free individuals.

The giving of the linguistic freedom from the learned to the learning, moreover, comes to signify something more than what we can word as the determinate truths about the world and ourselves. First, not a single term, or a phrase, or a language can exhaustively explain the constitution of the community of the free speakers, precisely because our speech act in any specific form of language presupposes the very community as its foundation. The human communities as the enabling grounds of their linguistic communications are already too much for any specific language to articulate determinately or express exhaustively. Second, the notion of the *compassio essendi* of the free speakers as the precondition for the single individual to exercise his linguistic *conatus essendi* takes us to another question on the origin of such freedom; namely, how do the whole of the communicative relations of the human individuals come to be? In relation to the transmission of linguistic freedom, we have seen that the learning receives the capacity to express itself freely from the learned and then the former, in turn, gives the same freedom and capacity to the others. And this series of their communicative relations seem to extend indefinitely in the course of human history. But what enables the continuous transmissions of the human capacities to communicate through languages to be? What gives the first giving of the receiving/giving of the human communications? Where lies the source of the *compassio essendi* apropos of our linguistic freedom as a whole?

The endless chain of our communicative relations as the receiving/giving of the linguistic freedom highlights another astonishing fact that the infinite desire (to communicate the truths about the world and ourselves) is mysteriously minted into the finite framework of our existence as the metaxological beings. This means that there is another source of communication (i.e., the infinite source of our communicative transcending) that radically possiblizes our linguistic self- and intermediations in immanence. As the self in its agapeic transcending sees the infinite restlessness as the transfinite sign of the divine transcendence in human immanence, those who remain attentive to the prior givenness of their linguistic freedom can come to see that the foundation of their communicative relations as their *compassio essendi* with each other is signaling their porosity to the infinite transcendence beyond themselves. This means that the linguistic interrelations of the finite selves are ultimately given and that they are sustained by the infinite source of their transcending—the inexhaustible source that is irreducible to, and yet intimately involved with, their determinate and self-determining communications. Divine transcendence communicates its infinite power of communication to the finite beings for the finite; and thanks to this primal giving of the communicative power, the single individuals and the communities of such singulars can continuously engage in their receiving/giving of their linguistic capacity and freedom.[91] As Desmond rightly says, "[o]ur speaking, as responding [to the givenness of our being], is an *endowed wording* of being."[92] Thus, in reference to the interrelations of free speakers in immanence, we see how our *compassio essendi* in immanence further points to the first giver of our (linguistic) freedom beyond ourselves. This is one instance in which we can reflect on the agapeics of community, namely, the hyperbolic presence of the divine transcendence in the heart of our free communicative relations in immanence.

From the hyperboles of being to the metaxological absolute

The four "hyperboles of being" have demonstrated the intimate signs of the divine transcendence in immanence. In reference to these signs, we witness how metaxological metaphysics configures the finite, the infinite, and their interrelations quite differently from the Kantian and the Hegelian philosophy of religion. The German philosophers have a tendency to regard (either consistently or initially) the single individual as the indeterminate particular in its oppositional relation to reason's universal: consequently, the significance of the singular (whether it is a human subject or a natural object) is always understood in its subordinated position to that of the rationalistic universal. Unlike these metaphysical formulations, metaxology recognizes the overdeterminate absolute in the inner depth of the finite. As the "idiocy of being" and the "aesthetics of happenings" have shown, there is something in a singular that we cannot exhaustively explain or entirely subordinate vis-à-vis the immanent universality of our determinate or self-determining thinking. The enigmatic givenness of its "to be" in the single individual shows the undeniable porosity of the singular to the infinite absolute before the rational universal.[93] Thus, the sensible particular demonstrates its ontological plentitude in immediacy and shines forth the enigmatic presence of the infinite transcendence in its finite framework of existence in immanence.

The third and the fourth hyperbole highlight the presence of the divine transcendence in the heart of human self- and intermediations. The "erotics of selving" accentuates the communicative interrelations of the single individual and the infinite transcendence in reference to the former's (self-)becoming. This chapter has demonstrated that the determinate or self-determining process of a single individual to move from its lack to fullness in the realm of the finite presupposes its porosity to the infinite transcendence as the inexhaustible source of its transcending energy. Since a human being both exists as a finite and exhibits his desire as infinitely self-surpassing, he cannot help but suffer from the overwhelming sense of ontological destitution in immanence—an overdeterminate poverty that it cannot possibly reconcile through itself or compensate with any other finite goods. Yet there is always hope to be found beyond this misery. Through burning despair, the finite self comes to forge its unshakable conviction that the ultimate satisfaction of his desire lies in the infinite good beyond itself. The self, in this case, is called to exercise agapeic transcending, that is, to give up the temptation to bring its ultimate satisfaction only through itself and to transcend itself to the infinite other as the other to itself. Whether the self makes this agapeic transcending or not, what we see here is the single individual who, with its intense self-awareness, finds in itself its openness to the infinite absolute beyond itself.

The "agapeics of community" shows how the communicative interrelation of the infinite and the finite shines through the intermediations of the finite individuals in immanence. In reference to the *conatus-passio* distinction along with the example of linguistic communications, I have shown how the freedom of a single individual presupposes its communicative interrelations with the other single individuals: accordingly, the *conatus essendi* of the singular is always already dependent on the *(com) passio essendi* of the other individuals. This does not mean, however, that the individual *conatus essendi* is fully accounted for through the community of the free individuals (this is what Kant and Hegel essentially tried to achieve through the "individual self-legislations of the *Reich*" or the "collective self-determination of the *Stadt*"). Rather, the community as the horizontal intertranscending of the free individuals requires the ultimate *compassio essendi* of the divine transcendence as its enabling ground. This point is exemplified in the continuous transmissions of our linguistic freedom: viz., the infinite series of our receiving/giving of our capacity to express ourselves cannot be originated from a determinate giving of the humans, but from the primal giving of it by the divine transcendence. No finite individual can be for itself through itself, but only through its (oft-unrecognized) interrelations with other agapeic individuals; and further, this communicative interrelation of free individuals points to the *incognito compassio essendi* of the absolute infinite beyond themselves. Thus, the community of free individuals (or what Desmond calls "agapeic servants") shows its porosity to the divine transcendence in the midst of their self- and intermediations.

With the first three hyperboles, Desmond invites us to think of the singular as the singular and, in doing so, see the various ways in which the single individual can communicate the infinite significance of the divine absolute beyond the limits of rational universalism. The last hyperbole pays special attention to the communicative foundation of our endowed freedom as the finite self. This account, however, is far from subsuming the significance of the individual freedom to the interrelations of multiple singulars (as we have witnessed in Hegel's formulation of it as the self-determining absolute). Instead, Desmond paints the community of the compassionate "servants" who recognize the ultimate foundation of their both individual and collective freedom in their interrelations with the divine absolute beyond themselves. For these free and agapeic individuals, their relative *compassio essendi* to each other in immanence originates from the ultimate *compassio essendi* of the divine love beyond their self- and/or intermediations. Thus, through the four hyperbolic signs of the divine transcendence in immanence, metaxology shows both the irreducible significance of the singular as the singular and its undeniable relativity to the divine absolute beyond the immanent universality of human self and interrelations.

6

The Metaxological Absolute and Its Interrelation with the Singular

Agapeic origin and the archeology of the between

Metaxology recognizes the divine otherness to what is determinable in immanent terms through the transfinite signs of what transcends immanence in immanent particulars. Since what is shown through these signs as the glimpse of the divine absolute exceeds the bounds of determinate intelligibility, the biggest challenges to the metaxological philosophy of religion would be to make sense of the divine transcendence and additionally to communicate what is truthful regarding the nature of the absolute. We will encounter some limit to this endeavor. If there is an ontological asymmetry between the divine infinite and human finite as the hyperboles of being clearly indicate, then a human understanding of the divine or any finite expression of the infinite absolute will suffer from some contraction in the process of making it intelligible. Nevertheless, the divine ultimate, as Desmond often articulates, is always communicative in its constitutive relation to what is finite and always already communicating itself through the hyperboles of being in the process of our (self-)becoming in immanence. This constant invitation to our intellectual quest of the ultimate comes from the side of the ultimate, and I can only respond to this call as I write this text on the philosophy of religion.

There are many ways in which metaxology articulates the senses of the divine and its "reciprocal asymmetry"[1] with the finite. It communicates the relations of the thereness of the finite to the divine infinite with different names, such as, agapeic origin, agapeic transcendence, hyper agathos, (huper)arche, (over)origin, the Good beyond good and evil, actual infinite, the intimate universal, God of creation, God beyond the whole, and trans-objective and trans-subjective God, etc. These names stress different aspects of the divine and one is not always irreducible to the other. There is the "plurality of ways of thinking about the divine."[2] For this reason, Desmond engages in a series of critical reflections on the different sense of the divine ultimate as well as the different modes of thinking about the absolute (e.g., polytheistic, monotheistic, transpersonal, personal, gnostic, pan(en)theistic, theistic, and mystic god). Instead of univocalizing these senses or dialectically sublating them into one consummate form, the metaxological philosophy of religion listens to the truthfulness of each form and, through its mindfulness, expresses the underlying attributes of the absolute original that allows such plurivocal senses of the divine—the multiplicity of divine infinite communicated through different forms of religious faith.[3] I would like to name and examine, in the following, at least three of these underlying attributes of the ultimate, which are distinctly the metaxological senses of the divine absolute.

Three metaxological characterizations of the divine absolute are: (1) intimate overdeterminacy, (2) agapeic transcendence beyond dualism, and the (3) radical origination of the finite for the finite. These three aspects of divinity are interrelated with each other: hence, a description of one both presupposes and overlaps with that of the other, and because of this, we have to keep all three in mind in order to understand properly the metaxological ultimate.

First, with regard to the intimate overdeterminacy, recall the previous discussions on the hyperboles of being. In most of these notions, we have witnessed the absolute as "too muchness" or the ontological richness of the "to be" that both exceeds and originates the determinate "becoming" of all things. In reference to the process of our becoming, Desmond repeatedly calls us to think about divine excess.

> We "negate" what is present in the presentiment that the determinate present does not exhaust the full reserves of being; in our negating, we incarnate intimate of the beyond of that present. Even when we negate our determinate selves as present, and with the view to a fuller self-affirmation, the "negation" can serve as a witness to reserves of being, beyond determinate presentness, and hence reaffirm presenting, as newly seen in light of a more ultimate, giving plentitude. Our negative energy, in this understanding, arises from a more reserved, affirmative source in intimate, original selving, beyond complete objective determination. The source of transcending in us is drawn to the overdeterminacy of the origin as inexhaustibility.[4]

Think again of the process of becoming and consider this process now in terms of our selving. We have seen that in order for A to become B, A must have its openness to become something more than A and transcend itself to become what is other than itself, namely B. Desmond is saying that A's self-negation does not exterminate its existence but enables it to transcend itself and thereby fulfill its promise as becoming B. In this dynamic transformation from A to B, metaxology witnesses the overdeterminate source that radically possiblizes the *dunamis* of becoming. This ontological ground of our becoming is both intimate and irreducible to the very process of becoming since it signals, in our determinate immanence, something more than what we can account for in immanent terms. The determinate process of our becoming is always already granted by what both intimates and exceeds our becoming, and this overdeterminacy is the sign of the divine absolute in the midst of our self- and intermediations.

This inner otherness of the overdeterminate that signals the primal ontological position of our reality as "given to be before we give ourselves to be"[5] constantly points us toward the source of our being as the inexhaustible plentitude beyond ourselves. However, since the richness of the metaxological absolute exceeds the limits of our determinate knowing and the determinate sense of richness does not apply to this excess, we are always tempted to deem it as an indeterminate lack. In this sense,

Desmond argues that the "the overdeterminate origin has been described as negativity by Hegel, and as nothingness by Sartre, for the good reason that it is not a finite determinate entity with the univocal identity we frequently ascribe to such entities."[6] The Irish thinker further articulates,

> If it is no thing in that sense, it is so, not because it is less than any thing, but because it is in excess of every determinate thing. The prior "something other" is an excess, over and above the determinations ascribed to finite entities, precisely because it is a determining source, not a determined delimitation. It is an originative surplus. It is a source of transcendence. The "trans" here not only points to a subsequent surpassing of every finite limit—though this is true; the "trans" refer to the other origin itself as over and above, beyond the beings.[7]

The metaxological sense of the divine absolute starkly differs from the practical postulate of the critical idealism or the dialectical god of the sublationary infinitism. Kant refrains from talking about the absolute beyond the confine of (practical) reason, while Hegel is much more audacious in his attempt to conceptualize the constitutive relation of the absolute and the particular in terms of the universal logic of self-determination. What Desmond finds problematic in these formulations of the divine ultimate is that they are not faithful to the "affirmative indeterminacy of inexhaustibility"[8] or overdeterminate richness that we detect in the ontological origin of our being. This divine original even exceeds the universality of our determinate rationality, for the latter always already presupposes the former. Consequently, both Kant and Hegel cannot see the notion of the divine as anything more than the indeterminate lack that needs to be either dismissed as empty absurdity or dialectically sublated as the necessary (and yet transitional) moment for reason's self-concretizing self-determination. The agapeic origin in metaxology points to the constitutive relation of the absolute both to the particular and the universal via the hyperboles of being in immanence. This means that the metaxological absolute possesses the hyperbolic richness that exceeds the immanent terms of the particular or the universal while grounding both of them: it releases each single individual to be the single individual and enables it to mediate itself with the other individuals to form the (intimate) universal, while the absolute itself is irreducible to either one of these terms in immanence.

Second, the agapeic origin preserves the robust sense of divine transcendence in its intimacy with the finitude of immanence. This statement should sound problematic to those who hold either the Kantian or the Hegelian viewpoint. To them, the statement would sound like declaring the aloof divinity in its dualistic opposition to the immanence of the particular and the universal. To discern the metaxological understanding of the divine transcendence, therefore, it is both important and helpful to discuss the three types of transcendence Desmond specifies in the beginning of *GB*. They are: (T^1) externality of beings, (T^2) self-transcendence, and (T^3) the superior beyond the distinction of the exterior and the interior.[9] T^1 understands the relation between the sacred transcendence and the profane immanence in their dualistic opposition. This is how Kant (almost always) and Hegel (initially) conceived the relation between transcendence of the infinite and immanence of the finite. However, as the dialectical metaphysician acutely shows, this juxtaposition is problematically one-sided, since it pictorially conceives of the infinite as another determinate finite standing over against the finitude of immanence, while the finite is raised to the level of the infinite as what equals the infinite; hence, it fails to understand the true meanings of the infinite and the finite in their mutual implications.

Desmond agrees with Hegel to the extent that we must reconsider the divine absolute in its profound mutuality with the immanence of finite beings. However, what he finds problematic in Hegel's concept of the divine—which was clarified in Chapter 3—is that his dialectical thinking conflates divine transcendence with the immanent logic of self-determination, that is, T^2. The "trans" in Hegel's dialectic only gives the *immanent transcendence*, where the initially abstract infinite goes out to the finite as its self-alienation and comes back to itself as the self-determining infinite in immanence.[10] We have seen that this logic of self-determination makes it impossible to distinguish between the self-concretizing self-mediation of the divine absolute and the self-competing self-determination of humanity.[11] At the end of this logic, we cannot find anything other to the world-historical manifestation of human self-mediation and, therefore, everything seems to be explained away in immanence. Hegel rightly criticizes position T^1 as being inadequate for understanding the divine infinite, yet his equation of the divine transcendence to T^2 prevents him from understanding anything beyond the immanent terms of self-determining reason.[12]

Desmond proposes T^3 as the proper sense of the divine transcendence. This sense of transcendence stresses its ontological superiority both to the exteriority of T^1 and the interiority of T^2. To grasp these points, we must keep in mind the overdeterminacy of the agapeic origin. Given that the origin is at work in immanence of every being, the processes of its becoming point to the transfinite otherness of the divine transcendence in the immanent processes themselves. This radical immanence to the finite happenings testifies that it cannot be completely divorced from the dynamism of becoming in immanence, nor can it be reduced to any immanent term that determinately explains the process of becoming. The agapeic origin, in other words, is transcendent to the finite happenings because it goes across to each of them and constitutively grounds its "becoming" and "self-becoming" in immanence.[13] In this configuration of the divine absolute in its intimacy to the finite relatives, there is no determinate dualism between the divine above and the profane below; for the overdeterminacy of the above is both at work in the dynamism of the below, while the above, seen in the midst of finitude, cannot be equated to a single being or a single process of self- or intermediation in the below: that is to say, the above cannot be fully conceptualized in, or equated to, any determinate terms of the below.[14] In this sense, Desmond argues:

> God as the absolute original is not an absorbing god. The profane is not dissolved in the sacred: while remaining itself, it is manifested as more than itself. Nor is the sacred reduced to the profane, immersed in it without difference and so destroyed by absorbing homogeneity. The sacred as sacred entered into the profane: as the transfiguring power it both remains itself and communicates itself, broadcasts its reality as other to what is other to itself. Sacred and profane are bound together in a mutuality deeper than dualistic exclusion. Though consecration sets apart a

place of worship, the transfiguration there effected returns us differently, newly, to the profane "outside." Worship stands in the space between sacred and profane: it endures the tension of their difference, yet mediates their reconciliation. This mediation is a metaxological intermediation of an open community, not a dialectical self-mediation of an absorbing totality.[15]

The metaxological configuration of the divine absolute keeps open the space of interrelativity between the sacred transcendence and the profane immanence. The sense of the divine cannot be thought as standing over against the finite immanence in terms of dualism (as if the sacred had nothing to do with the profane). Also, it cannot be totalized into the single process of self-transcending from the side of the profane such that the former is drained into the self-sanctification of the latter. Rather, since the divine superior is intimately at work in every fiber of immanence and also since it, out of its ontological surplus, reserves its otherness to the finite between, we see the intimate strangeness between the sacred above and the profane below. This intimate strangeness between agapeic origin and the finite between allows us to conceive of the divine transcendence in its profound relativity to the finite immanence beyond the confines of dualism.[16]

Third, with regard to agapeic origination of the finite, Desmond emphasizes its "radical origination of the new; its giving to be of the 'never before' into its unique 'once.'"[17] This creation of the finite particular *ex nihilo* points to the different sense of the origination of the finite from its dialectical production as the self-particularization of the self-determining universal. As I have shown earlier, Hegel's God creates the finite other as its self-alienation and then mediates itself in and through its finite. Put differently, Hegel's God needs to create the finite to create itself as the infinite absolute. It absorbs the finite into the process of its self-determination and leaves no room for the finite to be there for itself. In agapeic origin, contrariwise,

> [t]here is an other transcending not from lack but surplus, and that communicates out of itself, not for purposes of mediating with itself, but for going to the other as other. This transcendence is not lack completing itself, it is surplus giving out of self, giving for the other as other, as well as for selving. This is the way of agapeic self-transcending.[18]

The agapeic power transcends toward the finite out of its overdeterminate surplus and creates the finite other for the finite. This agapeic empowering, according to Desmond, looks more like "nothing" for two interrelated reasons: (1) it cannot be seen as any determinate power and (2) it "makes way for the other as other."[19] It is not the absorbing power of dialectical god, but

> Absolving power, releasing others beyond itself. It does not bind but unbinds. And it binds by unbinding, in that the deeper bond of agapeic togetherness and service is only thus allowed. Absolute absolving power is agapeic as power that gives the power to give. Only if absolute power is an absolving agape, is the absoluteness of the divine togetherness with the relativity of the finite.[20]

This mysterious giving that calculates no return to the giver but continuously keeps giving the good of the "to be" to the finite many—this "non-possessive dispensation of being"[21] is the agapeic origination. Desmond conclusively states that

> This is what is creation is: gift of the power of being to make come to be the finite other, itself a definite concretion of the original power of being, invested with its own integrity. The sovereign power of the divine, one might say, abdicates its own self-possession and gives the gift of being: gives it away, so to say, gives it from itself.[22]

Once again, agapeic richness is a kind of "nothingness" both because it exceeds our determinate knowing of all that is determinate and also because it is a "willing poverty" that is "in willing to be nothing, that the genuinely other maybe be endowed as something and as good"[23]—the "poverty that wants nothing for itself to want the good for the other."[24] The agapeic origin, in this sense, constitutes the divine kenosis that empties itself, its infinite richness, for the relative to be. The divine absolute as the "fertile void"[25] takes on the position of a servant who dies to himself as nothing, and out of its nothing, gives everything to the other.[26] The agapeic origination of the metaxological divine gives the finite other to be for the other, empowers each singular to be the singular with its original power to be, and endows the singular with the irrepeatable mark of the worthy "once."

What does this agapeic giving look like? C.S. Lewis, with his mastery of the English language, likens it to the image of pouring a "magic wine" that creates even a glass to be filled.[27] It is an act of giving that even creates the possibility of receiving in the receiver of the gift. There is no determinate language of philosophy that can give an accurate calculation of this overdeterminate power of giving. Our ability to talk about it is already a result of receiving the gift and, hence, it exceeds our conceptual articulation. This is where the silence of philosophy before religion might be the most appropriate response to the gift received.

But "woe to those who remain silence, for those who speak much are as the dumb."[28] There is no determinate language of reason that can capture the height and the depth (*altus*) of the agapeic origination. But a metaphor, Desmond argues, can carry across the image of the agapeic origin and awaken us to the transfinite "more" that is communicated in finite happenings.[29] As a metaxological exercise for cultivating our mindfulness of the agapeic origination, therefore, I would like to give another image from Dostoyevsky's *Poor People*: a young girl, Varvara Dobroselova, comes from a very poor household in St. Petersburg. She falls in love with her neighbor, a young scholar who loves poetry, but barely lives hand to mouth as a private tutor. His father, Mr. Pokrovsky, is a hopeless drunk who does everything he thinks best to receive approval from his son. But, perhaps because of the lack of consistent sobriety, or due to his inexperience in education, or of his last pride to present himself respectable before his son, his labor bears no fruit. The young girl with no education decides to give a birthday present to the young scholar as a token of her love. She goes to buy the complete works of Pushkin in eleven volumes. Out of her selfless care, she knows that her beloved would love to have it for himself, but the price of the poetry is too high. Mr. Pokrovsky stumbles upon the same bookstore with the same intention of buying a present for his son and starts to look through a shelf filled with dirt-cheap paperbacks of no intellectual value. She offers him to join their humble fund and give the present as their present to the young man. A few hours before their gift-giving, the father feels embarrassed and proposes that she would give the first ten volumes and he the last. She thinks for a second to herself, looks at the moral exactitude with the last remaining pride, thinks about the beloved they both care, and then offers to let the father give them all to his son as his gift.[30]

There is a tremendous power of agape in this gift-giving. The girl thinks solely about the good of her beloved, and because of her selfless love of the other for the other, she can let go of her desire to be recognized as the giver of the gift. Her happiness and joy are not diminished in her "making way" for the other from the gift. By giving herself over to nothing, she gives her beloved not only the books but also his reconciliation with his father. As a result, her joy from giving the gift is doubled. In this image, we see an overdeterminate richness that is communicated through the act of agapeic gift-giving. Beyond our ordinary exchanges of goods that demand determinate return, the ontological excess is found in our act of giving ourselves to nothing. This overdeterminate foundation of our ethical selving enables each of us to give for the other beyond ourselves and enriches our community as the (net)work(s) of love. In the lives of poor people, Dostoyevsky sees the hyperbolic wealth that empowers the agapeic transcendence of one to another from the richness that comes beyond ourselves.[31] This image of "making way for giving oneself for the other" communicates the signs of the selfless absolute or the "kenotic agapeics of the God"[32] that nonpossessively gives being beyond itself and "freely reserves itself to make way for the finite other to be itself as free."[33] Our agapeic transcendence in the economy of generosity, thus, communicates the divine fullness beyond ourselves and elucidates the divine origination of the finite other as the agapeic gift of the "coming to be" to the free becoming of the other for the other.

There are many similar metaphors that bring forth our metaphysical reflections on the agapeic origination. Victor Hugo, for instance, shows a thief receiving more goods from his victim in the form of gifts. Kierkegaard likewise depicts an ordinary scene in which a mother gently pushes her child's stroller until the point where he is let to push it for himself.[34] The best image is probably the religious one: the last mite of a poor woman. Jesus says that this giving is far better than giving half of a wealthy man.[35] Of course, these images are images; hence, they cannot equal the magnitude of the agapeic origination. All these gift-givings in the realm of the finite are enabled by the radical origination of the "coming to be." But what the infinite origin ecstatically endows to the universal transience of the finite other manifests through this nonpossessive giving that the finite gives itself to nothing for the other. The agapeic service of the finite for the sake of the other in this extreme form of self-sacrifice shows the energy of transcendence radiating with the infinite reserve of the divine giving in immanence. Thus, the transfinite wealth of the original gift, exchanged in the network of loving finites, shows us a shine of the agapeic origination in the midst of our finitude.[36]

Heteroarchic relation of the divine absolute and the single individual: What calls for the finite in its communicative relation to the absolute?

The metaxological sense of the divine absolute communicates the intimate over-determinacy of the divine transcendence in immanence of the finite singulars. Also, this divinity originates the finite for the finite beyond dualism. Naturally, the metaxological philosophy of religion calls for a different understanding of the divine-human relation from its previous formulations of the rational universalists. Kant has a tremendous difficulty conceiving the (metaphysical) relation of the divine absolute and the human as anything more than a heteronomous relation in which freedom of the latter is compromised. In relation to the mysterious call for the moral necessity of joining the *Reich*, Kant states as follows:

> We can form a concept of the universal and unconditional subjection of human beings to the divine legislation only insofar as we also consider ourselves his creatures; just so can God be considered the ultimate source of all natural laws only because he is the creator of natural things. It is, however, totally incomprehensible to our reason how beings can be created to use their powers freely, for according to the principle of causality we cannot attribute any other inner ground of action to a being, which we assume to have been produced, except that which the producing cause as placed in it.[37]

The determinate rationality of Kantian reason cannot comprehend the divine origination of the finite particular due to two interrelated problems: first, it strives to conceive of the divine-human relation in terms of the determinate category of causality; and second, in order for us to think of the causal relation of two things, we have to think of them as two determinate objects (or at least quantifiable forces) that can causally determine each other. Suppose a scene in which one jumps from a boat to the sea: within the Kantian framework of thinking, either one can freely determine oneself to jump into the water or someone else can kick one off the boat. The former is the autonomous determination of one's action, while the latter is the heteronomous subordination to the unwilled deed. When Kant is trying to understand the divine origination of one's freedom, he is implicitly thinking that it must be formulated in relation to the determinate category of causation; viz., he is thinking that there are two determinate particulars that can causally determine each other within the universal framework of understanding. This is like saying that God is another passenger on the boat, where he can either let one jump off in accord with one's own will or invade one's autonomy through the external force; hence, to think that God can causally generate one's free action, for Kant, is a contradiction. What is problematic in this contradictory picture is clearly that Kant is applying the determinate category of causation to the divine-human relation. He must be misconceiving the divine infinite as another determinate finite.

Hegel's dialectical formulation of the divine-human relation is much more finessed than Kant's understanding in the sense that divine freedom in its process of self-completing self-determination lets "what is other to itself" (i.e., the finite freedom of humanity) be and recognize this other as a necessary moment for the ultimate determination of itself as the divine freedom. The divine absolute in Hegel, in other words, dialectically constitutes the freedom of the finite not in terms of the finite (i.e., the determinate category of causation), as Kant wrongly tries to do, but in terms of the self-determination of the infinite. Hegel's use of the term *lassen*, which insinuates the dialectical *Gelassenheit* of the finite, led many commentators to think that the Hegelian formulation of the divine-human relation can allow the plurality of the infinite and the finite without falling victim to Kantian dualism. However, Desmond warns thus in HG:

> The plain sense of [Hegel's term "lassen"] is refashioned as more hospitable to robust otherness and irreducible plurality than can be read from the reiterated language of self-return that is all pervasive in Hegel. A few little fishes of "lassen" swim in the engulfing waters of self-return from self-othering, and these few "free" fishes are fastened on to give us the feeling of free plurality, while all around us there swirls the silent engulfment of the holistic sea.[38]

Once again, Desmond emphasizes that the logic of self-determination in Hegel's dialectic carries the problematic emphasis of the "self-return." This means that the "let be" of the finite is not ultimately made for the finite, but for the infinite to determine itself in and through the finite. What does it mean, then, to say that the divine allowance of human freedom is bestowed for the sake of the divine? This is like saying that Hegel's absolute allows one to choose freely to jump or not to jump into the water, but whatever the choice that one makes cannot give the irrepeatable significance of "once." The significance of the individual choices is ultimately subordinated to the totalizing circuit of the divine self-determination in immanence.

Again, since Hegel does not allow the divine self-mediation to be ontologically superior to the human/societal self-determination, it is not clear whether the freedom of the holistic sea stands for the infinitely self-mediating self-consciousness of a world-historical mind or its manifestation as the state. But what is clear is this: the freedom of a single individual is a necessary means for the divine absolute to affirm itself as the ultimate freedom. Thus, the instrumental value of the singular freedom for the anonymity of self-determining universal makes us wonder what significance our choice of a finite leap can have when "all around us there swirls the silent engulfment of the holistic sea." Whether we are to jump or not to jump, what does it matter since the individual vessel of our human freedom is eventually sucked into the self-determining whirlpool of the dialectical god?

Instead of trying to understand the divine-human relation in accordance with the determinate category of causation, the metaxological sense of the agapeic origin recognizes that the divine absolute cannot be reduced to another determinate particular in the realm of finite. As the "hyperboles of being" communicate in our posthumous mindfulness, divine transcendence does not stand in its external opposition to the finite (T^1), but it is intimately at work in the deepest interiority of the finite in immanence (T^2) as what is superior to the interiority (T^3). Nor does the agapeic origin need the finite other to overcome its initial lack to achieve its fullness in the end of its self-determining development (T^2). The divine transcendence exceeds such dialectical configuration of the self-transcendence in immanence because it, out of its ontological surplus, gives the finite other to be for itself in its genuine otherness. It releases the finite to be without the "self-return" but accompanies every step of its "becoming" as the selfless giver of the "coming to be."

Desmond's description of the divine-world relation, therefore, gives the nondualistic pluralism that comprises the irreducible centers of multiple mediations in their intimate togetherness. In this sense,

> Creation need not generate oppositional dualism but a different sense of plurality, a communicative enabling of others as others. That the world is not God need not mean the "not" yields overwhelming negation. In creation as agapeic origination the "not" is defined in agapeic transcending, for it allows an arising of the other that is there for itself: origin is not the creation, but creation is not at all without the origin. Nor is world void of traces of the divine as a work is not without signs of its originator or speech without some signature of its speaker. Transcendence is not nugatory, if the limit is with respect to the enigma of agapeic origination out of which the "It is good" is addressed to creation.[39]

This formulation of the divine-world relation applies to the metaxological understanding of the divine-human relation. The divine absolute as the agapeic transcendence is neither a determinate finite that externally impedes our exercise of freedom within the nexus of efficient causes nor the self-determining whole of the finite reality that allows our freedom for the sake of creating itself as the infinite absolute. But the agapeic origin nonpossessively releases each of the finite being to be for itself and lets it and other finite freely intermediate with each other for themselves.

The divine transcendence or otherness to the finite between is "a 'more,' a plentitude as other to the middle, but with an otherness that marks a community, not an antithesis, with the middle."[40] Desmond describes this relation of the overdeterminate absolute to human autonomy as *heteroarchic* community or the community of free beings originated from the other (i.e., the *heteros* as the *arche* of the finite between).[41] This term can certainly carry the risk of being interpreted as the heteronomy in the sense that the *nomos* of *autos* are given from the *heteros*. However, since the agapeic absolute points to the radical origination that enables the possibility of our autonomous becoming as a whole, its constitutive relation to the finite freedom cannot represent a heteronomous relation in which one determinate particular causally determines another within the realm of the finite. Nor does it dictate the dictatorial sublation of the finite freedom for the infinite totality of the human/societal self-relation.

> For this [divine] heteronomy is not imposing or dominating; primordially it is giving; it is the giving of the free promise of the finite creation as good for itself. Nor does it simply impose its law and make demands of what it has given; it lets the promise of what is given come to itself out of itself. It is not an other that imposes an external determination but an other that gives the promise of self-determination. And in the realization of that self-determination it again

does not impose itself, but it does companion the efforts at self-perfection of the creature. As companion alongside, it is an other that is with the freedom of the creature, even as this freedom strays from its own integral perfection, and turns against the original as primal giver. It retracts its power to impose itself; it constrains its own possible sovereignty; for it is an agapeic servant and not an erotic sovereign.[42]

In this sense, the "heteros" of the agapeic origin "is the compassionate companion that travels incognito the way of transcendence."[43] It gives a "joyful heteronomy" in one's reverence toward the divine that "frees [one] from [oneself] in a love that transcends towards the worthy superiority of another."[44] Desmond gives various metaphors to communicate this heteroarchic ground of human freedom. If we are to return to the image of one's diving from the boat into the sea, the agapeic origin is an invisible passenger who allows everything (including one's freedom, the boat, the sea, the light, and everything there is) to be and allows one to choose to do what one wills for oneself. It is like the overdeterminate pouring of wine that creates the possibility of its reception.[45] Though one's leap might be finite, one's freedom is an irrepeatable gift from the overdeterminate infinite that allows one to be free for oneself.

What are the implications of the communicative relationship between the agapeic origin and the single individuals for the freedom of humans? How can we account for the givenness of our autonomy in its relativity to the divine absolute? What is the promise of our freedom in relation to the heteroarchic origin of the agapeic transcendence? Desmond provides at least four different metaxological themes to respond to these ethico-religious questions, namely, (1) agapeic mindfulness, (2) agapeic transcendence in human self- and intermediations, (3) transformation of the humans, and (4) our witness to the agapeic origin as the Good beyond good and evil.

First, we are called to cultivate our agapeic mindfulness in our communicative relation to the agapeic origin. Desmond's understanding of the divine absolute points us to creation as an unmerited gift: that is "an agapeic communication which radically possiblizes both the primal good of selving and of being together with others."[46] This divine origination of our finite freedom communicates a kind of hyperbolic knowing—the hyperintelligible knowing that shows its utmost fidelity to the ontological worth of our freedom in the realm of finitude:

> God's (over)all-knowing as hyperbolic is transfinite finesse for the finite, and hence must be creative and responsive, and hence while responsive to the equivocities of the between cannot be only responsive. We run into this paradox: a knowing that is originative, that yet is responsive; a knowing that in originating the finite other does not univocally determine that other; a knowing that frees that other, allowing it as free to go its own way, to which way then the originating knowing responds, and respond creatively; a knowing that in creating the other, not only frees that other, but dwells with that other, even as it is genuinely other. Such a knowing of finesse, beyond the determinacies of universal geometry, will point us finally towards the being true of agapeic mindfulness.[47]

What the agapeic origin knows is immediately given to be for the known, and this divine knowledge/knowing of the known is both actively creative and patiently receptive in relation to the free manifestation of the known. It is certainly impossible for us to practice this originary knowing. By coming to be aware of the nature of agapeic origination, however, we can know what the divine knowing of the finite other must be like. Then what Desmond is indicating in this passage is that this hyperbolic knowing of the divine absolute indicates the significance of our agapeic mindfulness as a kind of intellectual *imitatio Dei*. As the divine absolute ecstatically endows the freedom of the finite for the finite and lets the finite determine itself for the finite,

> Agapeic mind makes a welcome in the manner it prepares the way for the other to come to self-manifestation. Preparing a way is making a space in the middle, a space for the freedom of the other. … To make way for the other is to create an opening for freedom that is not for oneself, though in that opening one is fully there for whatever may eventuate along the way. One is fully there, but not there as filling the between, but as opening it for the other, such as to seem not to be there. One is fully there for the fullness of the other to come into the between. Come what may, agapeic mind makes a way. It is a way that is no way, in the sense of a completely determinate track. It is no way, since it is a space of openness: it is space of expectation; it is space of faith and hope.[48]

The agapeic knowing of the divine original looks very much like the agapeic mindfulness of the humans, and there is an obvious mutuality between them: for humans to know the divine absolute beyond themselves, they have to cultivate their openness to what is other to themselves, while the agapeic origination points to the divine knowing as a kind of minding that both creatively and patiently lets the finite other be for the finite.[49] This means that we are free(d) to become mindful of the primal position of our ontological givenness and released to realize that being as what is other to our mind is also marked with the same ontological richness exceeding our speculative minding. This also means that we are equally allowed to deal with the equivocal givenness of reality as the indeterminate thereness and calibrate its value through the determinate knowing of our mind, no matter how misguided and contracted this constructive knowing of reality would turn out to be in the end. The metaxological origin does not make a demand that we ought to cultivate our mindfulness with its openness to what is other to ourselves or go astray with our self-determining propensity to absolutize our determinate knowing as the rational universal. The "heteros" of the agapeic *arche* is "not imposing or dominating." But precisely because of its nature as agape, it gives us a space to do what we will.[50]

How, in an undemanding way, does the agapeic origin "demand" us of our agapeic mindfulness? The answer lies in the nature of freedom as a hyperbolic gift. As we have seen above, our being is given to be before we freely determine ourselves to be and this ontological truth exceeds our determinate knowing that is bound to the process of our becoming. But when each of our determinate being/knowing reflects on its once/never, we are pushed back to what is prior to, and foundational for, our determinate process of becoming and knowing. Hence, in face of our being "nothing," we come to recognize the hyperbolic givenness of our "to be" with sheer astonishment. This awareness of the agapeic origin constitutes our agapeic mindfulness. Once again, this is not a logical necessity but a free choice: one can still choose to ignore the ontological fact, dismiss it as an indeterminate absurdity, and carry on to think itself as being entitled to squander the gift as his own wealth. Desmond frequently reflects on the divine allowance of our freedom in the tale of the prodigal son:

> A favorite son, still young, asks, demands his patrimony from the generous parent. The parent gives, since there is no forcing impetuous natures greedy for all that life offers. The son goes afar and spends the patrimony in unrestraint and riot. He comes to have nothing. But he comes to himself only when he has come to nothing. He finds himself feeding among swine. He has had his day in the sun, and now he makes friends with the muck of things. It is only when he comes into the knowing that he has come to nothing that he wakes up to himself differently, and to the generous other that gave him his freedom and resource. And then? He turns around and sets off for home. He is not greeted with admonition but in joy and celebration: generosity in welcoming back, generosity in allowing the youth to go forth and be for self.[51]

The point of the story is the infinite generosity and its meta-ethical allowance. The agapeic origin does not demand our homage even at the point of our ultimate realization that we are nothing without the generosity of the divine other. Our rude awakening to the ontological truth that what we have as our own is not really what we have given to ourselves still gives us a choice to face or turn away from the truth. If there is any homage to the origin at all, therefore, it is neither forced nor demanded, but it is our free homecoming that awaits an ecstatic welcome with "immediate song and dance."[52] The agapeic giver does not reprimand the ungrateful but shows its love of the singular for the singular by continuously giving it to be *this* singular. Thus, it gives in excess of human measure, and no human exactitude can measure the gravity of all that is as a gift. Like the wretched thief in *Les Miserables*, each of us is greeted with hospitality beyond every right to be welcomed and further set free with more gift than what we deserve in the first place. Our agapeic mindfulness is a free consent to creation as an overwhelming gift. Each of us are always already free(d) to join the feast of thanksgiving and forgiveness in our homecoming to the primal position of our givenness as this singular being.

Second, the agapeic mindfulness calls for the genuine transcendence in human self- and intermediations. The agapeic origin is "already agapeic community, communication with the other in its primordial oneness with itself, a communication itself the ground of its going outside of itself in relation to the world it creates."[53] In the same manner, our communicative relation to the agapeic origin does not leave each of us in a solitary inner meditation of a philosopher in his office.[54] Nor is it our contemplation of what is solely beyond ourselves such that our thinking of the divine other will set us apart from the concrete happenings of the finite world. But since the divine absolute gives each single individual as a concretion of its communicative power of being,

> The ontological integrity of [the] being is always open to the integrities of other beings. It is self-transcending from the beginning, not only as self-becoming, but as transcending self to what is other. There is an already given space of reception to the transcending of the others toward it. Thus we come to a doubly mediating, an intermediating (co)unity rather than solely a self-mediating unity. ... it is an open (comm)unity, allowing the self-becoming of each, the surpassing of this and that unity into the between, the interplay of one with the other allowing each its own integral otherness, and all of this from the origin. This last sense of "unity" points to the richest expression of "being at one" as agapeic community.[55]

This agapeic community is

> The community that tries to live in the between in light of its acknowledged metaxological relation to the divine: in light of the generous finitude of its being, given the goodness of the "to be," out of nothing and for nothing but the good of being. This is the religious community of agapeic service that enacts the intermediation of the good beyond erotic sovereignty, and in ethically likening itself to the generosity of the agapeic origin.[56]

As the agapeic origin brings itself over to nothing and gives everything to the finite other for the other, each of us must practice the nonpossessive dispensation of the good to the other for the other through bringing ourselves to nothing. This "community of agapeic service" is a religious community in two senses: (1) our communal relation to each other in immanence shows our utmost fidelity to our communicative relation to the agapeic transcendence as the origin of our determinate becoming and (2) our agapeic transcendence to each other in immanent communities mirrors the overdeterminacy of agapeic giving. Hence, it shows our transfinite transcendence to what is other to ourselves, namely, the agapeic origin. In the communal practice of the agapeic service, Desmond argues, "we try to live the agapeic being,"[57] and also, "this life makes us mindful of the life of the origin as agapeic."[58] Without living our lives in manner of agapeic transcendence, we cannot have a genuine thought of the divine ultimate as the agapeic absolute. Thus, to be mindful of the origin, we are called to practice an act of divine love.

This call for the self-sacrificial love of agape is certainly easier said than done. The ordinary process of our becoming goes from an indeterminate lack to a determinate fullness (i.e., potency to actuality), and also the primal position of our being qua *passio essendi* only signals a nonpossessive dispensation of being by the incognito absolute. This means that we can easily get self-absorbed into our daily struggles of *conatus essendi* and come to think that this mode of being is the sole process of our self- or intermediations. The erotic ascent of the self from its lack to fullness, in other words, tempts us to think that we can totalize the plurality of our self- and intermediations into a single form of self-completing self-mediation. We have seen this in the erotic mode of self-transcending. Why are we obsessed with such totalizing unity of our self-becoming? Because the irreducible plurality of our self-

and intermediations will introduce something more than what human autonomy can account for in its immanent terms. Our self-absorption in *conatus essendi* in this manner drives us to absolutize our autonomy and assimilate the open community of different centers of selving into the single process of self-determination. We are prone to make ourselves to be the *erotic* absolute and serve nobody but ourselves for our (given) desire to be.[59]

Our erotic tendency to eradicate the otherness of the open community between different centers of selving has resulted in horrific facts about the world we live today. Just as we have lost the feel for the sacred otherness of the divine absolute at work in immanence, we have lost the feel for the inherent value of nature as irreducible to our determinate knowing of it.[60] The result is our instrumentalization of what is other to ourselves in many spheres of our being: we have defiled the lands through unsustainable agriculture, slaughtered countless animals to be packaged into Styrofoam trays, and polluted the air to the point of climate change.[61] Things are disposable for the sake of our self-determining desire and people, too, are human capitals to be exploited, if they are not enemies to be exterminated. What our mindfulness of the agapeic origin asks us to do is not to make determinate solutions to the specific issues that pertain to these general problems of our present age, but to let go of our inherent tendency to insist on the absolute status of our freedom—the root metaphysical problem of all these problems. Our communicative relation to the agapeic origin asks us to open our minds to see something more than valueless thereness of each singular in nature and to see the inexhaustible richness of the "to be" in each center of our various becomings. To do so, we have to engage in the act of agapeic transcendence. With compassion of agape, we have to let go of the logic of "self-return" and give space for the inherent goodness of the other to its self-manifestation. It is the girl's willingness to dispense her gift nonpossessively for the other in *The Poor People*; it is the priest's forgiveness in his compassionate giving to his thief in *Les Miserables* or the motherly support that lets her toddler walk on his own in Kierkegaard's reflections. St. Francis' mortal kiss to a leper or Buddha's compassionate descent to the others in suffering are historical examples. The best pictures of this, I think, are the last penny of the poor woman and the father's welcoming of his prodigal son in the Bible. These generous acts of compassion tip the scale of our self-determinations and show that we are also given to live agapeically and capable of creating the space in which the other can come to its fullness for itself.[62]

Third, the life of agapeic mindfulness gives the transformative purification of human desire. Our inherent attachment to ourselves (i.e., our freedom) prevents the release toward the transcendence as other. However, the prior givenness of our freedom makes us realize our deeper nothingness of the process of our self-transcendence: "everything that [we are] from the ground up is nothing, were [we] not for the gift of the origin."[63] The genuine otherness and integrity of the "I" in its irreducible singularity is itself sustained as the gift of the divine absolute. This realization suddenly shows us the hitherto unacknowledged companion of our free selving and breaks our pride for determining ourselves to be the absolute. The divine solicitation in the process of our becoming, in other words, breaks us down and brings us back to the original posture of ontological patience and humility:

> A humility hard to describe for it seems to make the soul dwindled to nothing and yet it expands the soul with a serene exhalation, for it rejoices just in the divine generosity, melting in its glory even as it undergoes the suffering that delivers it over to nothing. In the undergoing of this patience, so much of what seems of ultimate significance fades to secondary significance. Previous importances can taste of insipidity; compared to this other sweetness, they are bland, and even repulsive.[64]

When we find ourselves purified of our desire to determine the absolute worth of our self-mediation and emptied out of the "self-clinging that blocks the passing of the divine through it,"[65] we suddenly come to realize something laughable about our overinflated seriousness in our attempt to absolutize our autonomy. The incessant philosophical argument for determining the infinite significance of our self-thinking thought melts away in front of a simple act of kindness that shows the secondary significance of our freedom in relation to the very kindness that allows our freedom.[66]

The metaxological metaphysician detects in this agapeic transcendence a kind of spiritual askesis—an enactment of detachment from self-insistent self to no-self, in which the other can be approached in its otherness. In this transformative practice of no-self, "The soul waits quietly in itself as in a nothing, but a nothing that is readiness and expectancy," and this openness as the nothing gives the "silence into which the fullness of the reserved divinity is worded."[67] The best record of this silence in the West is Augustine's mystic assent at Ostia, while the best image of this silence in the Eastern tradition is Xiāngyán Zhìxián's enlightenment.[68] The life of the metaxological mind requires the transformation from one's insistence on erotic self-transcendence to one's agapeic transcendence from oneself to the other. This conversion may allow us to taste the insipid insignificance of our self-determining process in relation to the fullness of the divine life and laugh at our previous seriousness of or mad self-obsession with our erotic desire.

Fourth, the agapeic origin represents the excessive "good" beyond our determinate concepts of good and evil. Given that the agapeic origin releases "all that is" into being out of nothing, it is ontologically prior to, and foundational for, the possibility of anything or anyone to be good or evil. This is to say, without the agapeic origination, one cannot even *come to be* good or evil in one's process of becoming. This "holy good" of the divine absolute remains hyperintelligible to our determinate understanding of what it means for us to be good or evil. However, this "holy good"

> flows out into an ethical life of agapeic service. Touched by this holy good, one is transformed into some likeness to it, and this likeness is expressed in a transformed participation in the world, human, and natural. We can be touched by the promise of universal love for all things, not just for human beings. The great monotheistic religions point in this direction. One thinks also of the compassion of the Buddha.[69]

This is to say that our religious porosity with the agapeic origin throws us beyond the bounds of moral good and evil and enables us to relate ourselves to the rest of creation (i.e., both humans and animals) as the origin relates to each and every one of us. The imitations of agapeic giving can be found in the images of the agapeic servant we have discussed previously; recall the sensible suggestion that the miserable father gives to the compassionate girl. Out of the last residue of his self-respect, he proposes to give the gift in accord with the merits of his contribution. The same expectation of moral exactitude is strongly felt in *Les Miserables*: Jean Valjean should receive the same punishment for stealing the candleholders from the priest, just as for stealing a loaf of bread from the baker.

What astonishes us is what follows after these ordinary expectations of moral exactitude. The agapeic heroine, out of her excessive love of her beloved, renounces her determinate entitlement to the gift and makes a way for the others to have it as their gift. The priest as the servant of agapeic God does the same thing by renouncing his entitlement to the goods in his house and celebrating the return of his ungrateful guest with more goods. These gift-givings are stupefying for our determinate concepts of morality because they commend (if not command) us that what is good should not go unrecognized or what is bad go unpunished. We can almost feel the silent indignation of the watchdog of the state, Javert. For him, it is outrageous that Jean Valjean gets away with theft and what further infuriates him is that the thief is even rewarded with more than he deserves. To those who hold on to the human measure of what is good and evil, an act of generosity, as *imtatio Dei*, looks more like a "reckless disregard of justice."[70]

However, to those who can regard the source of human justice higher than our determinate concepts of good and evil, these acts of generosity show the shimmer of divine transcendence. Desmond frequently reflects on the parables of the workers in the vineyard and the prodigal son. The owner of the vineyard gives equal payment even to those who merit no reward and, thus, turns the reward into gift. With regard to the parable of the prodigal son, we have also seen that the feast of welcome is given for the one who has wasted his father's legacy. These images communicate that "good is given gratuitously, for no reason beyond its goodness,"[71] and also that "[the agapeic origin] gives in excess of the measure; there is no measure that is proportioned to human exactitude; all are given their due, and more again, and in a sense, nothing is due, for all is gift."[72] This is to say that there is something more in the reward to our labors than we can determine as our merit. Those of us who see the divine measure beyond human measure witness that the fruits of our labors are not entirely what we have given to ourselves; and because of this, even the ungrateful, the lazy, and the bad are rewarded for no reason beyond their goodness to be. Each of us are given to be before we determine ourselves to be and our *conatus essendi* is always already empowered by the incognito *(com)passio essendi* of the agapeic absolute. In light of this ontological truth, we can see ourselves as the unmerited gift of agape in the divine announcement of creation as the good. The generosity of the agapeic origin, in this manner, shines through the generosity of the agapeic servants among us, and we are, therefore, called to love each singular for the singular no matter how ungrateful and bad it turns out to be. This is religious amen to every life or every good as a gift from God.

The hyperbolic measure of the "holy good" also calls for our forgiveness beyond the determinate exactitude of Kantian moral law or the self-reconciliation of the Hegelian Spirit.[73] Desmond reflects that the absolutization of moral law would make

Kant grumble like the older brother in the parable of the prodigal son.[74] I also see the same spirit of moral exactitude in Hugo's Javert. Kantian morality, in other words, would make the same demand that the virtuous alone deserves the feast of welcome. It is both illogical and unjust that the vicious is invited to the same table.[75] What is problematic with this logic of moral exactitude? It forgets that the fruits of our labors are first given from the source beyond ourselves; accordingly, the primal givenness of our moral labors as the gift is contracted to the determinate reward (or the moral worth) that we can give to ourselves. The agapeic transcendence, contrariwise, requires that we bring ourselves to nothing and recognize that we are nothing without the gift of our "coming to be" from the origin. Hence, paradoxically, the prodigal son who has come to recognize his fundamental poverty without his relativity to his generous father at home is much more attuned to the holy good of the agapeic origin than his diligent brother. Most importantly, moreover, the generosity of the giver does not discriminate whether the wicked comes to ask his forgiveness or the self-righteous feels indignant with his hyperbolic measure of agapeic love. He continues to love both of his sons equally, extends his steadfast generosity to both of them at all times, and remains forever willing to forgive their iniquities or disgrace against him. As the agapeic absolute continues to give each and every one of us to be for ourselves, we too must extend our generosity and forgiveness in the networks of divine love. The promise of human freedom, therefore, is to live the life of agapeic service.

Metaxological responses to the fundamental problems of the philosophy of religion

It should be clear by now that the metaxological accounts of the single individual, the divine absolute, and their interrelations have given responses to the Kierkegaardian concerns with the Kantian and the Hegelian notions of religion. In this closing section, I will recapitulate some of the key points of metaxology in relation to the five fundamental problems of the philosophy of religion.

1. *The reduction of the divine-human relation to the immanent universality of human/societal self-relation*: The divine-human relation, according to Desmond, is by no means irreducible to the immanent universality of human/societal self-relation or the self-circling self-mediation based solely on the autonomy of our reason. There are at least two reasons for this point. First, the metaxological sense of being communicates the intimacy of the divine absolute as the agapeic origin through posthumous thinking. In this self-reflection of finitude from the side of its never, a single individual is led to recognize the divine agape as being *neither* exterior to its determinate being (T^1) *nor* reducible to the self- or intermediating process of its self-becoming with other single individuals (T^2). The metaxological divine, in this sense, shows *both* its radical intimacy to our dynamic process of being or becoming in immanence *and* its ontological excess to any of the immanent terms (e.g., singular individual, particular, and universal). The overdeterminacy of the agapeic origin, therefore, points to the intimate source of our existence beyond ourselves.

Our posthumous thinking, which releases us beyond the bounds of the rational universal, also cultivates our attentiveness to the divine otherness at work in determining processes of becoming. This is the second reason. As Desmond demonstrates in relation to the distinction of "coming to be" and "becoming," every determining process from potency to actuality is marked with ontological givenness prior to the process of its determinate actualization. The radical origination of the process of becoming, therefore, points to the infinite originator beyond the finitude of the very process. Since our mind can only understand what kind of thing an object is only in reference to the dynamic process of its becoming in nature, the radical origination of this process escapes our mind's determinate knowing. Hence, the metaxological sense of the divine and our relation to it cannot be explained in the immanent terms of the rational universal. Rather, it requires a different kind of thinking from the self-thinking thought of the rational universal, that is, the agapeic mindfulness that remains attentive to the divine transcendence as being always already at work in the determinate processes of becoming and of knowing in immanence. We witness here the renewed sense of agapeic universalism that Desmond calls the "intimate universal."

2. *The eclipse of divine transcendence*: Metaxology clearly realizes that the robust sense of divine transcendence is requisite for making sense of the religious faith. The rational universalism, however, would hold that this divine otherness to the self- or intermediation of humanity problematically ends up compromising the unconditional worth of reason and its autonomy. Kant, in this sense, postulates an empty echo of practical reason that poses no threat to human autonomy as the unconditioned absolute, while Hegel goes so far as to say that the dialectical process of human self-determination is the absolute. What these thinkers presuppose in their avoidance of divine transcendence is that it would generate oppositional dualism vis-à-vis the immanent process of human self-becoming. Metaxological mindfulness testifies that this does not have to be the case, since it recognizes the transfinite otherness of the divine transcendence in the immanent processes themselves. This means that the agapeic origin, because of its ontological overdeterminacy, can neither be reducible to any immanent term that determinately explains the process of becoming nor be completely divorced from the dynamism of becoming in immanence. Once again, in this configuration of the divine absolute in its intimacy to the finite relatives, there is no determinate antithesis between divine transcendence and human immanence; divine transcendence is at work in the dynamism of the finite relative without being reduced to any process of self-mediations in immanence. The metaxological philosophy of religion, thus, conceives the divine infinite in its profound relativity to finite immanence and accounts for their essential pluralism without trapping us in dualism.

3. *The extirpation of the single individual in its relation to the rational universal as the immanent absolute*: Given that the hyperbole of being in the idiocy of the singular points to the proper relationship between divine transcendence and human self- or intermediations in immanence, the metaxological account of religious faith does not subordinate the single individual to the rational universal as the immanent absolute. We have seen through posthumous thinking that the incontrovertible oneness of the singular indicates its ontological richness of "to be" and this ontological excess

in the deepest interiority of the singular challenges universal reason that sees the mere indeterminacy in the singular. This metaphysical attentiveness to the transfinite "more/superior" in our finite "interior" points us to the intimate source of our existence beyond ourselves. In this manner, metaxology both recognizes the divine absolute beyond the rational universal and remains attentive to the ontological excess in the overdeterminate significance of the single individual. Thus, in metaxology, the agapeic origin is not reducible to the rational universal in immanence, nor is the single individual exhaustibly explained away in terms of the rational universal. Rather, it proposes the intimate strangeness or open community of the divine transcendence and human immanence as the intimate universal.

4. *The one-way movement of the self-negating self-transcendence of the finite individual to the infinite absolute*: The self-negating self-transcendence of the finite individual to the infinite absolute is always a two-way communication in metaxology. The relation of the overdeterminate absolute to human autonomy is described as the *heteroarchic* community of free beings wherein the agapeic absolute radically possiblizes our autonomous becoming. This is precisely what Desmond means by the phrase "*passio essendi* before *conatus essendi*."[76] We have seen that the communicative relation of the infinite to the finite neither represents a heteronomous relation in which one determinate finite causally generates another nor constitutes the dictatorial subordination of the finite freedom to the infinite self-determination. Rather, the agapeic origin as the infinite absolute releases the finite beyond itself and, as it brings itself over to nothing, makes way for the finite to determine itself to be. In this case,

> Wee are led to think of God as an eternal agapeic origin: always already having given the other its being as for itself—and the giving of "coming to be" is not its own coming to be but is given for the other as finite creation that comes to be. The agapeic giving releases this "coming to be" into its own otherness; hence, from this "coming to be" arises the gift of time, as an ecstasis of originated original being.[77]

The finitude of our timed existence, therefore, is an unmerited gift from the agapeic origin. We are empowered to be with our original power for our self-becoming and free(d) to make the process of our becoming for ourselves. Again, "creation is [the] gift of the power of being to make come to be the finite other, itself a definite concretion of the original power of being, invested with its own integrity."[78] Our self-negating transcendence of ourselves to divine otherness is always already enabled by the incognito *compassio essendi* of the metaxological absolute.

Since our autonomy is a gratuitous gift from the agapeic origin, we are allowed to be for ourselves in our self-determining process of *conatus essendi*. Divine allowance does not impose upon us to practice our self-negating self-transcendence in the face of the divine infinite, but secretly sustains us in the original position of *passio essendi*; regardless of our awareness of it, the divine empowers us to exercise our autonomy for ourselves. Because of this metaphysical account of creation as a free gift, our transcendence to the agapeic origin must be also a free consent of religious amen; and this movement from the finite to the infinite, made possible through agapeic kenosis of the origin, constitutes the ethico-religious community of agapeic service—the community in which "[t]he agapeic relation reveals richness to be a kind of 'being nothing' that the other maybe everything."[79] There are the horizontal interrelations in which the single individual gives oneself to the finite other in immanence, while this human community of agapeic servants is sustained by the divine transcendence of the agapeic origination. Certainly, the transcendence of the finite self cannot match the ontological magnitude of divine transcendence, for the former cannot even begin to reveal the hyperbolic wealth of "to be" unless it is already blessed with the agapeic transcendence of the divine source.[80] Nevertheless, the relation that we constitute through our agapeic giving shimmers the transfinite "more/superior" of the divine transcendence and brings us closer to the infinite source of our love. The self-negating self-transcendence of the finite toward the infinite in metaxology, therefore, gives this human-divine porosity in which the human self finds the divine lift in its freedom to give itself for the other and sees his freedom as a divine gift.

5. *The worth of the singular for the singular*: The metaxological metaphysic strives to account for the worth of the singular for the singular in reference to the agapeic absolute beyond the rational universal. Desmond argues that the seemingly indeterminate thereness of the contingent singular is a result from our mind's forgetfulness of its primal position where itself and what is other to it are equally given to be for themselves. However, because of that, a finessed observation of the singular (i.e., posthumous thinking) can remind us of the hyperboles of being—namely, the transfinite sign of overdeterminacy irreducible to, and foundational for, our rational conceptualization of all that is. In this case, the mind that has calibrated the singular merely as an indeterminate particular comes to realize that something in the particular exceeds its comprehension and simultaneously grounds its mindful existence. Stated otherwise, the hyperrational ground of being in the deepest interiority of the singular communicates divine transcendence in immanence. In this metaphysical light, the single individual is not merely the indeterminate particular understood in its subordinate position to the rational universal. Rather, because the transfinite sign of the divine is seen in the enigma of its "to be" beyond the abyss of nothingness, we are called to be mindful of the singular as something more than what we can exhaustively conceptualize in immanent terms. We see the singular in reference to the agapeic origin. Thus, the finite singular in metaxology must be accounted as the singular in relation to the absolute beyond the contracted notion of the rational universal.

How, then, does the metaxological relation of the singular and the absolute avoid the "extirpation" of the singular in the process of their intermediation? How does it help us account for the singular as the singular without instrumentalizing the singular for the ultimate affirmation of the absolute? To answer these questions, it is important to note that the nature of the divine absolute (communicated through the hyperboles of being) is uncompromisingly agapeic. Accordingly, its intermediation with the finite other in the metaphysical process of creation gives their agapeic intermediation, where the finite is given to be for the finite. The nonpossessive dispensation of the hyperbolic good, that is, the "to be," from the infinite to the finite is not given for the infinite, but for the finite to be for itself and come to be for itself. In this image of creation as the agapeic gift, the divine absolute cannot be seen as subordinating the worth of the singular to itself for creating itself to be the absolute, but only as the absolute spirit of generosity that brings itself to nothing and nonpossessively empowers freedom of the finite for the finite.

To see the singular in reference to this metaxological metaphysics of creation, we must cultivate in ourselves the agapeic mindfulness. We have seen that the agapeic mindfulness in metaxology is described in two ways: (1) divine (over)knowing of the singular for the singular and (2) human knowing of the singular as the singular in reference to the divine (over)knowing. The first is not equal to the second (since the former creates the possibility of the latter), but both require a kind of compassionate knowing that allows the known as free to go its own way without univocally determining the known or dialectically sublating it for the knower. As the divine absolute ecstatically endows the freedom of the single individual for itself and prepares the way for it to come to its free self-manifestation, the human knowing of the singular must cultivate our openness to the singular as other to ourselves and patiently lets the finite other to come to its self-creative self-manifestation for itself. This patient and selfless knowing of the singular for the singular enables us to recognize the worth of the singular as given by the absolute to be for the singular, and the worth of the singular is affirmed for itself in relation to the incognito divine companion that releases everything, if it is anything at all, to be and to be good. Once again, this is the sense of the intimate universal that Desmond communicates through the agapeic mindfulness beyond the limit of rational universalism. Thus, metaxological mindfulness allows us to think agapeically the worth of the singular as the singular, and in its process of doing so, our mindfulness can remain faithful to the way in which it is free to be what it is and recognize the infinite significance of the divine absolute beyond ourselves.

The metaxological philosophy of religion has shown that faith as our awareness of the divine absolute beyond the confines of the rational universal is not incompatible with autonomy of human reason but shows the picture of the divine absolute as an agapeic service to the self- and intermediation of the other. There is a clear message that the single individual is given to be what it is in its relation to the divine absolute beyond determinate or self-determining boundaries of the rational universal, and the universal framework of reason's conceptualization cannot exhaustively explain away the ontological worth of its "to be" as an incontrovertible *this*. The metaxological relation between the absolute and the single individual does not prescribe a heteronomous subordination of mind to the mindless precepts of faith in the dictatorial absolute, but instead provides a heteroarchic interrelation in which the mind can freely come to be mindful of the overdeterminate origin as the indispensable foundation of its mindful existence. The finite singular, in this case, is accounted for as the singular without disintegrating its relativity to the divine absolute, while the sense of universal communicated in this framework of metaphysical thinking is intimate universal beyond rational universal. Thus, metaxology gives a full response to the metaphysical perplexity of the ultimate, the singular, and their interrelation with each other beyond the confines of the Kantian and the Hegelian philosophy of religion.

Part Four

Metanoetics and the Problems of the Philosophy of Religion

7

Tanabe Hajime and Buddhism for the Philosophy of Religion

Tanabe Hajime Zenshū and Tanabe's philosophy of religion

Tanabe Hajime is a complex thinker. Unlike Desmond, who consistently argues for the significance of metaxology and its relevant notions from his earliest work, Tanabe's massive literary output in the course of fifty-two years (1910–62) marks several significant transitions in addition to a series of minor revisions made from one work to another.[1] His later obsession with his own version of dialectical thinking (i.e., absolute dialectic)—as well as his coinage of the new type of philosophy (i.e., metanoetics) that *both* subsumes the earlier metaphysical outlook on reality in terms of social ontology (i.e., logic of species) *and* existentially sustains the truth of absolute dialectic—makes it even more difficult to pin down what he means by each of his notions. In this sense, his philosophical takes on a variety of issues that emerge from his critical engagement with a number of thinkers from the history of philosophy (both from the East and the West) necessarily demand a dynamic approach that takes into account the various contexts in which Tanabe deals with these issues. This chapter will, first, specify which part of his oeuvre we will be consulting to answer fundamental problems in the philosophy of religion. From there, I show how Tanabe's formulations in these works of key notions in the Mahāyāna Buddhist and the Judeo-Christian traditions will help us respond to these very problems.

The Complete Works of Tanabe Hajime (*Tanabe Hajime Zenshū*, 田辺元全集) is generally divided into four parts in accordance with the historical development of Tanabe's philosophical thinking. The first part belongs to the period spanning 1910 to 1918, when Tanabe mainly worked on the philosophy of mathematics and science. His educational background in mathematics, coupled with his lifelong orientation toward metaphysics, enabled him to publish the first Japanese text on the philosophy of science in1915. With regard to this achievement that Tanabe made when he was teaching the "Introduction to Science" at Tohoku University, this publication, some argue, marked the beginning of philosophical thinking in Japanese academia.[2] This might have been an exaggeration on the critics' part but Tanabe's achievement was significant enough to draw Nishida's attention on the other side of Japan. The second part of Tanabe's works marks the period between his appointment as an assistant professor of philosophy at Kyoto University in 1919 and a decade after his return from studying abroad in Germany in 1924. During these years, his philosophical interest much more explicitly moves toward the works of Kant and Hegel. The representative works from this period are *Kant's Theory of Teleology* (1924) and *Hegel's Philosophy and Dialectic* (1932). Allegedly, Nishida insisted that his younger peer should continue studying Kant, while Tanabe's uncompromisingly metaphysical mind was unable to silence its increasing dissatisfaction with the limitation of Kantian philosophy. Because of that, nothing could stop him from continuing his investigation into the comprehensive framework of Hegel's dialectical thinking beyond Kant's critical idealism.[3] It is not surprising, in this sense, to see that Tanabe's first critique of Nishida's philosophy appeared in 1930 under the title, "Requesting the Teaching of Nishida-Sensei."

As I mentioned briefly in Chapter 2, Tanabe was increasingly frustrated with Hegel's configuration of dialectical thinking and eventually came to recognize its inability to deal genuinely with the concrete reality as what is irreducible to self-thinking thought. The self-concretization of the idea as the self-determining process of the absolute spirit, for Tanabe, seems to remain incapable of explaining the nonrational substratum of social existence, that is, species, in its contradictory relations to the freedom of each human being (i.e., individual), as well as the conceptual whole of humanity as rational being (i.e., the universal or genus). Consequently, while taking into account his prior critical assessments of Hegel's dialectic and Nishida's philosophy, Tanabe began to develop his own philosophy, that is, *The Logic of Species*, in the second half of 1930s and strove to reconfigure the intermediation of three metaphysical terms differently from the ways in which Hegel or Nishida laid out their intermediations. After the Second World War, Tanabe continued to rearticulate this logic of species in more explicitly existential and religious terms, which he explains much more clearly in his monumental work, *Philosophy as Metanoetics* (1946). This final formulation and completing essay of the logic of species was published as "The Dialectic of the Logic of Species" in 1947. This completion of the logic of species was just a few years after his retirement from the position of professor at the Kyoto University in July 1945. Most scholars mark the period between 1934 and 1945 as the third part of Tanabe's oeuvre.[4]

Finally, the fourth part of the historical development of Tanabe's philosophy consists of his later works published after his retirement. In his quiet resident in desolate Kitakaruizawa, he continuously worked on a variety of philosophical topics and published the following titles: *The Urgent Mission of Political Philosophy* (1946); *Existence, Love, and Practice* (1947); *Philosophy as Metanoetics* (1948); *Dialectic of Christianity* (1948); *Introduction to Philosophy* (1949); *Philosophy of Art in Paul Valéry* (1951); *The Historical Development of Mathematics* (1954); *Dialectic of the Theory of Relativity* (1955); and *A Memorandum on Mallarmé* (1961). Toward the end of his life in 1962, Tanabe still remained creative in his process of thinking and proposed the notion of the "philosophy of death" in opposition to the popular notion of the "philosophy of life" shared among notable thinkers at that time in Japan and abroad. Besides the text on Mallarmé, he set forth this most serious and urgent existential thought through a series of essays such as "Either Ontology of Life or Dialectic of Death," "*Memento Mori*," etc.

There are both merits and demerits for mapping out the whole of Tanabe's philosophy in four parts. It is extremely important to keep in mind which period a text under consideration belongs. For instance, I was once asked to explain how Tanabe's small essays on freedom from 1917 (i.e., "Moral Freedom" and "On Moral Freedom Revisited") would help us understand his logic of species or how these essays led Tanabe to construct the very logic of his own.⁵ This could be a misleading question if the questioner thinks that there is a continuous development from these articles from the first period to the formation of Tanabe's original philosophy in the third period. The significance of the early works mostly lies in the fact that they show Tanabe's preparation for the further engagement with Kantian and Hegelian philosophy in the second period, while there are hardly any direct or positive links between these essays and the formation of the major work in the period of 1934–45. In this sense, the four divisions can remind us to pay closer attention to the specific contexts in which Tanabe is addressing various philosophical questions.

Of course, there are also some unavoidable problems with this imposition of the rigid historical distinctions with regard to the dynamic development of Tanabe's metaphysical thinking. First, from the systematic viewpoint, the four distinctions do not always correspond to the possible demarcations of the philosophical transitions in Tanabe's works. For example, most of the early works from the first period and the works that pertain to Tanabe's sympathetic engagement with Kantian critical idealism in the second period clearly share the same systematic standpoint from which Tanabe sets forth his own insight. Then, as his philosophical interest shifts from Kant to Hegel, the method of his philosophical argumentation becomes much more consonant with the dynamic unfolding of the dialectical thinking in the latter. In this case, we could say that Tanabe had adopted a Hegelian framework of thinking that intended to sublate his earlier standpoint of (neo-)Kantian rationalism. If I were to borrow Desmond's terms, Tanabe goes through a transition from transcendentally univocal to dialectical thinking in the second half of the second period.

The logic of species from the third period, as I have argued in Chapter 2, does not mark a clear break from the dialectical thinking of Hegel in the second period; it albeit does reveal the origination of the term "Tanabean Philosophy." In this sense, Heisig is right in saying that "[a]part from the role accorded species [as the irrational substratum of historical reality], ... the logical scheme of what Tanabe is doing again looks like vintage Hegel."⁶ Nevertheless, once Tanabe clearly introduces the notion of absolute nothingness, metanoetics, and absolute dialectic as the foundations of the logic of species in his mature works published after 1945, the philosophical significance of the logic, as Tanabe's original contribution to the field of philosophy, becomes much more evident. This means that the logic of species systematically belongs both to the third and the fourth periods, thereby signaling a transition (*tenkan*) from an immanent ontology of Hegelian dialectic to an absolute dialectic based on the Mahāyāna concept of absolute nothingness.⁷ Thus, the four historical divisions of Tanabe's complete works do not neatly capture the two philosophical transitions that mark three systematic divisions of Tanabe's works: namely, the transitions from the standpoint of Kantian rationalism to that of Hegelian dialectic and from Hegelian dialectic to the ultimate standpoint of absolute dialectic.

Holding fast to the four historical divisions or three systematic divisions in relation to *Tanabe Zenshū*, moreover, these divisions themselves could misrepresent Tanabe as a fragmentary thinker. Many of the small essays from his early works seem to have nothing to do with the development of his later works. Because of that, the difficulty of tracing a seamless development in Tanabe's lifelong engagement with philosophy can discourage many scholars from examining all of his works in a comprehensive manner. Since the most interesting part of his works (especially for comparative theorists) is where he develops his own philosophy in the third and fourth parts, as well as the transition from Hegelian dialectic to absolute dialectic, why, then, can we not simply look at his mature works published after 1945, along with the essential part of the logic of species from the third period? Why can we not just disregard any of the earlier works? I do not necessarily reject this method of ruminating on Tanabe's later works in order to illuminate his original contribution to the history of philosophy. But I have some reservation toward the presupposition of this approach, namely, that Tanabe had suddenly arrived at interesting takes on various philosophical issues toward the end of his career, while none of his earlier works contain anything meaningful to offer with respect to these issues.

Take, for instance, the question of freedom in one of the early essays entitled "On Moral Freedom Revisited" (1917).[8] The most interesting thing about this small article is that Tanabe refers to Shinran's teaching called, *akunin-jōbutsu* (悪人成仏). It advocates the "salvation of an evil person as he is being evil." Put differently, it discusses the entrance of the finite relative as the finite into the realm of infinite absolute. Tanabe does not fully lay out how this unity of the contradiction between the finite and the infinite or between good and evil is possible in this text. Nor do I think that he can do so successfully, since he is trying to get clear about the nature of ethical oughtness in general merely from the standpoint of Kantian epistemology.[9] However, these texts offer us a view of the passage through which Tanabe's philosophy undergoes its development. Kōyama Iwao (高山岩男) (1905–93) reports that when Tanabe attended a philosophy colloquium at the Kyoto University, their discussions happened to touch on *Tannishō* (歎異抄) and Tanabe went on to criticize the well-known idea of *akunin-shōki* (悪人正機)—a teaching that a sinner is truly equipped with the ability to be saved through the Original Vow (*hongan*, 本願) of the Amida Buddha (i.e., *tariki-hongan*, 他力本願), precisely because he is a sinner. Tanabe argued that this teaching, which is equivalent to *akunin-jōbutsu*, leads to the nullification of ethics. So, he firmly concluded that "he could not agree with it."[10]

Kōyama explains that Tanabe's standpoint on this ethico-religious teaching significantly shifts in the course of twenty years (1925–45), which is especially evident in his later philosophy of religion that considers these teachings of Pure Land/Shin Buddhism to be of the utmost significance. Without them, it would have been impossible for Tanabe to ground the unity of the contradictory division between ideality and reality. Hence, Tanabe's positive interpretation of *akunin-jōbutsu* in "On Moral Freedom Revisited" demonstrates that he did not suddenly change his mind about Shinran's teaching from the negative to the positive for the sake of his arguments. Rather, Shinran's life and thought haunted him for at least three decades, which indicates why Tanabe struggled over the significance of Shinran's wisdom in the years to come. I will later explain these key notions developed by the Pure Land School in detail, but what is important here is the fact that some of Tanabe's early works can still shed some light on the central questions that he struggled with throughout his life as a philosopher.¹¹ As the exemplary interpretations of the small articles from 1917 demonstrate, we should not forget to stay vigilant to the surprising connections between different parts of Tanabe's *Zenshū*, albeit there are general divisions through which we cannot seamlessly draw a continuous development of his philosophical thinking.

By weighing the merits and the demerits of implementing the fourfold division of Tanabe's complete works, I would like to point out that Part Four will mainly focus on Tanabe's three central works on the philosophy of religion from the fourth period, namely, *Philosophy as Metanoetics*; *Existence, Love and Practice*; and *Dialectic of Christianity* (hereafter cited as *PM, ELP,* and *DC*). The *PM*, which was originally delivered as a year-long lecture at the end of the Second World War, sketches out Tanabe's definitive take on the interrelation of philosophy and religion in consonance with the religious teachings of Pure Land/Shin Buddhism. This text shows Tanabe's emphasis on the re-configured status of philosophy in relation to the Mahāyāna Buddhist notion of absolute nothingness. *ELP* explicitly argues for the logic of species specifically as the trinitarian network of love based on the notion of absolute nothingness and aims to unfold the social significance of metanoetics. This text accentuates the significance of the self-sacrificial act of love for understanding the interrelation of the divine absolute and the human relative. Finally, *DC* accounts for the logic of species based on the notion of absolute nothingness as the communal (net)works of love—namely, the communal concretion of divine absolute through the constant praxis of love and continuous self-awareness of metanoesis. Tanabe calls this final standpoint from which he elucidates the intermediation of universal, particular, and individual the "absolute dialectic" and argues that this dialectic, different than Hegel's dialectic, subsumes all of his key notions in the philosophy of religion just mentioned. As the title of this text suggests, Tanabe explores the special significance of Christian faith in light of absolute dialectic and thereby carries out the comparative examination of Christianity and Mahāyāna Buddhism for his philosophical understanding of religion. These three texts from the fourth period are indispensable for examining Tanabe's response to the fundamental problems of the philosophy of religion.

The general problem of Buddhism for the philosophy of religion

Before getting into the central arguments and the key notions in Tanabe's mature works on the philosophy of religion, I would like to discuss the general problem of engaging in a comparative philosophy of religion in relation to Christianity and Buddhism. Tanabe's stances toward different sects of Buddhism, as well as Christianity, slightly vary from one text to another, and these variations in his reflections on different religious traditions tacitly deal with the general problem of the interphilosophical and interreligious dialogues between Buddhism and Christianity. It is certainly possible to deal with this problem as we further investigate Tanabe's philosophical approach to the Western and the Eastern religious traditions. Not only because most readers of this book are presumably Western academics in the field of philosophy but also because this problem is pertinent to the general framework in which anyone can comparatively examine Christianity and Buddhism, I would like to address this issue as a preparation for our engagement with Tanabe's later texts on the (comparative) philosophy of religion.

The general problem of examining the Judeo-Christian and Buddhist traditions together can be summarized as the question as to whether or not we can use the term "religion" in the same sense. Regardless of the fact that Christianity and Buddhism are often classified as world religions, we seem to have much more certainty regarding the monotheistic tradition of Christianity or Islam as religions, while the spiritual exercises and the beliefs based on the words of the Buddha often seem to have nothing to do with supernatural divinity or miracles or anything that we can deem as being transcendent to the natural development of humanity in immanence. Hence, we hear the oft-repeated apothegm "Buddhism is much more philosophy than religion." This problem may seem trivial for some specialists of religions and perhaps even insignificant for most Buddholigsts. However, I think, it emphasizes the crucial point for understanding the significance of Tanabe's takes on Buddhism and also helps us understand the unavoidable difficulty of bringing Buddhism into dialogue with problems concerning the philosophy of religion. Let me explain this point in reference to the best-known book on the teachings of the Buddha in the West: Walpola Rahula's *What the Buddha Taught* (1959).[12]

Rahula mainly refers to the "earliest extant records of the teachings of the Buddha" in the Pali texts of the *Tripitaka* when explaining the main tenets of Buddhist teachings. The two major traditions of Buddhism, Theravada and Mahāyāna Buddhism, represent different beliefs and practices, but, according to Rahula, they both agree on the core teachings of the Buddha. Thus, Rahula's text, in this sense, constitutes one of the greatest achievements in the field of religious studies in terms of introducing the basic tenets of Buddhism to the general audience in the West. I simply cannot think of any other texts that exceed this one in terms of accessibility, clarity, and succinctness. However, the first *bhikkhu* (i.e., Buddhist monk) who became a professor of religious studies in the Western world opens this most influential introduction to Buddhism with an interpretation that sounds extremely controversial for the philosophers of religion.

Rahula emphasizes the importance of the human aspect of the Buddha in the opening chapter "The Buddhist Attitude of Mind."[13] The Buddha, according to Rahula, did not only claim himself to be anything more than just a simple human being but also "no inspiration from any god or external power either [but] attributed all his realization, attainments and achievements to human endeavour and human intelligence."[14] In this sense, "man's position, according to Buddhism, is supreme. Man is his own master, and there is no higher being or power that sits in judgment over his destiny."[15] This supremacy of human status in reference to the Buddha and the rest of humanity echoes the famous line from the *Dhammapada* (Jp. *Hokkugyō*, 法句経): "One indeed is one's own refuge; how can others be a refuge to one?" (*Atta hi attano natho ko hi natho paro siya*).[16]

Along with the strong orientation toward autonomy of the human individual, Buddhism conveys a series of equivocal claims, that is, the standpoint of absolute relativisim, the extirpation of individualism beyond the part-whole duality, and the complete rationality of Buddhist self-awareness. First, Rahula gives a short and powerful answer to the question, "What is Absolute Truth?"

> According to Buddhism, the Absolute truth is that there is nothing absolute in the world, that everything is relative, conditioned and impermanent, and that there is no unchanging, everlasting, absolute substance like Self, Soul or Atman within or without. This is the Absolute Truth.[17]

With regard to the notion of the single individual or the self, the venerable monk further articulates,

> according to the teaching of the Buddha, the idea of self is an imaginary, false belief which has no corresponding reality, and it produces harmful thoughts of "me" and "mine," selfish desire, craving, attachment, hatred, ill-will, conceit, pride, egoism, and other defilements, impurities and problems. It is the source of all the troubles in the world from personal conflicts to wars between nations. In short, to this false view can be traced all the evil in the world.[18]

So, to attain absolute truth through self-awareness—the realization of the truth that there is no such thing as an eternal substance like Self, Soul, Over-soul, or God—we must bear in mind that "to see things as they are without illusion or ignorance, is the extinction of craving thirst, and the cessation of *dukkha*, which is Nirvana."[19] Thus, freedom from the illusion of egoity—that is, to extirpate our misconception of ourselves as the self in its oppositional relation to the other and to see ourselves as who we are in the absolute relativity of reality in the present—provides the fundamental access point to the unconditioned state of Nirvana beyond the duality of good and evil or the division of self and other. This state of perfection, or more precisely, the complete lack of suffering or impermanence (*dukkha*) beyond reason and logic, requires seeing the world and ourselves as they are; and nothing in this art of living in the present moment calls for any superrational divine aid or irrational faith that challenges our rational thought. In this sense, Rahula points out that, unlike all religions that seem to be built on (blind) faith, "in Buddhism emphasis is laid on seeing, knowing, understanding and not on faith, or belief."[20]

Certainly, there are awfully a lot of other essential teachings of Buddhism that would call for finessed interpretations of Rahula's claims regarding the essential teachings of the Buddha. Some Mahāyāna Buddhists, who would not agree with Rahula's point that these essential teachings are unambiguously shared among various sects of the tradition, can also refer to a massive collection of Mahāyāna Sutras to amplify or suppress some of the abovementioned points. But for those who are not well versed in the teachings of Buddhism, Rahula's claims seem to propose some conundrums. First, how is it possible to claim the absolute truth when there is no absolute, and second, if there is nothing absolute, how could we say that "Niravana is"? Finally, if the unconditioned state of Nirvana is beyond reason or logic, how much emphasis can we actually place on the rational aspect of seeing, knowing, and understanding in Buddhism? Perhaps Rahula may accuse me for asking these speculative questions for intellectual pastime and kindly advise me to live a holy life in accordance with the words of the Buddha.[21] I cannot agree more about the danger of speculative thinking with its propensity to prevent us from actually dealing with the pervasive suffering in life. But also I cannot help but to think about these questions as an admirer of other Buddhists, who have tried to answer these life (and indeed religious) questions. These thinkers, after all, have left us with some texts to revisit these questions again and again.

Yet, despite the call to give up the selfish life that is the root of so much suffering in the world, the difficulty in accepting the precepts of Buddhism pertaining to the category of religion also lies in these equivocal claims. If everything is in immanent flux and there is nothing outside or beyond oneself to overcome the selfness and/or to realize the unconditioned state of Nirvana in immanence, it is hard to imagine that there is any intermediation between humans and what is superior to human autonomy.[22] The path to one's salvation, namely, one's freedom from suffering (*dhukka*), lies only in one's attainment of self-awareness through nothing but oneself.[23] Then, nothing seems to distinguish Buddhism from the rational ethics that is solely based on human autonomy, as both of them will equally regard each individual as the self-sufficient ground for his or her attainment of the divine perfection as who she or he really is. If I were to use Kierkegaard's critique of rational universalists, the straightforward presentations of the Buddhist teachings seem like unequivocally advocating an eclipse of divine transcendence, as well as one-way mediations of the self from the conditioned (*dhukka*) to the unconditioned (Nirvana). In the same way that we faced the difficulty of granting that the Kantian and the Hegelian philosophy of religion are faithful to the religious precepts of the Judeo-Christian faith—the precepts that are supposedly irreducible to the confines of philosophical thinking—we face here the philosophical difficulty of regarding Buddhism as presenting anything more than the self-sufficient self-fulfillment of ethical life.

Philosophy and two world religions in the later works of Tanabe

Tanabe is, first and foremost, a metaphysician. It is inaccurate, however, to describe him according to what Rahula has critically portrayed as a typical metaphysician of the present age, that is, as one who is preoccupied with highly speculative questions for pastime and forgets to live out the ideas represented in the religious teachings. Nor does Tanabe use dialectic for sport, like the depiction that Socrates gives as the sign of immature thinkers in *Republic*.[24] Philosophy for the cofounder of the Kyoto school is much more in consonance with Plato's notion as the art of dying or the "path toward freedom in which one must die to oneself."[25] Indeed, because of that, Tanabe claims,

> philosophy cannot be an object of enjoyment like other academic studies or art. To achieve philosophy cannot mean to make cultural refinement of ourselves or to receive enjoyment as we usually do in relation to the works of art. In other words, philosophy cannot be simply enjoyed as a part of cultural life in general, but each self must risk its own life to accomplish it. Thus, philosophy follows the same path as the life of religious faith.[26]

If philosophy and religion constitute different passages to the ultimate—the different ways in which we can be called to become aware of the truth of the world and ourselves—the philosophical questioning of the truth about the precepts of faith does not need to be detrimental to concrete living in accordance with religious teachings. Precisely in this sense, Tanabe claims that "like religious faith, philosophy, too, is a standpoint of death-and-resurrection."[27] Philosophical questioning, in this sense, could be a sign of the intellectual honesty of the rich enigma offered by any religious passage to the ultimate. Accordingly, Tanabe's engagement with the doctrines of Buddhism could provide a proper metaphysical response to the spiritual significance and the existential imports of religious teachings.

Tanabe's philosophical approach to the religious, therefore, comprises a dialogue between philosophy and religion. This intermediation of philosophy and religion in his later works is first made in relation to two major sects of Mahāyāna Buddhism, namely, Zen (in light of Dōgen, D.T. Suzuki, Nishida, and others) and Pure Land/Shin Buddhism (in reference to Shinran, Soga Ryōjin, and Takeuchi Yoshinori, to name but a few) in relation to his lifelong study of the Western philosophy of religion. His scope of philosophical investigation further extends to Christianity, which had long remained a mystery to his philosophical mind since his youth.[28] It is obviously impossible to cover the entire canons of Buddhism and then to map out the essential similarities and differences between pre-Sectarian Buddhism and these two forms of Japanese Buddhism by tracing the development of the various branches of Buddhism. There are also complicated issues related to the ways in which superficial "Occidentalism" and one-sided "orientalism" affect the interreligious dialogues between Christianity and Mahāyāna Buddhism.[29] Interpreting the agreements on the doctrines of Buddhism in the field of Buddhology is certainly valuable for solving some of the philosophical questions that I have raised in relation to Rahula's introductions to the teachings of the Buddha. The problems related to interreligious dialogues have influenced many comparative theorists to focus primarily on Tanabe's philosophical interpretations of Buddhism and, thus, prevented them from taking into account his engagement with Christianity. In order to deal with some of Tanabe's concepts that are closely related to Buddhist terms, it could be extremely valuable for us to reevaluate and overcome the conventional limitations of the Occidentalist, or even the orientalist, approach to Buddhist notions that run through his thought.

This genealogical inquiry into the history of Buddhism and its systematic dialogue with Christianity, however, anticipates another line of investigation into Tanabe's works. Once we question the interpretive differences or similarities regarding what counts as Buddhism within the Buddhist tradition(s), as well as its various receptions in the Western intellectual sphere, we will have to examine these differences and similarities with respect to the relations that these religious doctrines bear on Tanabe's understandings of them. To what extent is Tanabe's take on Buddhism faithful to what the Buddha taught? Can his understanding of Christianity be considered to be orthodox or heretical? Is his dialogical understanding of the relationship between Buddhism and Christianity truthful to their differences and similarities? The answers to these questions could constitute highly valuable scholarship on Tanabe's philosophy of religion and, undoubtedly, shed some light on its relation to the different religious doctrines. Nevertheless, it is not only impossible to lay out all the traditional forms of Buddhist faith and differentiate them from Tanabe's philosophical interpretations in this limited space but also detrimental for our search for the answers to the questions posed by the philosophy of religion. In the following sections, therefore, I will aim at presenting Tanabe's philosophical notions in their close affinity with Pure Land/ Shin Buddhism and then examine how these ideas, which provided him with a way to approach the different religions in his later works, can help us respond to our questions regarding the philosophical significance of religious faith.

The historical development of Buddhism also gives polyphonic records of the Buddhist thinkers who have struggled with the teachings of the Buddha (not unlike the ways in which the majority of the history of Western philosophy has struggled with the significance of the Judeo-Christian faith). Some of the interpretative differences among various sects of Buddhism have clearly resulted in distinct editions of Sutras, different styles of spiritual exercises, diverse religious rituals, and a multiplicity of beliefs that cannot always be univocalized. Since there is no central text in Buddhism that is universally consulted as the undeniable authority of faith like the Bible (in conjunction with the idea of universal church) in Christianity, it is quite natural that different groups of Buddhists in different parts of the world compiled their own religious texts by translating, editing, and even occasionally modifying the older editions that they have inherited from their ancestors. I have no doubt that a closer and comprehensive genealogical study of the Buddhist scriptures alone can provide us the keys to solve some of our questions concerning the ambiguities that we saw in Rahula's Theravada introduction to the Pali texts.

What is important for the purpose of the comparative philosophy of religion, however, is not to accentuate these benefits of diving into the vast ocean of Buddhist texts with philological attention, but to look at the hermeneutical stance that the Buddhist monks take in view of their scriptures. These thinkers have critically digested a variety of sutras and constituted their own traditional interpretations of Buddhist teachings, while their endeavor to remain truthful to their inherited traditions of Buddhism does not eliminate the possibility of deviating from the previous interpretations of these teachings. In some cases, we can even say that their interpretive differences were made for the sake of living truthfully to the teachings of Buddha in diverse historico-cultural contexts. What is called for a great scholar of Buddhism, then, is not just to look at their differences among the multiplicity of Buddhist sects but to see how their different interpretations of the religious texts were made sense in different historico-cultural viewpoints.

In the same manner, what I would like to propose to do in the next chapter is not to examine the deviations of Tanabe's critical approach to the two sects of Mahāyāna Buddhism, as well as to Christianity, from the traditional interpretations of these religious doctrines. Instead, we will view Tanabe's later works on the philosophy of religion as a single intellectual and existential effort to make sense of the religious faith(s) pertaining to these religious traditions. Therefore, despite their occasional defiance to the "original" orthodoxies, we will look at Tanabe's interpretations of the religious ideas pertaining to Buddhism and Christianity in their own light and bring them to the ongoing discussions of problems in the philosophy of religion. Tanabe's treatment of ideas pertaining to Christianity (e.g., God, divine kenosis, incarnation, resurrection, the trinity of love, and the city of God) heavily depends on his understanding of metanoetics established through his engagement with Pure Land/ Shin Buddhism. Some of them may sound controversial or counterintuitive for those who know their original contexts, and yet, they are also surprisingly harmonious. Because of that, they are quite useful for critically comparing Tanabe's takes on these notions in metanoetics with Desmond's elucidation of similar concepts in metaxology. For this reason, I will proceed to focus on the establishment of metanoetics through Tanabe's engagement with Mahāyāna Buddhism with some useful references to shared concepts in Judeo-Christian tradition.

8

Tanabe Hajime and the Problems of the Philosophy of Religion

A trilogy of faith: Two layers to Tanabe's later works on the philosophy of religion

There are two interrelated layers in Tanabe's later works on the philosophy of religion. The first pertains to Tanabe's approach to religion from the side of philosophy and the second pertains to his reconfiguration of philosophy in its openness to religion. With regard to the first, Tanabe argues in various occasions that his lifelong engagement with the history of Western philosophy (extending from Plato to Heidegger) has culminated in the painful conclusion that philosophy must face its destruction at the end of its self-inquiry, especially when it tries to claim its knowledge of itself as the absolute truth or to achieve this end of philosophical knowing only through itself. Tanabe calls this realization that philosophy cannot stand on its own reason alone "absolute critique" and shows that this radical self-critique of philosophy anticipates the constitution of "absolute dialectic" as the most comprehensive framework in which we can achieve (or more precisely be granted with) the philosophical awareness of the ultimate. Although the Japanese thinker makes these points in relation to the whole history of Western philosophy, it is important to note here that the term "absolute critique" implicates a critical stance mostly aimed at Kant's critique of reason, while "absolute dialectic" also denotes a kind of thinking that goes beyond the limitations of Hegel's dialectic. With regard to the most important term in his philosophy of religion, that is, "metanoetics," it is also important for us to bear in mind that Tanabe sometimes refers both to "absolute critique" and "absolute dialectic" under the general rubric of "metanoesis," and yet, at other times, he discusses the act of metanoesis as the necessary condition for the possibility of "absolute critique," which subsequently leads to the constitution of the "absolute dialectic." Thus, in the following, I will, first, explain what Tanabe means by the term "absolute critique," second, show how it leads to the "absolute dialectic" as that which maintains philosophical openness to religious faith, and finally, demonstrate how the notion of metanoetics, along with its core concepts, constitutes and characterizes Tanabe's philosophy of religion.

From the absolute critique to the absolute dialectic: The death and resurrection of reason

Tanabe explains that absolute critique represents the "theoretical side of metanoetics" and describes the intellectual path through which one could reach the "inevitable consequence of philosophical inquiries pursued as the critique of reason."[1] What this theoretical side of metanoetics essentially signifies is the downfall of philosophical inquiries based solely on the autonomy of reason, as well as the subsequent freedom of philosophy from its obsession with the self-identity of reason. This movement from the deconstruction to a reconstruction of philosophy or from the breakdown to a breakthrough of reason can be best seen in Tanabe's critical stance toward the historical development of German philosophy from Kant to Hegel.

Tanabe admits in *ELP* that Kant's critique of reason is far more radical than Descartes's methodological skepticism, because "the Cartesian ego is negated through Kantian critique and its existence is approved as the object of knowledge insofar as it appears to consciousness."[2] Tanabe, however, finds the critical method of Kantian philosophy highly problematic. That is because "the subject as the unity of such consciousness still continues to subsist as the core of critique, i.e., reason, and substantially exists as the universal that grounds the practical freedom of the subject and the self-consciousness of his will."[3] What the Japanese philosopher is trying to get at is the point that Kant never comes to question *self-critically* the possibility of the critique of reason itself. That is to say, he never comes to ask the crucial philosophical question of how one can thoroughly practice the critique of reason without calling into question one's critical project as a whole. Tanabe explicitly lays out his critique by saying that

> Though a critical philosopher, [Kant] did not venture into criticism of the very possibility of criticism. It would seem he was convinced that if criticism is the proper task of reason, as he believed it was, philosophy becomes possible only when we presuppose and admit criticism; and moreover, that the possibility of criticism itself cannot be called into question without negating reason and abandoning philosophy. In this, he was from first to last a philosopher of reason. Yet it takes no more than a moment's reflection to locate the problems with such an idea of criticism.[4]

If the subject of reason's critique is exempted from the critique itself, the critique of reason can never be fulfilled (as Kant wants to claim in the *Critique of Pure Reason*). But the flip side of this negative assessment of the Kantian project is that we ought to remain truthful to the spirit of criticism. To do so, we must turn the critiquing subject into the object of critique and further put our critical reason to the task of self-critical questioning. If, however, we keep trotting this path of radical self-criticism, Tanabe thinks,

> We end up in an infinite regress where each critique gives rise to a critique of itself. We would then be forced to conclude that the thoroughgoing critique of reason in

its entirety is simply impossible, involving a contradiction beyond the means of analytical logic to resolve because of the antinomies into which the infinite process of self-awareness is doomed to fall.

... [T]he self-criticism of reason [must] run aground on the impassable antinomies of the one and the many, the whole and the individual, infinity and finitude, determinacy and spontaneity, necessity and freedom. Criticism has no alternative but to surrender itself to this crisis of self-disruption, and to overcome it by allowing itself to be shattered to pieces.[5]

The absolute critique represents this intellectual passage of human self-awareness, where the thinking subject recognizes its inescapable fate of his self-disruption in the end of the uncompromising critique of his reason. What this deconstruction (or "absolute crisis"[6]) of reason reveals is the fact that the self-critique of human reason cannot make itself complete through itself alone, and in order for it to be a thorough self-criticism, it requires something other than itself. This sign of finitude in the self-reflection of human reason indicates that philosophy (especially in light of Kant, German Idealism, and some forms of contemporary phenomenology) has faced the deadlock in which it cannot sufficiently mitigate the discontinuity between reason and being; subject and object; universal and particular; absolute and relative; rational and irrational; ideality and reality; and self and other in addition to the other relevant metaphysical terms that Tanabe just mentioned.

But is this not exactly what Hegel saw at the end of Kant's critical project? Did Hegel not further emphasize the undeniable mutuality between these opposing terms beyond their simple dualism, while taking into account their undeniable differences? Tanabe admits that Hegel has great insight into the problem of Kantian reason as standing outside of criticism and also particularly praises the *Phenomenology of Spirit* as an excellent account of the historical development of philosophy from Kant to Hegel, which accords with the theoretical movement of absolute critique.[7] Hegel's thought thus significantly resonates in Tanabe's system. They both realize the one-sidedness in Kant's critique of reason. Also, they both come to propose, in one way or another, dialectical thinking as the consummate form of philosophical thinking. As I mentioned in Chapter 2, there are some earlier forms of dialectical thinking in the works of Tanabe (especially in the 1930s) that sound almost identical to Hegel's development of *Begriff*. Because of this, the problems that we previously saw in the works of Hegel are still inherent in the works of Tanabe from the third historical period. However, the Japanese thinker in these later works from the fourth period explicitly indicates the limitations of Hegel's dialectical thinking and diagnoses its inability to rise to the level of metanoetics.

There are several occasions in which Tanabe criticizes Hegel's dialectic in light of absolute critique. The common thread by which the Japanese dialectician weaves his objections, however, lies in Hegel's equivocal obsession with the self-identity of reason. Recall the standard model of Hegel's dialectical self-determination that we saw in Chapter 3, as well as Desmond's presentation of the modern formulation of dialectical thinking in Chapter 4: the initially abstract universal takes the particular as its own self-alienation and determines itself in and through the particular as the concrete universal. We can also simplify this point by saying that "unity mediates itself in and through multiplicity as the unity of multiplicity."[8] In reference to this dialectical process of self-determination, Hegel consistently uses the expression of "returning to self" and thereby tries to maintain that what we have in the end of the dialectical circle is what was essentially found at the beginning.[9] In addition to the apparent difficulty in maintaining that the process of concretizing the universal gives the same universal in its beginning and in its end, Tanabe sees the problem in Hegel's propensity to recover the "original unity" and place emphasis on *unity* in the final stage of the "unity of multicipity." Tanabe thinks that Hegel remains incapable of subjecting reason to the complete rupture between reason and being, which is evident in the fact that Hegel strives to eradicate this disruption by privileging the self-identity of dialectical reason.

Tanabe often argues that Hegel's dialectic does not take the negative into full account, but gives instead only the "nondialectical, self-identical philosophy," which marks a "simple return to Kantian reason, as well as to Schelling's philosophy of identity" or a "degeneration away from authentic dialectic."[10] This point is clear from the following passage in *ELP*:

> The special characteristic of Hegel's dialectic is the activity of sublation (*Aufhebung*), which, in order to establish the stage of synthesis, abandons both thesis and antithesis and simultaneously raises them [to the level], where both of them are preserved. This moment of preservation in sublation gives nothing but a residue of identity and indicates that Hegel makes a quantitative compromise without completing the negation. Since the antithesis stands in opposition to the thesis as a negation, their preservation in synthesis superficially appears as an identical preservation of the thesis and thereby the negativity of the antithesis comes to be included into the shadow of the synthesis. In this sense, Hegel's dialectic has the developmental rather than the negative characteristic.[11]

The mutual implication of thesis and antithesis in Hegel's dialectic is reduced to the immanent synthesis, where the opposing terms are preserved as the transitional moments for the constitution of the higher synthesis.[12] What bothers Tanabe is that the antithesis is assimilated into the further (self-)determination of the thesis as the syn-thesis; hence, it loses the full implication of the antithesis as something seriously negating the self-identity of the thesis. The synthesis as the comprehensive self-determination of the thesis blinds Hegel from the consequences of reason's self-criticism, that is, an uneradicable gap between reason and being, one and many, and self and other that we cannot intermediate only from the side of reason, unity, or self.[13] This recalcitrance of the negative vis-à-vis the self-determination of reason/unity/self is precisely the ground in which Tanabe continuously argues that Hegel's dialectic eventually maintains the standpoint of being (i.e., "both/and" in relation to the opposing metaphysical terms), while the consequence of absolute critique leaves no room to stand on but the standpoint of nothingness (i.e., neither/nor in relation to the opposing terms). This meontic standpoint that shreds apart reason's confidence of its self-identity is the consequence of following the absolute critique of reason to its logical consequence. What calls for such radical critique of reason is our full metaphysical commitment to the task of "tarrying with the negative," the task that Hegel celebrates in his overture to the *Phenomenology of Spirit*, yet fails to accomplish.[14]

What, then, does it mean to say that we arrive at the standpoint of nothingness through absolute critique? What do we have to do to reach this standpoint and what is the aftermath of the death of philosophy? Tanabe argues that we must first submit to the destiny of the radical self-critique where the self comes to realize that it can neither intermediate the gap between itself and other only from its own side nor absolutize itself as the comprehensive synthesis of relative self and other. We have to be truthful to the self-destruction of philosophy as the inevitable consequence of self-questioning as the finite relative. Nevertheless, as the second pillar of the Kyoto school continues,

> if we submit obediently to this destiny, choose this death willingly, and throw ourselves into the very depths of these utterly unavoidable contradictions, reality renews itself from those depths, and opens up a new way, urging us to head in the direction in which actuality is moving and to collaborate with this movement. Accompanying reason's option for its own death, the gate of contradictions, which was barred as long as reason clung to self-reliance, is thrown open. Contradictions do not thereby cease to be contradictions, but restore reason to a transrational dimension, where it can serve as a mediator to, or collaborator in the transformative activity of the absolute.[15]

As Tanabe repeatedly argues, "reason must fully break down in the pursuit of full autonomy through its self-critique."[16] But this passage clearly indicates that the breakdown of reason does not conclude with the mere annihilation of philosophical thinking altogether or our total degeneration into complete irrationalism. But because reason's confidence in its self-identity is shattered into pieces, philosophy can for the first time find a "foothold from which to break out its crisis by breaking through itself and to be transfromatively resurrected into a new being."[17] This new kind of philosophy is transrational in the sense that it cannot be reduced into any rationalistic framework of thinking that we saw in the Kantian and the Hegelian obsession with the (self-)identical univocity of reason. This anticipation of a breakthrough to the new direction in which transrational philosophy can embrace the radical difference between itself and what is other to itself in the very process of its breakdown constitutes the essence and *telos* of absolute critique. Thus, reason's openness to what is other to itself or capacity to think beyond itself (i.e., *metanoesis*) enables us both to conceive and to practice philosophy beyond the limit of rational universalism (i.e., *noesis*).

This might sound like an extremely charged statement to make. Some may even think, as Tanabe rightly anticipates, that this could be misread as a sign of strong orientalism.[18] But if we think about this death of philosophy in the context of the philosophy of religion, Tanabe is not saying anything more than Kierkegaard's critique of Kant and Hegel. Philosophy, insofar as it tends to base itself solely on autonomy of reason, cannot understand the significance of faith in what exceeds philosophical thinking, nor can it open itself to be in a communicative relation with what is more than its reason can dream of on its own terms. So long as the absolute-relative or infinite-finite relation is reduced to the immanent self-relation of the human relative(s) as the infinite absolute, there is no way for the self-thinking thought of the finite relative(s) to think what is truly absolute and infinite beyond itself because it erroneously thinks itself to be the absolute infinite in immanence. Once again, however, the "final result of the demand for self-identical unity in reason is the self-consciousness that all things are in absolute disruption because of antinomies and self-contradictions."[19] When reason forgets its original finitude and misconceives itself as the infinite absolute, it is destined to the end of absolute critique, namely, an absolute contradiction and disruption.

When philosophy loses its confidence in reason's self-identity and its presupposition of reason's absolute autonomy is brought into serious question, philosophy wakes up to a different kind of absolute that is other than itself. In this awakening to the absolute as what is other than what we can conceive of only in philosophical terms, we can, for the first time, begin to reconsider the intermediations of the irreducibly contradictory metaphysical terms, including the relation between philosophy and religion. And precisely when we realize our inability to bridge the gap between these opposing terms within the conventional form of philosophy alone, we can be led to a kind of philosophy that is "reborn out of the denial of philosophy." As we have seen earlier, Tanabe calls this "philosophy that is not a philosophy because, on the one hand, it has arisen from the vestiges of a philosophy I had cast away in despair, and on the other, it maintains the purpose of functioning as a reflection on what is ultimate as a radical self-awareness, which are the goals proper to philosophy."[20] The death-and-resurrection of philosophy does not mark only the inevitable consequence of absolute critique but also the proper reflection of the ultimate through the renewed sense of philosophy. In this case, humbled reason comes to hear the Buddhist notion of nothingness as the absolute beyond the immanent absolute of universal rationalism— the absolute reducible *neither* to reason *nor* to being. This awareness of ultimacy outside the conventional form of philosophy based solely on reason's autonomy now leads Tanabe to reconstruct a dialectical thinking—a new form of dialectic that, in reference to the otherness of absolute nothingness, recalibrates the intermediation of the opposing metaphysical terms with full attentiveness to the result of absolute critique (i.e., their irreducible difference). Tanabe calls this new form of dialectic that constitutes metanoetics "absolute dialectic" and holds it as the consummate standpoint for delivering his own take on the philosophy of religion.

The second layer to Tanabe's philosophy of religion: A reconfiguration of philosophy through its openness to religion

When reason goes through its rigorous self-criticism, it is forced to recognize its inability to completely assimilate the otherness of being into the self-identity of its reason. In this case, reason comes to abandon its desire to absolutize itself. The humbled reason with its full awareness of its own finitude comes to open itself to what is other to itself and thereby, it is "restored to a transrational dimension," where it serves as the collaborative mediator of the absolute. This transformative absolute that restores reason in the transrational level, according to Tanabe, comes to resonate with the Eastern notion of absolute nothingness, and this transformation of reason, through its submission to the notion of nothingness, constitutes *zangedō* (懺悔道), which Tanabe translates (in consonance with a biblical passage) as "metanoetics." To understand his philosophy of religion, in this sense, it is crucial to examine some of the philosophical notions pertaining to Mahāyāna Buddhism (especially of the Pure Land School) and elucidate how they provide a passage for Tanabe to develop a renewed sense of philosophy as "metanoetics" or "absolute dialectic." In the following, I will approach the second layer of Tanabe's philosophy of religion by introducing some key Buddhist notions and analyze how some of them play a central role in conveying Tanabe's response to the problems of the philosophy of religion.

From the philosophy of *jiriki* (自力) to the metanoetics of *tariki* (他力) I: Mysticism of sages and the penitent confessions of sinners

Tanabe describes a type of philosophy that is based solely on the autonomy of reason as the "philosophy of self-power"[21] and his metanoetics as the renewed sense of philosophy that recognizes its ground in the "other-power."[22] This distinction refers to the Buddhist notions of *jiriki-hongan* (自力本願) and *tariki-hongan* (他力本願).[23] The *jiriki-hongan* is often translated as "salvation through self-power" and this means that a human being makes the original vow of Bodhisattva (Skt. *pūrva-praṇidhāna*, Jp. *Hongan*, 本願) and realizes this vow as Tathāgata (Jpn. *Nyorai*, 如来) through his or her own effort toward perfection, or what is called the impermanent state of Nirvana (Jpn. *Nehan*, 涅槃).[24] In the context of the philosophy of religion, this is equivalent to saying that the movement from the finite to the infinite or the relative to the absolute is made only through the self's own effort to overcome its finitude and, therefore, the self becomes the infinite absolute through nothing but itself. The self-negating self-transcendence in philosophy of self-power, in this sense, makes the one-way movement from the human relative to the divine absolute.

Under the label of "self-power philosophy" (*jiriki-tetsugaku*, 自力哲学), Tanabe includes not only the Kantian and the Hegelian philosophy of religion but also what he characterizes as mysticism, Zen Buddhism, Heideggerian phenomenology, and Nishidian philosophy. Although he never explicitly names Nishida as a target of his criticism, it is obvious that some of Nishida's key notions are under serious scrutiny. This has caused many controversies among (Japanese) scholars of the Kyoto school, and most of the works published on this issue have tried to demonstrate how Tanabe's criticism is uncharitable (if not completely off the mark), in that he misrepresents the profound complexity of Nishida's metaphysical insight.[25] Furthermore, Tanabe's criticism of Heidegger, despite its great historical significance, is virtually untouched among the scholars in the field of comparative and Japanese philosophy. Since Tanabe was one of the earliest critics of Heidegger, a close analysis of his criticism from the third and the fourth period can undoubtedly bring forth some valuable contributions to Heidegger studies not unlike the way in which Tanabe's conflict with Nishida has enriched the field of Nishida studies. That being said, what I would like to emphasize here is the larger picture in which Tanabe is challenging all of mysticism, Zen Buddhism, Heidegger, and Nishida, along with the Kantian and the Hegelian philosophy of religion, that is, the general rubric of "philosophy of self-power." What Tanabe finds problematic in *jiriki* philosophy is the common ground from which he criticizes different variations found in these particular thinkers or schools of thought. Allow me to unpack the core of his arguments by referring to the example of mysticism.

Tanabe argues that "Mysticism is nothing other than a body of assertions meant to confirm an experience of the transcendent somehow made immanent in our finite beings" and also that "it maintains the position that we can have an intuition of the self as transcending itself to become one with that transcendent."[26] Given the division between divine transcendence and human immanence, the standpoint of mysticism claims that we can somehow both intuit and realize our continuity with divine transcendence from the side of human immanence. Tanabe describes this as the "contemplative speculation,"[27] following the path of the ascending movement of the self from the finite to the infinite. This mystic union of the infinite and the finite or the absolute and the relative, according to Tanabe, anticipates the following four problems: (1) divine transcendence is reduced to the ontic realm of finite immanence,[28] (2) autonomy of each human individual has to be subjugated to the necessity of the divine transcendence,[29] (3) this path is accessible only for saints or sages who, with their superhuman capacity, achieve their moral perfection through themselves,[30] and finally, (4) this contemplative self-overcoming of the finite self hardly touches on the indispensable significance of sociality for the praxis of religious faith.[31] For the sake of keeping these points relevant to our ongoing discussion, I will refer to the first three in the following.

The first problem in relation to the tradition of mysticism straightforwardly repeats Kierkegaard's doubt concerning the continuity of faith and reason in universal rationalism. If the mysticism claims to remain truthful to the precepts of the Judeo-Christian faith, this reduction of divine transcendence to the human immanence would be a major obstacle for claiming the orthodoxy of their faith. Tanabe often argues that this problematic absolutization of human immanence in mysticism is also pertinent in the self-overcoming of finitude in the works of Nishida and Zen Buddhists.[32] The eclipse of the divine transcendence—or more precisely the exhaustive reduction of the divine absolute to the ontic realm of the finite relative—constitutes a great problem for the Eastern thinkers, especially when they hold that the notion of absolute must be based on the Eastern concept of absolute nothingness—the notion that is supposedly irreducible to any of the ontic terms.

The seamless continuity between divinity and humanity inevitably suffers from the problem of either/or: either the necessity of divine transcendence or the contingency of humanity in immanence. The first problem of the reduction of the divine above to the human below holds the second horn, while the second problem points to the consequence of holding the first horn, that is, the conflation of human freedom and divine necessity. A particular variation of this problem has recently drawn much attention from scholars as one of the most difficult problems in the history of philosophy, that is, the problem of divine foreknowledge. This problem can be summarized with a single question: If the divine knowledge of contingent finite is necessary, how can we maintain the contingency/freedom of the finite relative? What is problematic in asking this question is the foundational presupposition of the abovementioned "either/or" prior to the emergence of the question itself. In other words, the direct continuity of infinite absolute and finite relative makes it impossible and problematic for us to account for the autonomy of finite relative (as much as this divine-human continuity causes the difficulty of maintaining the necessity of the divine knowledge in its identical relation to human contingency). This is precisely the reason why Tanabe argues that

> The contemplative unification of the absolute and the relative is based on a demand for supreme identity that is beyond our human ability, and can only end up in the dissolution of the mind into mystical unity. Mysticism does not allow us to regard what is relative as free and autonomous.[33]

The solution to this problem (which indeed would also be the solution to the problem of divine foreknowledge) is to rethink the continuity in the contradictory relationship between divine transcendence and human immanence beyond the logic of self-identity. Without breaking through this either/or by contemplating on the unity of opposites, we can solve neither the first problem regarding the reduction of divinity to humanity nor the second problem related to the dissolution of human freedom into divine necessity.

The third problem represents the existential side of Tanabe's critical stance toward the self-power philosophy. If the finite relative can overcome its own limitation and rise to the level of the infinite absolute, the consequence of following the logic of *jiriki-hongan* would amount to saying that only those who can autonomously realize the ideality of moral perfection or successfully manifest their Buddha nature without relying on anything other than themselves can access the path to the absolute. Tanabe gives a complex response to this logic of self-power. On the one hand, he praises this path as representing the "sacred way" (i.e., *shōdōmon*, 聖道門) of the saints and sages who can realize their Buddha nature by fully exercising their self-power.[34] There are many occasions in which Tanabe expresses his deep admiration for the Buddhists (especially in reference to the Zen tradition) who are known to have gone through a variety of spiritual exercises and managed to pass through this existential passage to enlightenment.[35] Perhaps this would be one of the responses that he would give to Rahula's emphasis on self-reliance in the teachings of the Buddha, as well as to the Theravada practice of Buddhism in general. On the other hand, Tanabe also expresses his concern that, if he were to say that this sacred path to the realization of Buddha nature is accessible to him, he would end up being disingenuous with regard to the state of his own historical existence.

There are at least three reasons for Tanabe's existential hesitation to believe in the sacred way of the religious self-realization that surface in his text. First, as the opening of *PM* testifies, Tanabe was greatly torn over his inability to reconcile his responsibilities, both as a philosopher and a citizen of Japan, during and following the end of the war. What we see in the overture of this masterpiece is a confession of an intellectual who strongly felt the responsibility to speak against the evildoing of his nation and to express his strong disagreement with the military government. But at the same time, as the citizen of a nation, Tanabe was compelled to refrain from causing a split among his people at the time of war.[36] In face of destructions that his nation had caused outside and inside the islands of Japan, Tanabe's health had also greatly degenerated at this time. In this state of intellectual and physical depression, Tanabe found it difficult to continue his life as a philosopher, while facing the self-destruction of his nation in the 1940s, let alone to believe in the sacred path of self-power (*jiriki-shōdōmon*).

Second, Tanabe repeatedly argues that he is hardly the wise and righteous man who is capable of ascending the sacred path of self-power to his perfection, but rather a "sinful, the ordinary, and the ignorant" man that can do nothing but admit to his incapacity to rise to the level of the absolute through his own self-power.[37] This existential self-awareness does not only accord with the historical circumstance in which he found himself as a failure in philosophy but also demonstrates the realization that the *shōdōmon* of self-power is disingenuous to the reality of his moral existence. Tanabe often refers to Kant's account of religion and the confession of St. Paul. As we have seen above, Kantian moral religion makes it clear that a human being is equipped with the natural disposition toward the good and, thus, he is fully capable of autonomously bringing himself to moral perfection. However, even the best of humanity, such as St. Paul, suffers from the so-called "propensity to evil" (or more specifically the "frailty of heart"), as he confesses, "For the good that I would I do not: but the evil which I would not, that I do" (Romans 7:19).[38] Tanabe emphasizes that this confession of St. Paul demonstrates existential honesty, essentially testifying to one's inability to achieve moral perfection through oneself, and because of that, we must admit with St. Paul (and Kant) that we need grace for our salvation, which always provides something more than the mere autonomy of reason can conjure.[39]

Lastly, from the theoretical viewpoint, Tanabe's rejection of self-power philosophy resonates with his insight into the inevitable consequence of reason's radical self-criticism. The absolute critique concludes that reason is incapable of accounting for its unity when it attempts to carry out a thorough criticism of itself and also that such reason cannot fully account for the unity of contradiction between itself and what is other to itself by maintaining its alleged self-identity. Given the inherent finitude (i.e., antinomies) of reason, Tanabe argues that the idea of the "sacred way," where the rational self is supposed to be able to bring itself to self-identical unity, as well as to the unity of itself and other, leads to the absolute crisis:

> The absolute self-disruption brought about in absolute critique is unavoidable for reason awakened to consciousness of itself. The self-consciousness that all things are in absolute disruption because of antinomies and self-contradictions is the final result of the demand for self-identical unity in reason. Pure self-identity is possible only for the absolute. Insofar as reason forgets its standpoint of finitude and relativity and erroneously presumes itself to be absolute, it is destined to fall into absolute contradiction and disruption.[40]

In face of the unavoidable consequence of absolute critique, however, the self has the following choices: either submit itself to the death of its own reason and humbly admit that its inherent finitude prevents itself from claiming its infinitude by itself or to exploit its own relative independence over against the absolute and commit the hubris of self-apotheosis. In this sense, Tanabe often argues that mysticism and Zen Buddhism, which tend to unite the absolute and the relative on the principle of self-identity, have the serious tendency to ignore the fact that "a human being as the finite relative cannot possibly have the power to break free from the sin through himself [and consequently,] the salvation or freedom (Skt. *mokṣa*, Jpn. *gedatsu* 解脱) from sufferings through self-power is impossible for humanity."[41] The *jiriki-shōdōmon* of Zen Buddhism and the absolute-relative identity of mysticism as the variations of self-power philosophy, therefore, falls victim to the greatest temptation of the religious, that is, the rebellion against the divine absolute.[42]

From the philosophy of *Jiriki* to the metanoetics of *Tariki* II: Through the lens of the threefold history of Buddhism

Tanabe's critical stance toward *jiriki* philosophy in reference to Western mysticism and the Eastern Zen tradition seems to vary significantly from the admiration to the existential reservation and to even go so far as to claim the outright theoretical rejection of them. This might tempt many of us to regard Tanabe as being disingenuous or even too cynical, if not being merely inconsistent, in praising his ancestors who are now known to have gone through the sacred path of *jiriki-hongan*, while claiming that this path is not only existentially inaccessible for him personally but also theoretically misleading for all of us. This complex response, however, makes sense if we understand it in reference to a Buddhist narrative of history that culminates in what many Buddhist thinkers hold as the philosophy of *mo-fa* (Jpn. *mappō-shisō*, 末法思想).

One of the most important texts from the middle period of Mahāyāna Buddhism, *Mahāsaṃnipāta Sutra* (Ch. *Dà Jí Jīng*, Jp. *Daijikkyō*, 大集経),[43] led many Buddhist thinkers to hold a world picture that divides history into three periods in reference to the notion of the "decline of the Dharma." The three major distinctions (or what they call three ages of the Dharma) are roughly translated as: (1) the Age of the Right Dharma (Ch. *zheng-fa*, Jpn. *shōbō* or *shōhō*, 正法), (2) the Age of Semblance Dharma (Ch. *xiang-fa*, Jpn. *Zōbō*, 像法) and finally, (3) the Latter Age of Dharma (Ch. *mo-fa*, Jpn. *Mappō*, 末法). The *zheng-fa* or *shōbō* indicates the right law or right teachings. It refers to the period of 500 years after the "death" (*nyūmetsu*, 入滅 or Nirvana) of the Buddha when the religious teachings, praxes, and witnesses of the laws of Buddhism follow the original forms given by the Buddha, while most disciples who are in direct contact with his life are capable of achieving enlightenment by upholding the sacred teachings. This age indicates the immediate togetherness between the enlightened master and the disciples, where there is hardly any disagreement among the latter concerning the inspirational message received from the former.

The *xiang-fa* often indicates the period between 500 and 1500 years after the death of Śākyamuni. As the historical distance of the followers of the Buddha to the original transmission of the Dharma increases, the corresponding teachings, praxes, and witness (*kyō-gyō-shō*, 教行証) go through more variations. As a result, they increasingly suffer from fragmentations and deviations. At this Age of Semblance Dharma, the teachings and praxes of Buddhism are said to be well preserved, while the witness of the Dharma significantly declines. In other words, there are the right laws of Buddhism, as well as a great number of those who earnestly follow the laws. However, the number of those who can actually achieve the state of enlightenment becomes null. Even though the natural disposition toward the laws of Buddhism among the people at this age of *xiang-fa* is much more inferior to that among the *zheng-fa*, it is still important to note that the formalized teachings and practices of Buddhism can still benefit for the spiritual ramification of the people.[44] Finally, the *mo-fa* indicates the period of 10,000 years following the *xiang-fa* period. During this period of the history, not only the witness of the truth of Buddhism becomes impossible for the sentient beings but also the proper praxes and the orthodox teachings of the Buddha undergo serious decline. In reference to the outlook of this period, it is believed that no one is capable of attaining one's enlightenment by abiding the Buddhist teachings, and consequently, every human society suffers from the utmost degree of moral degenerations.

The view of history based on the three distinctions of *zheng-fa*, *xiang-fa*, and *mo-fa* (termed as the *shōzōmatsu-no shikan*, 正像末の史観, in Japanese) can be found in various forms in the Mahāyāna tradition.[45] The leading thinker of Shin Buddhism and student of Tanabe, Takeuchi Yoshinori (武内義範) (1913–2002), points out that Shinran alone gives three different versions of the *shōzōmatsu* view of history in reference to *Mahāsaṃnipāta Sutra* and *Mappōtōmyōki* (末法燈明記).[46] Obviously, it is impossible to determine theoretically which version of the threefold view of history is the "correct" one. Even in relation to the works of a single thinker, there are several different versions that are in conflict with each other. I would imagine that my readers would have some difficulty in dealing with these distinctions as anything meaningful for the philosophy of religion. Takeuchi, in this sense, makes some great points in his masterpiece, entitled *Philosophy of Kyōgyōshinshō*:

> Some may think that these are meaningless and dry historical distinctions and representing an insignificant view of history. However, as the third category of the history [i.e., *mo-fa*] shows, this view of history is firstly based on the feelings and the reflections brewed [in the hearts-and-minds of the Buddhist thinkers] in accordance with the facts in the history of Buddhism, and hence, it provides an insight into the very history of Buddhism. Secondly, this view of history conveys the practical intention that directs us from the *mappō* in the present to our freedom (Skr. *mokṣa*, Jp. *gedatsu*, 解脱) in the future.[47]

The significance of the tripartite divisions does not lie in its capacity to provide a theoretical ground for illustrating the proper outline of the world history. Nor does it give any internally coherent system for providing an explanatory description of the ages. Rather, they are the self-critical narratives of the lived history shared among numerous Buddhist thinkers that merely propose an existential ground for expressing their pursuit of freedom from suffering. Takeuchi, for instance, argues that one of the central notions of the Shin Buddhism, namely, the salvation of all sentient beings through the three vows of Amida Buddha (*sangan-tennyū*, 三願転入), can make sense when seen through the notion of the "present" in reference to the *shōzōmatsu* view of history: that is to say, the intermediations of three vows of the Amida Buddha and the threefold view of the history must be internalized and seen as a development of self in the form of self-criticism.[48] This is precisely the reason why "Shinran, on the one hand, judges the world around himself as the impermissibly immoral picture of the age, but, on the other hand, sees the picture as the picture of the self and both repents and mourns over the problems of the age through turning his critique of it into his own self-criticism."[49]

The complex narratives of the threefold history in Mahāyāna Buddhism, therefore, require us to see them as the various forms of self-narratives shared among the Buddhist thinkers and also to understand each of them as representing an internal development of the self from whichever present (in which the self finds itself in relation to the *shōzōmatsu* view of history) toward its freedom in the future. When we see this peculiar view(s) of history in Buddhism and recognize the significance of its internalization in terms of self-development, we can see how this viewpoint is operative in Tanabe's complex response to the *jiriki-shōdōmon* of self-power philosophy. In one respect, Tanabe has clearly lived the most tragic point of contemporary Japanese history, where the optimistic modernization process (that quickly raised the military and economic power of his nation to the level of many other Western nations during Meiji era) led to the blind faith in the superiority of his country over all others in the world. Then, this modernization/Westernization process further paved the way toward the madness of right-wing nationalism, which was no doubt responsible for the greatest crime of the twentieth century, that is, the Fifteen Years War (1931–45). This might seem like a simplistic presentation of the modern history of Japan, but what is really relevant here is the fact that Tanabe felt simultaneously helpless and greatly responsible as a philosopher for the terrible direction in which his nation was heading during these years—the very fact that Tanabe himself confesses in the opening of the *Philosophy as Metanoetics*.

Granted that some of the dialectical arguments provided in the *Logic of Species* in the 1930s convey some dictums that seem to justify the Japanese totalitarianism, it is still remarkable to see how one of the most prolific thinkers from the Kyoto school, who always had something to say about social and philosophical issues through his articles and books, kept silent almost throughout the duration of the Pacific War (1941–45). This specific historical period that constituted Tanabe's "philosophical deadlock" had to be rather depressing and defeating, to the point that he could not help but to realize the powerlessness of his finite existence, as well as to recognize his responsibility for the immorality of thinking along with the self-apotheosis of Japanese imperialism. He not only felt but also thought seriously the truth of the *shōzōmatsu* view of history with every fiber of his existence, especially at the end of the war.[50] Indeed, the historical circumstance had to be compelling for him to cultivate his self-reflective understanding of the historical reality as the *mo-fa*, where philosophy based solely on the autonomy of human reason cannot sufficiently account for its freedom from sufferings and/or its reconciliations with the evildoings of finite humans. The time in which Tanabe lived as a philosopher more than sufficiently allowed him to think that nobody was capable of attaining his or her enlightenment merely by abiding oneself according to the teachings of the Buddha, and moreover, that his society had fallen victim to the utmost degree of its moral degenerations.

The self-reflective nature of the *shōzōmatsu* view of history shows that it does not straightforwardly reject the standpoint of *jiriki hongan* but also recognizes its possibility in a certain historical circumstance (i.e., the *zheng-fa*), where the relative is placed in its unprecedented proximity to, and harmony with, the absolute. Also, the threefold view of history, including one's self-realization of living in the Latter Age of Dharma, is not a theoretical statement made in relation to the linear representation of time. Rather, it always remains subject to the self-narratives of different selves and to various interpretations of history in reference to each given "present." Therefore, each statement that Tanabe makes in relation to the philosophy of self-power should be seen as a kind of his self-narrative made in specific historical circumstance in which he lives and philosophizes. In this sense, the first admiration of self-power philosophy and the second existential reservation toward it are clearly consistent with the ground in which he makes the division between *jiriki hongan* and *tariki hongan*— namely, the *shōzōmatsu* worldview—whereas the third rejection of any possibility of self-power philosophy should be contextualized relative to the profound sense of helplessness that the Japanese philosopher felt as a single individual in his given historical context.

Because the Buddhist view of history in question is always relative to the existential state and the particular surroundings of the single individual who holds that very view, the straightforward rejection of *jiriki hongan* should be always read as a self-criticism of the one who mourns over one's evildoing and suffering as an ordinary and ignorant person (Skt. *prithag-jana*, Jpn. *Bonbu*, 凡夫). This brings us to the second important point that Takeuchi is pointing out through Shinran's diverse interpretations of the *shōzōmatsu* viewpoint: viz., the cycle of the three divisions of the Buddhist history should be internalized in such a way that the self can find a foothold in which it can reorient itself (or let itself open) according to the practical intention of moving toward its freedom beyond its suffering in the present. The structure of this argument, which applies the threefold view of history to the threefold development of self-awareness in Buddhism, comes really close to the notion of selving or the development of the intermediating relationship between mind and being in metaxology. As we have seen in Parts One and Three, Desmond argues that there are a few occasions in life where the immediate unity of mind and being is felt as aesthetic presence, yet their inherent disunity gives rise to different ways in which we can strive to recover the original unity. This development from the immediate unity through disunity to the more concrete unity of difference between mind and being in metaxology explains both the development of the history of philosophy and the development of human's mindful existence (i.e., selving). To wit, metaxology is a clear example of a philosophical system that accounts for both the internalization of the historical development of philosophical thinking and the externalization of philosophical self-knowing as the history of human thinking.

In the same manner, Tanabe acknowledges that there are a few occasions in life where the unity of historical reality and moral ideality can be in perfect harmony with each other and reserves the possibility of the direct embodiment of moral perfection.[51] This acknowledgment alone shows that he would not see the *shōzōmatsu* view as representing the theoretical outline of the universal history that rejects any instances of the absolute-relative unity in terms of self-power in the present. And as Desmond would maintain in relation to the rapturous unity of mind and being, he would also say that the self cannot help but go through the division between itself and other, and hence, it must find an appropriate passage to recover the proper intermediation between itself and what is other to itself. Thus, the double posture toward *jiriki* philosophy can be understood in relation to the subject-relative nature of the *shōzōmatsu* viewpoint, and the second significance of this view (manifested through the process of internalization) indicates that it should be understood in relation to the development of self in philosophy of other-power.

What, then, is metanoetics as the philosophy based on "other-power"? This question brings us back to the second half of the distinction between self-power and other-power, namely the notion of *tariki-hongan* (他力本願). The *tariki-hongan* is often (mis-)used to mean the heteronomy of faith, where one is seen to leave everything up to the heaven and makes no effort whatsoever to match the ideality of moral perfection. However, in the original sense of the term in the Pure Land traditions (and especially in the works of Hōnen and Shinran), this term actually means that Amida Buddha's original vow ultimately saves sentient beings—that is to say, the self-negating self-transcendence of the finite relative to the infinite absolute must be accompanied by the divine kenosis of the compassionate other. What clearly differentiates the common (mis)understanding of the notion of *tariki* and its original configuration in the Pure Land traditions is the fact that the former maintains the rigid opposition between *jiriki* and *tariki*, while the latter construes a paradoxical relationship in which *tariki* denies the ultimacy of *jiriki* and yet, at the same time, sustains its possibility. For this reason, Tanabe maintains that, by means of one's total submission to the consequence of absolute critique, "what is impossible with *jiriki* becomes possible with *tariki*, though both *tariki* and *jiriki* remain complementary to one another."[52]

Naturally, the question is whether or not the compassionate lift of the absolute that comes from outside the finite impedes the self-power of the relative self or compromises in any way self's autonomous movement from the finite relative to the infinite absolute. Put succinctly, how does the complementary relationship between self-power and other-power affect our understanding of human autonomy? Tanabe's answer (once again much in consonance with Shinran) describes the other-power as the transformative power of the divine absolute (i.e., absolute nothingness) that noninsistently enables the self-power of each human to move from the finite to the infinite. Tanabe further articulates this "correlativity" of the absolute and the relative by saying that

> As nothingness, the absolute is absolute mediation and, therefore, permanently correlative to being; it is a circularity of unceasing mediation. The absolute is not an ideal or goal that ultimately sublates the relative; it is, rather, a principle that supports us continually wherever we stand and makes it possible for us to

engage in authentic action. It is not a point that lies forever beyond the reach of our advance, but the very force that moves us here and now. Wherever the relative exists, the absolute is there as its correlative. In the realm of being, nothingness always mediates and is mediated. The absolute coexists with the relative and becomes manifest through its confrontation with the relative.[53]

The other-power of the absolute, in this sense, grants the relative selves (i.e., being) their self-power (i.e., freedom), and each of these selves, in turn, can play its mediatory role of manifesting the absolute other-power *in concreto*. This mediatory concretization of the absolute is possible when the relative self transforms itself or more precisely lets itself to be transformed (through the transformative support of the other-power) into the natural embodiment of the other-power. This is precisely what Tanabe means by the death-and-resurrection of the self or the self-negating process in which each self becomes the "empty being" (*kū-u* 空有) that embodies the ideality of the absolute in relative reality.[54]

This transformation of self from its obsession with its own self-power into the self-power as the realization of the other-power requires that one should give up oneself for the sake of the other and engage in the act of charity with the heart-and-mind of great compassion.[55] This point becomes much clearer as we continue our investigation into the nature of the absolute and its intermadiatory relation with the relative in the following sections. But what is clear at this point is the fact that Tanabe calls for the necessity of recalibrating our understanding of autonomy as something made possible through its relativity to the power that is irreducible to our own self-power. In this sense, the proper formulation for understanding our autonomy should not be the dualistic framework in which the autonomy of reason (*jiriki*) opposes the heteronomy of faith (*tariki*), but the dynamic interrelation in which *tariki* empowers *jiriki*, while *jiriki* is transformed to realize *tariki* in concrete reality. Tanabe, in this manner, maintains that we should properly formulate the nature of human self-power as the *jiriki-soku-tariki* (自力即他力) or self-power-*qua*-other-power.[56]

Absolute nothingness: Self-awareness of Tathāgata or Amida Buddha

The absolute-relative relation beyond the self-power of the relative self, according to Tanabe, does not compromise the autonomy of human reason. To see this point, it is crucial to take into consideration the nature of the absolute in Buddhism and its transformative power as Tathāgata or Amida Buddha. The divine absolute, for Tanabe, is neither a rational postulate nor an ontic object of cognition, nor even the self-determining concept, but it is inspired by the Buddhist notion of nothingness, whose significance has a long lineage in the Eastern intellectual traditions under the term Śūnyatā. In Tanabe's account, this absolute represents an infinite activity of self-negating compassion or the divine kenosis of Amida Buddha that makes itself both transcendent to and immanent in the existence of the finite relatives.[57]

It is extremely difficult to visualize this notion of the absolute, since it refuses to be intellectually grasped as a static concept but represents the dynamic intermediation of itself as nothing and what is other to itself as all things. Hence, this notion has full existential significance for those who claim to understand its meaning as sentient beings. To emphasize the practical implications of the notion, therefore, Tanabe often qualifies this term with other names—for example, the absolute mediation, transformative power, the Great Compassionate Action (*taihigyō*, 大悲行), the act of love, self-negation, self-sacrifice, etc. These qualifications are also made against the standpoint of *jiriki* philosophy, which (Tanabe believes) wrongly claims to reach the standpoint of the infinite absolute merely through contemplative activities of *noesis noeseos*, which fails to capture the dynamic nature and practical implication of the notion of the absolute as absolute nothingness. How, then, do we reach this notion of the absolute that Tanabe sets forth through metanoetic philosophy? The answer lies in the end of the "absolute critique":

> Unlike the philosophies of sages and saints, which presuppose a standpoint of the infinite and the absolute, metanoetics is thoroughly conscious of its finite and relative limits. Since the critique of reason cannot avoid entangling itself in antinomies, and is finally brought by "absolute critique" to its complete undoing, reason has no choice but to let go of itself and acknowledge its own ineffectiveness. But once reason itself … decides to die in the midst of contradiction, the gate to a "middle way" (*chūdō* 中道) that is neither thesis nor antithesis opens up unexpectedly, and one is taken up into transcendent nothingness.[58]

Once the single individual realizes its finitude through its genuine self-criticism, it comes to realize its ground in what is other than itself. The otherness of this foundation as the absolute nothingness is recognized as being transcendent because it is neither identical to nor exhaustibly explicable by any of the relevant metaphysical terms (i.e., the single individual, the particular, and the universal). Rather, "it lies beyond the alternative of 'to be' and 'not to be'"[59] or the relative notions of being and nothing. The ultimate as nothingness, thus, gives the me-ontic ground that exceeds any of the ontic terms. Notice also how the realization of "death" is crucial for this awareness of transcendent nothingness in the interiority of one's existence as the finite individual. Tanabe emphasizes this point by describing the consequence of one's being "taken up into transcendent nothingness" in the following passage:

> Transformed into a mediator of an absolute transformation that supersedes the opposition between life and death, one is brought to faith-witness of the Great Compassionate Action (*taihigyō*, 大悲行) …. This is why we may speak of self-consciousness of the Great-Nay-qua-Great Compassion (*daihi-soku-daihi*, 大非即大悲), or of Nothingness-*qua*-love (*mu-soku-ai*, 無即愛), as the core of metanoetics. Here the self is resurrected from the death it once died of its own decision and is raised up to a new life beyond life and death, or a "life-in-death." The self is restored to a state of "empty being" as a mediator of absolute nothingness. … It is here that the Great Compassion of the absolute, which revives the relative self

by its transcendent power, realizes its quality of absolute mediation: it makes independent relative beings a skillful means (Skr. *upāya*, Jp. *hōben*, 方便) to serve the workings of its own Great Nay, and yet allows them their relative existence as an "other" to serve as mediators of absolute Other-power.[60]

The full awakening to one's finitude, which is to submit oneself to the painful truth that one's existence (i.e., life) must come to an end (i.e., death), leads to one's consciousness of oneself as being given to be by absolute nothingness (i.e., life beyond life and death). In this state of being "made to live its own life" from the perspective of death or the actuality of "living, or being restored to life, as one who is dead," the self comes to experience the renewed sense of "dying life" or "living death" based on the fundamental principle of life beyond life and death.[61] Tanabe argues that this self-consciousness of a finite being as being finite, that is, for each of us to recognize that we are mortal beings, constitutes a "self-consciousness based not on the continued existence of the self but on the passing away of the self"[62] and further elaborates the significance of this self-awareness by saying that

> It is a self-consciousness established in the witness of a self that lives as it dies. Even though the self has been restored to life, this does not mean that life reappears after death to replace it .... The dialectic of death and life consists rather in this, that just as death does not follow life but is already within life itself, so is life restored within death and mediated by it. The point at which the mutual transformation of life and death takes place is not a universal locus where death and life together are subsumed into a relationship of both/and. It is rather in the dynamic of the neither/nor itself, in the very transformation itself.[63]

The absolute nothingness is the absolute dialectic of neither/nor (or the open dialectic that preserves the "middle way" between self and other), since it represents *neither* life *nor* death within the confines of life's becoming and yet possiblizes them without subsuming them into itself in immanence of *both* life *and* death as Hegel's absolute spirit or Nishida's logic of *basho* (*à la* Tanabe) would maintain.[64] This means that the notion of absolute nothingness that appears in Tanabe's mindfulness of his own finitude through his self-reflection on death points him to the true meaning of life: viz., his life along with its self-power is ultimately given to him as his own by the other-power of absolute nothingness. This is precisely the sense in which he says that the relative self, when it submits itself to its finitude and recognizes itself as the dying life, experiences its resurrection through the self-negating fulfillment of absolute nothingness.

This existential awakening to the presence of infinite otherness within the self-consciousness of the finite life wakes the relative self to the truth that this absolute is also immanent in all sentient beings.[65] The transcendent nothingness is immanent because, through its self-negating compassion (*daihi-soku-daihi*), it continuously empties itself to let the finite self be and let the relative self freely determine itself through its own self-power. That is to say, the divine act of great compassion as nothingness never lords over the sentient beings for its self-determining self-affirmation, but always already enables everything to be what it is and "makes room"⁶⁶ for the relative self to freely determine itself.⁶⁷

Even if we understand the significance of discarding the dualistic framework for understanding the proper relationship between *jiriki* and *tariki*, self and other, and finite and infinite, it is still challenging for many of us to eradicate our suspicion that the heteronomous relation between the absolute and the relative in this Buddhist format is still problematic—problematic in the sense that the absolute seems to impede an autonomy of the relative self. To deal with this problem, we must recall our earlier discussions on Desmond's configuration of the "heteroarchic" relationship between the absolute and the relative: that is, the condition for the possibility of the heteronomous relation of the absolute to the relative that becomes a problem for reason's autonomy is always the dualism, where one of these terms can causally determine the other. In other words, we would have to be thinking about the absolute as another determinate self that can causally determine the action of the other self within the ontic realm of sentient beings.⁶⁸ However, the absolute nothingness, by definition, refuses to be conceived as any part or the whole of being.

> Nothingness is always nothing and cannot be that which directly works [on beings] as a being. It always mediates being for its work. Being as a mediator of nothingness takes nothingness as its principle and acts as it is acted on [by the absolute nothingness]. Also, since what makes this [being] act is not a being but nothingness, to be made to act [by the absolute] is [for the relative being] to act for itself. This precisely gives the other-power-*qua*-self-power (*tariki-soku-jiriki*). To be made to work by the other-power of nothingness means freedom in the sense that self is not restricted by any other existence than itself and acts in accordance with its own decisions.⁶⁹

As Tanabe repeatedly argues, a proper understanding of mediation or intermediation of two things cannot give "a relationship in which one party is subordinated to the other, but one in which both enjoy and maintain an independence made possible by the other; and there is no question here of a causal connection that would make one party subordinate to the other as its effect."⁷⁰ It is crucial to keep in mind, therefore, that the proper intermediation of absolute nothingness and self-power of the relative self does not diminish the integrity of the latter in the same sense. But since the other-power as the foundation of self-power refuses to be identified with anything that we can grasp as "being," the self-power of the relative self is fully granted for itself. This means that absolute nothingness can empower the self-power of sentient beings without getting trapped into dualism, precisely because it gives the transcendent ground as transformative power that is inexplicable in any of the determinate/finite terms.⁷¹

In this manner, metanoetic philosophy based on the other-power of nothingness as Tathāgata or Amida Buddha, in consonance with the religious teachings of the Pure Land/Shin Buddhism, preserves a peculiar sense of the divine transcendence that exceeds the realm of sentient beings, and yet, precisely because it exceeds the ontic domain of sentient beings as the meontological absolute, it remains forever at work in the self-power of all beings and the free processes of their continuous efforts toward the unconditioned state of the divine perfection, that is, Nirvana.[72] Thus, the me-ontic picture of the absolute in the works of Tanabe successfully demonstrates the "infinite reserve" of divine nothingness as the transcendent ground of all things, while avoiding the problem of conceiving divine transcendence in its dualistic opposition to the immanence of sentient beings.

The intermediations of the absolute and the relative as the networks of love: *Ōsō-Soku-Gensō* 往相即還相 and *Gensō-Soku-Ōsō* 還相即往相

The self-mediating self-power of the relative self is impossible without the "mysterious" support from the suprarational compassion of absolute nothingness. However, since the absolute claims itself to be nothing and takes nothing away from the freedom of the relative self, the relative self can easily think that it enjoys its integrity of being and self-power without recognizing the presence of the divine mediator in the way of its being. The autonomy of self-power is empowered to be for itself by the other-power; hence, it can mistake itself to be the absolute. Tanabe repeatedly reminds us that this way of self-centered thinking is guilty of "radical evil" against the other-power of absolute nothingness and criticizes various forms of self-power philosophy as committing this crime.[73] For the process of becoming itself, therefore, the relative self must see that the divine absolute selflessly grants it to be and to become conscious of itself as an empowered self-powering being, that is, to become the "empty being" or "being there for the emptiness" (*kū-u*). In order to achieve this true self-awareness of the finite individual as the mediator of absolute nothingness, then, the self must dwell in its inability to fulfill its own desire to determine itself only through its own power and let go of the very self-centered desire to ground its own existence only through itself. This achievement of true self-understanding—or the praxis of no-self—requires the transformation of the self from the self that is incapable of coming to know (and determine) itself through itself alone to the self that opens itself to the other and comes to know (and fully becomes) itself through its intermediation with the other.[74]

Tanabe argues in many occasions that this transformation from the self-determining self to the self-negating self requires an act of metanoesis—that is, a penitent confession of one's selfish tendency to think about oneself through oneself and also an earnest praxis of following the self-negating logic of divine nothingness. To know the presence of divine nothingness in the foundation of one's self-consciousness means that one must existentially engage in the act of true generosity and dedicate oneself to the other by learning to let go of its self-determining desire. To do this, we must go through the conversion from the standpoint of *eros* to that of *agape*.[75] This means that I must dedicate myself to you not for the sake of myself, but for you, and when I succeed in doing so, I will be filled with the overflowing spirit of great-negation-qua-great-compassion (*daihi-soku-daihi*). Only then, I will truly come to realize that I am enabled both to be and to know my autonomous existence through the generosity of what is other to myself. In order to see the essential logic of this self-negating self-transcendence toward the divine absolute, one must "sacrifice one's own self compassionately for the sake of others"[76] and continuously engage in the act of love, for the self-negation of absolute nothingness stands for nothing but love.[77] This practice of "dying" to oneself through the self-negating act of love, therefore, is indispensable for achieving one's self-awareness of absolute nothingness.

There are at least two important points that we can draw from this existential/practical implication of the metanoetic philosophy for the ongoing discussion of the philosophy of religion. The first can be found in the following passage summarizing Tanabe's take on the absolute-relative relation:

> [M]etanoesis seeks throughout to maintain a standpoint of action-faith through Other-power, and thereby to insist on a relationship of reciprocal mediatory transformation between the absolute and the self. The redeeming truth that the absolute can function only as the power of absolute mediation can reach self-consciousness by way of reciprocal mediatory activity between relative selves. In this sense, the transformation through vertical mediation between the absolute and the self must also be realized in horizontal social relationships between my self and other selves.[78]

Tanabe clearly points out in this passage that there has to be a two-way intermediation between the relative self and absolute nothingness. In various places in his later works, he describes this absolute-relative intermediations in terms of the Buddhist notions of *ōsō-ekō* (往相回向) and *gensō-ekō* (還相回向). The *ōsō-ekō* literally means the "going toward the Pure Land from this world" and the *gensō-ekō* the "returning of Amida Buddha from the Pure Land to this world."[79] To make these terms relevant to the general context of the philosophy of religion, however, Tanabe slightly modifies the notion of the *ōsō-ekō* to represent the upward movement of the self to the absolute or the self's ascent from the inferior to the superior, while the *gensō-ekō* indicates the downward movement of the absolute to the relative or the self's descent from the superior to the inferior.[80] What Tanabe is trying to say in this quoted passage is that one's vertical movement from the relative to the absolute (i.e., *ōsō-ekō*) must be accompanied by the *gensō-ekō* of the absolute to the relative, and at the same time, this vertical transformative intermediation(s) of the absolute and the relative is inaccessible unless the relative is practicing the act of generosity and compassion to other relatives by transforming himself within the realm of sentient beings.[81]

Tanabe incorporates these notions of *ōsō-ekō* and *gensō-ekō* into the mediatory relation of the absolute and relative by referring to the *Larger Sutra* and the *Meditation Sutra*.

> The mediatory significance of relative being may be understood in the two senses [in relation to the *Larger Sutra* and the *Meditation Sutra*]. First, the relative has being and significance only as a mediator of the absolute as an *ōsō*. But second, this function is fulfilled in a higher stage of self-consciousness: the vertical relation of *ōsō* must also be mediated by the horizontal relation between relative beings, which is the true import of the *gensō*. In other words, the absolute-relative relationship has

also to be mediated by a relative-relative relationship wherein each relative being fulfills a mediating role in the salvation of other relative beings. This is the concrete form of "returning to" mediated by the activity of the relative. Hence the absolute itself is able to perform its *gensō* function only when it is mediated by the relative.[82]

This *ōsō-gensō* relation shows that the transformation of self-centered self-power to the selfless use of the self-power for the sake of the other (i.e., to become the other-power and to function as the mediator of absolute nothingness) in the network of love is always made effective through the *gensō* movement of the other-power to the relative self; the intermediations of the self-negating relatives are the concrete manifestation of the transformative power of absolute nothingness.[83] The relative *gensō* movements among the finite selves are a kind of *imitatio Dei*, an imitation of the absolute *gensō* movement of Tathāgata as nothingness toward the communities of the finite selves themselves.[84] Thus, Tanabe's metanoetic philosophy of religion clearly demonstrates its attentiveness to the two-way mediations of the divine absolute and the relative selves by understanding their intermediations as the "two-fold dynamic of Amida Buddha,"[85] namely, the *ōsō-qua-genso* (*ōsō-soku-genso*, 往相即還相) or the self-power-as-other-power.

With respect to the absolute-relative intermediations as the *ōsō-qua-genso*, Tanabe emphasizes that there is an essential asymmetry between the *ōsō* movement of the relative to the absolute and the *genso* movement of the absolute to the relative despite their inseparability from each other. This would be the second point that we can draw from the practical implication of the other-power philosophy as *genso* metanoetics. Besides the transcendent status of absolute nothingness in relation to the realm of sentient beings, there are at least three reasons for Tanabe to emphasize the asymmetry between the *ōsō* and the *genso* relationship between the absolute and the relative: (1) the nature of religiosity (*shūkyōsei*, 宗教性) emerges from the nature of the absolute, (2) the "bridge from the relative to the absolute" (i.e., *ōsō-ekō*) cannot be made from the side of the relative, and (3) the essential nature of humanity as the finite relative prevents us from either engaging in the *genso* movements or initiating our act of metanoesis through our self-power alone.

In reference to Kierkegaard's three stages of life's way (i.e., the aesthetic, the ethical, and the religious), Tanabe gives an elaborate argument for demonstrating that the sense of the religious or religiosity originates from the side of the absolute and not from the relative standpoint of human beings.[86] First, he focuses on the self-contradictory nature of ethical reality (in the manner of absolute critique). Here he argues that ethical existence cannot achieve its completion due to the inherent contradiction in the stage of the ethical itself.

> The self as the subject of ethics is in search of the absolute goodness while it is entangled with the fundamental evil that it cannot escape in any way. This means that the self cannot reach what it seeks in ethics. Rather, the more it tries to make its improvement in the realm of the ethical, the clearer its awareness of the fundamental evil [in itself] becomes; and the more it tries to do the best it can in its search of goodness, the deeper its remorse comes to be as it continues to feel the greater regrets.[87]

The inner struggle of the ethical subject results from the inherent contradiction of ethics as an existential enterprise, and the rate of its intensification is directly proportional to the clarity of the awareness of his own finitude. The realization of the finite relativity in self-awareness of the single individual means that the content of moral imperatives assigned to the self gives "the unattainable ideal,"[88] and this split between ideality of ethical law and reality of human existence (Tanabe thinks) leads to the conviction that the origin of ethics does not lie in the "incomplete and finite self, but the highest good (i.e., God) that is both complete and absolute."[89] Here the self's responsibility for the crimes against the ethical exceeds the mere sense of self-responsibility (as Kant would like to maintain in *Groundwork*) but brings forth the sense of the religious rebellion against the divine absolute, namely, sin (*dazai*, 堕罪).

So far, this may sound like a standard model of describing the continuity between ethics and religion that we can find in the works of Kant and Hegel. But the following argument follows the Kierkegaardian tack, which points to the paradoxical relationship of these terms. In the process where one's self-awareness of ethical imperfection turns into one's crime against the absolute, Tanabe detects the origin of human existence beyond the realm of the ethical:

> The sin is no longer the mere self-awareness of the crime, but the rebellion against God: hence, it cannot appear unless God provokes it (*yūhatsu-suru*, 誘発する) from the self. The rebellion does not take place unless the power of the superior (i.e., God) … stimulates the inferior (i.e., humans) and allows it to pride in itself and to take over the power of the superior. The rebellion means that the inferior imitates the superior and brings itself to the level of the superior as the superior allows this rebelling to take place in the inferior. In this sense, [their contradictory relation] cannot be established only with the inferior, but requires the superior's collaborative allowance as the foundation of the rebellion: viz., it takes place where the superior allows the spontaneity of the inferior and puts it in temptation.[90]

The consequence of this realization that the self always falls victim to the antinomies of its existence and recognizing its moral imperfection as a sign of its rebellion against the absolute signals the following paradoxical truth: unless the relative self is given to be free by the absolute, it cannot even begin to rebel against God. There is something infinite in the very finitude of single individuals. The fact that we are morally imperfect, in this manner, comes to point toward the truth that the notions of moral perfection and righteousness do not originate from us, but from the absolute beyond us. In this sense, Tanabe concludes,

> Religions have their ground in the absolute (i.e., God) that enables them and they are not originated from humans. This is the precisely the reason why eastern and western religions claim that faith is something given by God or it is the faith (*shin* 信) granted by Tathāgata. There is no bridge that we can cross from the humans to the absolute. The bridge must be built from the side of the absolute to the humans.[91]

If the sense of the religious is built on this asymmetry of the absolute and the relative in their intermediations, then what can we do as humans in face of the utmost tension constituted by the contradictory relation between ourselves as the relative and God or Tathāgata as the absolute? What sense of religiosity emerges from this (me-)ontological asymmetry resulting from radical evil? Tanabe's answer is this: the finite individual must "throw away its relativity and return to the absolute in obedience."[92] From there, the absolute allows humans to transcend their limitations and "through the self-emptying of the finite individual that strives to die completely to its immediacy and recognize its emptiness before God, his relation to the absolute is turned over, and thereby he is taken up to salvation; and this represents the religious (*shūkyōsei*)."[93] Thus, the sense of religiosity communicated through Tanabe's philosophy of religion is that humans must maintain their self-awareness that they cannot do anything by themselves to accomplish the task of moral perfection. This is precisely what Tanabe means when he says, "Religion is established primarily through self-awareness—awareness of the self as being empty" before the absolute.[94]

The priority of the absolute as the foundation of the two-way mediations between the absolute and the relative is best described with the image of the bridge, where the passage from the relative to the absolute cannot be made only from the side of the relative. To elucidate this point, Tanabe points to the "greatest contradiction" lurking in the foundation of religion, namely, the fact that the "self must free itself from the heart-and-mind of seeking freedom of the very self and desiring its own salvation [through itself alone] because the heart-and-mind that seeks the faith in itself could be the biggest obstacle for the same faith."[95] What is emphasized here is that only when the self can forget itself, empty itself before the absolute, and dedicate itself for the other through the act of love—that is, to engage in the act of nothingness—there is the conversion (metanoesis) of the self from the self-centered use of its self-power to the selfless transformation of it as the mediator of absolute other-power. This *gensō*-mediation of human *ōsō*, Tanabe argues, is "not something that we can achieve only through *jiriki* but only originates from the grace of the absolute."[96]

The contradiction in one's effort to make oneself absolute or to attempt to travel the *ōsō* passage only through self-power is for the self to think that its act of nothingness (i.e., to love the other for the sake of the other) is its own. This contradiction is often condemned as the temptation of the "making of the Buddha" (*sabutsu*, 作仏) by problematically "desiring to become the Buddha who desires nothing." To force one's salvation through the other-power by means of one's own self-power is to commit this religious self-contradiction of *sabutsu*, which amounts to the radical evil of absolutizing the relative self. Tanabe clearly criticizes this attitude of egoity: "The salvation through *sabutsu* is impossible for human beings; for the bridge to absolute cannot be built from the side of the relative."[97] What should we do to restore the proper position of the relative in relation to the absolute? How can we realize that the bridge between the absolute and ourselves as being built from the side of the absolute? Tanabe's answer is in complete harmony with the traditions of the Pure Land Buddhism and Christianity, that is, to engage in the act of prayer. The importance of prayer is to demonstrate one's attentiveness to the status of its own finitude. Through praying or reciting the name of

Amida Buddha, the self can be reminded of the priority of the absolute not only in the midst of exercising the act of nothingness for the other relative selves but also in the midst of its hubris against the absolute.

This brings us to the final point: the act of metanoesis—the very transformation of our self-power into the other-power as the manifestation of absolute nothingness—is also impossible unless the other-power of the absolute is operative in our self-powering existence as the relative self and our interactions with each other.

> [M]etanoesis does not come about merely as a result of self-reflection carried out under self-power. It suffices to ensure conversion and salvation only when the Other-power of the absolute is performing the work of transformation. Metanoesis is not simply a process of human consciousness, not merely an intellectual dynamic within consciousness brought about through the self-power agency of the soul. It is not through a mere idea but through a real power that the soul is converted and turned in a new direction. Accordingly, metanoesis may be termed an inner action determined by Other-power.[98]

The transformation of ourselves through the inner act of metanoesis and the external act of love has to originate from the *gensō-tariki* of absolute nothingness. This is because we are finite individuals. Finite individuals are incapable of engaging in the infinite act of *gensō* to the same degree as the infinite absolute. Nor can we love each other at all times without failing to empty our egoity and dedicate ourselves entirely for the other. Nor can we initiate any of these activities through our own self-power alone. The very self-power that enables us to intermediate with the absolute as the skillful means (*upāya*) and/or tempts us to mistake ourselves for the absolute is ultimately the gift of the great compassion. Thus, the nature of the religious, the intermediating relation of the absolute and the relative, and the absolute *gensō* of nothingness as the foundation of our *ōsō(-qua-gensō)* movement point to the superiority of the absolute to the relative, thereby signaling the priority of the divine *gensō* in relation to the *ōsō* movement of the finite relatives toward the absolute.

The worth of the singular as the singular before the absolute: *Akunin-shōki* (悪人正機) and the salvation of the ordinary and the ignorant (*bonbu*, 凡夫)

The standpoint of metanoetic philosophy based on the other-power of absolute nothingness fully accounts for the singular status of the relative self as the relative self at least in two interrelated ways. First, as we have seen above, *zangedō* constitutes the *tariki* philosophy that abandons the "sacred way of saints and sages" (i.e., *jiriki shōdōmon*), where the relative self is seen to be equipped with a capacity to rise to the level of the absolute only through its own self-power. Tanabe has argued that this one-way passage from the finite relative to the infinite absolute makes it impossible to account for the freedom of finite individuals (since it would have to be ultimately subsumed into the necessity of the divine absolute). On the contrary, the path of the Pure Land (i.e., *tariki jōdomon*, 他力浄土門) requires that the single individual must recognize the finitude of its own existence as the relative self, and in its painful self-awareness that it cannot bring itself to the level of the absolute solely through its own self-power, it comes to find an inner openness to the genuine absolute through the sense of its failure to fulfill the great ethical responsibility, responsibility toward the absolute beyond the ontic realm of sentient beings. The act of metanoesis in confrontation with this sense of religiosity and its openness to the otherness of the divine absolute demand that the self would remain attentive to the singular status of itself and never lose its awareness of its own finitude in relation to the intermediation of itself and absolute nothingness as what is other to itself.

Tanabe has also shown that absolute nothingness is irreducible to any of the immanent terms (i.e., the single individual, the particular, and the universal), and yet, precisely as the compassionate ground of all sentient beings, it enables each of them to be for itself through the self-negating act of great compassion. Thus, Tanabe's absolute, despite its irreducibility to any of the ontic terms, can be manifested through the *gensō* intermediations of one relative self to another—namely, the horizontal interrelations of the finite individuals that constitute the *tariki* networks of love.[99] This self-negating transcendence (or the kenotic descent) of the absolute to each finite singular and the community of the finite relatives is not imposing or causally determining in any domineering way. It does not compromise the self-powering autonomy of relative selves. Rather, since the absolute, out of its self-negating compassion, lets each relative be for itself and "makes room" for the relative to freely determine itself, the freedom of the single individual is seen to be given for itself through the other-power of the divine nothingness. This kenotic interrelation of the absolute to the relative, according to Tanabe, constitutes the absolute dialectic of the single individual, the particular, and the universal (i.e., the logic of species), where the meontic absolute allows the intermediation of each term with the other while preserving their contradictory differences. This open community of the relative selves as the mediatory concretization of the absolute nothingness systematically implicates the consecration of the singular as the singular in its metanoetic mediation of the absolute. The Japanese philosopher makes this point by (a) emphasizing the significance of metanoesis as the intermediation of ethics and religion and also by (b) referring to the notion of *akunin-shōki* (悪人正機)—the notion that an evil person can be saved because he is evil.

First, Tanabe argues that by both recognizing and confessing one's finitude and powerlessness, the relative self as an ethical subject can co-operate with the *gensō* movement of the absolute nothingness—that is, to assist the manifestation of religion through its intermediation with other ethical subjects. In this sense, Tanabe argues, "religion mediates itself to ethics through metanoesis in order to actualize an absolute mediation of absolute-qua-relative."[100] In this intermediation of ethics and religion (or the movement from the breakdown of ethics to its breakthrough to religion), Tanabe sees the significance of the act of metanoesis as a way toward a consecration of a single individual as an individual in relation to the absolute.

It is only through metanoesis that ordinary sentient beings, the finite and relative subjects of ethics, are received into the grace of God or the Buddha and thereby restored to life as coworkers of God or the Buddha, without ceasing to be the ordinary, ignorant persons (*bonbu*) they are. In metanoesis, relative, finite beings forsake their vanity of aspiring to identity with the infinite and the absolute. Conscious of their own finitude and relativity, they abandon their claim to existence through self-power. This enables them to participate in Nirvana without being released from bondage to worldly passions (*bonnō*).[101]

What Tanabe means by the evil person is the ordinary and the ignorant (*bonbu*), whose essential character of being finite and individual prevents him from rising to the level of the infinite absolute only through exercising his autonomy. What enables him to be transformed into the other-power of the absolute is paradoxical in the following sense: First, he must abandon his hope for achieving his ethical perfection through himself and continue to remain attentive to his own finitude and imperfection. Second, in his penitent confession and awareness of his helplessness as the finite individual—or rather, precisely because he is the finite individual—he can find its openness to absolute nothingness as the foundation of its limited existence and be transformed into the mediator of the divine love or the *gensō-ekō* of Tathāgata.

This transformative *ōsō* movement of the single individual from the finite (i.e., the evil status of *bonbu*) to the *gensō* mediatory role of absolute nothingness (i.e., *kū-u*) points to the notion of *akunin-shōki*. Tanabe further elaborates on this idea in the context of the philosophy of religion:

> with respect to the *ōsō*-aspect of religion, every sin of a human being can be the mediator of compassionate grace as it is being sinful, and this does not mean that it becomes a value when he goes through an ethical improvement; but rather, the evil is forgiven as it is being evil [by the absolute] and turned into a cause for participating in the collaboration of divine work, and the evil itself becomes the occasion for [the manifestation of] the absolute value. There is no longer any evil that needs to be improved, nor is there any crime that needs to be removed. This is what it means to say that a human being is saved as he is. In this manner, there must be an aspect of "transcending" both good and evil in a certain sense to religion. The "beyond good and evil" is precisely the characteristics of religion.[102]

The metanoetic transcendence of the self from self-centered egoity to the selfless act of nothingness demands not only that the self must remain attentive to the limitation of its self-power as the finite and the sinful but also that the act of forgiveness transcending the ethical realm of good and evil be exercised between the absolute and the relative and between relative selves. When the single individual recognizes that it is incapable of making the *ōsō* movement or the self-negating metanoesis through itself alone, the absolute can allow the single individual to transcend its limitation and participate in the absolute *gensō* movement of its great other-power. This participation in the self-negating self-transcendence of the absolute to the relative (which shines through the mutual *gensō* mediations of the relative selves) does not deprive the singular status of each relative self that dedicates itself for the other. Nor does this compromise the self-power of the single individual. But because the self-emptying determination of absolute nothingness allows the free determination of each individual and selflessly grounds the communities of individuals prior to their ethical determinations, the absolute can forgive (and has always already forgiven) the single individuals who are constantly tempted to take their given freedom for granted and to regard their autonomy as the unconditioned over against the other-power of absolute nothingness. Regardless of *bonbu*'s commitment to radical evil, this absolute continues to empower selflessly the self-power of the individuals.

The absolute nothingness as the great act of divine love, in this sense, lets the finite sentient being be for itself and always already forgives its iniquity beyond its ethical determinations of good and evil precisely by letting the finite individual be.[103] In the same manner, the single individual is called to practice its self-sacrificial self-transcendence to the other relative self for the other as the coworker and concrete manifestation of absolute nothingness. This means that, in the act of love, forgiveness beyond good and evil is required among the finite individuals and *gensō* communities of such individuals in order to constitute the network of great compassion.[104] The intermediation of the relative and the absolute in Tanabe's formulation, which refers us to the Buddhist notion of *akunin-shōki*, therefore, not only reminds us to remain always attentive to the singular status of the single individual but also demonstrates how the single individual can be accounted for itself as the single individual beyond the universal ideality of its ethical determinations. To see this truth, we are called to practice the act of metanoetic conversion and forgiveness in love.

A concluding remark: Tanabe Hajime and the fundamental problems of the philosophy of religion

We have seen the general outline of Tanabe's later works on the philosophy of religion. In the previous chapter, I explained the intricacy of extracting Tanabe's complex take on the philosophy of religion from his oeuvre. Because of the later standpoint that requires a religious transformation of philosophical perspective(s), an approach to any work of the *Tanabe Zenshū* requires a series of rigorous contextualization or a dynamic interpretation that does not fixate on a single framework of a historical or systematic division, which could methodologically allow us to dismiss some of the important continuities and/or raptures inherent in these works as a whole. In relation to Tanabe's mature works on religion, I have also pointed out the general difficulty (especially for many of the scholars specializing in western philosophy of religion) for treating Buddhism as a religion. A short presentation of Rahula's Theravada introduction to the teachings of the Buddha shows how a straightforward reception of Buddhist teachings will not help us get away with some of the problems that I have extracted from Kierkegaard's critiques of the Kantian and Hegelian theories of religion. The basic precepts of Buddhism, without cultivating some awareness of the historical contexts in which they were developed and received, should remain great enigma to many of the thinkers in the field of the philosophy of religion.

The twofold approach to Tanabe's philosophy of religion in this chapter has demonstrated how his lifelong engagement with the history of (Western) philosophy led him to the renewed standpoint of philosophy based on the Eastern notion of absolute nothingness. The first layer demonstrates both the deconstructive and the reconstructive process of philosophical thinking that moves from the breakdown of its old framework that thinks itself to be based on itself alone to its breakthrough to the renewed sense of philosophy that finds its inherent openness to the otherness of religion. The second layer of Tanabe's philosophical works based on this sense of the religious gives at least four sets of notions derived from Pure Land and Shin Buddhism. This re-entrance to philosophy from the side of religion, contextualized in reference to the *shōzōmatsu* view of Buddhist history, has enabled us to see how Tanabe overcomes the limitation of the Theravada introduction to the teachings of the Buddha and deals with the five fundamental problems of the philosophy of religion. In this concluding section, I will recapitulate these points as Tanabe's short answers to the central questions of this book.

1. *The reduction of the divine-human relation to the immanent universality of human/ societal self-relation*: The Buddhist tradition does not suffer from the dualism of divine transcendence and human immanence in the same way as the history of philosophy based on the Judeo-Christian tradition usually does. As Rahula's introductory account demonstrates, the Buddhist tradition has a strong tendency to conceive of given reality primarily in monistic (or more precisely "nondual") terms. However, as the distinction between *jiriki-hongan* and *tariki-hongan* in reference to the *shōzōmatsu* view of the history demonstrates, the same concern of whether or not the unifying relation of the divine (i.e., Tathāgata) and the nondivine (i.e., sentient beings) can be achieved from the side of the latter has entered into the intellectual discourses among Buddhist thinkers roughly through the rise of the Pure Land/Shin school. The standpoint of *jiriki-hongan* in consonance with the Theravada introduction to the teachings of the Buddha (and some forms of Mahāyāna Buddhism) would maintain that the passage from the nondivine to the divine or from the sentient beings to the state of impermanence (i.e., Nirvana) can be achieved through the self-power of the nondivine or sentient beings.

Tanabe clearly criticizes that this direct unity of the divine and the nondivine from the side of the latter, which he detects in the works of Mystics, Zen, Heidegger, and Nishida along with the rational universalists, is guilty of conflating the divine-human relation with the human self-relation in immanence. Contrary to this notion of *jiriki-hongan* and *jiriki-shōdōmon*, Tanabe proposes the paradoxical path of Other-Power Pure Land (*tariki-jōdomon*) tacitly based on the threefold history of Buddhism. This configuration of the divine-human relation does not straightforwardly reject the standpoint of *jiriki-hongan*. But it enables the metanoetic thinker to realize that the self-negating self-transcendence of the relative self to the divine absolute relies on the *gensō* movement of the absolute. The manifestation of this absolute is achieved through the transformation of self-power into compassionate other-power through self-sacrificial acts of love for the other relative selves. In relation to this continuity between the divine-human relation and the community of humans, Tanabe still reserves their asymmetry, since the possibility of the self-negating self-transcendence of each relative self to the other (whether it is the absolute or the other relative self) is still made possible and sustained through the absolute other-power. Thus, the metanoetic philosophy of religion constantly reminds us not to reduce the divine-human relation based on divine other-power into the self-relation of humanity based solely on our self-power.

2. *The eclipse of divine transcendence*: At the end of the rigorous self-criticism of reason as the absolute critique, metanoetic philosophy presents the notion of nothingness as the divine absolute that is irreducible to the autonomy of human reason or what it calls "philosophy of self-power." Tanabe often identifies this notion with the transformative (other-)power of Tathāgata or Amida Buddha and continuously emphasizes its practical and existential implications as the act of love or of great compassion. Regardless of the different terms under which he describes this notion, Tanabe essentially presents it as the meontological absolute—the absolute, in its otherness to the philosophical language of universal reason, points to the divine infinite that refuses to be grasped merely as a concept or to be explained away as any part or the whole of beings. Because this transcendent ground of all beings is irreducible to any of the ontic terms, and yet, simultaneously represents the act of self-negating compassion in relation to the sentient beings, we can conceive of its constitutive relation to relative selves without constraining this relation to the problematic form of either/or: either the freedom of human self-power is compromised or divine transcendence is reduced to human self-power in immanence. Since the essential nature of the absolute is presented as the self-negating compassion or the Great Compassionate Act of nothingness, we can see the absolute as continuously emptying itself to let the relative self be in order to ground its self-power for the relative self. Thus, in consonance with the tradition of the Pure Land/Shin Buddhism and its faith in the other-power of absolute nothingness, Tanabe preserves a peculiar sense of divine transcendence that both exceeds and remains at work in the free process of all sentient beings' striving toward the unconditioned state of Nirvana.

3. *The extirpation of the single individual in its relation to the rational universal as the immanent absolute*: Unlike the *jiriki* philosophy, which tends to reduce the freedom of a finite individual to the necessity of the divine absolute in immanence, *tariki* philosophy reminds us to remain attentive to the singular status of the finite individual in relation to the irreducible transcendence of the absolute. The path of *tariki* Pure Land, according to Tanabe, demands that a single individual must continuously recognize the finitude of its own existence through an act of metanoesis, and in its self-awareness of unavoidable finitude, the relative self finds in itself its openness to absolute nothingness beyond the ontic realm of sentient beings. Throughout the continuous act of penitent confession, the self must keep in mind that it is essentially incapable of surmounting the absolute status of divine nothingness as the ordinary and the ignorant (i.e., *bonbu*). This point is further emphasized with the notion of *akunin-shōki*, which is most relevant to the fifth problem concerning the worth of the singular, but what is important to note in relation to the notion and praxis of metanoetics is that it points to the inevitable truth of each of our human existence uncompromisingly as a finite individual.

4. *The one-way movement of the self-negating self-transcendence of the finite individual to the infinite absolute*: The self-negating self-transcendence (i.e., *ōsō-ekō*) of the relative self in view of absolute nothingness is always accompanied by the self-negating self-transcendence of the absolute toward the relative (i.e., *gensō-ekō*). Tanabe expresses this two-way mediation of the absolute and the relative always as the *ōsō*-qua-*gensō* and *gensō*-qua-*ōsō*. This understanding of the absolute-relative intermediations, deriving from the notion of *tariki-hongan* in Pure Land Buddhism, indicates that the autonomy of human reason is always already empowered to be for its own self-power by the other-power of absolute nothingness. Tanabe, in this sense, clearly argues that the movement from the relative to the absolute cannot be a one-way movement, whereby the relative self determines itself to be the absolute (which he sees as the central structure of various *jiriki* philosophies), but must adopt the standpoint of intermediation.

The Kyoto school philosopher further emphasizes that this point can be understood through a transformation of a relative self from its obsession with its own self-power to its self-less application of self-power for the sake of the other—thereby transforming itself into a mediator of absolute other-power as an "empty being" (*kū-u*). This means that the truth of the absolute-relative intermediations in the metanoetic framework of thinking can be witnessed by actively constituting open communities of compassionate selves. The intersubjective networks of love, however, by no means exhaust the transcendence of absolute nothingness because the continuous act of metanoesis always reminds us to sustain our self-awareness that our self-power is ultimately given through the other-power of absolute nothingness. This means that the *ōsō*-bridge from the relative to the absolute cannot be built from the side of the relative merely with its self-power, but the divine absolute, which remains irreducible to the intersubjective constitution of such ethical subjects, must solicit every step of their transformative movement of *ōsō* through the act of *gensō*. Hence, the movement of the finite relative to the infinite absolute always provides the intermediation of the absolute and the relative as the *ōsō*-qua-*gensō* and *gensō*-qua-*ōsō*. Thus, the notion of the absolute in the later works of Tanabe essentially represents the divine kenosis of absolute nothingness that always already makes possible the self-negating transcendence of the finite relative to the divine absolute; and the interrelation of the absolute is understood as the two-way mediation of the divine and the human without conflating this relative-absolute relation to the self-relation of relative selves.

5. *The worth of the singular as the singular*: The metanoetic self-awareness of finitude and powerlessness paradoxically leads to the consecration of the finite individual as the finite individual through its inner openness toward absolute nothingness. The *tariki* philosophy, which abandons the standpoint of *jiriki shōdōmon*, best explains this worth of the singular with the Buddhist notion of *akunin-shōki*—the notion that an evil person (i.e., *bonbu*) can be saved precisely because he is (self-aware of his being) the ordinary and the ignorant. Tanabe takes two existential steps to explain the legitimacy of this notion: First, through the act of metanoesis, the finite individual must recognize the finitude of its own existence and its inability to bridge the gap between itself and the infinite absolute as what is other to itself through its self-power alone; and second, in practicing the act of metanoesis, the finite relative not only abandons its impossible

dream of self-identity as the infinite absolute but also finds its openness to the genuine absolute as the foundation of its finite existence prior to its ethical determinations of good or evil. The great compassionate act of the meontic absolute, in this case, is always already empowering the self-power of the finite individual before its ethical determinations to be good or evil and always already allowing the single individual to be (transformed into) the mediator of the *gensō-ekō* of Tathagata without losing its status of being the singular. Thus, the notion of *akunin-shōki* in the path of *tariki* Pure Land (i.e., *tariki-jōdomon*) affirms the worth of the singular for the singular insofar as the singular humbles itself as the ordinary and the ignorant before the inexhaustible compassion of great Amida Buddha.

Thus, Tanabe's metanoetic philosophy, which achieves great insight into some of the key notions in the Mahāyāna Buddhist tradition through rigorous self-criticism, has shown us a way to respond to the fundamental problems of the philosophy of religion. The absolute critique that signals the end of philosophy based solely on the self-power of human reason brings forth the new sense of philosophy based on other-power of absolute nothingness. The reconfiguration of self-power through other-power, as well as the conversion of the self-centered self to the selfless self, beyond the breakdown of self-power, points us toward the metanoetic openness to the Buddhist sense of the absolute beyond the confines of rational universalism. Just as Desmond is capable of recuperating the sense of religion as being irreducible to philosophy from the side of the Western intellectual tradition, Tanabe maintains the open mediation between philosophy and religion through his attentiveness to both the Eastern and the Western intellectual traditions.

Conclusion

We have carried out an extensive examination of two contemporary forms of philosophical thought on the divine absolute, the relative self, and their relation to each other. As an overture, I have undertaken a series of methodological reflections that justify the way in which this book has approached prominent works of Tanabe Hajime and William Desmond. This book has elucidated the central questions of what I take their work to be about, namely, the philosophical significance of religious faith, through my critical engagement with the Kantian and the Hegelian texts on the philosophy of religion. Some patient readers, who have carefully followed my arguments, should be able to notice that my reflections on these issues in relation to metaxology and metanoetics have been conducted with a great deal of attentiveness to the method(s) of philosophizing at work in the two thinkers. In some ways, my exposition of their ideas, originating from different intellectual traditions, is my "active receptions" of their insight. I have made an effort to provide the space in which each of these philosophical systems can speak for itself and clarified the notions that could help us formulate the proper interrelation of philosophy and religion beyond the limits of rational universalism. Since my comparative examinations of Tanabe and Desmond have been conducted with agapeic and metanoetic mindfulness, we can say that the methodological approach adopted in this text is essentially in accord with the underling metaphysical assumptions inherent in the way of both *metaxu* and *zange*.

Some readers may still wonder if my receptions or noninvasive articulations of metaxological and metanoetic thinking have satisfactorily voiced my own answers to the problems that we have found in the Kantian and the Hegelian philosophy. No matter how active these articulations or receptions might sound, it still seems that I lack my own thought on the questions. It may be so. I do have to confess that I do not yet have any systematic framework of thinking that I can call "my own"; nor do I know how to articulate my original responses to the questions of religion in my own terms. However, no man begins his life as a giant. As these contemporary thinkers themselves had to develop their own thought on philosophy and religion through their intense reflections on the works of their intellectual forefathers, I do have to do the same in relation to their works.

What I can offer as a passage to go beyond the confines of the metaxological or the metanoetic framework of thinking, moreover, is not to come up with my own technical terms to describe my solutions to the problems at hand, but to amplify their astonishing consonance unexamined hitherto. Given that these contemporary thinkers can guide us to respond to the fundamental problems of the philosophy of religion and that they both successfully recuperate the sense of the religious, as that which is irreducible to the bounds of philosophical reasoning, their basic agreements can show us the general outline of the possibility for a renewed sense of philosophy that shows its fidelity to the proper sense of the divine absolute. In other words, to talk about the incredible harmony between the two philosophical standpoints that we have seen in the works of the Japanese and the Irish thinkers here can propose a viable option to those who find themselves asking the twofold question of philosophy, either from the Western or the Eastern tradition or both. In this concluding chapter, I would like to illuminate the profound convergences between metaxology and metanoetics in the general context of the philosophy of religion and discuss the significance of these profound agreements as a way to voice my answers from the shoulders of the giants— answers to the philosophical questions of religious faith(s).

The divine transcendence and its intimacy to the finite relatives

In order to recuperate the sense of the religious as being irreducible to the sense of the philosophical, and to account for their open communication with each other, it is necessary to reserve some kind of transcendence in the notion of the absolute. Yet, as the rational universalists have rightly recognized, a dualistic presentation of the absolute over against the relative inevitably leads to a series of the problems that could compromise the significance of human autonomy and ultimately undermine the significance of philosophical thinking. In face of this dilemma between divine transcendence and human immanence (or religion and philosophy), both metaxology and metanoetics preserve some sense of divine transcendence, while taking into account its intimate relativity to the self- and intermediations of the human.

Desmond describes this transcendence of the divine absolute as the overdeterminate origin of all things and shows that its relation to the self- and intermediations of human individuals is the heteroarchic relation of the agapeic origin to relative selves. Tanabe derives his notion of the absolute from the Mahāyāna tradition, which he calls "absolute nothingness," referring to it as the infinite activity of absolute mediation that empowers the self-power of all sentient beings. His understanding of this absolute in his later works is laid out mostly in reference to the religious notion of Tathāgata or Amida Buddha and further solidifies the significance of this notion in reference to the idea of God in the Judeo-Christian tradition. When he discusses the *gensō*-movement of the absolute to the relative as the divine kenosis of agapeic love or the great compassionate act (i.e., *daihigyō*, 大悲行), he clearly suggests that his notion of the absolute is applicable both to the Mahāyāna Buddhist and Judeo-Christian traditions.

At times, Desmond seems to be much more clearly setting forth the robust sense of divine transcendence (T^3) as the hyperbolic origin of all things (especially when he calls it "agapeic transcendence"). It is undeniable that he shows it to be the ontological condition for the possibility of all determinate/determining processes of human becoming or knowing and also that this condition is neither identical nor reducible to any part or the whole of these processes. Tanabe occasionally uses the term "transcendence" to describe the nature of absolute nothingness, but precisely because this notion, by definition, refuses to be equated with any ontic terms, he acknowledges that it cannot be exhaustibly explained away by reference to finite objects or determinate/determining processes of their self-becoming in immanence, regardless of the fact that the former can only be manifested through the latter. This is one of the advantages that he has when describing the notion of the absolute as "nothingness," and Desmond, too, recognizes the effectiveness of calling the absolute "nothing" or the "fertile void." These thinkers equally strive to remain faithful to the sense of the religious as they reflect on the nature of the absolute as divine transcendence. They each illuminate this notion as both infinitely exceeding and intimately grounding the self- and intermediations of the relative selves in immanence.

The absolute as love beyond heteronomy or instrumentalization

What is remarkable in comparing these two thinkers' reflections on the ultimate is their agreement on two important points: (1) the divine absolute is conceived as selfless compassion or agapeic love; and (2) the absolute-relative relation does not fall victim to the problematic notions of heteronomy or dialectical instrumentalization that we saw respectively in the works of Kant and Hegel. These two points of convergence particularly highlight the fact that Desmond and Tanabe recognize the danger of defining the notion of the absolute as divine transcendence; and what they aim at achieving through these points is to show that their notions of the divine absolute do not threaten the freedom of finite relatives in immanence. Rather, they demonstrate that our proper reflections on the nature of the absolute and of the single individual can reveal that the former grounds the true significance of the latter, while our realization of this proper relationship between the absolute and the relative can free us from the dualistic formulation of the relationship between divine transcendence and human immanence, which have chained us to the abovementioned dilemma in the works of Kant and Hegel.

We have seen that Kant conceives of the absolute as the practical postulate and fails to account for the constitutive relation of the absolute and the relative. Hegel's mind is much more attuned to their mutual implications, and yet, as Kierkegaard rightly criticizes, the notion of the absolute in Hegel's dialectic is conflated with the self-determination of (human) reason as the immanent absolute; hence, Hegel's understanding of their mutuality is one-sided. Kant and Hegel have clearly presented different ideas of the absolute. Nonetheless, they both equally avoid attributing "transcendence" to their notions, precisely because they thought that the introduction of the robust sense of divine transcendence, which, I think (in accord with Kierkegaard and two contemporary metaphysicians) is indispensable for grounding the authority of religion as something irreducible to that of ethics or philosophy, ends up compromising human autonomy.

Additionally, Hegel's formulation of the divine-human relation, regardless of the fact that the immanent absolute seems to be limited to a human self-determining self-relation, poses a problematic "intermediation" of divinity and humanity, that is, the self-determination of absolute spirit. Hegel's god ultimately needs the finite particular as its self-particularized moment as a means for determining itself to be the absolute *in concreto*. The dialectical logic of Hegel, in this sense, risks the divine instrumentalization of finite humans. If we are to grant that there is a constitutive relation between divinity and humanity beyond the self-determination of humanity and that divinity grants the freedom of humanity for determining itself to be the absolute, then we find it extremely difficult to acknowledge that Hegel offers a meaningful notion of freedom.

Pace Hegel, Desmond and Tanabe recognize that there needs to be a porous relativity between the divine absolute and the human relative. *Contra* Hegel, however, they have emphasized that the absolute cannot be the "erotic absolute," which grants existence and freedom to the finite relative ultimately as a means for itself to become the infinite absolute, but rather the "agapeic servant" who empties itself and brings itself to nothing so that everything is given to the finite for the finite. We have seen this understanding of the divine absolute in the literary examples and religious images through our examination of metaxology in the periphery of philosophical thinking. The same idea is also essential to Tanabe's presentation of absolute nothingness as the great-negation-qua-great-compassion (*daihi-soku-daihi*, 大非即大悲) or nothingness-qua-love (*mu-soku-ai*, 無即愛). If the absolute is understood to be the act of giving existence and freedom to the finite relative and this divine gift is given in the manner of self-negating, self-sacrificial love, as these contemporary thinkers maintain, then we would have to conceive of the absolute-relative relation as the heteroarchic relation or the metanoetic intermediation, where the absolute constitutively grounds the existence and freedom of relative selves not for itself, but for the relatives in immanence. Since the absolute "releases" each of the finite beings to be for itself and to be with the other as the community of such free subjects, the between or the "inter" of the absolute-relative intermediation is always kept open. Hence, the freedom of the relative is always preserved for itself. In this sense, the absolute-relative bridge, always built from the side of the absolute, is the token of divine love or boundless hospitality that maintains this open communication between the divine absolute and the human relatives. We are always already (invited to be) crossing and criss-crossing this bridge as we receive our own existence and freedom, even before coming to know the truth and the worth of these gifts.

We have also seen that the metaxological and the metanoetic interrelation of the absolute and the relative pay closer attention to the significance of divine transcendence, and because of this, they are capable of avoiding the problems that we have diagnosed in the works of Kant and Hegel. In reference to Kant's passages, where he confesses his difficulty in conceiving the possibility of "created freedom," I have shown through the example of the seafarers that Kant must be thinking about the relation of the creator and the created in terms of causal relation—the relation applicable only to the objects in the phenomenal realm. In this case, the absolute is erroneously conceived to be another determinate finite that can compromise the autonomy of the human individual (as the empirical character). Contrariwise, Desmond and Tanabe maintain that the divine absolute, if it is the overdeterminate origin or absolute nothingness, should not be conceived as another determinate finite standing over against the relative other. But since the absolute as the overdeterminate origin or nothingness cannot be reduced to any of the self- and intermediating processes of becoming in immanence, its constitutive relation to the free act of the finite relative must be conceived beyond the entire nexus of efficient causes. Since their absolute represents agapeic love or self-negating compassion, the absolute-relative relation cannot impose a dictatorial sublation of finite freedom for the infinite totality of the human/societal self-relation. These thinkers continuously communicate the sense of the absolute as intimate transcendence that enables the self- and intermediations of the finite relatives by giving them the space (i.e., the between or the middle way [*chūdō* 中道]) to exercise their freedom for themselves.

On the significance of the singular as the singular

The singular status of finite existence plays an enormously important role in Desmond's and Tanabe's reflections on the nature of the absolute, precisely because the proper understanding of ourselves as single individuals leads to the proper understanding of the absolute as the ultimate ground of our (given) existence. Kant has difficulty in conceiving the inherent ontological value in the sensible particularity, while Hegel, too, sees in it mere indeterminacy that needs to be overcome by the self-determining universal. Metaxology, however, recognizes the idiocy of the singular, namely, an ontological surplus in the singular that resists its complete subordination to the determinate knowing of the rational universal. But rather, it communicates intimate signs of the divine transcendence in immanence. The flipside of this argument is that we can recognize the overdeterminate absolute only through the intense reflections on the inner depth of the finite singular. By thinking about the singular as the singular (i.e., an irreducible *this*), we find the passage to the divine origin from which its incontrovertible oneness is derived.

Tanabe's metanoesis and the notion of *akunin-shōki* also point in the same direction. The Japanese philosopher reflects on the nature of the relative self as the finite individual in the given historical context and recognizes its inherent incapacity to intermediate the gap between itself and what is other to itself through its reason or self-power alone. This breakdown of reason's confidence in its ability to comprehend itself (and its relation to what is other to itself) through its self-power alone is the unavoidable consequence of the radical self-criticism (i.e., absolute critique). Yet this breakdown of reason's confidence in its absolute self-power does not leave us in despair or end with some kind of radical skepticism of reason shared among many postmodern thinkers. The self's profound awareness of its own finitude leads to penitent confessions of its egoity; that is to say, the self repents its tendency to regard itself as the determiner of its continuity with what is other to itself and to (mis-)take itself to be the infinite absolute.[1] In this process of submitting the self to the inevitable consequence of absolute critique, the relative self reaches the state of enlightenment, where she or he recognizes its own true state as being the finite relative. In this case, the self recovers its genuine relativity to the ultimate ground of its existence and discovers the foundation of its self-power in the other-power of the absolute as absolute nothingness beyond itself. Just as the idiocy of the singular in metaxology breaks down the confidence of reason in its radical autonomy and releases the self and its reason to the genuine absolute from itself as the counterfeit absolute in immanence, the absolute critique of reason in metanoetics achieves a similar "breakthrough" to the renewed sense of philosophical reason, which maintains its openness to the divine absolute beyond the ontic realm of sentient beings.[2]

This transformative transition (*tenkan*) of reason from its self-centered absolutization of itself (i.e., egoity) to the self-less act of nothingness beyond itself (i.e., *meta-noesis* or no-self) has also led us to the consecration of the finite individual as the individual. The metanoetic conversion of the self not only demands that the self would remain attentive to the limit of its self-power but also implies that the act of forgiveness transcending the ethical realm of good and evil be exercised between the absolute and the relative, as well as among the relative selves. Given that the relative self cannot make the *ōsō*-movement or the act of metanoesis through itself alone, the self must recognize that only the absolute can allow the self to transcend itself and participate in the *gensō*-movement of great other-power through its act of compassion. This means that the kenotic movement of the absolute to the relative allows each finite being to be for itself and always already forgives its iniquity beyond its ethical determinations of good and evil precisely by enabling it to be and to be free.[3] This religious consent to the ontological worth of the singular as the singular beyond its ethical determination of good and evil is practiced both in the metanoetic and metaxological lines of thinking.

The (net-)works of love as the religious communities of the finite relatives and the divine absolute

The metanoetic and the metaxological configuration of the absolute, the relative self, and their interrelations call for our existential and practical applications of these notions as the "(net)works of love." This establishment of the religious community is a concrete manifestation of our intellectual fidelity to the notion of the divine absolute, which signals a fulfillment of the promise of our freedom as a hyperbolic gift.

Metaxology accounts for the givenness of human autonomy in reference to the communicative relation of the divine absolute and the single individual(s). Desmond has shown that we are called not only to cultivate our agapeic mindfulness (as a kind of hyperbolic knowing as an image of divine over-knowing) but also to exercise our agapeic transcendence in terms of human self- and intermediations. Since the absolute gives each single individual as a concretion of its communicative power of being, the single individual carries within itself the same communicative openness to the other single individuals. Then, what kind of communicative openness is this? How should we exercise our intermediations with each other such that we most concretely realize this openness? As the agapeic origin gives itself over to nothing and gives everything to the finite for the finite, Desmond has argued, each of us must practice the nonpossessive dispensation of the good for the other. The Irish philosopher calls this interrelations of humans in reference to the divine absolute "community of agapeic service," and in this community, we exhibit our utmost fidelity to our communicative relation to the agapeic absolute (as the origin of our free self-becoming). In this case, our humble acts of love in our intermediations in immanence mark our transfinite transcendence toward the absolute beyond ourselves.

Metanoetics sets forth the same outlook on the intersubjective communities of the relative selves as the coworkers of absolute nothingness (i.e., empty being or *kū-u*). This point is particularly clear when we focus on the two-way mediation between absolute nothingness and the relative self as the *ōsō*-qua-*gensō* and *gensō*-qua-*ōsō*. In order for the self to achieve its true self-awareness as the mediator of absolute nothingness, Tanabe argues, the self must dwell in its inability to fulfill its desire to determine itself only through its own self-power and give up the very self-centered desire to ground its existence only through itself. This praxis of no-self comprises the conversion of the self from the self-determining self that loses sight of itself to the selfless self that can open itself to the other and come to know (and fully become) itself through its intermediation with the other. This transformation of the relative self, according to the Kyoto school philosopher, requires an act of metanoesis, that is, a penitent confession of one's selfish tendency to think about oneself through oneself, as well as an earnest praxis of following the self-negating logic of divine nothingness through constant act of love.

To know the presence of the divine absolute in the deepest foundation of one's existence means, therefore, that one must existentially engage in the act of true generosity and learn to let go of one's self-determining desire. Desmond has shown that in order to think metaxologically about the ultimate and one's proper relation to it, one must cultivate agapeic mindfulness and thereby engage in the act of agapeic transcendence. That is what it means for us to think and live beyond the confines of self-thinking thought. Through this existential transformation, we will be able to find the absolute beyond ourselves. In tune with the language of Pure Land/Shin Buddhism, Tanabe echoes this point by saying that one's movement of *ōsō-ekō* from the relative to the absolute must be accompanied by the *gensō-ekō* of the absolute to the relative, and at the same time, the vertical transformative intermediation(s) of the absolute and the relative must give the relatives that are practicing the acts of generosity and compassion to each other. Only when we act in manner of *gensō* toward each other can we have the feeling for the *gensō*-movement of the infinite absolute toward the finite relative in our own self-awareness. Thus, as both Desmond and Tanabe have argued, we must existentially engage in the transformation of our desire from the standpoint of *eros* to that of *agape*, and this calls for the constitution of our religious community in reference to the divine absolute through acts of generosity and compassion. In this network of love, the self can truly come to see its own face as the finite relative and find the light of the divine absolute as the agapeic origin of all beings.

Beyond the harmonious finale to the new overture in the philosophy of religion

The basic harmony between metaxology and metanoetics signifies something of the greatest importance in the contemporary field of (comparative) philosophy of religion. These philosophical standpoints not only draw their inspiration from different intellectual traditions but also propose their central ideas in very different technical terms. But they both provide ways in which we can move beyond the confines of rational universalism, which helps us to respond to the fundamental problems of the philosophy of religion. Desmond has called this the "agapeic mindfulness" that constitutes the intimate universality of divine transcendence in immanence, while Tanabe advocated "a philosophy that is not a philosophy." If, however, we focus our attention to the ways in which their views resonate, I think that these renewed senses of philosophy provide theories of religion that demand this much, at least; namely, it does not matter whether or not we start from the Eastern and/or the Western intellectual tradition in order to unfold the philosophical significance of religious faith, along with the open communication of philosophy and religion, the point is that we must examine the state of ourselves as a single individual. These contemporary philosophers have demonstrated through self-reflection that the finite singular resists subordination to the rationalistic universal. This reconsideration of the singular *as* the singular breaks down our prior confidence of reason in its universal as the immanent absolute. This means that we must also reconsider the possibility of the divine absolute beyond the rational universal and subsequently its relation to ourselves as the singular in immanence.

Metaxological and metanoetic metaphysics both essentially assert that reconfiguring the notion of the single individual is the key to unlock the door beyond consideration of ourselves in mere egoity to thereby aim toward the absolute. At the outset, they do look like contradicting positions that compete with regard to the ways in which to reach the absolute. The metaxological shows that the ontological plentitude of "to be" in the singular as an incontrovertible *this* points us to the agapeic origin that grounds the communivocity of mind and being—the profound togetherness from which the ontological surplus of the singular is derived. The metanoetic focuses on the extreme poverty of the relative self in its isolation. That is to say, the self can neither mitigate the gap between itself and other nor even complete its own self-examination through its own self-power alone. Notice, however, how they are getting at the same thing: namely, the inadequacy of the rationalistic universal for comprehending the whole nature of the singular or grasping the undeniable orientation of the singular toward the absolute beyond such a contracted notion of the universal. This double-directionality in our philosophical reflection on the singular has something to do with the paradoxical nature of the single individual in relation to the absolute. Ontologically speaking, the finite individual is both rich and poor: It is rich because its worth and existence as the singular is ultimately derived from the inexhaustible wealth of the absolute and poor because it cannot ground its worth and existence through itself alone. The inexhaustible richness of the self in its openness to the otherness of the absolute is consistent with the powerlessness of the self in its self-enclosed insistence on its self-power. These two modes of "being human" (*ningende arukoto*, 人間であること) indicate the importance of practicing the radical self-criticism through which we can break down the wrong-headed confidence that we have in ourselves as the sole foundation of our own existence. It also shows the fact that, in the face of our own impoverishment, we can come to make a breakthrough to the renewed sense of our "selves," a move that finds our relativity to the inexhaustible source of our existence and self-power beyond ourselves. Again, Desmond explicitly names this reason's fidelity to its foundational openness to the divine absolute as the "intimate universal," while Tanabe existentially strives to establish it as the metanoetics.

Through such intense self-reflections and renewed sense of philosophical thinking, what we will encounter as the sense of absolute can neither be a projection of our minds nor the self-apotheosis of human self-power as the immanent absolute, nor even the god that subordinates the finite relatives for its own self-determining self-affirmation as the infinite absolute. Rather, as metaxology and metanoetics have communicated in dialogue with the Judeo-Christian and Mahāyāna traditions, it must represent the notion of *agape* or the act of great compassion; it gives the picture of the divine as unconditional love, as the selfless act that brings itself to nothing so that the finite other as its beloved would have everything for itself. This agapeic release of the finite relative for the finite is indispensable; it allows us to conceive of the absolute as divine transcendence without contracting our understanding to the dualistic framework of thinking. The notion of the divine, in this case, must be conceived of as the intimate transcendence that enables the finite relatives to be and to be for themselves in immanence. Only in this sense of the absolute as unconditional love or great compassion can we understand its irreducibility to the realm of the finite without losing sight of it as the enabling ground of all things.

What can we do in the present age of "godlessness" or *Mo-fa*?

What calls for our philosophical thinking on religious faith in reference to the works of Tanabe and Desmond? What does this renewed sense of philosophy in its open relation to religion asks us to do in the present age of "Godlessness" or the Latter Age of Dharma? It is the practice of self-negating compassion and self-sacrificial love as a kind of *imitatio Dei*. The very philosophical notion of the divine absolute that allows us to respond to the fundamental problems of the philosophy of religion requires a transformation of our desire, which begins in the self-centered self and moves toward the selfless dedication of itself to other selves. This means that without our active intermediations with each other through acts of generosity and compassion, it is unlikely that we will recognize our communicative relation to the absolute in the foundation of our existence, let alone, coming to realize that our existence and our intermediations with each other are at all possible because of the communicative relation of the infinite absolute to ourselves as being finite relatives.

It is not difficult to imagine how impossible it would be for us to acknowledge the agapeic release of the finite for the finite by the absolute unless we pay close attention to the agapeic release of the finite for the finite among ourselves as the finite relatives. Notice how any part of our self-becoming is impossible unless there is some relativity involved in the self-negating compassion of other selves. No one brings oneself to this world through oneself, but all depend on those who can take good care of us. Unless there is someone like the priest from *Les Miserable* or the young girl from *The Poor People*, the chance of our coming-of-age is very slim. Remember this: even Thrasymachus had to blush when he realized that his outrageously self-centered doctrine of "might makes right" requires the generous audience that let him speak for himself. Without our continuous attentiveness to the transfinite signs of agapeic love in immanence and active involvement with such transrational embodiment of divine generosity, we will never come to know the most generous absolute in the foundation of our existence.

Last, the path to the glory of the absolute and our genuine self-knowledge in relation to it always lies in details. Of course, they are not the scholarly details that could result in *commentaria ad nauseam*, but the ontological details hidden in the details ordinary of our everyday lives. I certainly do not deny that the long hours (if not years) of reading *God and the Between* or *Philosophy as Metanoetics* can help us gain some insight into the twofold question of philosophy. This is indeed what I have tried to accomplish in this monograph. Nevertheless, both Desmond and Tanabe praise the ordinary and the ignorant (and sometimes even the bad and the ugly) as transmitting something of the utmost importance in the philosophy of religion. We have seen that the "ray of sunshine" can communicate the mystery of divinity and creation to Plato, Dostoyevsky, Solzhenitsyn, and Desmond. The other-power path (*tariki-jōdomon*, 他力浄土門) of the Pure Land Buddhism is about the salvation of the ordinary and the ignorant (*bonbu*, 凡夫). Many Buddhist thinkers (including Tanabe) have recognized this movement from the relative to the absolute as the constitution of historical reality with a simple image of a pompon dahlia. The flower blooming in the midst of muddy swamp symbolizes our embodiment of divine perfection, despite the basic condition of our life as the ordinary finite.[4] It is this kind of attentiveness to the details of our daily lives that can save us from our insane self-obsession as self-thinking thought. Sometimes, our salvation from the self-inflicted sufferings of egoity is, too, lying in front of us in our everyday lives. Philosophers of religion should not shy away from writing the poetry of these details, since, as we saw in relation to metaxology, we often find a surprising solicitation of the divine absolute in the periphery of philosophical language.

The act of great compassion or the agapeic dedication of the self for the other that we have examined through literary and religious images does not only remind us that we are always already the participants of the networks of love but also demonstrates that it does not take much effort of reasoning to achieve this end. In fact, too much talk about love might prevent us from doing the actual act of dedicating ourselves to the other. This is another important point about the ordinary. To love one another and to act for each other in love is something that anyone can do (with as little as a penny according to the Bible), and no academic degree or license is necessary for living in accordance with such religious significance. If the ultimate is the agapeic absolute, and genuine knowledge of this truth requires us to go beyond the *noesis* of the human mind—as I maintain in line with Desmond and Tanabe—then the task of the philosophy of religion should never exhaust itself with the textual analyses of scholarly books. Nor should we be obsessed only with the publications of "scientific" articles. But our task of asking the twofold question of philosophy and striving to give an answer to it should extend to the actual living of the life with agapeic mindfulness and making the agapeic transcendence of the self to the other without the sly qualification of "self-return." In this act of the ordinary and ignorant self for another ordinary and ignorant through the metanoetic transformation of the self, we will find the most extraordinary attunement of the self to the true notion of the absolute.

To be truthful to what we have found in the answers to the fundamental questions of the philosophy of religion through metaxology and metanoetics, therefore, we have to remind ourselves the following as to where this book closes with its answers to the questions of religion: we will only find the commencement to the actual life in which our philosophical convictions on the notions of the absolute, the relative self, and their relation to each other will have to be tested. As Dostoyevsky tells us through *The Brothers Karamazov*, it is one thing to talk about the idea of love and another to love a single individual.[5] We must go back to the world of our everyday lives and that is exactly where we have the choice to be or not to be an agapeic servant. We can choose to be full of ourselves and face our spiritual bankruptcy or seek to find our true self-fulfillment through becoming an empty being. Either way, we have to go back to the world and find what we are made of. One thing is clear: without our *gensō*-movement to the ordinary as the ordinary with the sacred heart of agapeic emptiness, all that I have written as our reason's fidelity to the divine absolute will signify much less than straw. What we hear is the call for our performance in the worldstage of our life's way and what I will prove as the single individual goes beyond what I can provide with a single text on the comparative philosophy of religion. Thus, the end of this text is only the beginning of the lifelong answer to the twofold question of philosophy.

Notes

Acknowledgments

1 Rebecca Solnit, *Wanderlust: A History of Walking* (London: Granta, 2014).

Introduction

1 Augustine, *The Soliloquies*, trans. John H.S. Burleigh (Philadelphia, PA: The Westminster Press, 1953), 26.
2 Augustine, *On Order (De ordine)*, trans. Silvano Borruso (South Bend, Indiana: St. Augustine's Press, 2007), 2.18.47.
3 If some readers find themselves less concerned with the questions raised in the preamble, I would advise them to jump straight to the main philosophical issue further described in section "The Main Philosophical Question."
4 By Western canon of philosophy, I mean what is usually taught as the history of philosophy at any philosophy department across Europe, North America, and Asia. The dominant model of an academic program in philosophy consists of teaching the history of Western thought as the only way of philosophizing. For this reason, if a philosophy department looks for a specialist in comparative philosophy (which happens quite often these days), a candidate who can compare two intellectual traditions or multiple thinkers from two different cultural milieus in the West would be usually disqualified. More detailed discussions on this issue are given in Chapter 1.
5 Perhaps we do not have to go out of academia to see this point. Consider, for instance, the discipline of history. No history department in the field of academia would claim that its curriculum covers the entire history of humanity when it, in fact, covers the history of Western civilization alone. It seems to be a matter of simple logic that no philosophy department should be able to claim that its curriculum covers the entire history of philosophy when it only covers the history of Western thought. But somehow many of us as philosophy scholars seem to have a shared habit of ignoring the force of this logic both in the East and in the West.
6 A Sinologist, Nicolas Standaert, points out an interesting fact that the field of Sinology as one of these area-studies is facing the same methodological challenge. The general contention against the discipline of Chinese studies lies in the fact that their notion of area-study, regardless of the fact that their scholars do cultivate their "profound knowledge of the Chinese language, culture, and history in all its diversity necessary to understand China," seems to lack a specific methodology that we can find, for instance, in the disciplines of history, sociology, anthropology, etc. This problem seems to be much wider than the methodological problem of comparative philosophy that we are dealing with here. What interests us the most in Standaert's account,

however, is the following two points: First, he argues for the significance of practicing (new) Sinology as the art of "in-betweenness"—a finessed mode of thinking or a kind of intellectual dance that pays special attention to the ambivalent, and yet both (re-)formative and dynamic, interrelations between various academic disciplines in the process of cultivating one's insight into the truth of the Chinese world. Second, Standaert draws the philosophical ground of this art of "speaking the word(s) of the between—wording the between" from Desmond's metaxology. I will refer to this second point again in Chapters 1, 5, and 6. For these points, see Nicolas Standaert, "Don't Mind the Gap: Sinology as an Art of In-Betweenness," *Philosophy Compass* 10 (2015): 95, 97–99. Desmond's phrase that Standaert quotes in his argument is from *BBCIT*, 11.

7   Cf. Katrin Froese, *Nietzsche, Heidegger and Daoist Thought: Crossing Paths In-Between* (Albany, NY: State University of New York Press, 2006), 6. Froese argues that this signifies philosophical chauvinism but can also be attributed to our general emphasis on specialization in the field of philosophy in Western academia. I am not sure if we can dismiss all contemporary works on Western philosophy in the West that are demonstrating no openness to the non-Western intellectual traditions as exclusively the signs of our academic chauvinism. But I cannot agree more with her point that comparative philosophy in principle requires a dialogical thinking in which we must refrain from specializing in the subfield of philosophy or creating a niche in the conventional frameworks of philosophical scholarship just mentioned. Rather, it should redefine the boundary of philosophical thinking beyond the conventional split between East and West.

8   It is unlikely that Tanabe came to a direct contact with Karl Jaspers, who just started teaching philosophy at the University of Heidelberg in 1921, but it is a well-known fact that Tanabe regarded much more highly of Jaspers' existentialism than Heidegger's phenomenology and even extended his support to Jaspers and his wife during the early 1940s. For a glimpse of this connection, see Tanabe's telegraph to Jaspers sent for celebrating Jaspers' sixtieth birthday on February 23rd 1943 in Nawata Yūji (縄田雄二), "Tanabe Hajime's Telegraph to Karl Jaspers" (田辺元のカール・ヤスパース宛電報), *Shisō*
(思想), no. 1053 (2012): 217–218.

9   Tanabe, *Filosofía como metanoética*, trans. Rebeca Maldonado with Andés Marquina, Sasha Jair Espinosa, Christina Pérez (Barcelona: Herder Editorial, 2014); *Filosofia come metanoetica*, trans. Tiziano Tosolini (Milan: Mimesis Edizione, 2011).

10 For a detailed account of Tanabe's life and its relation to the development of his philosophy, see my "The Singular Life and Philosophy of Tanabe Hajime," in Appendix to *PM*, 447–488. I will be referring to the second edition of the English translation of *PM* (Nagoya: Chisokudō Publications, 2016) in the following, while the pagination of the first edition (Berkley: University of California Press, 1986) is indicated in parentheses.

11 John Caputo makes the same assessment of Desmond by saying that "he is best known as an original philosopher in his own right, having been at the forefront over the years in cultivating a singularly contemporary style of metaphysics" (*WDR*, vii).

12 Several scholars argue that Desmond's philosophical and scholarly achievements are remarkable and epoch-making. See Cathrin Pickstock, "What Shines Between: The Metaxu of Light," in *Between System and Poetics: William Desmond and Philosophy after Dialectic* (Aldershot: Ashgate, 2007), 107.

13 *THZ* 3; 9.

14 It is absolutely crucial to note Tsujimura Kōichi's choice of Tanabe's word for the epitaph on his grave stone: "My search is for truth, and it alone." In reference to this epitaph, James Heisig makes a succinct and acute assessment of Tanabe as a thinker: "Everything I have heard and read about Tanabe portrays him as a man who never hesitated to rise to the demands of a new idea whatever its source—be it books or teachers or students or colleagues—and never let go of what he judged valuable, even when it meant parting company with those whose influence on him had been most decisive" (*PM*, 2 [viii]). For Desmond's emphasis on the matter at hand in philosophy, see *PU*, 9; *AOO*, xi.

15 Cf. Peter Henneberg, "Faith and Grace in the Thought of Tanabe Hajime and of Søren Kierkegaard" (Ph.D. diss., Université catholique de Louvain, 2010), 70: "Tanabe and Kierkegaard can be read as reactions to what Kant and Hegel had written [and because of that], it is reasonable to start with reviewing the salient characteristics of the religious philosophy of these two thinkers as a lead into the philosophy of Kierkegaard and of Tanabe." In the same manner, I will examine these two German thinkers as a way into the works of Desmond and Tanabe.

16 The following four books are exclusively on Hegel: *Art and the Absolute: A Study of Hegel's Aesthetics, Hegel and His Critics: Philosophy in the Aftermath of Hegel, Beyond Hegel and Dialectic: Speculation, Cult and Comedy, Hegel's God: A Counterfeit Double*? Three titles, contributing a few chapters on Kant and Hegel, are *Art, Origins, Otherness: Between Art and Philosophy; Philosophy and Religion in German Idealism*; and *Is There a Sabbath for Thought*?

17 Alexander Solzhenitsyn et al., *From under the Rubble*, trans. Michael Scammel (London: Little, Brown, and Co., 1975), x.

18 See *BB*, xvi for the importance of this "daring" for a philosopher; *PU*, 179 for Desmond's emphasis on the audacity of self-questioning as the possibility of refreshing our philosophical quest; and *GB*, 281 for the metaphysical foundation (i.e., *hyperboles*) for the possibility of this daring in its humility and reverence. Notable contemporary Japanese thinkers tend to share this spirit of intellectual boldness. In reference to a poem written by a Zen priest, Sengai (仙厓) (1750–1837), D.T. Suzuki discusses with Nishitani Keiji.

> Suzuki: "Scholars often base their opinions on the words of others, saying, 'The Buddha teaches,' 'Socrates says,' 'Hegel states' and so forth. I don't agree with this way of thinking. Instead, scholars should express themselves more freely, saying, 'My view is as follows, and the Buddha is in agreement with me.' This may sound arrogant, but it's not. Even if you are a student of the teachings of Hegel, Kant, or the Buddha, you must still be able to say, 'I feel this way,' and if you can do that, there is no longer any need for Buddha or Christ…."
>
> Nishitani: "Yes, it's just as you say."

For this dialogue held among the leading Zen and Pure Land thinkers in contemporary Japan, see "Shinran's World: A Dialogue of Shin Buddhism and Zen Buddhism: Nishitani Keiji (moderator) with Suzuki Daisetsu, Kaneko Daiei, and Soga Ryōjin," in *Listening to Shin Buddhism: Starting Points of Modern Dialogue*, ed. Michael Pye, 249; hereafter cited as *Listening*.

19 However, the diligence of scholars can sometimes bridge the historical, cultural, and thematic gulf between two (seemingly) independent islands of thought. There have been a number of scholarly works on the general outline of Dōgen's thought, while his reflections on language are considered to be one of the important aspects of his thinking. One of his most important texts, *Shōbōgenzō* (正法眼蔵), has been

translated multiple times into English. Many of the excellent works on Dōgen in Japanese are slowly but surely becoming available to the general academic audience in the West. It hardly bears repeating here that there are a good number of Western scholars of Dōgen today. Contrariwise, Ōmori's texts have not enjoyed the same fame as those of Dōgen or generated many intellectual followers in Western academia. Despite the brilliance of his works, much of his legacy is unknown to us. In this case, we seem to be able to tip the scale in favor of (2) due to the maturity of scholarship available on Dōgen and his thought on language.

20 Given the closeness of Tanabe and Desmond, one may wonder if it is appropriate to categorize this comparative examination of these thinkers as a work of comparative philosophy. If Tanabe begins his philosophic journey from the viewpoint of Western philosophy and reaches the comprehensive framework of thinking that takes into account both the Eastern and the Western intellectual tradition, then, it seems more appropriate to characterize this project as a dialogue between a leading Western philosopher and a notable comparative philosopher of the Eastern origin. I have, however, some reservation toward this simple acceptance of Tanabe as an established comparative philosopher in the history of philosophy and place him next to Desmond as if they are from the same background of "contemporary philosophy." The biggest concern is that Tanabe is virtually unknown and hardly studied among the scholars in the field of philosophy in the West. Coupled with the minor status of comparative philosophy and the general lack of interest in non-Western thought, most of Tanabe's works have remained out of our reach or never made it to be our common scholarly interest. Under the current academic circumstance, Tanabe's later works that make extensive references to the Buddhist concepts will sound very foreign to most of the Western audience even in the field of contemporary philosophy. Consequently, the comparative examination of Tanabe's metanoetics and Desmond's metaxology will bear the basic feature of interculturality—the feature that seems to characterize every form of comparative philosophy. Unless Tanabe's major texts will be widely read in original language and/or through critical translations, there will not be an educated consensus that Tanabe is definitely a contemporary comparative philosopher emerging both from the Western and Eastern intellectual tradition. In this sense, because of the general lack of our familiarity with Eastern intellectual tradition in the West, I think it is appropriate to label my examination of Tanabe and Desmond as a work pertaining to the field of comparative philosophy.

21 Bret Davis, "The Stimulating Doubleness of the Japanese Philosophy of Religion: Thinking through Nishida and Zen" (日本の宗教哲学における刺激的な両義性：西田と禅を中心に), in *The World-Significance of Japanese Philosophy: Its Receptions and Future Overseas* (日本哲学の国際性：海外における受容と展望), ed. James Heisig (Tokyo: Risōsha, 2006), 300.

22 Kant, "The Conflict of the Faculties," in *Religion and Rational Theology*, eds. Allen W. Wood, George di Giovanni, and trans. Mary J. Gregor and Robert Anchor (Cambridge: Cambridge University Press, 1996), 270 (7: 48), hereafter *Conflict*. The pagination of *Kants gesammelte Schriften*, ed. the German Academy of Sciences (Berlin: Walter de Gruyter & Co., 1900–) will be indicated in parentheses.

23 Davis, "The Stimulating Doubleness of the Japanese Philosophy of Religion," 310–314. See also BR, 176; *ITST*, 110, 116. The general emphasis on the "*reasonableness* of religion" among philosophers and scientists prevents them from recognizing the genuine interplay between religion and philosophy or science; and just like Nishida's or Tanabe's philosophy of religion, metaxology focuses on this philosophy-religion interplay.

24 Cf. Taitetsu Unno and James Heisig, "Editor's Introduction," in *The Religious Philosophy of Tanabe Hajime: The Metanoetic Imperative*, eds. Taitetsu Unno and James Heisig (Berkley, CA: Asian Humanities Press, 1990), vii, hereafter *RPTH*: "[the vision of applying the rigors of the Western philosophical tradition to the intellectual tradition of Japan and… cultivating a more Oriental expression to philosophical questions] led Tanabe away from the separation of philosophy and religion that has characterized philosophy in the West and towards a standpoint in which the two work symbiotically, distinguishable but inseparable."

25 See Henneberg, "Faith and Grace in the Thought of Tanabe Hajime and Søren Kierkegaard," 18–70. Henneberg sets forth this kind of "objective method" for his examination of Tanabe and Kierkegaard. Henneberg's "Model of Analysis," in its effort to make itself be applicable to anyone in any given place and time, relies on the objective language that remains almost completely foreign to the ways in which Tanabe or Kierkegaard describes his existential self-reflections. (This is understandable, since Henneberg wrote this dissertation after his retirement as a research scientist [7, 9].) Precisely because this "objective" model for the analysis of two thinkers abstracts from the actual method(s) through which the thinkers in question communicate their thoughts, it remains extremely ineffective for grounding the comparative analysis. What is needed, then, is to articulate the method(s) of thinking operative in the works of the thinkers and to show that one's reflections on these works remain faithful to the very method(s) of thinking. This is exactly what Heidegger says in "A Dialogue on Language": "nobody can in just one single leap take distance from the predominant circle of ideas, especially not if he is dealing with the well-worn tracks of traditional thinking…." See Heidegger, *On the Way to Language*, trans. Peter D. Hertz (New York: HarperCollins, 1971), 36. Both Desmond and Tanabe make the same critique of the "view from nowhere": cf. *BB*, 45; *PU*, 111; and "Historical Reality," *THZ* 8: 128–129.

26 For the sake of keeping the endnote in a manageable size, Kierkegaard's criticism of rational ethics will be derived mainly from *Fear and Trembling*, ed. and trans. Howard V. Hong and Edna H. Hong (Princeton, NJ: Princeton University Press, 1980), hereafter *FT*.

27 Kierkegaard does not directly articulate these criticisms, but his literary invention, Johannes de Silentio, guides us to see them through contemplating Abraham's sacrifice of Isaac in *FT*. In facing this religious image, Johannes summarizes the relation of a single individual to the immanent universality of the rationally articulated ethics as follows:

   1. The ethical as such is the universal and rests immanent in itself, has nothing outside itself that is its *telos* but is itself the *telos* for everything outside itself (*FT*, 54 and see also 68, 82).
   2. The single individual has his ethical task continually to express himself in the universal and annul his singularity in order to become the universal (*FT*, 54).
   3. As soon as the single individual asserts himself in his singularity before the universal, he sins, and only by acknowledging this can he be reconciled again with the universal (*FT*, 54 and see also, 61–62).

   "If this [universal] is the highest that can be said of man and his existence," Johannes further articulates, "then the ethical is of the same nature as a person's eternal salvation, which is his telos forevermore and at all times" (*FT*, 54). Put differently, if the highest end to which human freedom must be determined is this universal, to be religious ultimately is to be ethical, and thus a single individual cannot relate herself or himself to the divine absolute without determining herself or himself to be the universal through negating his or her singular particularity; for the absolute in this framework of rational ethics is the ethical universal. If this general structure of rational ethics is inherent in the Kantian or Hegelian configuration of the divinity-humanity relation, Kierkegaard's concerns come to the fore: God is reduced to the immanent totality of the ethical universal, and human relation to this divine absolute requires the extirpation of one's singularity in the process of determining oneself to be the universal.

28 Graham Parkes, ed., *Heidegger and Asian Thought* (Honolulu: University of Hawai'i Press, 1987), 9, 106; hereafter, *HAT*.

Chapter 1

1 This does not mean that legions of papers in comparative philosophy have never given their thoughts on the methods of comparative philosophy. As Thorsten Botz-Bornstein once said, if we look at the leading Anglo-American journal in the field of comparative philosophy, *Philosophy of East and West*, we would notice that almost every single article from its inaugural volume spent a page or two explaining why the author is justified to talk about the topic (with some thought on its underlining methodology). But then in the 1970s, most authors stopped writing these justificatory reflections. Now the question is whether or not many of these justifications were well-founded. In this sense, I think it is necessary and significant for any comparative work today to re-examine its methodological foundation.
2 Hegel, *Phänomenologie des Geistes*, eds. Wolfgang Bonsiepen and Reinhard Heede (Hamburg: Meiner, 1980), 10–11, hereafter *PhG*; *Phenomenology of Spirit*, trans. A.V. Miller (Oxford: Oxford University Press, 1977), 2–3 (§3), hereafter *PhS*.
3 Robert W. Smid, *Methodologies of Comparative Philosophy: The Pragmatist and Process Traditions* (Albany: State University of New York Press, 2009). It is important to note, however, that the pragmatist tradition itself has not always been open to the idea of comparative philosophy. According to Anindita N. Balslev, Rorty attended the Sixth East-West Comparative Philosophy Conference at the University of Hawai'i in 1989, where he delivered a paper expressing his doubts concerning the legitimacy of comparative philosophy. Wei Zhang summarizes Rorty's points: "[t]he main thrust of Rorty's argument was that since philosophy is a uniquely Greek concept and a specialized form of intellectual inquiry instituted in the Western academy, any comparison of philosophy can create more awkwardness than collegiality among fellow philosophers." On this, see Balslev, ed., *Cultural Otherness: Correspondence with Richard Rorty* (Atlanta, GA: Scholar Press, 1991), 59; Zhang, *Heidegger, Rorty and the Eastern Thinkers: A Hermeneutics of Cross-Cultural Understanding* (Albany: State University of New York Press, 2006), 12. This does not mean, however, that what Rorty sets forth as the methodology of pragmatic philosophy is not conducive to the idea of cross-cultural understanding. In fact, there is something ironic about the fact that he actually attended a conference on cross-cultural understanding in the field of philosophy and delivered that paper (with an assumption that his point will be understood cross-culturally). In the same manner, we should not eliminate Desmond as a potential resource for inter- and cross-cultural communication. As I mentioned in Introduction, Standaert applauds

(in reference to the Chinese notion of the "betweenness") the relevance of metaxological thinking as methodological grounding of Sinology. This article alone shows how Desmond's ideas, despite their Western roots, are highly relevant for the theoretical grounding and practice of comparative philosophy.

4 Neville provides an interesting remark on metaxology in the back cover of *BB*: "What I like most about the book is that it is a fully developed, comprehensively argued, philosophical system. There are previous few of these, for reasons Desmond discusses, and here is one, all in one book. Although anticipated in Desmond earlier books, here is the system fully expressed in Western Philosophy. His erudition is exquisite, yet his expositions make this book wonderfully useful for philosophy majors who would be exited to read a philosopher interacting with the figures to which they have been introduced." Neville's assessment clearly indicates that metaxology belongs to "Western philosophy," and that its use will be relevant to students in the history of Western philosophy. Although this assessment is quite positive, it is not positive enough to extend the scope of metaxology beyond the confines of the Western intellectual tradition. Neville's half-positive comment on metaxology in *BB*, therefore, clearly anticipates his later criticism of *GB*: "[Desmond] does not engage the Confucians and Daoists, the Hindus and Buddhists, or even the Muslims and Jews, the way he does the philosophers and theologians of the European Greek and Christian West. They rarely enter into any of his critical analyses of strengths and limitations.... Unless he treats his whole approach as an hypothesis and makes it vulnerable to correction by the other great traditions of philosophy, his analysis remains strangely private to the Western tradition." See Neville, "William Desmond's Philosophical Theology," *Louvain Studies* 36 (2012): 247. For Desmond's rejoinder to this criticism, see his "Responses," *Louvain Studies* 36 (2012): 304–308.

5 The best discussion concerning the methodical foundation and the philosophical significance of comparative philosophy that I have seen so far is Chris Goto-Jones' review of Smid's *Methodologies of Comparative Philosophy*. Cf. Goto-Jones, "What Is (Comparative) Philosophy?" *Philosophy* 88 (2013): 133–140. *Pace* Smid, Goto-Jones argues that the professionalization of philosophy in Western academia implies the "*de facto* establishment of the 'non-Western' world as the 'non-philosophical' world" (133) and comparative philosophy aims to promote the formation of broader philosophical views. *Contra* Smid, however, Goto-Jones argues that comparative philosophy cannot be in principle a subfield of philosophy, as it has been practiced in academia precisely because "[it] requires a radical rethinking of the dimensions of the entire philosophical enterprise," which can be expressed in the basic question of "*What is philosophy?*" (140). Goto-Jones claims that Smid is avoiding this question and only giving descriptive accounts of the ways in which comparative philosophy has been practiced among the thinkers in the tradition of American pragmatism. My methodological reflection sides with Goto-Jones, insofar as I maintain that to ask what is at work in the foundation of philosophical thinking cannot be exempted from the method in which one practices one's thinking. The methodological reflection on comparative philosophy, insofar as its self-reflective nature is concerned, does not really matter whether it comes from the Eastern or the Western intellectual tradition. In this sense, Desmond's philosophy is fully qualified as a methodology of (comparative) thinking. I do not think, however, that we can so quickly ask and answer the question regarding "What is (comparative) philosophy?" without any reference to the historical, cultural, and linguistic backgrounds in which it is asked, nor can we set aside the intricate problems of communicating various philosophical

questions from vastly different historical, cultural, and linguistic backgrounds. In this sense, Smid's descriptive examination of American pragmatism apropos of (comparative) thinking is still indispensable for answering the question that Goto-Jones poses as the ultimate methodological question of comparative philosophy.
6 As to the formation of metaxology, Desmond often articulates the significance of his particularity as a single thinker (or what he calls "idiocy") at work in the depth of his systematic thinking. In this case, his particular background of being Irish (as well as having studied in the United States and teaching in Belgium for a few decades) must have some great effect on his ways of communicating his thoughts. This point will be further discussed in Chapter 5, but for these passages, consult *PU*, 1–2, 41; and also Christopher Ben Simpson, *Religion, Metaphysics, and the Postmodern: William Desmond and John D. Caputo* (Indianapolis: Indiana University Press, 2009), 24.
7 This is what Tanabe demonstrates through his reading of Kant's texts on the theory of teleology, namely, to think systematically with Kant and then to articulate an answer to the question—that is, the question that Kant famously raises in the third *Critique*. Cf. Tanabe, "Kant's Theory of Teleology," *THZ* 3: 4.
8 This is quite similar to the ways in which Ram Adhar Mall discusses the task of intercultural and comparative philosophy as the interplay of univocity and equivocity, uniformity and radical difference, and the hermeneutics of total identity and total difference. See Mall, *Intercultural Philosophy* (Lanham, MD: Rowman & Little Field Publishers, Inc., 2000), 4, 25, 37, 42–43.
9 For Desmond's brief exposition of these four senses of being, see also *DDO*, xix, 8; *PO*, 4; *PU*, 12; *EB*, 2, 51; *GB*, 9–10; *ISB*, 368, *IU*, 164. For other scholarly expositions of the ontological fourfold, see Simpson, *Religion, Metaphysics, and the Postmodern*, 28–35; Giacomo Rinaldi, "Metaphysics as a Cultural Presence: Dialectical and Metaxological Thought in the Philosophy of William Desmond," in *Being and Dialectic: Metaphysics as a Cultural Presence*, eds. William Desmond and Joseph Grange (Albany: State University of New York Press, 2000), 158–164; Sander Griffioen, "Towards a Philosophy of God: A Study in William Desmond's Thought," *Philosophia Reformata* 75 (2010): 5–6; Jere O'Neill Surber, "Metaxological Metaphysics and Idiotic Style: The 'Conceptual Persona' of William Desmond," in *Between System and Poetics: William Desmond and Philosophy after Dialectic*, ed. Thomas A.F. Kelly (Aldershot: Ashgate, 2007), 55–61, hereafter, *BSP*.
10 Cf. *BB*, 49, 75.
11 Cf. *BB*, 58–62, 124; *EB*, 28, 67, 72n, 421, 472–473; *GB*, 64–65. See also Cyril O'Regan, "Repetition: Desmond's New Science," *BSP*, 67.
12 Cf. *BB*, 89; *PO*, 4; *ISB*, 48.
13 *BB*, xii.
14 *ISB*, 36.
15 *ISB*, 36.
16 *ISB*, 36.
17 *BB*, 408. This is precisely what the dialectical understanding of being tries to demonstrate.
18 *DDO*, 200–201.
19 *BB*, 324, 392n; *PU*, 15; *PO*, 60, 151; *GB*, 54; *ISB*, 63.
20 Because of this refusal to think of being in terms of its own self-mediation or to favor one way of thinking over the other, Rinaldi's criticism that the metaxological is guilty of subordinating all the other senses for determining itself as the consummate sense or claiming itself to be the totality that either negates or sublates all the others is off

the mark (cf. Rinaldi, "Metaphysics as a Cultural Presence," 165). I also find Rinaldi's eleven objections to the metaxological metaphysics in this article almost as good as Gaunilo's objections to Anselm's *Proslogion*: viz., they are useful for testing our true understanding of Desmond's arguments. I will try to give my replies to some of these objections *en passant* in endnotes to this chapter and Chapters 5 and 6.

21 Cf. Mall, *Intercultural Philosophy*, 36.

22 Cf. Elena Anikeeva, "Orthodox Religious and Philosophical Aspects of Intercultural Communication," in *Communication across Cultures: The hermeneutics of Cultures and Religions in a Global Age*, eds. Chibueze C. Udeani et al. (Cardinal Station, Washington, DC: The Council for Research in Values and Philosophy, 2008), 241–242.

23 For the historical development of the notion of otherness in the context of comparative and intercultural philosophy, see Zhang, *Heidegger, Rorty, and the Eastern Thinkers*, 34–38. Zhang finds Desmond's analysis of otherness in *DDO* as being consistent with Lars-Henrik Schmidt's analysis of the category of otherness in "Commonness across Culture," in *Cross-Cultural Conversation: Initiation*, ed. Anindita N. Baslev (Atlanta, NY: Scholar Press, 1996), 121–122.

24 The majority of the thinkers in the history had no means to travel over the extended distance between Europe and Asia. The materials that are available for them to conduct philosophical investigations were much more scarce than what we enjoy today in Europe. Keeping this in mind, one should be much more reluctant to accuse Descartes for not paying attention to Dōgen's discussions on the mind-body relation than any contemporary thinkers (such as Popper and Searle, etc.) revisiting the same problem with no reference to the ways in which this relation was conceived outside the usual starting points of the discussion: Plato, Aristotle, Descartes, Kant, etc.

25 For Schopenhauer's (mis)appropriation of Indian philosophical works and Buddhism, see Richard White, "Schopenhauer and Indian Philosophy: On the Limits of Comparative Thought," *International Philosophical Quarterly* 50 (2010): 58–60, 71, 75–76. For the general proximity between Schopenhauer's philosophy and Indian thought, consult Stephen Cross, *Schopenhauer's Encounter with Indian Thought: Representation and Will and Their Indian Parallels* (Honolulu: University of Hawai'i Press, 2013). Cross gives a very generous reading of Schopenhauer by arguing that Schopenhauer displays a consistent and advanced knowledge of Indian philosophies in comparison to his contemporaries (14). Cross states that more accurate interpretations of the Indian philosophies available today demonstrate their closer affinities with Schopenhauer's thoughts (102). What I find unsatisfactory with Cross' efforts to trace the parallels between Schopenhauer's and Indian philosophies is twofold: (1) the limitation that Cross recognizes in the former in relation to the latter (viz., philosophy for Schopenhauer remains within the boundary of experience, while the Indian philosophical traditions exceed such limits with its openness to the religious) seems to highlight the essential difference between them (cf., 15–17, 97, 216); and (2) none of the parallels that Cross provides in this text seem to dissolve some of the issues that White and others have recognized as Schopenhauer's problematic/contracted reading of the Eastern philosophical traditions. Desmond provides a similar criticism regarding Schopenhauer's interpretation of Buddhism: cf. *EB*, 496n.

26 Mall, *Intercultural Philosophy*, 29.

27 Mall, *Intercultural Philosophy*, 29–30, 56. Graham Parkes points out an important point that Jasper's "thoroughly nihilistic" account of the Buddhist attitude toward death in *Psychologie der Weltanschauungen* is "influenced by the (rather unreliable) interpretations given by Schopenhauer and Nietzsche," and thus, clearly fails to take

into account the Mahāyāna tradition. See Parkes' complementary essay, "Rising Sun over Black Forest: Heidegger's Japanese Connections," in Reinhard May's *Heidegger's Hidden Sources: East Asian Influences on His Work*, trans. Graham Parkes (London: Routledge, 1996), 84. Unlike Jaspers, Heidegger hardly ever mentions any non-Western philosophy as a significant source of his thinking, but many contemporary scholars (including May, Parkes, Steven Burik, and Katrin Froese) have argued that there is a profound consonance between Heideggerian and Daoist thought. According to Parkes' personal correspondence, Gadamar reported in 1985 that "Heidegger studies would do well to pursue seriously comparisons of his work with Asian philosophies," and this has been proven to be true. What this shows, however, is that it is one thing for a Western thinker to acknowledge the significance of non-Western thought and another for him or her to understand it properly. It is important to praise Jaspers for the fact that he has demonstrated his tolerance and respect toward the non-Western philosophy. But it is also necessary to investigate further in detail whether or not his understanding of a non-Western philosophy is actually an accurate one and even further if his own philosophical thinking corresponds in anyway to what we can find in the non-Western intellectual tradition. Unless we make these in-depth comparative examinations, it seems quite superfluous to condemn Heidegger on the ground that he hardly ever makes any positive remarks on non-Western philosophy, while pardoning Jaspers for paying respect to the non-Western intellectual tradition through his misinterpretation of it. For Gadamar's quote and Parkes' reflection on the significance of comparative examinations, see *HAT*, 1–4, 5.

28 Edmund Husserl, "The Vienna Lectures," in *The Crisis of European Sciences and Transcendental Phenomenology: An Introduction to Phenomenological Philosophy*, trans. David Carr (Evanston, IL: Northwestern University Press, 1970), 274.
29 Husserl, "The Vienna Lectures," 274.
30 Husserl, "The Vienna Lectures," 275.
31 Steven Burik, *The End of Comparative Philosophy and the Task of Comparative Thinking: Heidegger, Derrida and Daoism* (Albany, NY: State University of New York Press, 2010), 35.
32 Heidegger is known for making several problematic remarks, such as, the Western European philosophy alone has the basic framework of understanding reality in terms of "beings—in being," the preservation of the European peoples from the Asian, and the notorious equation of philosophy to the Western intellectual tradition. See Heidegger, *What Is Called Thinking?* (New York: Harper & Row, 1968), 224; and *What Is Philosophy?* trans. Jean T. Wilde and William Kluback (Lanham, MD: Rowman & Littlefield, 1956), 30–31: "The often heard expression 'Western-European philosophy' is, in truth, a tautology. Why? Because philosophy is in its nature; Greek, in this instance, means that in origin the nature of philosophy is of such a kind that it first appropriated the Greek world, and only it, in order to unfold." From the similar passages to this, we can see how unlikely it is for Heidegger to give the predicate of philosophy to non-Western thought. In recent years, there have been some great (that is to say, "well-balanced") critiques of Heidegger's one-sidedness with regard to the history of philosophy. See, Chung-Ying Cheng, "Preface: Origins and Relations of Philosophy: European and Chinese," in *European and Chinese Philosophy: Origins and Intersections*, eds. Chung-ying Cheng, Eric Nelson and Lyinyu Gu (Chi Chester, West Sussex: John Wiley & Sons, 2013), 1–2, hereafter cited as *ECP*; Eric S. Nelson, "Heidegger, Misch, and the Origins of Philosophy," *ECP*, 13–15. For Desmond's critique of this univocity in Heidegger's notion and praxis of philosophy, see *ITST*, 315; *PU*, 24.

33 *Contra* Burik, Nelson argues, "the other beginning is suggestive in that it might be taken as a beginning outside of Greece. Nonetheless non-Western thought cannot constitute another beginning for Heidegger insofar as it is not a differentiating confrontation (*Auseinadersetzung*) with the first Greek beginning." See Nelson, "Heidegger, Misch, and the Origins of Philosophy," *ECP*, 16. This seems to suggest that Burik's (and many other comparative theorists') reading of the other-beginning as the suggestive of comparative thinking in Heideggerian texts goes beyond the authorial intent of Heidegger.

34 This refers to Heidegger, "A Dialogue on Language," in *On the Way to Language*, trans. Peter D. Hertz (New York: HarperCollins, 1971), 1–56. In this dialogue, Heidegger claims that he once asked the following question to Tanabe: "Why it was that Japanese did not call back to mind the venerable beginnings of their own thinking, instead of chasing ever more greedily after the latest news in European Philosophy" (36–37). As far as Tezuka Tomio's recollection goes, it seems unlikely that Heidegger mentioned this during their conversations but it is possible that Heidegger has greatly encouraged his Asian colleagues and students to reflect on the roots of their intellectual traditions as much as he did to his own.

35 Burik, *The End of Comparative Philosophy and the Task of Comparative Thinking*, 38.

36 Cf. Katrin Froese, Nietzsche, *Heidegger and Daoist Thought: Crossing Paths In-Between*, 49 and Chang Chung-Yuan, *Tao: A New Way of Thinking* (New York: Harper Colophon Books, 1975), 96. Froese goes so far as to the say (*à la* Chang) that "Heidegger's appeal through the concept of *Ereignis* to constantly return to the 'other beginning' may in part have developed out of his encounter with Daoist philosophy." Otto Pöggler argues for Heidegger's substantial methodological contribution to the intercultural and comparative philosophy with a reference to the prominent student of Heidegger in Japan, Nishitani Keiji. According to Pöggler, "Nishitani made it clear to European and American readers, in his great book *Was Ist Religion?* (*Religion and Nothingness*), how Heidegger made possible a new encounter between Eastern and Western thought." For this point, see Pöggler, "West-East Dialogue: Heidegger and Lao-tzu," *HAT*, 48; Nishitani, *Religion and Nothingness*, trans. Jan Van Bragt (Berkley: University of California Press, 1982), 64ff.

37 Burik, *The End of Comparative Philosophy and the Task of Comparative Thinking*, 38. Cf. Martin Heidegger, "Only a God Can Save Us," in *Heidegger: The Man and the Thinker* (1981), ed. T. Sheehan and trans. by William J. Richardson (Chicago: Precedent, 1981), 61.

38 Burik, *The End of Comparative Philosophy and the Task of Comparative Thinking*, 38.

39 Desmond clearly recognizes this problematic tendency to univocalize the sense of philosophizing in Heidegger. See *ITST*, 315.

40 See Karl Jaspers, *The Origin and Goal of History*, trans. Michael Bullock (New Haven, CT: Yale University Press, 1953), 1–2. With regard to a more specific correspondence between Heidegger and Tanabe, see Parkes, "Rising Sun over the Black Forest," 81–87.

41 Burik, *The End of Comparative Philosophy and the Task of Comparative Thinking*, 50.

42 For a succinct exposition of the marvelous consonance between Derrida's notion of *différance* and the Chinese notion of *Dao*, see Chung-Ying Cheng, "Deconstruction and Différance: Onto-Return and Emergence in a Daoist Interpretation of Derrida," *ECP*, 40–50.

43 Davis, "The Stimulating Doubleness of the Japanese Philosophy of Religion," 296. To the group of postmodern thinkers, Davis includes in this passage, Derrida, De Vries,

Jeffrey Bloechl, and John D. Caputo. For Desmond's same critique against post-Hegelian philosophers, see *BHD*, 88–89.
44 Derrida, *Dissemination* (London: Routledge, 2004), 132–133.
45 *BB*, 47.
46 This is like the feeling of waking up to the bright morning in early summer and taking in the fresh air with a completely renewed self. There is no left over of any fatigue from the day before or no concern for the day's trouble in that moment of our unified existence. Tanabe also gives an example of this experience in "Thetic Judgment," an experience of looking at the stream of the clouds on blue sky while lying on his back against green meadow in a sunny spring day. Cf. "Thetic Judgment," *THZ* 1: 3. For Desmond's description of the metaphysical Eden, see *BB* 48; *EB*, 52; *GB*, 36, 76, 118.
47 *BB*, 8–13; *ITST*, 287, 332.
48 *BB*, 48.
49 *BB*, 48.
50 *BB*, 48. See also *PU*, 110.
51 John Stuart Mill, *A System of Logic: Ratiocinative and Inductive* (London: Savill and Edwards, 1842), 343 (3: 3.1) and see also 353–354 (3: 4.1). (The numbers of the book, the chapter, and the section are indicated in parentheses.) Mill argues that there are multiplicities of uniformities in the course of nature and they do not necessarily presuppose a hierarchical order in which they can be categorized in accordance with a higher unity (or unities); and so, he further maintains that the "regularity of nature" or "the fewest general propositions from which all the uniformities which exist in the universe might be deductively inferred" are "nothing but the uniformities [that] exist among natural phenomena." Tanabe translates the terms "uniformity" and "regularity" into the Japanese phrase, *seisei* (整斉). The ambiguity of the distinction between the regular uniformities that we simply observe in everyday life and the regularity of nature that becomes the foundation of scientific theories as the laws of nature is well expressed in this single Japanese phrase, for it conveys the interchangeability of "uniformity" and "regularity."
52 *BB*, 56.
53 *BB*, 56.
54 Cf., *BB*, 66: "What is now being stressed is the irreducible unity of the absolute self. There is significant ambiguity here, in that this absolute self is sometimes referred to as a pure logical condition, sometimes as a purely formal universal ego, and sometimes again in much more dynamic terms, as the source that generates all the categories, and as the source of all synthesis in experience."
55 *BB*, 67. Cf. *PU*, 141.
56 *BB*, 69.
57 *BB*, 69. For a fantastic reflection on this problem of self-obsessed self-loss in reference to the myth of Narcissus, see also *DDO*, 135.
58 *BB*, 69.
59 *BB*, 70.
60 *BB*, 70.
61 Cf. Griffioen, "Towards a Philosophy of God," 11.
62 This is precisely why, as Desmond rightly argues, the anti-Hegelian post-Hegelian thinkers are "often deeply in agreement with Hegel" in that they are "claiming to be entirely immanent in their view or in the practice of philosophy" (AWASN, 17). When a thinker fails to maintain his openness to being or the divine transcendence as other

to his own transcending, he cannot recover the primal communivocity between his philosophical thinking and what is other to it. For this point, see also AWASN, 18.
63 *EB*, 145.
64 *EB*, 146.
65 *EB*, 145 (my paraphrase). Cf. *HG*, 53–54.
66 Cf., Nishitani Keiji, "Reflections on Two Addresses by Martin Heidegger," *HAT*, 149. Nishitani gives a helpful illustration of how problematic the dialectical "inclusion of otherness" into self's self-determining self-affirmation with a reference to the dogmatic relation of religion to philosophy: "By the very causes that make the establishment of dogmatics necessary… religion is compelled to accept from philosophy as many concepts and theories as are useful to its purposes. Dogmatics comes in this way to contain elements which make a dialogue with 'outsiders' possible; it becomes in this way more or less open-minded it may become and is enabled to exist as an open system. But however open-minded it may become, even when its system is made as open as possible, so long as it remains dogmatics, that is, so long as it stands on an exclusively closed basis of faith and dogma, it can never avert the above-mentioned procedure: it must produce, in all its own efforts to become 'open,' a means to confirm itself alone. And thus, as it become more 'open,' it must become all the more firmly closed. It is compelled to return to its original enclosure, making futile all its 'openness.' It thus betrays itself, and allows mutual understanding to remain despairingly difficult." The dialectical process that we see in the dogmatic self-mediation of religion to philosophy shows the self that fails to genuinely open itself to the other as the other and suffers from the "despairing difficulty" in recognizing its free intermediation with the other.
67 *EB*, 146.
68 Cf. Hegel, *Lectures on the Philosophy of World History*, trans. Hugh Barr Nisbet (Cambridge: Cambridge University Press, 1975), 54. Cf. *HG*, "Evil and the Counterfeits of God in History," 147–151, 160–162.
69 I am aware that my reference to the "overcoming of modernity" might be seen to suffer from a gross generalization of the ways in which the Western intellectual tradition was received among Japanese thinkers in the 1930s and 1940s. The most controversial symposium of the "overcoming of modernity" was held in 1942 for the purposes of reviewing Western culture as a whole (in reference to its enormous influence on Japanese culture since the Meiji era), and of discussing the Japanese overcoming of the problems in Western culture. The four prominent thinkers (and students of Nishida and Tanabe) from the Kyoto school—Kōsaka Masaaki, Nishitani Keiji, Kōyama Iwao, and Suzuki Shigetaka—participated in this symposium. This historical event has particularly fueled the postwar criticisms against the Kyoto school philosophy for its support of the previous government. Karatani Kōjin, however, points out three important points: (1) the symposium itself suffers from some thematic incoherence among three general groups of the participants, that is, those who belong to the literary world, Japanese romantics, and the Kyoto school; (2) what these participants meant by the West or modernity was mostly German and French (despite this, many critics interpret their arguments as if they were pointed toward England and the United States during the Pacific War); and (3) the targets of the postwar criticisms (such as Nishida and Yasuda Yojūrō) were absent at the meeting.
As you can see, there needs to be more scholarly works in the West to clarify the fact and the nature of the symposium and to reevaluate the basis of the rampant

criticisms that it has generated following the Second World War in the East. Regardless of what was actually discussed at the meeting, however, I argue in this context of comparative philosophy that we can see the general tendency to talk about the self-determination of Japanese culture/philosophy in and through the Western intellectual/cultural tradition (if not the complete rejection of the latter in favor of the former) in many intellectual works from the 1930s, and that the presence of the logic of self-determination in minds of prominent Japanese thinkers at that time. This explains the fact that such a symposium as the "overcoming of modernity" received its support in the 1940s, and regardless of its success in critically reviewing Western culture or mapping out the future development of Japanese culture/philosophy, it fails to ground the open communication of diverse intellectual traditions or their intermediations necessary to ground the method of intercultural or comparative philosophy. In light of this argument, I find Christopher Goto-Jones' short remark (with a parenthetical reflection) on the Kyoto school philosophers' stance at the symposium most insightful: "The wartime Kyoto school was acutely conscious of the imperialist contradictions of the universalist aspirations of a particularly European history of philosophy. (They were not always so aware of similar contradictions in their own thought.)" For Karatani's analysis, see Karatani Kōjin, "Overcoming Modernity," in *Contemporary Japanese Thought*, ed. Richard F. Calichman (New York: Columbia University Press, 2005), 101–118; for Goto-Jones' remark, cf., Goto-Jones, "The Kyoto School and the History of Political Philosophy: Reconsidering the Methodological Domination of the Cambridge School," in *Re-Politicising The Kyoto School as Philosophy*, ed. Christopher Goto-Jones (Oxon; New York: Routledge, 2008), 8 (hereafter, *Re-Politicising*); and for the relation of this symposium to the Kyoto school philosophy in general (and especially to the philosophy of Nishitani), see Parkes, "The Definite Internationalism of the Kyoto School: Changing Attitudes in the Contemporary Academy," *Re-Politicising*, 176–77; Bernard Stevens, "La Seduction Du Nationalisme," in *Le Néant Évidé: Ontologie et Politique chez Keiji Nishitani* (Louvain; Paris: Peeters, 2003), 41–97.
70 For the most accessible terms in which Desmond articulates this double mediation, cf. *PU*, 56–57; *PO*, 230–231.
71 *BB*, 196.
72 *BB*, 196.
73 *PO*, 116; *GB*, 71.
74 Cf. *PU*, 99: BR, 195; *PO*, 209–210, 212; *BB*, 38, 46, 197–198, 206, 222, 332; *EB*, 111–112, 161–162, 196, 219, 223–224, *GB*, 168, 186, 275–277, 336. *ISB*, 148–151.
75 *DDO*, 158–159.
76 *BB*, 197–198. Cf., *BB*, 182–187, 308; *PU*, 99.
77 *PU*, 124. Cf. also *PU*, 178. Henneberg adopts the "principle of charity" (Henneberg, "Faith and Grace in the Thought of Tanabe Hajime and Søren Kierkegaard," 9) as the "indispensable ingredient for his comparative analysis of Tanabe and Kierkegaard." Despite his unsuccessful rendering of the methodology in "objective" terms, I find this to be one of the most important insights for the possibility of carrying out any comparative philosophy.
78 *PU*, 147.
79 *BB*, 368, 370, 408, 412, 434, 454.
80 This is precisely the reason why Nishida, for instance, advised his Japanese students to study Western philosophy so as to make it their own. Cf. Nishitani, *Nishida Kitarō: His Life and Thought* (西田幾多郎:その人と思想) (Tokyo: Chikuma Shobō, 1984), 97–98.

81 *BB*, 129: "There may not initially be a common language, but we find ways of making a new 'we'; then 'we' newly come across the gap, and at least partially mitigate the gulf occasioned by the initial absence of a common language. We are always in the between, never windowless monads confined to one side of a dualistic antithesis. Dialectical mediation may risk subordinating the other to the self-interpretation of the putatively 'strong' partner. By contrast, metaxological intermediation sees this strength as possible weakness, as failure to be open to the other in the fullness of its otherness, hence as failure to listen to the other on its own terms as best as possible." For the inter-religious dimension of the agapeic mindfulness, see also *IU*, 181, 359–360.

82 Cf. *PU*, 121–122; 233: "community of different centers of self-transcendence." See also, Standaert, 95. As I briefly discussed in Introduction, Standaert gives a marvelous exposition of how metaxological thinking as the art of "in-betweenness" can serve as the philosophical foundation of comparative thinking (especially in the area of Sinology), and I am more than confident that more works on the methodological reflections on comparative philosophy or world philosophies will recognize the significance of metaxology for interdisciplinary and comparative thinking.

83 To patient and vigilant readers, I would like to give the following passage from *PU*: "Philosophy might be an agapeic knowing. This relates to the metaxological view and its double mediation. The first movement of mind… is from the self to the other but for the other, perhaps even the point of sacrifice of self.… This is the death of the self in the knowing of the other.… The second movement concerns openness to the return from the other to the self. This is not a return to the self of itself; it is the self-revelation of the other to the self. In agapeic alert the other may come out of itself. This is *its* unfolding, not mine, *its self-unfolding* as given for the self, given in return from the other as the other. The coming of the other is welcomed" (*PU*, 121–122). This agapeic philosophizing, as Desmond further argues, requires "active patience" or "non-insistence vigilance" often in the state where "[we are] not sure what will emerge." But this patient willingness to let the other speak for the other is absolutely indispensable for the practice of comparative thinking.

Chapter 2

1 With regard to *Tanabe Hajime Zenshū* (*THZ*), I will cite the major works on the philosophy of religion, namely, *Philosophy as Metanoetics; Existence, Love and Practice*; and *The Dialectic of Christianity* with the abbreviations *PM*, *ELP*, and *DC*. The page numbers for the *PM* are from the English translations, while the page numbers for the *ELP* and the *DC* are indicated in accord with the vols. 9 and 10 of the *THZ*. The other texts of Tanabe are cited in accord with the *THZ* followed by the volume and the page numbers.

2 Cf. Naoki Sakai, "Resistance to Conclusion: The Kyoto School Philosophy under the Pax Americana," *Re-Politicising*, 189–191. For the Japanese translation of this essay, see Sakai, "The Kyoto School Philosophy under the Pax Americana" (パックス・アメリカーナの下での京都学派の哲学), in *"Overcoming of Modernity" and the Kyoto School: Modernity, Empire and Universality* (「近代の超克」と京都学派：近代性・帝国・普遍性), eds. Sakai Naoki and Isomae Junichi and trans. Takahashi Hara (Tokyo: Ibunsha, 2010), 3–28.

3. It is indeed surprising (as Heisig observes) that "it took [Japanese] only one generation to produce their first original philosopher in the person of Nishida Kitarō." Cf. Heisig, "The Religious Philosophy of the Kyoto School" in *RPTH*, 17.
4. Nishi Amane (西周), "Hyakuichi-sihnron" (百一新論), in *Nishida Amane Zenshū* (西周全集), ed. Ōkubo Toshiaki (大久保利謙) (Tokyo: Munetaka Shobō, 1960), 288–289.
5. This sense of philosophy corresponds to what Desmond elucidates as the univocal and the dialectical sense of philosophy that ultimately comprises the determinate or self-determining knowledge. For a detailed depiction of Nishi's sense of "philosophy," see Clinton Godart "'Philosophy' or 'Religion'? The Confrontation with Foreign Categories in Late Nineteenth-Century Japan," *Journal of the History of Ideas* (2008): 76; Kuwaki Genyoku (桑木厳翼), "Nishi Amane's Philosophy: The Philosophical Tendencies of Early Meiji Era," in *The Philosophies of Miji Era* (明治の哲学界) (Tokyo: Chūōkōron-sha, 1942), 71–79; Suzuki, Noboru, "The System of Knowledge and the Unifying Science in Nishi Amane Philosophy: In Search of the Composition toward Synthetization," in *Nishi Amane and Japanese Modernity* (西周と日本の近代), ed. The Nishi Amane Study Group at the Shimane Prefectural University (Tokyo: Perikansha, 2005), 286–291.
6. In this regard, the achievement of the *Japanese Philosophy: A Sourcebook* is monumental, revolutionary, and highly controversial for the scholars of Japanese intellectual history.
7. I am aware that this is quite a simplistic presentation of the philosophical world of Meiji and Taishō era and that I am skipping over a number of important Japanese thinkers between late nineteenth and early twentieth century. For a comprehensive presentation of the Japanese thinkers of this period, see Inoue Katsuhito (井上克人), "The Philosophical World of Meiji: The Philosophy of Organism and Its Genealogy" (明治の哲学界：有機体の哲学とその系譜), in *Fertile Culture and Philosophy of Meiji Period* (豊饒なる明治), ed. Inoue Katsuhito (Kansai University Press, 2012), 3–22; trans. Takeshi Morisato, *European Journal of Japanese Philosophy* 1 (2016): 9–30.
8. Among these thinkers, we can name Nakamura Hajime (中村元) (1912–1999), Maruyama Masao (丸山眞男) (1914–1996) and Izutsu Toshihiko (井筒俊彦) (1914–1993).
9. There are several passages in which Tanabe seems to think that his predecessor (i.e., Nishida) has already accomplished the task of raising the level of Japanese philosophy to that of Western philosophy. Because of that, Tanabe seems to sound as if he were completely oblivious to the fact that he is making the same contribution as that of Nishida.
10. Mall, *Intercultural Philosophy*, 5, 14–15.
11. Shimomura Toratarō (下村寅太郎) (1902–1995) praises Tanabe's philosophy as achieving the establishment of a "Herculean pole" that goes from the West intellectual tradition to the East and moves back from the East to the West. For this point, see Shimomura, "The Development and the Character of Tanabe Philosophy" (田辺哲学の発展とその性格), in *The Collected Works of Shimomura Toratarō* (下村寅太郎著作集) (Tokyo: Misuzu Shobō, 1990), 12: 333.
12. Again the distance between Tanabe and Desmond is not as wide as that between an Eastern thinker who stayed within the confines of the Eastern intellectual tradition and a Western thinker who stayed within the confines of the Western intellectual tradition. Since we have seen that Desmond's metaxology is also hospitable to the possibility of comparative thinking, we should keep in mind that there is neither a sharp opposition nor a clear historico-cultural break between the works of Tanabe and Desmond.

13 Henneberg, "Faith and Grace in the Thought of Tanabe Hajime and Søren Kierkegaard," 129. Henneberg argues that the Kyoto school philosophy as a whole belongs to this peculiar position of "world philosophy," beyond the East-West distinction: "It is… fair to say that the legacy of the Kyoto School should be understood neither as Buddhist thought forced into western philosophical expression, nor western universal discourse dressed up in traditional Japanese apparel. Rather, the output from this school may be best be understood as a set of unique contributions from a distinctly Japanese perspective to a nascent worldwide dialogue of cross-cultural philosophy, that is to say from a perspective that is fundamentally determined by its historical layers of traditional culture while at the same time… it is also conditioned by a recent layer of contact with the West. In this way, the Kyoto School may be regarded as a group of thinkers that stood between—or as some authors claim—moved beyond East and West."

14 See also AWASN, 19. Here, Desmond makes a good point by saying that whether we reside in the analytic or the continental side of contemporary philosophy, we equally suffer from "the aftermath of the self-inflation of idealistic thought"—the intellectual inflation which "led to a rational bubble which in time burst, leading to a painful deflation, and a long recession of reason, even to a depression, certainly diminution of our confidence in reason."

15 Yet, if we take the failure of modern philosophy as the final word on the destiny of any philosophical endeavors, then how can we qualify anything written in the twentieth to twenty-first century to be "philosophical" at all? When we say "postmodern thinking," the term "postmodern" may add the chronological index to the activity of thinking. What is worse is that this approach could also deny the possibility of philosophical thinking altogether. Within the impoverished ethos of postmodernity, it would constitute a contradiction in terms to say "postmodern *philosophy*." Thus, the usual classification of "postmodernity" spoken in the sense of radical skepticism cannot be used for defining Tanabe as a philosopher in the present age.

16 Tanabe, *PM*, 76 (5). Desmond also talks about the importance of this breakthrough after the breakdown. He argues that the contracted understanding of mind, being, and their relation to each other will go through a breakdown (as the self comes to realize that it is not the ultimate foundation of the self- and intermediation of the other), but this breakdown only signals the breakthrough to a renewed sense of mind and being that accounts for their open intermediations. For these accounts, consult *PU*, 35, 44; *BB*, 30, 192-193, 386, 415, 478-479, 500, 541; *EB*, 112, 181, 241; *GB*, 28-30, 136-137, 270.

17 Tanabe, *PM*, 54-55 (1).

18 Tanabe, "The Logic of Species and the World-Scheme," in *Tanabe Hajime Zenshū*, eds. Nishitani Keiji et al. (Tokyo: Chikuma Shobō, 1963), 6: 169-264, hereafter *THZ*. For a concise introduction and partial translation of this work by Ralf Müller, see *Japanese Philosophy: A Source Book*, eds. James W. Heisig, Thomas P. Kasulis, and John Maraldo (Honolulu: University of Hawai'i Press, 2011), 674-677.

19 Tanabe, "The Logic of Species and the World-Scheme," 184. For Tanabe's concept of transformation, see also *PM*, 207 (109).

20 Tanabe, "Eternity, History and Act," *THZ* 7: 101-170.

21 Tanabe, "Eternity, History and Act," 104-105.

22 Leopold von Ranke, *Über die Epochen der neueren Geschichte: Vorträge dem Konige Maximilian II. von Bayern im Herbst 1854 zu Berchtesgaden Gehalten* (Leipzig: Duncker & Humblot, 1906), 15-17. This text is translated into Japanese by a Kyoto

school philosopher, Suzuki Shigetaka, and Aihara Shinsaku and published in 1941 through Iwanami Shoten.
23 Tanabe, "Eternity, History and Act," 109. For Tanabe's view of history, consult also the essay published in June 1940: "Historical Reality" (*THZ* 8: 117–170). In *THZ* 8: 161–163, he clearly gives up the notion of history as a linear development and describes it as a series of concentric circles that never close on themselves but constantly get wider. For the clearest exposition of this essay and Tanabe's notion of history, see Goto-Jones, "The Kyoto School and the History of Political Philosophy," 11.
24 Cf. *BHD*, 71; *HG*, 141–145, 147–151.
25 This reflection alone should enable us to conceive of the history of philosophy as the history of world philosophies where Tanabe's and Desmond's frameworks of thinking are placed in an open community with each other.
26 Tanabe, "Eternity, History and Act," 110.
27 Tanabe, "Eternity, History and Act," 110–111. See also Tanabe, "Historical Reality," *THZ* 8: 133, 166–167.
28 For the qualification for what counts as an age that could overcome the other, see Tanabe, "Eternity, History and Act," 111.
29 Tanabe, "Eternity, History and Act," 111. Cf. Taguchi Shigeru (田口茂), "The Logic of *Tenkan*: The Generation of Tanabean Thinking and 'Logic as Ethics'" (「転換」の論理：田辺的思考の生成と〈倫理としての論理〉), *Shisō* (思想), no. 1053 (2012): 147. Taguchi acutely argues that Tanabe's works in the middle period (i.e., the *Logic of Species*, etc.) are already utilizing the concept of *tenkan* to the fullest extent as the "operative concept" (with a bow to Eugen Fink and his article on *Operative Begriffe* in Husserl) and this concept, accordingly Taguchi, is one of the main themes that propels Tanabe's thinking in his later works.
30 This means that the absolute dialectic found in Tanabe's metanoetics both frees us from the contracted sense of philosophy in modernity and simultaneously enables us to find the way out of postmodern skepticism. Cf. Murai Norio (村井則夫), "Baroque Philosophy of Tanabe Hajime: The Mechanics and Symbolism of the Absolute Dialectic," *Shisō* (思想), no. 1053 (2012): 117–119, 137–138, 139. Murai acutely indicates that "'absolute mediation' that plays the central role of Tanabe's thought does not aim at the static unity that dissolves contradictions or the endpoint that completely overcomes struggles but points at the movement itself in which the completely different things unexpectedly meet each other and in which a new life that neither of them could predict in the first place as they are denied by each other through their encounter" (117). In this sense, the "absolute dialectic does not constitute the synthetic system that takes absolute spirit as its pinnacle but rather the dynamic locus within which various fields [of studies] can differentiate from and negate each other: accordingly, philosophy as absolute dialectic does not only refuse to privilege any area [of studies], but also allow them to penetrate each other through mutual transcendence and gives the movement of hybrid thinking that self-reflectively takes in the changing processes of these [studies] and continuously changes its own topos" (119). Murai clearly recognizes that Tanabe's later formulation of absolute dialectic, which allows him to transcend from one field of study to another (i.e., science, art, religion, and philosophy) and constitutes the "purely crisscrossing philosophy" that "resonates with the Baroque world," clearly goes beyond the limit of Hegel's dialectic (138–139).
31 J. Kieth Hyde makes the same point for grounding his excellent comparative analyses of the concepts of power in Kierkegaard's and Nietzsche's existentialism. Cf. Hyde,

Concepts of Power in Kierkegaard and Nietzsche (Burlington, VT: Ashgate Publishing Co., 2010), 2.

32　Hyde points out that the concepts of power in the works of Nietzsche and Kierkegaard are crucial for comparing these two thinkers. He argues that they would agree on the concept of power as a kind of creative power and see it as the foundation of reality as well as the enabling condition of human existence. But clearly they locate the source of this power in two completely different things, namely, humans and God. Because of this, they come to form completely different forms of existentialism. Interestingly, however, this does not prevent them from criticizing the rational universalists (such as, Kant and Hegel) who locate this creative source of truth in immanence and identify it with the notion of the divine absolute. Nietzsche would see them as failing to recognize the source as lying in humans, whereas Kierkegaard sees them as being unfaithful to the true creative source of our reality beyond ourselves. Despite their great differences, they are equally dissatisfied with the Kantian and the Hegelian framework of thinking about reality and our existence.

33　Tanabe, "Kant's Theory of Teleology," *THZ* 3: 1–72, hereafter *KTT*.

34　Tanabe, "Hegel's Philosophy and Dialectic," *THZ* 3: 73–369, hereafter *HPD*.

35　For a detailed analysis of the *KTT* and of how Tanabe succeeds in understanding Kant's teleology as the consistent development of the will of reason, see Himi Kiyoshi, "Tanabe Hajime's Understanding of Kantian Teleology," *Campana*, no. 11 (2004): 139–146. The reflections on the third *Critique* in the *KTT* already show Tanabe's departure from the Kantian framework of thinking in several ways. First, he acknowledges, "Kant did not principally explain the unifying relationship among these three kinds of purposiveness" (4). So, he further articulates, "what appears as Kant in this text is what Kant ought to be rather than how he has been seen to be" (4). That is to say, Tanabe should be seen as developing his own thought on teleology through his reflection on Kant's theory of it. Second, Tanabe relies on Hermann Cohen's concept of the infinitesimals as the ground for completing the development of his own theory, namely the continuity between what is and what ought to be in Kant's philosophy. Third, as Himi rightly argues, Tanabe's elucidation of the relationship among three kinds of purposiveness "leads him inevitably to the study of Hegelian dialectical way of thinking" and marks "an apparent metamorphosis into a dialectical thinker" (145–146). The key arguments that Tanabe gives for proving the relationship among three kinds of purposiveness are much more Hegelian in their nature. With regard to the first, we can still maintain that Tanabe remains within the Kantian framework of thinking. Perhaps, we can say the same for the second. But with regard to the third, it is quite clear that Tanabe is moving from Kantian criticism to Hegelian dialectic in his way of thinking.

36　Tanabe, *KTT*, 9.

37　Note also the year of 1948 was just two years after the publication of *Philosophy as Metanoetics* (1946), the completion of *The Logic of Species* (1947), and the same year in which *Dialectic of Christianity* (1948) was published.

38　Tanabe, *KTT*, 7.

39　Tanabe, *KTT*, 8–9. See also Ōshima Yasumasa's emphasis on the notion of *tenkan* in his commentary to the *Logic of Species*, *THZ* 7: 384.

40　In his earlier essays, Tanabe shows his attempt to categorize the different aspects of Hegel's thought in the manner of a neo-Kantian thinker, while the later essays begin to elaborate on his critical interpretation that Hegel's dialectic falls victim to the problematic logic of emanation and therefore it belongs to the logic of being.

41 Cf., Tanabe, *THZ* 3: 532.
42 Tanabe, *THZ* 3: 9. Kōyama Iwao is right in saying that this text is a "document of a hard-fought battle of thought" for Tanabe in no less a fashion than was the text of *Intuition and Reflection in Self-Consciousness* for Nishida. Cf. Tanabe, *THZ* 3: 532–534; Nishida Kitarō, *Intuition and Reflection in Self-Consciousness*, trans. Valdo H. Viglielmo, Takeuchi Yoshinori, and Joseph S. O'Leary (Albany: State University of New York Press, 1987), xxiii. For the philosophical significance of this deadlock in Tanabe's later philosophy of religion, see *PM* 102–103 (26–27), 352 (224).
43 Cf. Tanabe, *PM* 61 (lvi), 104 (27), 109–110 (31), 352 (224), 391–392 (254).
44 Tanabe, "Dialectic of the Logic of Species," *THZ* 7: 254. For the translation of the first chapter of this essay, see David Dilworth and Taira Sato, "The Logic of Species as Dialectic: Shino ronri no benshoho, by Tanabe Hajime," *Monumenta Nipponica* 24, no. 3 (1969): 273–288.
45 Tanabe, *KTT*, 10. Cf. *HPD*, 83.
46 See, for instance, *KTT*, 39. Tanabe clearly shows a vision of the absolute dialectic in which the worth of an object as the other to the subject is granted for the object. Even in the midst of struggling with Kant, he uses Hegelian language to think about the end of nature and seems to be able to express what he will later develop clearly as the intermediation of the object and the subject in the absolute dialectic.
47 Cf. Tanabe, "Dialectic of the Logic of Species," *THZ* 253–254. If we compare the essays written in mid-1930s with the later ones, this key change is quite audible. The last essay written in 1946 seems to overhaul the language of self-determining dialectic in the earlier works and enable Tanabe to attend to the truly self-sacrificial transcendence of absolute nothingness through his praxis of metanoesis. I do not, however, mean by the "lack of religious tone" in Tanabe's works in 1930s as being completely devoid of any religious languages. As Heisig and Fujita have pointed out, there are some parts in the *Logic of Species* (e.g., *THZ* 7: 24, 99) where Tanabe equates the nation with Śākyamuni and likens individual participations in it as *imitatio Christi*, thus justifying the sacrificial dedication of the single individual for the specific state. In these occasions, Tanabe clearly utilizes the religious language but what is important, as Heisig rightly says, is that "Tanabe has lost touch with the original purposes of his logic of the specific" and fails to capture the true meaning of the religious language. For these points, see Heisig, "Philosophy as Spirituality," 380; Fujita Masakatsu (藤田正勝), "Tanabe Hajime's Thinking: Through the Concept of 'Absolute Nothingness,'" *Shisō* (思想), no. 1053 (2012): 177–178.
48 Tanabe, "A Clarification of the Meaning of the Logic of Species," *THZ* 6: 475. Cf. Heisig, Kasulis and Maraldo, *Japanese Philosophy*, 677–683.
49 Cf. Tanabe, "A Clarification of the Meaning of the Logic of Species," *THZ* 6: 460; *PM*, 425–428 (281–283), 432–434 (287–288). The best description of the logic of species in early parts of *The Logic of Species* can be found in Heisig's foreword to the English transition of the *Philosophy as Metanoetics*. Heisig explains that species for Tanabe is "an irrational substratum of human Existenz itself, the ground of the 'will to life' (xvi)" and further articulates, "Tanabe's species begins from a radical irrationality of pure desire for life at the core of human consciousness…." So, "the dialectic of absolute mediation" as the core of the logic of species comes to show that "[i]n mediating the will to life of its specific contingency, the individual exercises the will to power of its particular freedom, and vice versa." Thus, the dialectic of absolute mediation in the logic of species, demonstrating "the last vestiges of vitalism," represents Tanabe's philosophy of life. But his further attempt to complete his notion of absolute

nothingness leads him to give up this philosophy and formulate philosophy of death from *Philosophy as Metanoetics* onward. Now at the outset, Heisig's take on the logic of species and absolute dialectic seems to prevent us from seeing the logic of species as the *metanoetic* intermediation of genus, species, and individuals, that is, absolute dialectic. (Cf. Hase Shōtō, *What Is the Original Vow: What Shinran Saw as the Buddhism* (本願とは何か：親鸞の捉えた仏教) [Kyoto: Hōzōkan, 2015], 266–267.) But this does not have to be the case. First, the distinction between *The Logic of Species* and *Philosophy as Metanoetics* is not as clear as it seems since the term "metanoetics" begins to play its important role in Tanabe's reformulation of the logic of species toward the end of *The Logic of Species* (especially from "Eternity, History, Act") and this appearance dates before the publication of *Philosophy as Metanoetics*. Simultaneously, the completion of the former outdates the publication of the latter; hence, it is very likely that Tanabe continued to reformulate the logic of species as he pursued his metanoetic thinking. Second, if the logic of species, which Tanabe specifically defines as the absolute dialectic (*THZ* 6: 477), overcomes the framework of Hegelian dialectic, the logic of species must go through a "transfiguration" from philosophy of life to philosophy of death as Heisig also acknowledges. This means that the logic of species goes through the transition from the logic of self-determining dialectic to the self-negating dialectic of absolute nothingness just as Tanabe goes through the same transition in the course of his life as a philosopher. In this sense, we can claim both that Heisig's initial clarification of the nature of the logic of species is correct and that Tanabe's reference to the logic of species as the absolute dialectic in his later works needs our attentiveness to the transfiguration of the same logic seen in Tanabe's later religious philosophy.

Some commentators of Tanabe seem to suffer from this vacillation between the logic of species as the dialectical self-determination of humans and that as the transformative intermediation of human self and divine other. Matteo Cestari, for instance, clearly acknowledges that the state as intersubjective manifestation of the absolute nothingness in the logic of species differs from Hegel's objective spirit because of two points: first, the individual in the logic of species is not simply the irrational but "trans-rational" (65) and second, the logic itself has the "religious characterization… beyond dispute" (66). However, Cestari concludes, "notwithstanding his anti-Hegelianism, [Tanabe] is firmly convinced of the Hegelian identity of the Real and the Ideal: if the nation is the actualization of the universal, it can only be fundamentally rational, or at least a kind of 'the best possible nation'" (68). The difficulty of conceiving the clear break of the logic of species from Hegel's logic of dialectical self-determination lies in the fact that Tanabe does not insist on the religious dimension of the absolute mediation in this logic till the end of the massive text. Thus, depending on how religious this logic of species is going to be read and what we mean by the "religious" in reference to other texts on metanoetics, many commentators will continue to vacillate on the question of whether Tanabe's logic of species is an original contribution to the history of philosophy or, as Heisig once said, another "vintage Hegel." For Cestari's point, see his "The Individual and Individualism in Nishida and Tanabe," *Re-Politicising*, 49–74; and for Heisig's point, *PM*, 17–18 (xviii–xix).

50 Granted that the structure of the genus-species-individual intermediations in Tanabe's logic of species seems to be more complicated than the dialectical relation of the universal, the particular, and the individual in Hegel, but I suspect that they reach the same conclusion so long as the former follows the self-determining logic of the

latter. Just as the dialectical instrumentalization of the particular (including the finite individuals) for the sake of the self-determining universal, we could see how the earlier form of the logic of species (i.e., philosophy of life) could be seen to utilize the self-sacrifice of the finite individual for the universal (i.e., genus) to mediate with itself in and through the particular (i.e., species). For this point, see Tanabe, "The Logic of State Existence," *THZ* 7: 90–91.

51 Tanabe, "The Logic of Social Existence," *THZ* 6: 181.
52 Tanabe, "The Logic of the Social Ontological Structure," *THZ* 6: 325–327; "A Clarification of the Meaning of the Logic of Species," *THZ* 467–468, 476–477, 509. This is the way in which Tanabe talks about Hegel's inability to account for the evil (i.e., the irrational) in *PM*: cf. Tanabe, *PM*, 385 (249), 412 (270).
53 Tanabe clearly identifies the logic of species with the absolute dialectic through his criticism of Hegel and Nishida from "A Clarification of the Meaning of the Logic of Species" (*THZ* 6: 477).
54 This is the reason why often Tanabe explains that the knife of nothingness cuts through these terms to make their distinction, but since it is not any of these terms, it does not separate them. An analogy that he gives to this distinction is "Dedekind's cut": that is, a series of natural numbers is maintained as a series because there is a cut by irrational numbers that is not a part of the series but inseparable from it as its enabling condition. His reference to the notion of Dedekind's cut is consistently present from the early works (such as, "The World of Infinity," *THZ* 1: 231) and numerous throughout the *Tanabe Zenshū*. In relation to the religion of philosophy, see especially *PM*, 165; *ELP*, 449–450, 454.
55 Cf. Cyril O'Regan, *The Heterodox Hegel* (Albany, NY: State University of New York Press, 1994), 151–171.
56 Cf. Tanabe, *PM*, 269, *THZ* 6: 147: "The individual is mediated by nothingness by a self-negating mediation of the specific in which the being of the specific functions as a nothing-qua-being, thus making the individual a being-qua-nothingness." An English translation of this passage can be found in Heisig, "Tanabe's Logic of the Specific and the Critique of the Global Village," 279. See also Langdon Gilkey, "Tanabe and the Philosophy of Religion," *RPTH*, 78–81.
57 Tanabe, *PM*, 92–93 (18), 99–100 (23), 188–189 (94), 309–310 (190–191), 416–419 (274–276), 430 (285). See also Fujita, "Tanabe Hajime's Thinking," 169. Fujita points out that in the *Outline of Philosophy*, Tanabe describes this transcending movement in the interrelation of individuals and species as the activity (*hataraki*, はたらき): "by 'transcendence,' it means the act of transcending or more precisely nothing but the activity of absolute negation that denies the immanence and takes it as the moment of mediation" (*THZ* 3: 512). In this sense, the appearance of what transcends immanence (i.e., absolute nothingness) cannot be a static representation of the interrelations between individuals and species but has to be the dynamic empowering of their active intermediations through the genus or the absolute nothingness. Tanabe does not spell this out in his earlier works but already in them, we see his consistent effort to conceptualize the absolute as the dynamic enabling of the active intermediation of individuals and species.
58 For the agapeic nature of Tanabe's absolute, see Tanabe, "The Development of the Concept of Existence," *THZ* 7: 242–243; *PM*, 290 (175), 394–395 (256), 415–416 (273) and especially 238 (132–133) for the absolute dialectic as the open unity of two opposing terms: "dialectical unity is both a unity and an opposition. It is not the sort of unity that brings contradictions into synthesis by way of negation and

sublation, but a unity that leaves contradictions just as they are. Insofar as dialectical synthesis contains the idea of sublation or sublimation, it necessarily implies the removal or dismissal of the opposition between thesis and antithesis, and therefore cannot get beyond the realm of rational identity. But such a synthesis is different from the unity of the dialectic of love or the unity of the Great Compassion. In these latter, contradictory opposites are never abrogated. Rather, because the subject dies in the depths of the contradiction, the opposition ceases to be an opposition, but the contradictories are left as they are."

59 Tanabe, "Ethics and Logic," *THZ* 7: 195; *PM*, 415 (273), 439 (292).
60 Cf. Tanabe, "Ethics and Logic," *THZ* 7: 194–195. *PM*, 83 (10), 415 (273), 436–437 (290).
61 Absolute nothingness, for Tanabe, signifies the absolute self-negating self-mediation. So, it manifests itself through the intermediations among genus, species, and individual. For genus to be concretized through species, species must go through its self-negating self-mediation with genus, while for the species to intermediate with genus, the individual must go through the self-negating self-mediation, that is, a metanoetic conversion of its hearts-and-minds from the will to self-power to the will to other-power. The first explicit discussion concerning the importance of the metanoetic conversion for the completion of the logic of species occurs in "The Logic of State Existence" (*THZ* 7: 119), but the need of this transformative intermediations among genus, species, and individual from the self-determining will to self-sacrificing will for the other can be found in many other places throughout *The Logic of Species*: cf. Tanabe, "A Clarification of the Meaning of the Logic of Species," *THZ* 6: 473, 480–484; "Eternity, History and Act," 132–133, 167–168; "The Development of the Concept of Existence," *THZ* 7: 233–234; "The Dialectic of the Logic of Species," *THZ* 7: 272–273; *PM*, 79–80 (8), 83 (10), 124–125 (44), 412–416 (271–273).
62 Tanabe, "Dialectic of the Logic of Species," *THZ* 7: 313. Cf. *PM*, 249 (139), 332 (207–208), 337 (211), 389 (252).
63 Tanabe, "Dialectic of the Logic of Species," *THZ* 7: 355. Cf. *PM*, 388 (252). Note also how Tanabe translates the term *zange* as metanoesis in reference to John the Baptist in the Gospel of Matthew: "repent (*metanoeō*): for the kingdom of heaven is at hand" (Matthew 4:17). But clearly he recognizes the philosophical implication of transcendence (i.e., meta) vis-à-vis the philosophical endeavors based on reason (i.e., noesis). For this point, see Fujita, "Tanabe Hajime's Thinking," 180.
64 The *gensō*, *ōsō*, and their interrelation as *ōsō*-qua-*gensō* are the key notions in Tanabe's philosophy of religion, and precisely because of this, we can acknowledge the root of Tanabe's reflections on the philosophy of religion in the Pure Land Buddhist tradition. I will further discuss the philosophical importance of these notions in Chapter 8.
65 Tanabe, "Eternity, History and Act," 148. Cf. Tanabe, *PM* 335–336 (210), 356 (227), 363–364 (232–233), 366–368 (235–236).
66 Tanabe, "Eternity, History and Act," 117. Cf. Tanabe, *PM*, 186–187 (93).
67 Tanabe, "Eternity, History and Act," 111.
68 This is precisely why Tanabe's philosophy marks the transition from the modern framework of thinking that closes the boundary of its philosophical investigation within its own intellectual tradition to the contemporary framework of thinking that adopts the self-negating principle of great compassion (*daihi-soku-daihi*). This principle moves the thinker to extend the scope of his philosophical examination beyond the confines of the particular intellectual traditions.
69 *BB*, 198.

70 *BB*, 311. Think further with the following image the methodological implications of a metaxological community for the togetherness of Eastern and Western philosophy: "Community communicates itself in a plurivocity that looks to the redemption of equivocity. This communivocity is the metaxological togetherness of a pluralism of voices, where no one voice shouts down the other voices, or reduces them to itself. Even the voice of evil too is allowed its say, with its smirk and sneer of 'Polyannna'— allowed, let be, in the hope that, in time, its freedom will be converted into the redeemed voice of a good" (*BB*, 434). The task of comparative philosophy, therefore, is to create this plurivocal harmony of harmonies wherein "many voices sing together, none loses its integrity for itself, yet each also acts on behalf of, sings for, the beauty of all together" (*BB*, 324).
71 *BB*, 311. *PO*, 102–109.
72 Some self-reflective readers might have noticed that in the end of Part One, we have come full circle. The method of comparative philosophy that I have elucidated through the critical examinations both of metaxology and metanoetics has already been at work in the process of my elucidation. This again testifies to the important point that I have mentioned earlier: if a philosophical method is to be as comprehensive and coherent as it should be, then it will dictate philosopher's self-reflective description of it. My initial comparative investigations of Tanabe's and Desmond's works, in this sense, exemplify the method of comparative philosophy that I have reached through my self-reflective engagement with these thinkers. If I were to mention one shortcoming with this methodological reflection, however, it would be the tightness of space in which it had to present the key elements of metaxology and metanoetics. To mend the initial ambiguity that is likely to result from my dense presentations of Desmond's and Tanabe's thought and that is likely to cast some doubt on the legitimacy of my reflections, therefore, I must beg my readers to come back to Part One after proceeding to read the Parts Three and Four of this book. These later parts will give more concrete pictures of these thinkers' philosophical contributions and help us understand more clearly what is harmoniously at work in both of their foundations.

Chapter 3

1 There are some tendencies among the commentators of these contemporary thinkers to associate their thought with Kierkegaard's thinking. The extent to which Desmond and Tanabe criticize the problems of rational universalism, I think, is the right move, and certainly, there are a lot of places where they both explicitly side with the arguments that Kierkegaard makes against Kant and Hegel. Nevertheless, there are also some good reasons why we cannot explain metanoetics or metaxology merely in terms of Kierkegaardian existentialism. For this point, see *WDR*, 223–224, *ITST*, 17; *PU*, 61–64; *ELP*, 327.
2 I recognize, however, that those who wish to study the works of Desmond and Tanabe would find these textual analyses to be of utmost significance. To satisfy this scholarly need to a moderate extent, therefore, I will refer to their passages where we can find the same criticisms of Kant and Hegel in endnotes.
3 Cf. Kant, "Critique of Practical Reason," in *Practical Philosophy*, ed. and trans. Mary J. Gregor (Cambridge: Cambridge University Press, 1999), 141–142 (5: 6), hereafter *KpV*.

4 Cf. *Conflict*, 280 (7:58–59), 291 (7:72); *KpV*, 162 (5: 28–29), 166 (5:33), 174 (5:43), 267 (5:15); "Groundwork of the Metaphysics of Morals," in *Practical Philosophy*, ed. and trans. Mary J. Gregor (Cambridge: Cambridge University Press, 1996), 94 (4:446), 99 (4:452–453), hereafter *GMS*.

5 Cf. *GMS*, 69 (4:416), 81 (4:431), 84 (4:434); *KpV*, 158, 210, 267. For more detailed accounts of the criteria by which one can transcend the particularity of one's self-interest and enter into the universal community with the other rational selves, see the first section of Jacqueline Mariña, "The Religious Significance of Kant's Ethics," *American Catholic Philosophical Quarterly* 75, no. 2 (2001): 181–192. For Desmond's account of Kant's categorical imperative, see *EB*, 135.

6 Cf. *GMS*, 55–57 (4:400–401), 78–80 (4:428–429), *KpV*, 205 (5:81).

7 *GMS*, 80 (4:429). Cf. *KpV*, 210 (587).

8 Cf. *GMS*, 81–83 (4:431–433); *KpV*, 174–175 (5:43–44).

9 *GMS*, 83 (4:433). Cf. *KpV*, 243 (5:128–9).

10 *GMS*, 83 (4:433). Kant remains equivocal concerning the sovereign status of rational beings in the kingdom of ends because they need to postulate God as a moral legislator. For Kant's demotion of the sovereign status of rational beings, see *KpV*, 206–207 (5:82–83).

11 This point is explicitly stated in the opening of the *Religion*. Cf. *Religion*, 57 (6:3–4).

12 *KpV*, 226–227 (5: 108), 231 (5:113–114). Cf. *KpV*, 226–227 (5:108); "Lectures on the Philosophical Doctrine of Religion," *Religion and Rational Theology*, eds. Allen W. Wood and George Di Giovanni, and trans. Allen W. Wood (Cambridge: Cambridge University Press, 1996), 343–344 (28:996), 347 (28:1000–1001), hereafter *LPDR*; *Religion*, 58 (6:5), 137 (6:104).

13 *LPRD*, 406–407 (28:1072), 420 (28:1090). Johannes de Silentio makes the same observation by saying that "he who does not work does get bread, and he who sleeps gets it even more abundantly than he works," *FT*, 27.

14 Cf. *GMS*, 55 (4:400), 77 (4:425–426), 88 (4:439); *KpV*, 190 (5:62), 267 (5:159).

15 Cf. *GMS*, 70–71 (4:418).

16 *KpV*, 240–241 (5:125).

17 *KpV*, 240 (5:125).

18 *KpV*, 241 (5:126). Cf. *KpV*, 231 (5:113), 255 (5:143); *LPDR*, 349 (28:1003), 357 (28:1012), 406–7 (1071–1072), 415 (28:1083); "What Does It Mean to Orient Oneself in Thinking?" in *Religion and Rational Theology*, eds. Allen W. Wood and George Di Giovanni, and trans. Allen W. Wood (Cambridge: Cambridge University Press, 1996), 12 (8:139), hereafter *WDO*.

19 *KpV*, 241 (5:126). Cf. *Conflict*, 274 (7:51); *KpV*, 255 (5:144), 257 (5:146); *LPDR*, 356 (28:1011); "On the Common Saying: That Maybe Correct in Theory," *Practical Philosophy*, ed. And trans. Mary J. Gregor (Cambridge; Cambridge University Press, 1996), 282 (8:279); *Religion*, 184–185 (6:163–164); *WDO*, 14–15 (8:141–143).

20 Cf. Jacqueline Mariña, "The Religious Significance of Kant's Ethics," *American Catholic Philosophical Quarterly* 75, no. 2 (2001): 198. Mariña highlights the consonance between the categorical imperative and the commandment of loving one's neighbor as oneself with some references to Kierkegaard's *Works of Love*. But her analysis faces the same question: "While it is not doubt true that for Kant the moral law and the will of God must be conceived of as conforming to one another, the deeper question is whether the will of God must be thought of and defined in terms of the moral law, or whether the moral law must be thought of in terms of the will of God. The problem

is, therefore, which must be prior in the order of knowledge, knowledge of the will of God, or knowledge of the moral law?"
21 *Religion*, 165 (6:139). Cf. *LPDR*, 347–348 (28:1001–1002), *Religion*, 59–60 (6:6).
22 *Religion*, 165 (6:139).
23 Cf. *GMS*, 63 (4:408–409); *Religion*, 58 (6:5), 137 (6:104).
24 *LPDR*, 407–8 (28:1073–1074), my paraphrase. Cf. *Conflict*, 279 (7:57–58); *LPDR*, 447 (28:1122); *WDO*, 12 (8:139).
25 *LPDR*, 409 (28:1075).
26 *Religion*, 133–134 (6:99).
27 *Religion*, 168 (6:142). Cf. *GMS*, 90–93 (4:441–445). Note how Kant presupposes God as either an idea of moral perfection or (immoral) dark beyond subjugating humanity into its mechanical servility. See also John E. Hare, "Kant on Recognizing Our Duties as God's Commands," *Faith and Philosophy* 17, no. 4 (October 2000): 466. Like Mariña, Hare views the question as asking "either we derive the notion of God's perfection from our moral concepts or we do not." From there, Hare tries to solve this dilemma by deriving the obligation of the moral law from the human and divine joint-authorship, where Kant's systematic union of rational selves is seen as "a common wealth of ends" (*à la* J. L. Mackie). This solution seems to have two problems: (1) it does not take the nature of the Kantian God into account, and (2) deviates from (and highlights the problem of calling) the idea of the universal community of *ens rationis* as the "kingdom." For Desmond's criticism of this point, see *EB*, 137.
28 *LPDR*, 442 (28:1116). Cf. "Moral Philosophy: Collins's Lecture Notes (1784–1785)," *Lectures on Ethics*, ed. Peter Heath, J.B. Schneewind, and trans. Peter Heath (Cambridge, Cambridge University Press, 1997), 76 (27:283). Kant says "of the Lawgiver" that "nobody, not even the deity, is an originator of moral laws, since they have not arisen from choice, but are practically necessary; ... But moral laws can still be subject to a lawgiver (unter einem Gesetzgeber stehen); there may be a being who is omnipotent and has power to execute these laws, and to declare that this moral law is at the same time a law of His will and obliges everyone to act accordingly. Such a being is then a lawgiver, though not an originator." This position is held also in *GMS*, 91 (4:443): "unless we think of divine will in terms of morality, the concept of his will still left to us, made up of the attributes of desire for glory and dominion combined with dreadful representations of power and vengefulness, would have to be the foundation for a system of morals that would be directly opposed to morality."
29 For the equivocal showing of the divine absolute and its significance in the works of Kant, see *EB*, 136n, 136–138.
30 *KpV*, 249 (5:135).
31 *Religion*, 177 (6:154). Cf. *Conflict*, 284 (7:64), *KpV*, 244 (5:129).
32 *Religion*, 134 (6:99). Cf. *Conflict*, 292 (7:73–74).
33 *Religion*, 199 (6:181).
34 Cf. *Conflict*, 262 (7:36): "As far as its matter, i.e., the object is concerned, religion does not differ in any point from morality, for it is concerned with duties as such. Its distinction from morality is a merely formal one: that reason in its legislation uses the Idea of God, which is derived from morality itself, to give morality influence on man's will to fulfill all his duties."
35 *Religion*, 137 (6:103).
36 *Conflict*, 289 (7:70). Note here how Kant depicts humanity as a kind of divine being who is "the original maker of all his presentations and concepts" besides his absolute authorship of his own actions. See also *Conflict*, 289–290 (7:71).

37 Kierkegaard sometimes sounds much more critical of Kant's absolutization of human autonomy than de Silentio. In one of his journal entries, Kierkegaard states the following: "Kant was of the opinion that man is his own law (autonomy)—that is, he binds himself under the law which he himself gives himself. Actually, in a profounder sense, this is how lawlessness or experimentation are established. This is not being rigorously earnest any more than Sancho Panza's self-administered blows to his own bottom were vigorous," *Søren Kierkegaard's Journals and Papers*, ed. and trans. Howard V. Hong and Edna H. Hong (Bloomington: Indiana University Press, 1970), 1:76 (188), hereafter *JP*. In the same entry, Kierkegaard concludes that if a man does not place the law giver higher than himself, "the man is allowed to live on in self-complacent illusion and make-believe and experimentation, but this also means; utterly without grace." At any rate, this is exactly what Johannes anticipates: "If the ethical entirely equals the divine absolute, it is proper to say that every duty is essentially duty to God, but if no more can be said than this, then it is also said that I actually have no duty to God. The duty becomes duty by being traced back to God, but in the duty itself I do not enter into relation to God.... The whole existence of the human race rounds itself off as a perfect, self-contained sphere, and then the ethical is that which limits and fills at one and the same time. God comes to be an invisible vanishing point, an impotent thought; his power is only in the ethical, which fills all of existence." Cf. *FT*, 60 and 68.

38 By the fact that reason must postulate the divine absolute as the ruler of our ethical community apropos of the concept of morality, therefore, Kant has an ample ground for wondering if there are more things in heaven and earth than are dreamt of in his own philosophy. Cf. Hegel, *Lectures on the Philosophy of Religion*, ed. and trans. Peter C. Hodgson et al. (Berkeley: University of California Press, 1988), 173 (317), hereafter *LPR*: "inasmuch as we know something as a limit, we are already beyond it." The pagination of *Vorlesungen über die Philosophie der Religion*, ed. Walter Jaeschke (Hamburg: Felix Meiner, 1983-1985) will be indicated in parentheses.

39 Cf. *KpV*, 249 (5:135-135) and *Religion*, 189 (6:169): "Anthropomorphism... is highly dangerous with respect to our practical relation to [divine] will and to our very morality; for, since we are making a God for ourselves, we create him in the way we believe that we can most easily win him over to our advantage, and ourselves be dispensed from the arduous and uninterrupted effort of affecting the innermost part of our moral disposition." In endnote to this passage, Kant writes, "every human being must make [a God] according to moral concepts... in order to honor in him the one who made him. For in whatever manner a being has being made known to him by somebody else, and described as God, indeed, even if such a being might appear to him in person... a human being must yet confront this representation with his ideal first, in order to judge whether he is authorized to hold and revere this being as Divinity. Hence, on the basis of revelation alone, without that concept being previously laid down in its purity at its foundation as touchstone, there can be no religion, and reverence for God would be idolatry." But when the divine command is made to be the command of our reason, God is postulated to always favor our moral conduct, and therefore, we are obedient to nobody but ourselves—there is a kind of metaphysical anthropomorphism in Kant's moralization of the divine command. For Desmond's criticism of Kant's usage of notion of the divine absolute, as well as his equation of practical reason to divine command, see *GB*, 97-98.

40 Cf. "On Moral Freedom Revisited," *THZ* 1: 125. Tanabe is right in saying that "so long as we think humanity as a single object in nature, its action is necessarily determined

in accordance with character and circumstances, that is to say, it cannot escape its causal limitation and thereby, there is no room for discussing any freedom."
41 EB, 139. See also, EB, 319–320.
42 KrV, B 422–423 (A 361–362).
43 LPDR, 377 (28:1036). See also LPDR, 385 (28:1045), 421 (28:1091).
44 Cf. William Desmond, "Preface" to BB, xvi; Kierkegaard, "On the Occasion of a Confession" in *Three Discourses on Imagined Occasions*, ed. and trans. Howard V. Hong and Edna H. Hong (Princeton, NJ: Princeton University Press, 1993), 20. Desmond commends one's audacity to think metaphysically since "a philosopher is a seeker." Unless we dare to seek beyond the confines of Kantian philosophy, we will not be able to find our answer to the question of faith and reason. Kierkegaard also commends the cultivation of this audacity to think beyond the conventional framework of thinking.

Chapter 4

1 G.W.F. Hegel, *Early Theological Writings*, trans. T.M. Knox and Richard Kroner (Philadelphia: University of Pennsylvania Press, 1988), 144, hereafter *ETW*; *Hegels theologische Jugendschriften*, ed. Herman Nohl (Tübingen: Mohr), 212. The pagination of Nohl's edition will be inserted in parenthesis.
2 ETW, 144 (212). Cf. ETW, 164 (228). Here Hegel defines "piety" as the disposition that acts from respect for God as lawgiver beyond us.
3 ETW, 213–214 (267–268).
4 LPR, 89–90 (73–74).
5 LPR, 96 (79).
6 LPR, 170 (315).
7 LPR, 170–172 (315–317). Cf. Hegel, *The Science of Logic*, ed. and trans. George di Giovanni (Cambridge: Cambridge University Press, 2010), 102, 109–110, hereafter *SL*; *Wissenschaft Der Logik: Erster Teil Die Objective Logik*, eds. Friedrich Hogemann and Walter Jaeschke (Hamburg: Meiner, 1985), 117–118, 125. The pagination of the German text will be indicated in parenthesis.
8 LPR, 172 (316–317). Cf. SL, 108–110 (124–125).
9 Hegel, *The Encyclopaedia Logic (with the Zusätze): Part I of the Encyclopaedia of Philosophical Sciences with the Zusätze*, trans. T.F. Geraets, W.A. Suchting, H.S. Harris (Indianapolis, IN: Hackett Publishing company, Inc., 1991); "Enzyklopädie Der Philosophischen Wissenschaften Im Grundrisse (1830)," in *Gesammelte Werke*, eds. Wolfgang Bonsiepen and Hans-Christian Lucas (Hamburg: Felix Meiner, 1992) 20:§95, hereafter *Enc. I*.
10 Cf. LPR, 406 (190).
11 LPR, 172 (316).
12 Cf. Kierkegaard, "Four Upbuilding Discourses (1843): To Gain One's Soul in Patience," *Eighteen Upbuilding Discourses*, ed. and trans. Howard V. Hong and Edna H. Hong (Princeton, NJ: Princeton University Press, 1990), 166, hereafter *UD*. Kierkegaard also conceives of the human soul as "a self-contradiction between the external and the internal, the temporal and the eternal" and further articulates this internal division in human existence as the source of its self-determining development (or in Kierkegaardian terms "becoming") and requires the external divine power to close the

gap. For the passages evincing Kierkegaard's adoption of Hegel's concept of soul, see *UD*, 163, 166–167, 172.
13 *LPR*, 438–440 (220–223), 452 (233). See also Hegel, *Hegel's Philosophy of Right*, trans. T.M. Knox (London: Oxford University Press, 2008); "Grundlinen Der Philosophie Des Rechts," *Gesammelte Werke*, eds. Klaus Grotsch and Elizabeth Weisser-Lohmann (Hamburg: Felix Meiner, 2009–2010), 14.1–3:§7, hereafter *PR*.
14 For Hegel's discussions on the distinction between work of love and work of obligations, cf. *PhG*, 230–231; *PhS*, 255–256 (§425). It is highly questionable, however, that Hegel's conception of the ethical self-determination follows the logic of self-sacrificial love (i.e., *agape*) but, as this section will illustrate in detail, it seems to follow the logic of self-centered self-determination (i.e., *eros*). This is precisely what Tanabe and Desmond find problematic in the works of Hegel.
15 *ETW*, 212 (266).
16 Hegel describes this division between the self-consciousness and existent as the "wounds of Spirit [that] heal, and leave no scars behind." Cf. *PhG*, 360–361; *PhS*, 407 (§669).
17 *LPR*, 452 (233). Since, for Hegel, ideality is always inseparable from its actuality, the rationality of the human being must realize itself in and through its natural existence: see several arguments supporting this point in *Enc. I*, 153–154 (§96), 210–211 (§138–140). This second layer of the dialectical intermediation reminds us of the internal split that Dmitri Karamazov, for instance, discusses as the battle between God and devils within ourselves. Cf. Dostoyevsky, *The Brothers Karamazov*, trans. Constance Garnett (New York: The Modern Library, 1996), 118; hereafter, *Karamazov*. But the question still remains: Is this split between good and evil or rational and natural in ourselves, something that we can reconcile through the unifying process of our self-determining self-consciousness alone, or do we need something beyond ourselves to realize this redemption of our soul?
18 Kierkegaard inherits Hegel's conception of divine eternity as that which is at home with itself. See "Three Upbuilding Discourse (1844): The Expectancy of Eternal Salvation," *UD*, 266–267.
19 Cf. *LPR*, 437 (220). This elevation is required by the fact that human beings are essentially rational and the activity of our thinking is the soil in which our religious consciousness can come to flourish. God, as infinite spirit, is available for humanity as a thinking subject, while humanity, as finite spirit, faces the demand to overcome its statue of finitude/untruth and desires to know this divine truth.
20 *LPR*, 414 (197–198). See also, 172–173 (316–317), 405 (189), 447–449 (228–230).
21 *LPR*, 411 (194).
22 For a succinct presentation of this dialectical scheme, see *LPR*, 415–416 (198–199).
23 Cf. *LPR*, 104–105 (87), 415–416 (198–199), 469–470 (250–251), 474–475 (255–256); *PR*, §7.
24 Contrary to Kant's concern, this constitutive presencing of the divine self-determination to human self-determination is not a threat to our autonomy but rather the enabling condition for its possibility because our self-determining process mirrors the divine self-determination.
25 Hegel's dialectical configuration of the reconciliation, therefore, works without a free communication between divinity and humanity, but the former determines itself in and through humanity as the other. And this other does not exist as the other to the divine self, but rather as the self-othering. If we think of this in terms of human's reconciliation with God, Hegel's usage of the term "reconciliation" in

the third intermediation becomes troubling. If the finite is the self-alienation of the infinite, what is finite and evil is really a self-offense of the infinite good; and if the reconciliation is the latter's true self-affirmation through the negation of the finite as its self-othering, this reconciliation is really the self-forgiving of the concrete universal. For further discussions on the self-imposition and self-absolution of evil in Hegel's notion of the divine absolute, see *HG*, 62, 156.

26 Cf. *HG*, 136; *GB*, 167.
27 Hegel remains equivocal with regard to the question of whether there will be the same God (or humanity) in the beginning and the end of its development, since the logic of self-determination uses the expression of "returning to self" in closing its dialectical circle and tries to maintain that what we have in the end is what it essentially is from the beginning. But the language of implicit/explicit or abstract/concrete implies a change in the characteristics of divinity. Cf. Ludwig Feuerbach, "Zur Kritik der Hegelschen Philosophie," *Gesammelte Werke: Kleinere Schriften II (1839–1846)*, Hrsg. Werner Schuffenhauer (Berlin: Akademie, 1982), 25–26: "the first [das Erste] to which I return is no longer the initial, indeterminate, and unproved first, but it is now mediated and therefore no longer the same or, if it is the same, no longer in the same form." Thus, Hegel's God, influenced by Jacob Boehme's Gnosticism, significantly differs from the way in which Kierkegaard conceives of God in reference to James 1:17–22: "Every good gift and every perfect gift is from above and comes down from the Father of lights, with whom there is no change or shadow of variation." For Kierkegaard's reflections on God's unchangeable generosity, see "Four Upbuilding Discourses (1843): Every Good Gift and Every Perfect Gift Is from Above," *UD*, 125–155; "Two Upbuilding Discourses (1843): Love Will Hide a Multitude of Sins," *UD*, 56–57; "Four Upbuilding Discourses (1844); One Who Prays Aright," *UD*, 393.
28 Desmond clearly detects this problem in his analysis of Hegel; cf. *PU*, 50, 116, 176; *GB*, 167. Tanabe's critique of Hegel hinges on the fact that the negativity of the antithesis (i.e., particular) is not taken seriously in relation to the dialectical synthesis. As we will see further in Chapter 8, Tanabe argues that true dialectic (i.e., absolute dialectic) is supposedly capable of accounting for the unity of difference without compromising the irreducible difference between thesis and antithesis, identity and difference, and self and other.
29 In this sense, the dialectical relation of the universal and the particular cannot be conceived of as the work of love. For the contrast between the transcendent God of Christianity and Hegel's dialectical self-determining God in relation to the otherness of creation, see *HG*, 132–137.
30 *PhG*, 104; *PhS*, 105 (§167).
31 *PhG*, 104–105, 106; *PhS*, 106 (§168), 107 (§171). For the self-relating unity of self-consciousness, see *PhG*, 106, 107; *PhS*, 108 (§171), 109 (§173–174). For the dialectical scheme of the development of a living self-consciousness, see *PhG*, 108; *PhS*, 110 (§176).
32 *PhG*, 108; *PhS*, 110 (§176).
33 *PhG*, 108; *PhS*, 110 (§177).
34 *PR*, §187.
35 *PR*, §187.
36 For an interpretation of Chapter 6 of the *PhG* that describes how a historical self enters into the conflicting relationship with others in the manner of civil society, see George di Giovanni, "Faith without Religion, Religion without Faith: Kant and Hegel on Religion," *Journal of the History of Philosophy* 41, no. 3 (2003): 380.

37 *PR*, §260 and see also §257.
38 *PR*, §262.
39 *LPR*, 482 (262).
40 *LPR*, 482 (262).
41 *LPR*, 484n (264).
42 Hegel presents the concept of religion as a foundation for the manifestation of the political state, while making it clear that the latter's worldly freedom is more consummate than the spiritual freedom of the religious community. What he fails to clarify in the end is whether the Absolute Spirit, discussed as if it were more than just a political organization of the state, is ultimately human or something more than what we can determine in the immanent realm of humanity.
43 Cf. "Spirit that is certain of itself: Morality" in Chapter 6, the manifest religion (*die offenbare Religion*) in Chapter 7, and the sublation (*Aufhebung*) of religion to philosophy in Chapter 8 of *PhG*. Di Giovanni interprets the last section of Chapter 6 as showing that "[the protagonists of the *PhG*] should be able to understand that the secret of their Christian faith has been the structure of their social life all along, or, more graphically, that the spirit that they sought in a world-beyond is actually to be found—even as transcendent—within the realm of their community" (382). So, "[b]y the end of Chapter 6, religious faith (Christian or otherwise) is at an end" (382). For the religious dimension of *PhG* in Chapters 7 and 8, see H.S. Harris, *Hegel's Ladder II: The Odyssey of Spirit* (Indianapolis: Hackett Publishing Company, Inc., 1997), 649–763. Harris describes three ways in which Hegel's account of Christianity as the manifest religion compromises the integrity of orthodox representations of Christian fidelity: (1) the conflation of resurrection into Pentecost (694), (2) his concept of fall as a necessary moment for the dialectical development of the Absolute spirit (683–684, 686; *PhG*, §776), and (3) strong influences from Boehme on the heterodox view of the Trinity (678–681, 684). Besides these deviations, the transition from *Vorstellung* to *Begriff* (Harris believes) "entails the elimination of all transcendence. Nothing 'beyond,' nothing outside the circle can break in.... Christianity is the 'absolute religion,' because it makes 'God' conceptually interpretable without residue" (732). So, the move to absolute knowledge overcomes the transcendence that is a *sine qua non* for orthodox Christian faith. Cf. Cyril O'Regan, "The Impossibility of a Christian Reading of the Phenomenology of Spirit: H.S. Harris on Hegel's Liquidation of Christianity," *The Owl of Minerva* 33, no. 1 (2001–2002), 46, 84; Harris, 21, 711. O'Regan understands the "liquidation of Christianity" in Harris' commentary to mean that "while Christianity survives as a historical presupposition for what replaces it, its representational modality of discourse (*Vorstellung*) is surpassed, and with it any residual commitments to a transcendence reality that is beyond human historical existence." He thinks that this dialectical movement from *Vorstellung* to *Begriff* in Chapter 8 "leaves the interpreter in the following position: it is possible to be a Christian and a Hegelian, but not a Hegelian precisely as a Christian" and so, "by a very different route from Kierkegaard's, Harris gives credence to Kierkegaard's either-or: Christianity or Hegelian speculative philosophy." Thus, we can arrive at the same conclusion concerning the impossibility of (Christian) faith in the end of *PhG* as that which we have already seen in *LPR* and *PR*. For Desmond's succinct remark on this issue, see *GB*, 215, 215n.
44 Cf. Feuerbach, "Das Wesen des Christentums," in *Gesammelte Werke*, ed. Werner Schuffenhauer (Berlin: Akademie, 1974), 5:47–48: "our task [as thinkers] is to show that the antithesis of divine and human is altogether illusory, that it is nothing else

than the antithesis between the human nature in general, and the human individual: that, consequently, the object and contents of the Christian religion are altogether human.... The divine being is nothing else than the human being, or, rather the human nature purified, freed from the limits of the individual man, made objective—i.e., contemplated and revered as another, a distinct being. All the attributes of the divine nature are, therefore, attributes of the human nature." Whether Feuerbach understood all of Hegel's philosophy correctly is beyond the scope of this chapter but here he shows the same insight into the result of the Hegelian conceptualization of divine infinite. For the English translation of the text, see Feuerbach, *The Essence of Christianity*, trans. George Eliot (New York: Harper & Row, 1957), 13–14. Since this translation fails to italicize the phrases according to the original, the emphases above are Feuerbach's. Desmond gives the same reflection that the divine-human reconciliation in Hegel essentially denotes the self-reconciliation of humanity: cf. *HG*, 192–193.

45 This should remind us of Ivan Karamazov's controversial article or the end of Rousseau's social contract: the state should become the church and the church the state (*Karamazov*, 64–65). See also, Kierkegaard, *The Point of View*, ed. and trans. Howard V. Hong and Edna H. Hong (Princeton, NJ: Princeton University Press, 1998), 42, hereafter *PV*. Kierkegaard saw the same logic of civil religion in works of his contemporary Hegelians and criticized their conflation of the state and the church as an "enormous illusion," where becoming a Christian means the same as complying to the social norms rather than cultivating one's awareness of one's intimate relation to the divine absolute.

46 Regarding this equivocation of human "way up" to divine "way down" in twofold dialectical passage for their reconciliation, see *HG*, 60. For the "blurring" of the ontological distinction between humanity and divinity, see *HG*, 177; *GB*, 312.

47 *LPR*, 134 (282).

48 *LPR*, 138 (286), 142–144 (290–291), 150–152 (297–298). Cf. *Religion*, 145 (6:114), *Conflict*, 259 (7:33).

49 Cf. *LPR*, 153–154 (300–301), 419–420 (202–203). Augustine also deals with this immediate incomprehensibility of God's determinate characteristics in his *Confessions* (1. 4. 4). But notice the difference between Hegelian and classical interpretations of the divine attributes; namely, in terms of the dialectical reduction to the immanent universal and plurivocal unfolding that has an openness to the otherness of the divine absolute as that which is beyond the universality of linguistic communications in human term.

50 Cf. Hegel, *Philosophy of Mind: Being Part Three of the Encyclopaedia of the Philosophical Sciences (1830), Together with the Zusätze*, ed. Michael J. Inwood and trans. William Wallace and A.V. Miller (Oxford: Oxford University Press, 2007); "Enzyklopädie Der Philosophischen Wissenschaften Im Grundrisse (1830)," *Gesammelte Werke*, 20: §569–74, hereafter *Enc. II*. For further discussions concerning the secondary status of *Vorstellung* and its philosophical consequences, consult *HG*, 67–70, 126–127.

51 It should be noted how Hegel's conceptualization of a religious representation significantly differs from the classical/pros-hen-equivocal interpretations of the Scripture. Aquinas, for instance, argues that there can be four levels of meaning (i.e., literal, allegorical, moral, and anagogical) in one's interpretations of the Bible and the last level, which builds on the preceding three, has an openness to the divine transcendence. Dante Alighieri adopts this schema and makes it more explicit that

the anagogical meaning is incommensurable to the rational explications available in first three levels. Unlike these classical thinkers, Hegel consistently tries to transfer the religious representation to a conceptual form that is commensurable and explicable in terms of the immanent self-determining universal. Cf. Aquinas, (ST. Ia, 1, 10) and Dante, *Il Convivio*, Book II Chapter 1.

52 This is precisely what Kierkegaard is trying to show the possibility of through the traditional image of Judeo-Christian faith, i.e., *Akedah*. Abraham, who follows the divine command that is in conflict with his ethical obligations to others, looks like he is asserting himself as a single individual before the universal; and in relating himself as the single individual to the divine absolute without determining himself to be the universal, his action points toward the possibility of divinity as being transcendent to the immanent *telos* of the ethical universality. In this relation to the divine transcendence, the singularity of Abraham's existence is held as being irreducible to the rational totality of the ethical universal. Thus, the *Akedah* instantiates the tension between divine command (based on heteronomy of faith) and ethical interrelations of human beings (based on autonomy of reason) and calls for the necessity of examining "whether this story contains any higher expression for the ethical that can ethically explain his behavior, can ethically justify his suspending the ethical obligation to the son, but without moving beyond the teleology of the ethical" (*FT*, 57). If God is the highest expression of human destiny transcendent to the ethical universal and man's relation to this absolute in his singularity ought to be prior to and foundational for his ethical self/interrelations, the autonomy of human reason would have to be relativized in relation to such divinity as the highest end. This point of relativity to the divine absolute beyond the autonomy of human reason is impossible for Hegel to acknowledge within the confines of his dialectical thinking. For Desmond's agreement with this point in relation to Kierkegaard's presentation of *Akedah* against Hegel, see *PU*, 51.

53 For Desmond's criticism of Hegel's absolute as the immanent absolute, see *GB*, 42, 92.

54 *FT*, 68. See also *FT*, 60.

55 Kierkegaard highlights this point in his draft to the *FT*: "All Problemata should end as follows: this is the paradox of faith, a paradox that no reasoning is able to master—and yet it is so, or we must obliterate the story of Abraham," *JP*, 3:402 (3079). This obliteration of Abraham's faith seems to happen in the end of Kant's and Hegel's philosophy of religion since, as di Giovanni puts it, "Kant's system demands a moral faith but leaves no rational space for religion apart from the practical itself of morality… whereas for Hegel religion has autonomous as well as fundamental standing as a human phenomenon, but precisely for that reason, at the end no longer requires faith" (369).

56 Cf. *PU*, ix.

Chapter 5

1 Desmond recalls his visit to Paul Weis: "I would visit the philosopher Paul Weiss in his old age, and coming in the door he would ask me, almost shouting: 'How do you get from being to God?'" (*GB*, 282–283). I agree with Desmond. This is "a very good question" and, in fact, it is precisely the question that one must keep in mind when one reads his Trilogy, which explores the metaxological passages between being and the

absolute. Among the commentators of Desmond's works, Griffioen notices the same point. See Griffioen, "Towards a Philosophy of God," 15.
2. The earliest articulation of the "hyperboles of being" can be found in *DDO*, 245 and the most explicit articulation of it in context of the philosophy religion in *GB*, 8, 281, 312, 326, 338. Yet Desmond consistently refers to the significance of this notion in various contexts. For some of these references, cf. *DDO*, 173; *ITST*, 13.
3. *BB*, 48. See also *PU*, 110.
4. This also means that one cannot move from *BB* to *EB* and to *GB* as if they are three separate projects responding to determinate ques Circle, trans. Harry T. Willets (New York: tions in three different fields or that one can dispense with *BB* and *EB* once one reaches the height of *GB* (like Wittgenstein's ladder). They are companion volumes to each other, and one cannot get one of them right while failing to understand the others. What we often forget in our reading of comprehensive and systematic works in the field of philosophy is the singular status of the thinker behind the systematic expositions of thought. In this sense, *PO* as a companion volume to the *BB* is indispensable for reading the trilogy as well.
5. *GB*, 8 and 281. Desmond refers to these as "signs in immanence of what transcends immanence and cannot be fully determined in immanent terms" or "what is too much for immanence in immanence itself points to what is more than immanence"; and that, "in finitude, they communicate what is hyperbolic to finitude."
6. *GB*, 127, 313. I use this term much wider than most ongoing discussions on distributive justice would permit here. For instance, Kant's moral notion of happiness merited in exact correspondence with virtue would belong to this moral distribution of goods to the degree of one's moral uprightness (not unlike the way in which Aristotle talks about it in the *Nichomachean Ethics*). The divine economy of giving being exceeds these determinate categories of Aristotelian distributive justice or Kantian moral notion of happiness (let alone Rawlsian distributive justice). It is simply too much for our determinate knowledge of good and evil, whether it is calculated in Kant's and Aristotle's moral terms or in economic terms as described by Rawls.
7. *GB*, 193. Cf. *GB*, 202.
8. *EB*, 496.
9. *GB*, 127.
10. Cf. *ITST*, 43; *GB*, 11–13. Griffioen points out that no sufficient explanations of the relation of the fourfold sense of being and the four hyperboles of being are given in the works of Desmond. So, he tentatively defines the former as the "modes of understanding" and the latter as the "modes of selving"; and sees them as a "correlation between anthropological and epistemological distinctions" (6). I find this monolithic way of looking at the relation of the fourfold and the hyperboles misleading, since the former cannot be understood without including the sense of selving in the latter and vice versa. But I think that this raises a significant question (as Desmond admits and recognizes as worthy of another monograph in *GB*, 141). To answer this question briefly, I think we must exercise our *espirit de finesse*. The fourfold sense of being does systematically give different ways in which we can configure the relation of mind to being. But notice how these distinctions are neither univocally nor equivocally nor dialectically understood, but ultimately we must metaxologically see the legitimacy and limitation of each and recognize that each of them can have more than one meaning depending on which perspective one holds. (E.g., the univocal can carry more than one sense depending on how it is seen in relation to other senses.) This ultimate plurality of all the senses in which we understand the relation of mind and being is accessible only

through the metaxological viewpoint. To wit, the fourfold sense of being, only when it is seen in the light of the metaxological, correlates to the four hyperboles of being. In this sense, the idiocy of the singular points to the infinitely valuable "oneness" or the infinite worth of a singular beyond simple univocity; the aesthetics of happenings to the shimmer of what is beyond the equivocity of the historical reality in the midst of its equivocal presence; the erotics of selving to the infinite reserve of the overdeterminate transcendence beyond the dialectical self-fulfillment from its initially indeterminate lack; and finally, the agapeics of community gives the consummate allowance of these different senses of selving, as well as of being, in the overdeterminate fullness of the between.

11 *PU*, 41.
12 *FT*, 54.
13 Hence, Abraham's faith is impossible for both Kant and Hegel.
14 Cf. *PO*, 278, 282, 310; *EB*, 112, 177; *GB*, 32, 136–137, 249.
15 Take a look at the following sentence from the publication criteria for the Ph.D. in philosophy at KU Leuven: "For journal publications, the VABB list… only indicates a minimum criterion, i.e. the lowest limit that a scientific publication must meet." I am not sure what the lowest limit of a scientific publication means, but what strikes me here is the fact that philosophy professors and doctoral students (regardless of their infinite disagreement on what counts as a good philosophy) seem to equate the question of a good publication in philosophy with a "scientific" publication. If philosophy is higher than science, we will have to discuss whether or not we have to use philosophical criteria rather than scientific ones, but what is most important here is whether or not philosophical writing can be contracted to the universal framework of rational thinking that resorts (and limits us) to the public neutrality of scientific language. How can we talk about philosophy or the philosophy of religion when we need something other than scientific language to speak about these questions? For Desmond's concerns with the academic business of publishing articles, consult *AWASN*, 5; *BHD*, xi; *GB*, 202; *ITST*, 1–7.
16 Kierkegaard's caricature of Hegel usually hinges on this public/neutral aspect of Hegel's language that forgets himself as an individual thinker. Desmond also often refers to this significant contrast between the private intimacy of poetic language and the public neutrality of universal thinking in modern and philosophical discourses, which thereby calls for the necessity of recuperating the philosophical significance of the singular beyond the dualism of poetic intimacy and public neutrality in philosophical language spoken hitherto. This leads him to the poetic articulation of metaphysical and religious notions in the more comprehensive form of metaxological philosophy. For this point on art or poetry as having stronger affinity with the overdeterminacy of being, see *PU*, 49; *ITST*, 2, 7, 126; *DDO*, 97; *PO*, 103–107, 260.
17 If we look at the fact that every one of his books is dedicated to his family, friends, and fellow thinkers who have or had strong bearing on his personal and intellectual life as a single individual, this point seems very clear. Also, Desmond's texts often make references to poetry (of Shakespeare, Yeats, Keats, Blake, Joyce, to name but a few) and never refrain from conveying the points through his own poetic expressions. For example, some of the central notions of his works (e.g., posthumous thinking) are introduced through his reflections on the Irish folklore of Oisín or other tales that most thinkers in the continental European or North American tradition are either unlikely or hesitant to cite. As far as I know, he is the only one who has cited Luke Kelly for a philosophy article (*AWASN*, 23), and how more Irish can a thinker be for doing this

(and doing it well)? These personal elements in the texts of Desmond are testimonies to the significance of the single status of the metaxological thinker. More philosophically, Desmond repeatedly argues that poetic language has the feel for the ontological surplus of the particular and it is important to see how poetically his personal reflections are delivered in his texts.

18 Notice how the term "private" means something more than mere privacy or an isolated individual in opposition to the public and the universal, since this self-reflection on our existence as the single individual communicates something more than the indeterminate particular in our existence. It attunes us to the communicative relation with the source of our finite and individual existence. Just as Augustine's soliloquy does not give a private monologue, but turns instead into a dialogue between himself and God beyond himself, these intimate self-reflections in metaxology point to something beyond mere singularity in the single individual itself. Desmond calls this "intimate singular." Cf., *IU*, 49.
19 *PU*, 41–42. See also *BHD*, 324; *GB*, 186–187; *ITST*, 103.
20 *GB*, 52, 75.
21 Cf. *GB*, 129.
22 Among contemporary Japanese thinkers, Kuki Shūzō explicitly makes this point in his metaphysical work, *The Problem of Contingency*. Cf. Kuki, *The Problem of Contingency* (偶然性の問題) (Tokyo: Iwanami Shoten, 2012), 13–16. For Desmond's references to the metaphysical significance of onceness of the contingent singular, see *PO*, 119; 231–232; *ITST*, 63; *GB*, 52.
23 Desmond articulates the notion of "posthumous thinking" in many different ways; cf. *PO*, 278–282, 310; *GB*, 136–137, 185, 249. As we will see later, Tanabe would talk about this as a "standpoint of death-and-resurrection" and would go so far as to say that "there is no other study but philosophy that has to do with the not to be" (*ELP*, 280).
24 Joseph Frank, *Dostoevsky: The Years of Ordeal, 1850–1859* (Princeton, NJ: Princeton University Press, 1983), 55. Cf. Dostoyevsky, *The Idiot*, trans. David McDuff (London: Penguin Books, 2004), 71.
25 Frank, *Dostoevsky: The Years of Ordeal, 1850–1859*, 56–57 and *Idiot*, 71–72. Cf. *PO*, 231–232.
26 Desmond gives the same reflection in *EB*, 176fn. The legitimacy of this reflection can be seen in its profound resonance with Dostoyevsky's accounts of the mock execution day. Apparently, years later, he told his second wife: "I cannot recall when I was ever as happy as on that day. I walked up and down my cell in the Alekseevsky Ravelin and sang the whole time, sang at the top of my voice, so happy was I at being given back my life" (Frank, *Dostoevsky: The Years of Ordeal, 1850–1859*, 61). He can no longer look at his life in the same way, but in his conversion through posthumous thinking, he realizes the positive energy of his sheer being. A few hours after the execution, Dostoyevsky wrote to his brother the following: "[w]hen I look back on my past and think how much time I wasted on nothing, how much time has been lost in futilities, errors, laziness, incapacity to live; how little I appreciated it, how much times I sinned against my heart and soul—then my heart bleeds. Life is a gift, life is happiness, *every minute can be eternity of happiness*! *Si jeunesse savait*… ! Now, in changing my life, I am reborn in a new form. Brother! I swear that I will not lose hope and will keep my soul and heart pure. I will be reborn for the better. That's all my hope, all my consolation!" (Frank, *Dostoevsky: The Years of Ordeal, 1850–1859*, 62, emphasis mine). What a remarkable

reflection on life and how joyful he becomes after his posthumous thinking! He lives the same life in prison. But this time his life is received as a gift in joy.

27 Cf. *BB*, 184–185.
28 Plato, *Republic*, 515a.
29 Frank, *Dostoevsky: The Years of Ordeal, 1850–1859*, 58.
30 Cf., *GB*, 52. Reference to the significance of the recoil from the monstrous: *EB*, 180–181.
31 *BB*, 185: "The finite singular is given into being as uniquely itself, as the excess for now rides over nothingness, intoxicated with the elemental joy of simply being at all, indeed with the elemental good of the simple to be that cannot be reduced to anything other. During its span it is full with the 'once' of its to be, and this fullness is given out of the fullness or plentitude of the overdetermined source. It is full with being, packed tightly into its won integral ontological compactness, floating on nothing, because the overdetermined fullness gives it to be as full." See also, *ITST*, 7.
32 *BB*, 384. My emphasis. For the significance of the inward otherness, cf., *PO*, 116, 209–210; *AA*, 114–120; *AOO*, 109; *EB*, 37; *GB*, 43–44, 71–72.
33 *BB*, 384. Cf. *PU*, 144; *EB*, 481: "What cannot be absolutely incorporated into the power of the ascendant sovereign [i.e., the rational universal]? At one extreme, there is the idiot self—the void, you might say sometimes, the indeterminate source of innerness that is never exhausted by any determination, though its determinate existence be in bondage to them. The idiot is not absolute solitude but is intermediated prior to determinate mediation: God is in the immanence of the soul. From that deepest intimacy the call of agapeic service comes again, shattering the determinations that hold us spellbound, retuning us as to nothing, offering anew a recreation of our being, out of the plentitude that twines around our lack. There is the released religious 'sovereignty' of the idiot, the sacred fool." For the same point, see also *PO*, 231–232. *ITST*, 16–17; *IU*, 56.
34 Augustine, *Confessions* (10, 6, 9).
35 *GB*, 109. Cf. *ITST*, 66, 128; *AOO*, 5; *GB*, 52, 75, 248: "Creation concerns the kind of beings we find in the between, in so far as they show themselves as coming to be. The most insistent showing of coming to be is intimated in the *becoming* of such beings, but it is very important to distinguish 'coming to be' and 'becoming.' The becoming in the between is important, not because traditionally becoming was counterposed with being, as beyond all becoming, but because of the ontological dynamic of things. To think of origin by means of an escape from becoming risks depriving origin of that dynamic openness necessary for an origin to be an origin at all. Rather, the ontological dynamic shifts our attention to an originative source of dynamic being, an origin dynamic in a surplus sense to what is given in the between. The finitely dynamic does not arise from the static but from a more primordial *energeia*."
36 If we describe this in more modern terms, we can say that the acorn as the indeterminate has its openness to the oak tree and also that through the dynamic self-negating self-mediation, the former becomes the latter.
37 This argument is quite similar to what Desmond sees in Aquinas' Third Way. Cf., *GB*, 6; *DDO*, 216–217 and also Simpson, *Religion, Metaphysics, and the Postmodern*, 101–102.
38 *BB*, 384. In this sense, we cannot practice posthumous thinking once and do away with it. But constant practice is necessary for achieving the metaxological thinking. Cf. *GB*, 75: "The showings of nature in the universal impermanence are themselves ambiguous. They mingle creation and destruction, life and death. The aesthetic happening shows

the togetherness of these as dynamic processes. Process suggests not some static ground fixed by univocity, but a more primordial origin that is dynamic power in an even more original way. The thought of God looks through the presentiment of this more primordial original. This thought of God is not a univocal retreat from becoming to stasis but arises from honesty before the equivocity of givenness, from thinking into and through the constitutive ambiguity of creation as an aesthetic happening. There need be no flight from the world. The world itself is a givenness of aesthetic show that intimates a source that is more than aesthetic show." The same argument can be found in *GB*, 248–49 and other places throughout the works of Desmond: cf. *DDO*, 158; *ITST*, 13, 63–64, 287.

39 *BB*, 185.
40 Cf. *GB*, 52.
41 For an excellent explanation of the nature of hyperintelligibility, cf. *GB*, 245: "What, then, would it mean to say that creation is a hyperintelligible? Think of it this way. If we link intelligibility to determinacy and ask what grounds determinate intelligibility, the answer cannot be another determinate intelligible, for that too would be in question. If there is such a ground, it must be *a determining in excess of determinate intelligibles*. Suppose we link creation to such an overdeterminate grounding. Then, to call creation a hyperintelligible would be to say it concerns the beyond of intelligibility that sources the possible intelligibility of the determinately intelligible."
42 *GB*, 242.
43 *GB*, 236.
44 *GB*, 75. For Desmond's expositions of artistic attentiveness to the rich thereness of being and overdeterminacy of the ultimate, see *DDO*, 97; *PO*, 103, 106–107, 260; *ITST*, 126; *AOO*, 1–3; *IU*, 72–73. It is important here to note that philosophy should know what it can do the best and what the other disciples can do better than itself. The mistake of universal rationalism especially in the form of Hegelian dialectic is to think that philosophy can surpass every other disciple through the conceptualization of the truth of things. Desmond recognizes this power of poetry in relation to the otherness of religion to philosophy and puts poems to the beginning of each chapter and ends with a kind of religious poetry as ten metaphysical cantos. The metaxological mindfulness in its best form breaks into songs for what it thinks beyond itself. For the musical dimension of metaxological thinking, cf. *DDO*, 126, and the same reflection in relation to the art of painting, see *DDO*, 184.
45 *GB*, 338.
46 *GB*, 169. For the metaxological significance of the ordinary, see also AWASN, 22. Desmond goes so far as to say that even the bad, the ugly, and the monstrous can put us in the position of recognizing the divine transcendence in immanence. Cf., *PU*, 162: A smelly drunkard, picked up near Inchydoney in West Cork, gave Desmond the look of self in his irreducible singularity. With his frequent reference to St. Francis and his deadly kisses of the lepers, the metaxological philosophy argues that even the hateful must be loved for the goodness of its "to be."
47 C.S. Lewis, *Surprised by Joy* (New York: Hartcourt, Brace & Co., 1955), 211. Cf. *GB*, 274. Desmond talks about the bird singing in the bush and that is enough to set off the experience of his *ecstasis* toward the glory of creation. These testimonies show that the extraordinary moments of human conversions are found in the ordinary.
48 Solzhenitsyn, *In The First Circle*, trans. Harry T. Willets (New York: HarperCollins, 2009), 171. I must say that this first English translation of the uncensored version of the *First Circle* occasionally falls behind the poetic quality achieved by the previous

translations of the censored version. Especially in relation to this chapter, I would recommend Thomas P. Whitney's translation. Some readers may notice that I have slightly deviated from Solzhenitsyn's text in the sense that the glory of the creation is immediately seen by Sologdin as a miracle. while it will take a while for Nerzin to reach Sologdin's state of awareness. After rereading the novel, I thought of re-adjusting my recollection with the text but I was suddenly reminded of *The Dream of a Ridiculous Man*. The question of whether or not my poetic recollection of the "Sawing Wood" is textually accurate is not as important as that of whether or not it captures the truth of what the original points toward and, as ridiculous as it may sound, I believe my writing does the job.

49 Ippolit attributes this statement to Myshkins in Part Three and Chapter Five of *The Idiot*.
50 Consult Rilke's "Archaic Torso of Apollo."
51 Solzhenitsyn goes so far as to say that he is absolutely grateful for the opportunity to be imprisoned by the Soviet Union or else he could never understand the richness of creation. Thus, regardless of the extreme poverty and injustice that he had to suffer during and after his imprisonment, he thanks God for what he is offered in his life. This is a tremendous life testimony of awareness that one's life is given to be beyond one's determinate or self-determining reckoning.
52 *GB*, 12.
53 *BB*, 377. Cf. *GB*, 286–287.
54 *EB*, 209. Cf. *EB*, 12.
55 *EB*, 209.
56 *EB*, 209.
57 Augustine, *Confessions* (2, 10, 18).
58 Thank God that no hyperlink can be placed in this hardbound book! In this endnote, I would like to draw my readers' attention to the fact that there is something philosophically disturbing about the general requirement in academia to place endnotes to many sentences in philosophy papers. (Ironically, there is no better place but in a endnote to make this statement.) Sometimes a endnote can provide some crucial qualifications, insightful reflections, or supplementary arguments that are absolutely useful for the readers to follow the author's arguments. I would even argue that, in some occasions, these notes could help the author share the same philosophical insight with the readers. The practice of putting citations could also be a sign of the author's respect toward the fellow thinkers who thought about the same points or initiated the same discussions with some notable (if not original) contributions in the history of philosophy. But very often, I find myself being driven by mere curiosities in checking the endnotes, and many of the endnotes that I see in scholarly articles seem to be there just to show that the authors' points are original, common, controversial, etc., or that they (supposedly) read the impressive amount of the other scholarly works (including their own). But none of these points are essential for anyone to understand the significance of the arguments presented in the texts, and sometimes it does not even matter who actually made these points. Perhaps I am being too idealistic here, being as idealistic as Socrates in the *Meno* or the young Desmond who submitted his dissertation without any endnotes or bibliography. But I can only say this: there is no reason why one should look at a endnote to a sentence that ends with "amazon.com," unless one is simply driven by curiosity. I would like to both thank and apologize to any of my readers who have patiently and scrupulously read my texts and stumbled upon this insignificant endnote. But I would like to note

for the record how endnotes could easily distract us from the deeper metaphysical questions that we are going after in the field of philosophy.
59 Again, Augustine is right: the fruitless satisfaction of the insatiable desires is nothing but "a rich beggary and a base glory." Cf. Augustine, *Confessions* (1.12.19).
60 *Hamlet* (4.3.21–27).
61 I have heard from a couple of farmers in Nebraska that they have seen some mother pigs eating their piglets just to satisfy their hunger and then going back to eat from the feeder as if nothing happened. This reminded me of Dante's Ugolino: a treacherous Count imprisoned with two sons and two grandsons in a tower in Pisa for days without food. After all of his children died in a matter of days, his "fasting did what grief had failed to do" (*Inf.* 33.75). As we see Ugolino in hell, we must realize that the act of eating for humans is just not the same for some animals that can eat whatever they find edible for their survival. We need something more than just hunger to keep bringing food to our mouths.
62 Cf. Augustine, Confessions (1.19.14–1.10.16; 1.12.19; and 1.17.27). Listen again to Augustine's awareness of the problems in the ways we learn in the "stormy society of human life" (1, 8, 13).
63 *ISB*, 9–10. The earlier version of this chapter, "Being, Determination, and Dialectic: On the Sources of Metaphysical Thinking," can be found in *The Review of Metaphysics* 48 (1995): 731–769 and Chapter 1 of *Being and Dialectic: Metaphysics as a Cultural Presence*, eds. William Desmond and Joseph Grange (Albany: State University of New York Press, 2000), 3–36.
64 Cf. AWASN, 6–8, 20.
65 Cf. Simpson, *Religion, Metaphysics, and the Postmodern*, 38.
66 *EB*, 213. See also, *GB*, 107–108.
67 *EB*, 215.
68 On the disproportionality of will to know and the known in terms of curiosity, see BR, 185–186.
69 *EB*, 209.
70 *EB*, 215.
71 Oscar Wilde, *The Picture of Dorian Gray* (Oxford: Oxford University Press, 2006), 22.
72 Wilde, 19.
73 Wilde, 188.
74 Plato, *Phaedrus*, 230a.
75 See also *AOO*, 35–40 for Desmond's exposition of this notion of the "erotics of self-transcending" in reference to the works of Plato.
76 Cf. *ITST*, 132; *EB*, 232–234; *GB*, 143. This basic tenet of agapeic transcending (or agapeic mindfulness) provides the ground upon which we can give a full rebuttal to Rinaldi's 7th objection. To simplify his point, Rinaldi has difficulty in conceiving the possibility of a self-transcending process other than the erotic one from lack to fullness (Rinaldi, "Metaphysics as a Cultural Presence," 168–169). If the beginning is full, how is it possible for one to make the process of self-completing self-development? The notion of the agapeic transcending shows that there is something more than what we can provide through our own determinate/self-determining being or becoming such that we can move toward the more that infinitely drives us to transcend ourselves. The goal of this transcending process, in other words, is constitutive of the transcending movement: hence, the movement from the infinite lack to infinite fullness has to start with the fullness that drives us to go beyond ourselves. The agapeic process of transcending in metaxology, thus, shows the

movement of the self not from the lack to the fullness in self-determining/erotic process, but from the overdeterminate fullness to fullness through its self-awareness that it cannot make this movement through itself alone. For the difference of erotic and agapeic transcending, see *PU*, 70, 80.

77 Cf. *GB*, 142–143. For the agapeic transformation of the root will, see *EB*, 223–224; *PO*, 190.
78 *ISB*, 72.
79 *ISB*, 295.
80 *ISB*, 86. Cf. *ISB*, 83, 220.
81 *ISB*, 200–201. Desmond continuously argues for the importance of *compassio essendi*. For these arguments, see especially *HG*, 136–137; *GB*, 100.
82 I would like to note that the metaxological account of the divine-human relation is much more extensively discussed in the following chapter. Hence, some readers might find the later images to be more helpful for answering these questions. What follows in this section are only a few instances in which we can realize how the "agapeics of community" emits the presence of the divine transcendence in our human immanence.
83 Rowan Williams, *Dostoevsky: Language, Faith, and Fiction* (London: Continuum, 2009), 11.
84 Williams, *Dostoevsky: Language, Faith, and Fiction*, 11.
85 Williams, *Dostoevsky: Language, Faith, and Fiction*, 11.
86 This contrast between two types of teaching can remind us of two images: (1) *The Brave New World* and (2) *Phaedrus*. The first gives the fully industrialized society in which each individual is (hypnopaedically) conditioned to be able to repeat certain maxims—sayings that nonrationally encourage the speakers to conform to the stable order of the societal whole. The individual in this society is raised to become literal at the level where she or he can follow instructions appropriate to his or her own class, but never to the point of self-criticism or philosophical thinking. Notice how two things are categorically denied to citizens in the new world: (a) books and (b) flowers. The former will encourage the citizens to think for themselves, while the enjoyment of the "[primroses and landscapes] have a great defect: they are 'gratuitous'" (Aldous Huxley, *Brave New World and Brave New World Revisited*, New York: HarperCollins, 2004, 30–31). The ability to think for oneself is a threat to the order in which the value of one is subordinated to that of many and nothing is more contradictory to their instrumentalizing relation than the free gift of natural beauty. In contrast to this new world, the ancient dialogue gives Socrates, who goes beyond the city limits to follow his friend, both the intellectual and emotional ability to instruct his friend to rethink the nature of love as well as his servile, instrumental relation to the terrible (*deinos*) sophist, Lysias. What Plato shows through Socrates, his myth, and his relation to Phaedrus as the function of teachers (and also parents) is to make their children better than themselves (in likeness to the divine that the teachers/parents would see in their children). In these two stories, I see two diametrically opposing types of teachings and the world in which the agapeic teachings of Phaedrus is denied would have to be Huxley's Brave New World. Cf. Huxley, *Brave New World and Brave New World Revisited*, 30–31 and *Phaedrus*, 253B–C.
87 I suppose it is possible to live in a world where nobody speaks properly or speaks the truth about the world and themselves (like the most of interlocutors in Dostoyevsky's *The Possessed*).

88 All the receiving and giving of the linguistic freedom is in this sense a hyperbolic gift from the divine absolute. Desmond's reflections on this point can be found, for instance, in *ITST*, 305.
89 The constancies of the expressions shared among this community are usually framed as grammatical rules, and without these rules, we cannot freely express our thoughts and feelings, either.
90 Think, for instance, of Thrasymachus in *Republic*. Cf. *IU*, 138, 367.
91 Cf. *ITST*, 305.
92 AWASN, 23.
93 Here I am sticking to the Kierkegaardian rendering of the terms "universal" in his critical engagement with the Kantian and the Hegelian philosophy of religion. What emerges from this denial of the rational universal in metaxology is not a complete dismissal of any sense of the universal or any intermediation with singulars, but a renewed sense of togetherness or communicative relations. This is what Desmond calls "the intimate universal."

Chapter 6

1 *DDO*, 139. Cf., *DDO*, 200.
2 *GB*, 173.
3 This is precisely why there is the dimension of interreligious and intercultural dialogues in the metaxological philosophy of religion. For this point, see also *GB*, 173–176.
4 *GB*, 42.
5 *GB*, 21. This primal givenness of our determinate being is the *passio essendi*, that is, the patience of being. Since we have received our being rather than as having determined it for ourselves in our process of becoming, the *passio essendi* is always prior to our endeavor to be, that is, *conatus essendi*. We will see the significance of this point more in detail later. Cf. *GB*, 129–130; *IU*, 57, 113, 135, 173, 244.
6 *PU*, 142–143. Cf. Rinaldi's objection 3 in Rinaldi, "Metaphysics as a Cultural Presence," 166. Notice how his understanding of the overdeterminate origin is reduced to the indeterminate notion of "matter," and because of this, the sense of "givenness" with regard to being is conceived as a mere "passivity." Hence, Rinaldi thinks that metaxology runs the risk of undermining the foundation of metaphysical thinking, that is, freedom and activity of thinking. As we will see in the following quotation and the intricate argument concerning the interrelation of *passio* and *conatus essendi*, the overdeterminate origin is not a mere lack, nor the passivity of our freedom denotes the simple heteronomous relation in which one determinate object can causally determine the movement of another. Rinaldi would have to rethink these two notions of "overdeterminate" and the intermediation of the overdeterminate origin and the freedom of determinate/self-determining being.
7 *PU*, 142–43. See also BR, 180; *IU*, 49.
8 *BHD*, 80.
9 *GB*, 22. Cf. *HG*, 2–7, 93; Simpson, *Religion, Metaphysics, and the Postmodern*, 46–49.
10 Cf. *BB*, 77, 145–146; *PU*, 247; *ITST*, 91; *GB*, 92–93.
11 Cf. *GB*, 324.

12 *GB*, 201: "Self-transcending openness to transcendence as other to the self: this describes an ultimate porosity giving birth to the urgency of ultimacy, shaped now in more recognizable religious.... The agapeic origin is an effort to name this 'trans.'"
13 Cf. *PU*, 144.
14 Cf., *GB*, 123.
15 *BHD*, 101.
16 From this notion of (2) "agapeic transcendence beyond dualism," we can give a full response to Rinaldi's objection no. 4 and 6. His objection 4 basically contends that the concept of plurality in metaxology logically requires determinate entities, and accordingly, the metaxological plurivocity of being is, contrary to Desmond's claim, both determinate and exhaustible (Rinaldi, "Metaphysics as a Cultural Presence," 167). Objection 6 argues that the "radical otherness" of being or origin ultimately reintroduces duality. Notice how Rinaldi must be thinking about plurality and the otherness of origin only in accord with the determinate category of plurality, which requires two determinate entities to think of plurality or otherness. What Desmond means by plurality and otherness is quite other to this determinate understanding of quantifiable plurality or causally determinable otherness in dualistic terms. In other words, the origin that allows the multiplicity of beings and their self-/intermediating processes of self-becoming cannot be one of the many beings. Nor can it be reduced to one of these processes of becoming, for it is the enabling ground of the plurality of beings and of the processes of their self-becoming. Thus, the metaxological notion of plurality and otherness must be reconsidered beyond the determinate category of plurality and otherness applicable only to the determinate entities in immanence. For Desmond's succinct argument on the metaxological sense of "many" that radically differs from that in dualism, see *GB*, 252, 255.
17 *GB*, 242.
18 *GB*, 143.
19 *GB*, 320. See also *GB*, 275.
20 *GB*, 254.
21 *DDO*, 191. Cf., *BB*, 418; *PU*, 212; *HT*, 41; *BR* 224; *EB*, 207; *HG*, 136; *GB*, 307, 319–320.
22 *GB*, 319. Cf. *ITST*, 315.
23 *GB*, 252.
24 *GB*, 307. Cf. also *GB*, 283–284.
25 *GB*, 34. Cf., *GB*, 283–284, 287, 335; *IU*, 56–57, 147–148, 212–213, 401–403; *ITST*, 122–123, 275; *PU*, 142.
26 *PU*, 212; *BB*, 459, 499. Griffioen points out that Desmond's emphasis on the divine "letting be" of the finite relative for the finite would anticipate some commentators to recognize its possible parallel with Schelling's notion of *contractio Dei*, the self-negating god that retreats for the creation to freely determine itself, and names Richard Kearney as one of them. However, Griffioen further argues that this is misleading since the "[notion of *contractio Dei*] assumes a potential conflict between God and man when it comes to freedom" (which Sartre emphasizes), while "Desmond assumes a trust relationship" between them. This is a crucial distinction between a passive self-negation of the divine absolute that has a merely negative relation to the finite creation and the active self-negation of the agapeic absolute that selflessly constitutes the possibility of freedom for the finite relatives. This distinction must also be kept for our understanding of the self-negation of the divine absolute in Tanabe's works. For these points, see Griffioen, "Towards a Philosophy of God," 9 and Kearney, "Maybe Not, Maybe: William Desmond on God," in *Between System and Poetics:*

William Desmond and Philosophy after Dialectic, ed. Thomas A.F. Kelly (Albershot: Ashgate, 2007), 198.
27 Lewis, *The Four Loves* (London: Collins, 1960), 157. Cf. *ITST*, 305.
28 Augustine, *Confessions* (1. 4. 4).
29 For the significance of a metaphor for metaphysical thought on the divine absolute, see *PU*, 208–209; *BB*, 210–211; *GB*, 123.
30 This whole scene can be found in Fyodor Dostoyevsky, "Poor Folk," in *Poor Folk and Other Stories*, trans. David McDuff (London: Penguin Books, 1988), 37–41.
31 *GB*, 307: "Agapeic relation reveals richness to be a kind of 'being nothing' that the other maybe everything, a poverty that wants nothing for itself to want the good for the other, a richness that is an emptying of the absolute even of its absoluteness, to be there at the disposal of the free other, should the other seek aid and succor." See also, *EB*, 274; *ITST*, 68, 225; *GB*, 274.
32 *GB*, 284.
33 *GB*, 255. Cf. *DDO*, 200–201, 223.
34 Cf. Kierkegaard, "Christ as the Prototype," in *For Self-Examination. Judge for Yourself!*, ed. and trans. Howard V. Hong and Edna H. Hong (Princeton, NJ: Princeton University Press, 1990), 185–186. For the direct inferences to the nature of divine compassion in its constitutive relation to each individual's ethical self/intermediations, see also Kierkegaard, "The Halt," in *Practice in Christianity*, ed. and trans. Howard V. Hong and Edna H. Hong (Princeton, NJ: Princeton University Press, 1991), 58–60. Desmond gives the same example in *GB*, 237.
35 For Desmond's reflection on the last mite of the poor woman in contrast with Nietzsche's gift-giving virtue, see *ITST*, 225ff.
36 These are different ways in which we can witness the "agapeics of community" and these images might more efficiently communicate the divine absolute than the previous example of the linguistic community. To see how the agapeic origin is always already the agapeic community that "communicates with the other in its primordial oneness with itself, a communication itself the ground of its going outside of itself in relation to the world it creates," see *GB*, 284.
37 Kant, *Religion*, 168 (6: 142). Cf. *EB*, 137.
38 *HG*, 121.
39 *GB*, 252. Cf. *BHD*, 100, 113; *GB*, 252–255; *PU*, 212: "[Agapeic origination] is not a movement from lack through self-mediation to self-perfection, but from perfection to perfection, from pluperfection to an other perfection, not from imperfection to perfection. The pluperfect in itself is overdetermined in an affirmative sense, not in the privative sense of erotic transcendence. As in itself positively overdetermined, the being of agapeic transcendence is open to the origination of the other, which is let be as other. So the giving out of the other is not for the sake of the origin in itself, but for the other itself, as being constituted with its own ontological perfection and freedom. The reaching towards the other of the agapeic being is not the appropriation of the other for the purposes of the self-completion of the origin, but for the support of a community of plurality wherein otherness is not dualistic opposition."
40 *PU*, 209.
41 *BB*, 527–528.
42 *BB*, 537. Cf. *EB*, 158, 161, 201–202. Not all of the erotic sovereigns will claim themselves to be erotic absolute (i.e., *eros turanos*), but they are capable of harnessing the infinitely transcending energy of their existence to their ontological fullness in immanence and then, in face of their equivocal fate as a finite being (i.e., death),

they choose either to surrender to the fate of their finitude and thank in humility the infinite source from which their fullness was granted or to become obsessed with itself and fall victim to its self-deceptive apotheosis of itself as the absolute. The former gives the agapeic transcending in which the sovereign turns into a servant, while the latter gives the erotic absolute. Desmond provides the third possibility of *eros uranos* where the charismatic sovereign enjoys its fullness without falling victim to the tyrannical self-deception and exemplifies it in the "inspiration of genius" (*EB*, 452). I find the case of *eros uranos* to be extremely rare and wonder that most of us will fall into the ethico-religious either/or: either the erotic or the agapeic absolute.
43 *BB*, 537.
44 *BR*, 182.
45 Desmond gives some great image that, in my opinion, matches the imagination of Lewis. Cf. *BB*, 412: "The agapeic self: an intense space of fullness that listens for what is coming towards it; a space of fullness that goes towards what is coming, but that yet stays stock-still, where it is. Or: a space of emptiness in an open countryside that awaits patiently for the wind to blow through it, as it will, the wind of winter that bites, the breeze of summer that softens. Or: a thereness of availability, a nothing that does not shout itself, a meeting in the middle where the original powers of being communicate and fructify beyond themselves, and where the silent spaces sing."
46 *GB*, 320.
47 *GB*, 322.
48 *PU*, 147. For the metaxological notion of the space between the divine infinite and the profane finite as this agapeic granting of otherness, see *DDO*, 200–201; *GB*, 164, 168.
49 There is also an irreducible asymmetry between the human way up and the divine way down. This is evident in the abovementioned fact that an agapeic origination of finite freedom exceeds our determinable knowing, and in fact, the latter is always already grounded by the former.
50 Cf. Christopher David Shaw, *On Exceeding Determination and the Idea of Reason: Immanuel Kant, William Desmond, and the Noumenological Principle* (Newcastle: Cambridge Scholar Publishing, 2012), 113–114.
51 *EB*, 211. Cf. *EB*, 305; *GB*, 186.
52 *EB*, 212n. Tanabe also gives the same reflection on this parable and presents his metanoesis as holding the standpoint of the prodigal son. For this point, see *ELP*, 484–485.
53 *GB*, 301.
54 Why does this remind me of Kierkegaard's caricature of Hegel? I am not denying that some thought that thinks what is other to itself can be like a prayer or that a philosopher could practice this religious mode of thinking in his office. But the question here is what follows the thought that thinks what is other to itself as the foundation of its very thinking? I cannot think of any better point than the old adage: "faith without works is dead."
55 *GB*, 289.
56 *EB*, 481.
57 *GB*, 166.
58 *GB*, 166.
59 For the distinction between erotic absolute that moves from its lack to fullness by means of the other and agapeic absolute that, out of its overdeterminate fullness and generosity, grants existence and worth to the relative other for the relative, see *DDO*, 224; *HG*, 40, 113–118; *PU*, 70, 113, 230.

60 Cf. *PO*, 161; *EB*, 23–25.
61 For Desmond's reflections on the ecological impact of the lack of agapeic mindfulness, see BR, 196; *PO*, 161.
62 *GB*, 166.
63 *GB*, 274.
64 *GB*, 274. See also, *DDO*, 181.
65 *GB*, 274.
66 Desmond discusses the significance of realizing that freedom to practice philosophy is a given freedom or that philosophy is a gift from the source of thinking beyond itself through the notion of the comic in Hegel and its contrast with the philosophical praxis of Plato in his essay, "Can Philosophy Laugh at Itself?: On Hegel and Aristophanes—With a Bow to Plato" (*BHD*, 301–342). This is a crude summary of the point that Desmond is trying to show through this article, but my point is that philosophy (or philosophers) must be able to laugh at itself in order to go beyond itself in the mode of agapeic transcending. For this point, see especially *BHD*, 325ff.
67 *GB*, 274.
68 Sometimes he is known also as Guanxi Zhìxián, and in Japanese, he is widely know as Kyōgen Chikan (香嚴智閑) (?–898). He was a Zen monk from the Tang dynasty (618–907), equipped with the high intellectual virtue and encyclopedic mind. However, he was not able to satisfy his mind's desire through the acquisition of knowledge alone, and so, he became a practitioner of Zen under the master, Guishan Lingyou (潙山靈祐) (Jpn. Isan Reiyū, 771–853). Guanxi was unable to answer his master's question despite his effort to think through it while consulting all the books that he had at that time. With a great disappointment, Guanxi decided to mediate at a monastery where the famous monk Nanyang Huizhong (南陽慧忠) (Jpn. Nanyō Echū, 675–775) had previously trained himself. When he was sweeping the ground next to the graveyard, he hit a piece of a rooftile and it made a resonating sound by hitting a bamboo tree. In listening to this sound, he forgot all the knowledge that he accumulated up to that point and immediately achieved enlightenment (i.e., *satori*). It is a well-known story in the Zen and Buddhist tradition that one's obsession with knowledge and reason can prevent oneself from attaining *satori*, but by letting go of such craving, one can be awakened to the soundness of Buddhist enlightenment.
69 *GB*, 277. See also *GB*, 150: "The agapeic origin cannot be fully determined in the terms of determinate morality of good and evil such as its generally proportionate to our finite measure…. There is a power of the good that possiblizes beyond good and evil, but it is so beyond because it is an excessive good relative to the moralization of the good. We cannot be the measure of it; we are measured by it, even though we mostly do not know this and are oblivious to the way we are let be by this excessive good." For Desmond's reference to the compassion of the Buddha (sometimes in parallel to Western religious figures), see *PO*, 144, 190, 273; *PU*, 151, *ITST*, 19.
70 *GB*, 147. Cf. *GB*, 99. Hugo's description is especially attentive to the religious awareness that the house that the priest rules over is the house of God. What he has in his house is not really his but comes from the higher giving source that enables him to have them. The priest as an agapeic servant, therefore, never locks his door to secure his possessions as his but sees everything therein as belonging to all others as the children of God. This is an awe-inspiring practice of religious living that shocked the wretched thief like Milton's devil before Eden.
71 *GB*, 99.

72 *GB*, 186.
73 Hegel's dialectical configuration of the reconciliation, which presupposes only relativized notions of good and evil, works without a free communication of two terms; but one side of them determines itself in and through the other. And this other does not exist as the other to the self, but rather as the self's self-othering. Here, Hegel's usage of the term "reconciliation" becomes much more troubling. If the finite is the self-alienation of the infinite, what is finite and evil is really a self-offense of the infinite good; and if the reconciliation is the latter's true self-affirmation through the negation of the finite as its self-othering, then this reconciliation is really the self-forgiving of the concrete universal. Then what does it mean to call it a reconciliation if the offense is self-(im)posed and the absolution is self-given? This is like saying, "I offend myself through alienating myself but forgive my own wrongdoing because it serves for the true affirmation of myself as the good." Dostoyevsky calls this peculiar self-forgiveness as "self-laceration" and shows a variety of cases in which the human subject follows this logic in *Brothers Karamazov* (part II Book IV). The best example is found in the sensualist—Fyodor Karamazov—who says: "I am good and better than everyone else as long as I commit more evil and publicly declare that I am more sinful than everyone else!" To call this a reconciliation of the finite and the infinite is extremely problematic in relation to the human subject. And what is worse, this logic is supposed to work for God's self-determination. If the evil separation of the finite creation from the divine infinite is really God's own doing in his process of fully determining himself, I do not see how humans should feel responsible for their basic condition of being separated from the divine infinite, let alone should ask for the forgiveness to be reconciled with God in the community of his goodness: for this God can neither be devoid of evil nor possess the need to be patient for the free consent from the finite other as the other. Rather, God needs to use the other for Himself. Thus, Hegel's reconciliation suffers from the one-way self-relation of the infinite to the finite and fails to grasp the true sense of the term where two sides of the antithesis come to be in the community of goodness through freely receiving and giving the forgiveness.
74 For Desmond's critique of Kant's inability to let go of the moral exactitude, see *EB*, 144; *ITST*, 340–341; BR, 181; *GB*, 147. For the delicious retelling of the story of the prodigal son from the perspective of the Kantian and the Hegelian philosophy of religion through the voices of the elder brother, see DMA, 306–312. For Desmond's reflections on this parable, see also *EB*, 305, *GB*, 186.
75 Recall the passage from *Religion*, 134 (6:99): "God can be thought of as the supreme lawgiver of an ethical community, with respect to whom all true duties, hence also the ethical, must be represented as at the same time his commands; consequently, he must also be one who knows the heart, in order to penetrate to the most intimate parts of the dispositions of each and everyone and, as must be in every community, *give to each according to the worth of his actions*" (my emphasis). Kant's notion of the divine absolute is essentially the moral judge who cannot give to a single individual if his action is morally worthless. It would be impossible for this kind of divinity to welcome the single individual when the individual has strayed from the extremely narrow path of moral uprightness. For Desmond's critiques on this point, see *ITST*, 340–341.
76 Cf. *ITST*, 23, 46–47, 126, 245–247, 293, 330; *AOO*, 43; *EB*, 369; *GB*, 21; *IU*, 91, 113, 134–135, 233–236, 265.
77 *GB*, 297. Cf. *GB*, 109.
78 *GB*, 319.

79 *GB*, 307.
80 In this sense, the "way up" of creation to God and the "way down" of God to creation, therefore, are not the same.

Chapter 7

1 Cf. Heisig, "Philosophy as Spirituality," 374–375. Heisig points out the following: "Tanabe's writings show a more topical flow of ideas and a passion for consistency that contrasts sharply with Nishida's creative leaps of imagination. If Nishida's prose is a seedbed of suggestiveness where one needs to read a great deal and occasionally wander off between the lines to see where things are going, Tanabe's is more like a mathematical calculus where the surface is complex but transparent.... Tanabe—and for that matter, Nishitani also—were more thematic and produced essays that can stand on their own and be understood as such." This is very true about the ways in which Tanabe writes his works in comparison with Nishida, but in comparison with Desmond, I find the collection of thematically structured writings of Tanabe to contain more ambivalence and equivocity. Accordingly, it is harder to represent a coherent view of some philosophical topics in reference to the entire *Zenshū* of Tanabe than the entire work of Desmond. Heisig also recognizes this "Darwinian habit of argumentation" in Tanabe: Cf. Heisig, "Tanabe's Logic of the Specific and the Critique of Global Village," 279.

2 Cf. Heisig, "The 'Self That Is Not a Self': Tanabe's Dialectics of Self-Awareness," in *The Religious Philosophy of Tanabe Hajime*, eds. Taitetsu Unno and James W. Heisig (Berkley, CA: Asian Humanities Press, 1990), 284, hereafter cited as *RPTH*. In this article, Heisig identifies the shift from the logic of species to the metanoetics (i.e., from the third to the fourth period of *Tanabe Zenshū*) in terms of the "structure of [Tanabe's] dialectical understanding of the self" as the change of his "focus" from "concrete history" to the human "self-awareness": the "concrete history, which had once provided the central locus for the praxis whereby the self dies to itself to be reborn and where the ideal of the true self takes shape, is displaced to the periphery to make room for self-awareness of the finitude of all historical praxis." I agree with Heisig to the extent that the "concrete history," which is the primal focus of the logic of species, does not play the central role in the discourse of human self-awareness as the finite individual in the *PM*. But we must keep in mind that the discourse on the finitude of human existence in the latter comes to reappropriate the logic of species (especially in the last essay "The Dialectic of the Logic of Species"). In this case, it seems that Tanabe needed his self-reflection as the finite individual in the *PM* to (re-)formulate the proper understanding of the concrete history in the *Logic of Species*. As I will demonstrate later, the shift from the earlier form of the logic of species to the metanoetics (which results in the later form of the logic of species) marks not only the shift of topics from the concrete history to self-awareness but also a radical shift of thinking from that which is based solely on self-power to that which lives the promise of the other-power, the systematic shift that allowed Tanabe to reformulate and complete his understanding of concrete history. For this point, see also Johannes Laube, "The Way of Metanoia and the Way of the Boddhisattva," *RPTH*, 321. Laube clearly indicates that the eighth chapter of the *PM* discusses the "metanoia of the state"

and "in so doing, [Tanabe] sets out on a course of rethinking and reformulating the theory of the 'Logic of Species.'"

3   A philosophy and student of Tanabe, Kōyama Iwao (高山岩男) (1905–1993), recollects that Tanabe's lectures in 1920s incarnated analytic clarity but his tendency to lay out the complex arguments in the works of Emil Lask and Husserl as clearly and straightforwardly as possible began to disappear when he started to work on the *Logic of Species* in 1930s (*THZ* 3: 535). This clearly shows that Tanabe went through a methodological transition from the (neo-)Kantian or the univocal to the dialectical framework of thinking in the course of his philosophical career.

4   Cf. Takeuchi, "Commentary," *THZ* 9: 500.

5   Cf. Tanabe Hajime, "Two Essays on Moral Freedom from the Early Works of Tanabe Hajime," translated and introduced by Takeshi Morisato and Cody Staton, *Comparative and Continental Philosophy* 8 (2016): 144–159.

6   Heisig, *PM*, 17–18 (xviii–xix). See also, Himi, "Tanabe's Theory of the State," *RPTH*, 308, 310, 315. Himi clearly indicates that the basic structure of the logic of species as dialectic fully corresponds to the Hegelian dialectic commonly understood in terms of "thesis-antithesis-synthesis" (308), and there is a reduction of religion to the "service of the state" (310). This does not mean, however, the logic of species as the ontology of the state strictly echoes Hegel's notion of the state, precisely because the former comes to incorporate the metanoetics and further indicates a "kind of community administered on the basis of a fraternal relationship among its inhabitants in the *ōsō* and *gensō* phases of *pariṇāma* [i.e., *ekō*]" (315). We must further investigate whether or not Tanabe's notion of the state, as the manifestation of absolute nothingness or expedient means for concretizing the kind of absolute that he discusses as the absolute nothingness, is systematically reducible to Hegel's concept of the state or the dialectical manifestation of Absolute Spirit.

7   Some commentators of Tanabe's philosophy (as well as Tanabe himself) occasionally discuss the establishment of his original philosophy as representing the transition from the Western philosophical standpoint of being to the Eastern philosophical standpoint of nothingness, where the absolute is no longer conceived of as being, but as nothingness. I find that this simple presentation of the difference between the Eastern and the Western philosophical standpoints problematic for two reasons: (1) it tends to misunderstand what some Western philosophers (including Desmond) have tried to conceptualize as the absolute (whether or not they call it "being" or "being beyond being" or even "nothingness") and (2) it dismisses the fact that some formulations of the philosophy of nothingness (e.g., the early form of the logic of species) fail to represent the full implication of the conclusion that the absolute is nothingness or emptiness. Cf. Heisig, "Tanabe Hajime and the Hint of a Dharmic Finality," *Comprendre* 13 (2011): 61.

8   *THZ* 1: 131–140.

9   Cf. *THZ* 1: 483–484.

10 *THZ* 3: 534. See Yuien (唯円), *Tannishō* (歎異抄), ed. Kaneko Daiei (Tokyo: Iwanami Shoten, 1931), 40–41. The most accessible (and partial) translation of the passage can be found in Kaneko, "Shin Religion as I Believe It," Listening, 53: "In believing this Vow, deeds of morality are not required, because there are no deeds of morality that can surpass the Nebmbutsu, neither should one be afraid of evil because there are no evils powerful enough to obstruct the way of Amida's Original Vow." The *Tannishō* is based on the collection of Shinran's sayings (edited by his disciple Yuien). It tends to

convey in the most accessible manner the true teaching of Shinran, while lamenting the heretical views spread after his death.
11 Taguchi, "The Logic of *Tenkan*: The Generation of Tanabean Thinking and 'Logic as Ethics,'" 145 and especially 150–151 for the significance of these early essays on moral freedom in relation to the later development of metanoetics. Taguchi argues that Tanabe's philosophy after the middle period (or what comes after the logic of species) tends to integrate a lot of what he has discussed in the earlier works, and this alone makes it extremely difficult for the commentators to trace the origin of each idea. However, Taguchi further points out that "philosophical arguments in the earlier works provide intellectual moments that enable us to prepare for us to understand the development of Tanabe's ideas in the middle and the later works: and accordingly, we can differentiate these ideas from each other and search for what motivated Tanabe to develop them" (145). I cannot agree more with Taguchi on this benefit of reading Tanabe's earlier works in relation to his later works.
12 Walpola Rahula, *What the Buddha Taught* (London; Bedford: The Gordon Fraser Gallery Ltd., 1959).
13 Rahula, *What the Buddha Taught*, 1.
14 Rahula, *What the Buddha Taught*, 1.
15 Rahula, *What the Buddha Taught*, 1.
16 Alternatively, this can be read as "self is lord of the self" or "self is its own support."
17 Rahula, *What the Buddha Taught*, 39–40.
18 Rahula, *What the Buddha Taught*, 51.
19 Rahula, *What the Buddha Taught*, 40.
20 Rahula, *What the Buddha Taught*, 8.
21 It is extremely important to emphasize the existential and practical dimension of the ultimate in Buddhism and the following passage of Rahula is worthy of our attention: "Nirvana is beyond logic and reasoning. However much we may engage, often as a vain intellectual pastime, in highly speculative discussions regarding Nirvana or Ultimate Truth or Reality, we shall never understand it that way. A child in the kindergarten should not quarrel about the theory of relativity. Instead, if he follows his studies patiently and diligently, one day he may understand it. Nirvana is to be realized by wise within themselves. If we follow the path patiently and with diligence, train and purify ourselves earnestly, and attain the necessary spiritual development, we may one day realize it within ourselves—without taxing ourselves with puzzling and high-sounding words" (Rahula, *What the Buddha Taught*, 43–44).
22 This is precisely the way in which Desmond detects an apotheosis of *conatus essendi* in some forms of Buddhism. Consult *ITST*, 144, 152. Tanabe locates the same problem in Zen Buddhism. Cf. *DC*, 32.
23 This is, of course, not an entirely fair reading of the Pali texts. So, for instance, Buddha has a conversation in which he argues that human salvation through humanity alone (i.e., without the teachings of the Buddha) is like a blind man leading another blind man through the narrow path of enlightenment. These parables seem to indicate that humans would need something more than themselves for attaining their freedom from sufferings.
24 Plato, *Republic*, 539d.
25 *ELP*, 397.
26 *ELP*, 397–398. Tanabe criticizes culturalism as the typical expansion of life and starkly differentiates it from his philosophy of religion based on the notion of death. This is remarkably close to what Desmond tries to point out through his notion of

"posthumous thinking." Tanabe often describes this mode of philosophical thinking as a "standpoint of death-and-resurrection," and on the basis of this standpoint, he argues that philosophy that purses an art of dying to oneself has a very close affinity with religion. For these points, see *PM*, 116–117 (37), 276 (164). In relation to Desmond's metaxology, Shaw makes the same point of philosophy as a preparation for divine/religious knowing. Cf. Shaw, *On Exceeding Determination and the Idea of Reason*, 107–110.

27 *PM*, 116–117 (37). Cf., Robert E. Carter, *The Kyoto School: An Introduction* (Albany: State University of New York Press, 2013), 11. Carter rightly points out that Kyoto school thinkers share the understanding of philosophy as a "transformative activity and not just a cerebral exercise in logic or the analysis of words or propositions." In this sense, philosophy, for Tanabe (as well as the other Kyoto school thinkers), is about converting not only the ways in which we understand the world and ourselves but also the ways in which we live our lives.

28 *DC*, 3–7.

29 The issues at stake in relation to the study of Pure Land/Shin Buddhism are that the Occidentalists tend to impose their own understanding of religions on their interpretation of the Buddhist doctrines or that the orientalists generally dismiss the profound consonance between the core of the Pure Land/Shin teachings and that of Judeo-Christian faith. Cf. Galen Dean Amstutz, *Interpreting Amida: History and Orientalism in the Study of Pure Land Buddhism* (Albany: State University of New York Press, 1997), 68–70.

Chapter 8

1 *PM*, 115–116 (36–37).
2 *ELP*, 294.
3 *ELP*, 294.
4 *PM*, 117 (38). Cf. *PM*, 204 (107), *ELP*, 294–295.
5 *PM*, 118 (38). Cf. *DC*. 290. The same argument can be found in *PM*, 124 (43–44): "[T]he *Critique of Pure Reason* cannot provide the ultimate standpoint for philosophy that Kant claimed for it, since his solution of separating the phenomenal world from the noumenal is a mere compromise incapable of bringing reason to an ultimate state of peace. Quite to the contrary, reason is left exposed to antinomies that can only rend it asunder and cast it into a state of absolute self-disruption. As far as the critique of pure reason is concerned, reason as the criticizing subject always remains in a safety zone, where it preserves its own security without having to criticize the possibility of critique itself. Yet precisely because reason cannot thereby avoid self-disruption, the reason that does the criticizing and the reason that is to be criticized must inevitably be separated from each other. Reason thus forced to recognize itself as self-disruptive because of the critique must finally admit that the very reason that has come to think highly of itself in virtue of its capacity for critique must be shattered. Reason must recognize that it lacks the capacity for critique; otherwise the criticizing reason can only be distinguished from the reason to be criticized. In either case, there is no avoiding the final self-disruption of reason. In other words, reason that tries to establish its own competence by means of self-criticism must finally, contrary to its own intentions, recognize its absolute self-disruption."

6 *PM*, 124 (43). Cf. *PM*, 61 (lvi), 94–95 (20), 237 (132), 432 (286).
7 *PM*, 116 (37), 135 (52). See also his praise of Hegel in *PM*, 194 (99).
8 Cf. *HG*, 91, 107–108.
9 See how often Hegel repeats this same point for instance in *LPR*, 108, 102–103, 115–116, 394, 410–411, 416, 433, 485.
10 *PM*, 135 (52). Desmond also makes the same point in relation to the significance of "dia" in dialectic. *BB*, 210; *GB*, 271, 275.
11 *ELP*, 304.
12 The distinction of thesis, antithesis, and synthesis has been criticized as something that Hegel never proposed in his works, but I do not think it is impossible to conceive of them as proposing relevant metaphysical terms for generalizing such distinctions as universal/particular, unity/multiplicity, necessary/contingent, rational/real, self/other, etc., in relation to Hegel's dialectic.
13 This is precisely the reason why Tanabe criticizes Hegel's absolute to be ontic, while the proper absolute unfolded through metanoesis as the result of absolute critique must be meontic, that is to say, based on the Buddhist notion of absolute nothingness. Cf. *DC*, 321. Desmond also gives a similar critique of Hegel's sublationary infinitism as problematically providing an "absorbing god in which all differences are dissolved" in the end of dialectical development of the absolute spirit. For this point, cf. *HG*, 134–135.
14 Tanabe thinks that the fact that Hegel's absolute knowledge cuts itself off from the truth of absolute critique and retires once again to the direct affirmation of reason shows that he lets go of the spirit of the critique of reason itself and this is a result of Hegel's lack of a thoroughgoing metanoetics and of his lack of religious practice and faith. For this point, see *PM* 196–197 (101).
15 *PM*, 125 (44). Cf. *DC*, 49.
16 *PM*, 118 (39).
17 *PM*, 118 (39). This is identical with the way in which Desmond discusses the breakdown of reason that leads to its extreme poverty and then to its openness to the otherness of origin as its infinite source. The absolute critique in metanoesis is what Desmond would call "fertile self-skepticism that opens thought to otherness in the very act of its own self-questioning" (*PO*, 19). For the way in which Desmond would describe the absolute critique, see *PO*, 224.
18 *PM*, 391–392 (253–254). See also *PM*, 399–400 (260–261). Here Tanabe argues that he would have to reserve a special place for Pure Land Buddhism to show him the passage beyond the limit of self-power philosophy based solely on autonomy of reason, but further qualifies that the "grace of Tathagata's Great Compassion enables the development of Eastern and Western philosophy, in mutual dependence, toward the direction of metanoetics" (*PM*, 400 [261]: my translation). Tanabe is clearly thinking that despite its close affinity with the notions of Pure Land Buddhism, his metanoetics is a world philosophy that goes beyond the division between Eastern and Western philosophy.
19 *ELP*, 309. Cf. *PM*, 98 (23), 124–125 (44). Tanabe specifically argues that this antinomy of reason includes not only the impossibility of the theoretical unity between subject and object but also the practical unity of ethical personhood (*ELP*, 309).
20 *PM*, 55 (1). This death and resurrection of reason in Tanabe is harmonious with Desmond's notion and praxis of posthumous thinking. For Tanabe's emphasis on the significance of thinking from the side of never, see *ELP*, 280, 406–409, 474–475; *DC*, 25–26, 116.

21 There are several occasions in which Tanabe clearly equates philosophy based on the autonomy of reason as the self-power philosophy. For these references, see *PM*, 61–62 (lvi–lvii), 73 (2), 101–104 (25–27), 204–205 (107).
22 *PM*, 84 (11).
23 We must note that an emphasis on this distinction between *jiriki-hongan* and *tariki-hongan*, as well as that between *jiriki-shōdōmon* and *tariki-jōdomon*, that I will emphasize later on rather comes from the side of those who believe in the significance of *tariki-hongan* and *tariki-jōdomon*. The most famous example from Japanese Buddhism is found in the work of Shinran's master, Hōnen (法然) (1133–1212), entitled *Senchaku Hongan Nembutsushū* (選択本願念仏集). For the accessible and excellent edition of this text, see Hōnen, *Senchaku Hongan Nembutsushū: Teachings of Hōnen* (選択本願念仏集：法然の教え), ed. Ama Toshimaro (阿満利麿) (Tokyo: Kadokawa Shoten, 2007).
24 For the Pure Land/Shin Buddhist definition of the original vow (*hongan*), see Kaneko Daiei (金子大栄) (1881–1976), "Shin Religion as I Believe It," in *Listening to Shin Buddhism: Starting Points of Modern Dialogue*, ed. Michael Pye (Sheffield: Equinox Publishing, 2012), 47–48, hereafter, *Listening*. A great discussion on the difficulty of translating this term is provided by Pye ed., "Shinran's World," *Listening*, 233–243.
25 The fierce intellectual battle that Tanabe waged against Nishida played a significant role in the establishment of the Kyoto school of philosophy. This conflict, like any other in the history of philosophy, generates a series of complex questions and answers concerning the possibility of its resolution. Of course, the question can initially be put in a simple form: Was Tanabe right about his criticisms of Nishida? Many followers of Nishida's philosophy answer this question in the negative. They have tried to show, whether successfully or not, how Tanabe's criticisms do not accurately portray the fundamental notions provided in the framework of Nishida's thinking or how their interpretation(s) of Nishida's texts can escape the criticisms that Tanabe brings forth in his later works. But to say that Tanabe's criticisms of Nishida were not correct is not to say that Tanabe was wrong about what he said regarding the notion of absolute nothingness and its relation to human ethical development. Cf., Sugimoto Kōichi, "Tanabe Hajime's Logic of Species and the Philosophy of Nishida Kitarō: A Critical Dialogue within the Kyoto School," in *Japanese and Continental Philosophy: Conversations with the Kyoto School* (Bloomington, IN: Indiana University Press, 2011), 53; Makoto Ozaki, *Individuum, Society, Human Kind: The Triadic Logic of Species according to Hajime Tanabe* (Leiden: Brill, 2001), 138–139, 142–143. For the most notable English scholarship, attempting to unfold the underling commonality between Nishida and Tanabe, cf., James W. Heisig, *Philosophers of Nothingness: An Essay on the Kyoto School* (Honolulu: University of Hawai'i press, 2001); especially for Tanabe's critical adaptation of Nishida's notion of absolute nothingness, see pp. 118–122. There has been more Japanese scholarship on the Nishida-Tanabe relation: cf. Kōsaka Masaaki, "Nishida Philosophy and Tanabe Philosophy," in vol. 8 of *The Collected Works of Kōsaka Masaaki* (Tokyo: Gakujutsu Shuppankai, 2011), 298–307; Nakayama Nobuji, *Buddhism, Nishida & Tanabe Philosophy: On Tanabe's Criticisms of Nishida Philosophy and the Teachings of Shinran* (Tokyo: Risōsha, 1956), 73–129; Ienaga Saburō, *A Study of Tanabe Hajime from the Perspective of the History of Thought: War and Philosopher* (Tokyo: Hōsei University Press, 1974), 86–99; Himi Kiyoshi, *A Study of Tanabe Philosophy: From the Viewpoint of the Philosophy of Religion* (Tokyo: Hokuju Syhuppan, 1990); Mine Hideki, *The Confrontation between Nishida Philosophy and Tanabe Philosophy: The Logic of Locus and the Dialectic*

(Kyoto: Minerva Shobō, 2012). Nishitani and Kōsaka are the pioneers in the process of unfolding the complex co-influences of Nishida and Tanabe. Nakayama's treatment of Tanabe's criticisms of Nishida is an exemplar of what we have described as the one-sided defense of Nishida. Ienaga's analysis, which adopts Kōsaka's insight, begins with an acknowledgment that there are shared themes in the works of the two thinkers (e.g., sociality, species, dialectic, absolute nothingness, and living through dying) but its main focus shifts toward their intellectual engagement with the Pacific War. This analysis suffers from a simplistic interpretation of *The Logic of Species*, where Tanabe is presented as giving a straightforward endorsement of Japanese nationalism. Himi shares our sentiment that there are disproportionately more scholarly works available on Nishida than Tanabe (21–22), as well as the methodological problem of approaching the works of Tanabe from the standpoint of Nishida philosophy (23–24). In this work, Himi holds a clear position that "to understand the affirmative influence of Tanabe on Nishida philosophy, it ultimately suffices to investigate how Tanabe inherited the concept or the term 'absolute nothingness'" (84). Mine's analysis of the Nishida-Tanabe conflict is much more finessed and quite helpful, for it focuses on the philosophical themes in the works of Nishida and Tanabe, while demonstrating Tanabe's constructive influences on the development of Nishida philosophy, as well as how Tanabe's critical stance toward the works of Nishida contributed to the development of Tanabe's philosophical motifs. But Mine's analysis, which brings him much closer to Nishida than Tanabe in the end, maintains an inconclusive neutrality that leaves the question concerning the possibility of the profound agreement between Nishida and Tanabe unanswered. As Ienaga points out, this is "an immense theme that requires a monograph length" (86), and despite the recent publication on the issue by Mine in Japanese and the notable contribution by Heisig in English, further discussions on the issue of Nishida-Tanabe (dis)continuity might well throw light on the debate. I think that it is possible to show the deeper resonance between Nishida's and Tanabe's notion of absolute nothingness than what each of these thinkers could see in the works of the other or any of the commentators on their works. That discussion, however, will have to wait for another occasion.

26 *PM*, 164 (75).
27 *PM*, 73 (3). Or sometimes he calls it "*ōsō*-speculation" as opposed to "*gensō*-practice." Cf. *DC*, 15.
28 *PM*, 170 (80), 193 (98).
29 *PM*, 164 (75), 170 (80), 193 (98).
30 *PM*, 226–228 (124–125).
31 Cf. *PM*, 282–283 (169–170), 288–289 (174), 305–307 (187–188), 411 (270).
32 Cf., Carter, 54–56. Carter points out that Nishida differentiates his standpoint [of Zen philosophy] from mysticism by emphasizing the dualistic framework of thinking that separates the absolute and the relative. According to Carter, this is the same point that D.T. Suzuki makes in *The Japanese Mind*. But, as we will see later in this section, this differentiation does not enable Nishida to escape the problems of self-power philosophy that Tanabe puts forward under the label of "mysticism." The central problem that Tanabe sees both in mysticism and Nishidian philosophy is the one-way movement from the relative to the absolute that takes place as the immanent self-determination of the individuals. Interestingly, Carter points that Nishida mentions the complementary relation of the *jiriki* and *tariki* in his earliest work, *An Inquiry into the Good*. The reconciliation of Nishida and Tanabe philosophy in relation to the philosophy of religion, therefore, must lie in the formulation of the interrelation

between the *jiriki* of the finite relative and the *tariki* of the absolute or how to justify the statement that Nishida makes in his early work with the philosophical viewpoint(s) developed in his later works.
33 *PM*, 170 (80).
34 *PM*, 283 (170): "[T]his tendency [to put the emphasis on the in-itself mode of the original Buddhahood of sentient beings] follows naturally from Zen's preferential concern for saints and sages rather than the ordinary and ignorant, for saints and sages belong to an in-itself mode of being that recognizes the original Buddhahood of the self and thus has no need of the love and compassion of other-power. They are able to penetrate the self's true nature by self-power and the self's own freedom to dwell in the tranquility of unrestricted freedom of the authentic self. This is why the Zen Buddhist locates the most important aspect of human religious existence in the elemental fact of resting at home, eating when hungry, and sleeping when weary, which are also the essential marks of the wise and the holy."
35 *PM*, 283–284 (170).
36 *PM*, 53 (xlix).
37 *PM*, 197 (101).
38 Kant, *Religion*, 77 (6: 29).
39 *PM*, 133 (50): "Kant proposed a 'religion within the limits of reason alone' but in truth there can be no such religion. The principle of absolute goodness, which furnishes a basis for religion and is able to overcome the radical evil in humanity, belongs only to God. Religion consists in the faith of those who participate in the work of establishing the Kingdom of God on earth and who, as members of the Kingdom of God, submit to the supremacy of divine providence. The faith in God to which Kant was pointing was rational and universal, as distinct from faith based on God's revelation as a historical event. Genuine faith, however, is an absolute negation of reason, worthy of being termed religion only when it transcends mere rational thinking." For the general problem of Zen Buddhism, see *PM*, 236 (131); and for his critique of Kant, see also, *PM* 135 (52), 257 (148).
40 *PM*, 124–125 (44).
41 *ELP*, 344. For Tanabe's critical stance toward Zen Buddhism, see also *PM*, 170: "Even though sentient beings are originally Buddha, Buddhahood contains within itself the inevitable tendency to degrade itself to the level of sentient being…. But Zen puts the emphasis not so much on this inevitable degeneration as on the in-itself mode of the original Buddhahood of sentient beings…. Zen's exhortation to others to the attainment of *satori* and its advice on progress along the path to enlightenment dispose it to see the path as open and accessible to all, and hence to lay the stress on self-identity and the in itself. Moreover, this tendency follows naturally from Zen's preferential concern for saints and sages rather than the ordinary and ignorant, for saints and sages belong to an in-itself mode of being that recognizes the original Buddhahood of the self and thus have no need of the love and compassion of other-power. They are able to penetrate the self's true nature by self-power and the self's own freedom, to dwell in the tranquility of unrestricted freedom of the authentic self. This is why the Zen Buddhist locates the most important aspect of human religious existence in the elemental fact of resting at home, eating when hungry, and sleeping when weary, which are also the essential marks of the wise and the holy." For the similar criticisms of Zen Buddhism and Zen Philosophy, see *PM*, 172. It is also important to note that Tanabe's critical stance toward Zen Buddhism subsides once he pays attention to the Zen practice of death in reference to the works of Suzuki

Shōsan (鈴木正三) (1579–1655) in *ELP*, 473–475. For Dōgen's notion of *satori* and bodhisattva-ideal, see *PM*, 337 (211); *DC*, 238, 305, and the master-disciple relation in Zen in *ELP*, 318.

42 Tanabe specifically calls this as the radical evil. For this point see the following passage from the *PM*, 98 (22–23): "The relative self, then, as being that serves as the medium or means (*upāya*) of absolute nothingness and yet remains opposed to nothingness, contains within itself the relative independence of being independent of the absolute. The self, as relative being brought to existence as the medium or expedient of absolute nothingness, contains implanted within itself the possibility of securing its existence in opposition to nothingness and adhering stubbornly to its independence. This is what is termed the 'radical evil' of human existence."

43 The title of the text is often translated as the "Sutra of Great Assembly."

44 The *Mahāsaṃnipāta Sutra*, for instance, argues that more interpretations and teachings of the sutras are practiced among the religious thinkers in this age and thereby human communities manage to construct many towers and temples. These intellectual and constructive works of Buddhism are of great benefit for the communal life of the people insofar as they show people's veneration of the teachings of the Buddha. It is understandable in this respect why some Buddhologists simply interpret the significance of this change from the *zheng-fa* to *xiang-fa* as the rise of Mahāyāna Buddhism and its break from the tradition of Theravada Buddhism.

45 For an overview of the historical development of the Shōzōmatsu view of history in Japan from its reception to maturation in Kamakura Buddhism, see Michele Marra, "The Development of Mappō Thought in Japan (I)," *Japanese Journal of Religious Studies*, 15 (1988): 25–54 and "The Development of Mappō Thought in Japan (II)," *Japanese Journal of Religious Studies* 15 (1988): 287–305; hereafter cited as Mappō Thought I and II.

46 Takeuchi Yoshinori, *Philosophy of Kyōgyōshinshō* (教行信証の哲学) (Kyoto: Hōzōkan, 2002), 32–34. The first version of these three gives 500 years after Buddha's death as the *zheng-fa* but indicates the following period between 500 and 1000 as the *xiang-fa* and then the period between 1000 and 10,000 as the *mo-fa*, thus recognizing his own time as the beginning of the *mo-fa* and prophesizing the end of the world 10,150 years after the death of the Buddha. The second version of Shinran's *shōzōmatsu shikan* is faithful to *Mahāsaṃnipāta Sutra*: viz., he gives 500 years to each distinction, and then the third version, based on *Mappōtōmyōki*, gives more detailed (and yet somewhat contorted) account of the distinctions in accordance with the historical facts. For the significance of *Mappōtōmyōki* in relation to the historical development of *Mappō* thought in Japan, see Marra, Mappō Thought II, 287–290.

47 Takeuchi, *Philosophy of Kyōgyōshinshō*, 34–35.

48 Takeuchi, *Philosophy of Kyōgyōshinshō*, 43. Marra interestingly points out that "a coherent formulation of the theory of the Three Ages never developed in India" (Mappō Thought I, 27), but two centuries after the reception of Buddhism in Japan (especially from the time of Kyōkai (景戒) [757?–822]), the influence of the *mappō* thought gradually takes place in the history of Japanese Buddhism. The knowledge of *mappō* thought, Marra argues, was present in the works of Kyōkai; nevertheless, "[he] was still very confident in the power of the faith he had embraced" and "his age was still far from feeling the necessity of opening the way of salvation to all human beings" (Mappō Thought I, 39). Then, in the tenth century, especially in works of Genshin (源信) (942–1017), it begins to be seen as a "product of a deep inner crisis, not as a simple matter of dates" (Mappō Thought I, 40). Genshin's

reflection, for instance, moves toward the possibility for common beings (凡夫, *bonbu*) to find their way out of their historical suffering (Mappō Thought I, 46). In the second half of eleventh century, Fujiwara no Munetada (藤原宗忠) (1062–1141) believed that the "power of Buddhist spirit was active even in the most degenerated periods," and Marra further explains that "this would have been impossible without [his] confidence and faith in an external power (*tariki* 他力) able to help human beings, whose self efforts (*jiriki* 自力) were insufficient to stand the inexorability of the times" (Mappō Thought I, 51). Finally, the works of Honen and Shinran in that Kamakura period (1185–1333, immediately following the Gempei War [1180–1185]) shed light on the full implication of *tariki* faith as the enabling condition for the salvation of all sentient beings. As you can see, the *shōzōmatsu* view of history led the Buddhist thinkers to give up the idea of salvation through their self-power and simultaneously to their reflection on the absolute status of Amida Buddha's other power (cf. Mappō Thought II, 295). Paradoxically, in concluding that the salvation is available only through the other-power of Amida Buddha, the way of salvation becomes open to all human beings. Notice how Tanabe in 1946, immediately following the Second World War, tries to self-reflectively make the same point that his salvation cannot be achieved through his autonomous reason alone, but requires the other-power of the divine absolute.

49 Takeuchi, *Philosophy of Kyōgyōshinshō*, 38. In the same vein of this argument, Amstutz argues that the view of *mo-fa* (or *mappō* thought) intends to teach humility and reverence in the hearts and minds of the people, rather than representing a theoretically coherent view of historical reality. See Amstutz, *Interpreting Amida*, 12–13.

50 Cf. James Fredericks, "Philosophy as Metanoetics: An Analysis," *RPTH*, 47–48; John C. Maraldo, "Metanoetics and the Crisis of Reason: Tanabe, Nishida, and Contemporary Philosophy," *RPTH*, 247–249. Fredericks is absolutely right in saying that "[a]ny adequate reading of *Philosophy as Metanoetics* must be mindful of the biographical context" (given in *PM*, 71 [1]). *Pace* Fredericks, Maraldo also realizes that "A Startling central thesis of that philosophy is that it is impossible to philosophize apart from one's personal and historical situation" (247) but goes so far as to say, "ultimately, however, the removal of *Philosophy as Metanotics* from its concrete historical situation in wartime Japan raises the specter of massive deception and betrayal" (248). The historical context in which Tanabe lays out his metanoetic philosophy is crucial for our understanding of it. However, the significance of the historical narrative cannot be grasped in reference to the linear understanding of time, on the basis of which we can be tempted to think that metanoetics has its significance only in Japan circa 1945. Just as the *shōzōmatsu* view of history, along with one's awareness of living in the latter age of Dharma (i.e., *mappō*), is subject to one's intense self-reflection, the significance of the historical context in which Tanabe practices his uncompromising self-criticism does not rid us of the possibility of practicing the metanoetic thinking outside Japan or any point in the history of humanity. Tanabe clearly suggests this when he mentions Augustine, Hegel, Schelling, Kierkegaard et al. (in addition to many other Eastern thinkers) in the history of philosophy as sharing similar insight to that of metanoetics.

51 Tanabe often refers to Confucius' attainment of moral freedom in his old age as the possible embodiment of moral perfection: "one could give one's heart-and-mind free reign without overstepping the boundaries" (七十而從心所欲, 不踰矩). Cf. *THZ* 1: 127;

Confucius, *The Analects of Confucius: A Philosophical Translation*, trans. Roger T. Ames (New York: The Random House Publishing, 1998), 77.
52 *PM*, 81 (9).
53 *PM*, 190 (95–96).
54 *PM*, 269–270 (159).
55 *PM*, 83 (10). Cf. *PM*, 170–172 (80–81), 332–333 (208), 336–337 (211).
56 It is tremendously important to note that Tanabe clearly equates the notion of *soku* (即) in *jiriki-soku-tariki* (自力即他力) with the metanoetic intermediation where two opposing terms are conceived in their relativity to each other, and this intermediation does not conflate one with the other, unlike Hegel's dialectical sublation that Tanabe criticizes in the quotation above. See also Sasaki Genjun (佐々木現順) (1915–2010), *From Theravada Buddhism to Mahayana Buddhism* (原始仏教から大乗仏教へ) (Tokyo: Shimizu Kōbundō, 1978), 152–153. Sasaki argues that the abovementioned passage on the self-reliance in the original teachings of the Buddha essentially points to the Buddha as being in the state of absolute and also to the necessity of self-critique for one's attainment of such state; hence, there is no inconsistency between the Theravada emphasis on the self and the doctrine of the other-power in the works of Shinran.
57 Cf. *PM*, 415–417 (273–274). Cf. *DC*, 52–53, 184, 300–301. The term "kenosis" here should remind us of the theological notion of love in the Judeo-Christian tradition as much as its obvious reference to the Mahāyāna notion of compassion (i.e., *karuṇā*). This is precisely the reason why Yuasa Yasuo explains that "[Tanabe's] philosophy in his later years aimed for a universal love which synthesizes Christian love and Buddhist *karuṇā*, or compassion"—a love "awakened through a spiritual resurrection arising from facing death" or an "eternal love transcending death." For this point, see Yuasa, "The Encounter of Modern Japanese Philosophy with Heidegger," *HAT*, 158.
58 *PM*, 394 (256). The term *upāya* refers to the method through which one moves closer to enlightenment (i.e., *satori*) or the process through which one helps another move closer to it. For the transcendence of absolute nothingness, cf., *PM*, 55 (li), 80 (170), 259 (149); *ELP*, 350–351.
59 Nishitani, "Reflections on Two Addresses by Martin Heidegger," *HAT*, 151.
60 *PM*, 394–395 (256). Cf. *PM*, 405 (265); *DC*, 126.
61 *DC*, 25.
62 *PM*, 276 (164).
63 *PM*, 276 (164).
64 Cf. *ELP*, 467.
65 For Tanabe's arguments for the immanence of absolute nothingness to reality, see *PM*, 192–193 (97–98).
66 *PM*, 415–417 (273–274), 422 (279).
67 In this sense, Tanabe argues that the self-determination of Tathāgata is always other-determination and calls it "self-determination-qua-other-determination." For this point, cf. *PM*, 366–367 (235).
68 Cf. *PM*, 366 (234–235): "Between being and nothingness there can be no such relative relationship. The relative existence of sentient beings can be transformed into new being by absolute nothingness so that it can mediate Other-power. But the work of Other-power, because it is nothingness and absolute transformation, cannot appear in the pure passivity of the relative that is transformed by it, nor can it simply be set alongside the relative as a 'one' to an 'other.' If the absolute were to be placed in such an opposition to the relative, it would of necessity become another relative. Absolute Other-power means obedience to an absolute seen as a 'naturalness' that

supersedes the opposition between self and other. Hence, when we say that the self becomes a mediator of Other-power, we cannot mean that it cooperates with the Other-power that confronts it. Properly speaking, we mean that the self is transformed under the influence of an absolute nothingness which is neither the self nor an other, and is drawn into a 'naturalness' in which the self loses itself: Other-power is action (*gyō*) seen as the transformation of the self."

69 *ELP*, 284. Cf. *ELP*, 318; *DC*, 305; *PM*, 273 and especially 175: "[M]etanoesis may be termed an inner action determined by Other-power. But the real power of this Other-power does not simply function from without as a 'for-others.' In that case, metanoesis would degenerate from an inner activity into an outer dynamic. In order to be true inner action, what is determined by Other-power must at the same time be brought to self-consciousness through an act of self-determination: the real power from outside must simultaneously constitute the spontaneous ideal element of self-consciousness."

70 *PM*, 415–416 (273).

71 Cf. *PM*, 83 (10), 172 (81), 181 (88), 190 (95). Tanabe often describes this relation of the absolute and the relative in Shinran's term "Great Action" (*taigyō*) (*PM*, 172 [81] ff). For this point, see also Henneberg, 153 and especially 182, where he insightfully identifies nothingness as the "transcendent grace."

72 Cf. *PM*, 395–396 (257): "If philosophy is thought to attain absolute knowledge only by means of absolute mediation, then metanoetics is just such a philosophy. Only metanoetics considers the absolute as the transcendent ground of a self conscious of the fact that it can never be identified with the absolute, that it is no more than a finite relative mediating the absolute, and that as such it is bound inseparably to the absolute in the form of a 'unity-in-opposition.' Only metanoetics can bring about a mutual transformation of the absolute and the relative in which the relative transcends itself in an ascent to the absolute and the absolute makes itself immanent in a descent to the relative."

73 *PM*, 99 (23), 124–125 (44), 246 (139), 262–270 (153–159). Cf. Laube, "The Way of Metanoia and the Way of the Boddhisattva," *RPTH*, 318.

74 This overcoming of egoity is equivalent to Desmond's argument for the transition from *eros* to *agape*. He calls this act "a remembering of ontological-metaphysical dimensions [in our existential condition], and a *metanoia* with respect to granting that we are first granted to be," *IU*, 294. Desmond's rendering of metanoesis, see *IU*, 53, 292, 391, 496n(52). For Tanabe's articulations of the same *eros-agape* distinction, cf. *ELP*, 469, 471; *DC*, 135, 183–185, 205, 291.

75 *ELP*, 343, 417, 469; *DC*, 135, 205. Notice how Desmond talks about the same conversion that requires the breakdown of self-enclosed reason for a breakthrough of the agapeic mindfulness as the transition from the *eros* to *agape*: cf. *BB*, 10, 11, *PU*, Chapters 4 and 6 and *EB*, 354–356.

76 *PM*, 337 (211). The Shin/Pure Land tradition tends to talk about this in terms of "vicarious suffering," but as you can see, Tanabe purposefully introduces the notions of love (i.e., *eros* and *agape*) in reference to the Judeo-Christian tradition. For a Pure Land/Shin interpretation of the relation between vicarious suffering and self-sacrifice, see Kaneko, "The Buddhist Doctrine of Vicarious Suffering," *Listening*, 20–23.

77 *DC*, 126, 237–238.

78 *PM*, 63 (lvii). Cf. *PM*, 340–341 (214).

79 These are Heisig's translations of *ōsō* and *gensō* that can be found in *PM*, 3.

80 The modification of these Buddhist notions can be found in *PM*, 335–336 (210). The contemporary Pure Land/Shin takes on these notions as, however, not so different from what Tanabe lays out in his trilogy. See Kaneko, "Shin Religion as I Believe It," 55–56.
81 In the section of "From Philosophy of *Jiriki* 自力 to the Metanoetics of *Tariki* 他力 I," I have touched on the four problems that Tanabe sees in *jiriki* philosophy. Specifically the fourth one discussed its "lack of sociality for the praxis of religious faith." As you can see, with the notion of *gensō*-qua-*ōsō* or the relation of these two notions in the Shin/Pure Land Buddhism, Tanabe provides an alternative way to account for the indispensable sociality of religious praxis. For the social dimension of the single individual's metanoesis in reference to Tanabe's understanding of Christianity, see *DC*, 106–108, 139. For the Shin Buddhist discussion on the social dimension of religious faith, see Kaneko, "Shin Religion as I Believe It," 56–58.
82 *PM*, 338 (212). Cf. *ELP*, 374–375.
83 The addition of the "net" to the intermediation of the absolute and the relative selves as the networks of love is extremely important for Tanabe. In *Introduction to Philosophy*, he points out that "the absolute is essentially not something like a bag that can close the end and include everything in it. Rather, it is an infinite net. We can find a hole everywhere in the net. Hence, no matter how tightly one closes the opening, it does not mean anything. Everything can freely enter and exit the net. This is to say, insofar as it is the net, it is open contrary to the bag that is closed. The net allows everything to freely go in and out of it. We are in that kind of net [in our relation to the absolute]" (*TZH*, 11: 130; for the earliest treatment of this notion in Tanabe, see also *TZH*, 2: 238). The metanoetic intermediations of the absolute and the relative, therefore, are the open networks of love. For scholarly discussion on this theme of "net," cf. Carter, *The Kyoto School*, 73–74; Hase Shōtō, "The Structure of Faith: Nothingness-qua-Love," *RPTH*, 98. Tanabe seems to think that the Judeo-Christian notion of the "City of God" is the same as his notion of the metanoetic community of compassionate selves that he drew from the Pure Land tradition as the manifestation of absolute nothingness. See *DC*, 66–67, 106–108, 120, 146–147, 299–300. In his appendix to *DC*, Tanabe seems to think that his notion of the absolute nothingness is the underlining principle both for the Eastern and the Western religious traditions, thereby calling for the necessity of interreligious dialogues to become aware of this truth as the "absolute religion": cf. *DC*, 305–306, 312–313, 319.
84 *PM*, 418–419 (276).
85 *PM*, 335 (210): "For Pure Land Buddhism, however, Amida Buddha's vow of Great Compassion is mediated by the pre-enlightenment discipline and work of Dharmākara (*Hōzō-bosatsu*), which as a whole already presupposes the notion of *gensō-ekō* or the compassionate 'return to the world' of Amida Buddha. Thus the circularity within Amida Buddha sets up a twofold dynamic which we can only call a *gensō*-qua-*ōsō*: the Buddha's coming to himself (the reflection of the absolute within itself) is at the same time his going out to the relative world. And this corresponds, in turn, to a dynamic within sentient beings: their movement toward salvation is at the same time a return from Nirvana."
86 This means that, for Tanabe, an anthropological approach to faith completely misses its metaphysical and existential implication that you will see in the following.
87 *ELP*, 309.
88 *ELP*, 309.
89 *ELP*, 309.
90 *ELP*, 310.

91 *ELP*, 310.
92 *ELP*, 310.
93 *ELP*, 310.
94 *ELP*, 310. Cf. Whalen Lai, "Tanabe and the Dialectics of Mediation: A Critique," *RPTH*, 266. Lai indicates the priority of other-power to self-power in Tanabe's *PM*: "Other-power is clearly given precedence over self-power. Amida is not *totaliter aliter* from the human, but neither is Amida ever said to be totally the same as the human. For Tanabe, the sin-ridden human individual needs Amida to become whole far more than Amida needs men and women. The mutual mediation is thus asymmetrical, favoring a greater role for Amida."
95 *ELP*, 365.
96 *ELP*, 365. Cf. *PM*, 436–437 (290–291).
97 *ELP*, 365. In this sense, Tanabe clearly argues that for powerless beings like us, loving God and our neighbors is possible because of the love of God. For this point, see *ELP*, 329.
98 *PM*, 290 (175). Cf. *DC*, 141, 210. In the *Dialectic of Christianity*, Tanabe often calls the networks of love (i.e., the intermediation of compassionate selves, sustained by the love of absolute nothingness) "trinity of love" and presents the social implication of metanoetics as being in agreement with the notion of the community of agapeic service, while acknowledging the superiority of Christianity to Pure Land Buddhism for the explicit exposition of the social dimension of religious faith. For this point, see *DC*, 164, 223–224, 244, 292.
99 Many Japanese commentators rightly point out this manifestation of the absolute nothingness as the transformation of the self-power into the other-power, which constitutes the intermediations of compassionate selves. For this point, see for instance Hosoya Masashi (細谷昌志), "Preface to the Shisō Volume on Tanabe Philosophy: How Does the Absolute Appear in Thinking?" *Shisō* (思想), no. 1053 (2012): 5.
100 *PM*, 310 (190).
101 *PM*, 310 (190). Cf. Kaneko, "The Buddhist Doctrine of Vicarious Suffering," *Listening*, 20–23.
102 *ELP*, 352. See also *ELP*, 315, 485–486. Desmond gives almost an identical description of this religious notion of the work reflecting the superlative good beyond good and evil as the "works of mercy" (*EB*, 508–511). Perhaps the truth of this notion as the manifestation of religious faith (or the works of mercy) is much easier to present through literary works. From earlier on, Tanabe commends his readers to read Kurata Hyakuzō's The Priest and His Disciples (出家とその弟子); here the works of mercy based on the *tariki* faith are demonstrated through the relation of Shinran and his disciples. Cf. Kurata Hyakuzō (倉田百三), *The Priest and His Disciples: A Play*, trans. Glenn W. Shaw (Tokyo: Hokuseido, 1969); (出家とその弟子) (Tokyo: Iwanami Shoten, 2003).
103 *DC*, 291: "So long as there is no overcoming of egoity, the self cannot escape hopelessness. At the height of this despair, the self is turned to the grace of other-power and through its self-abandonment of metanoesis as the turning-point, it is resurrected in its faith-witness of nothingness-qua-love. At this point, the sin of egoity is forgiven and it is turned into the subject of neighborly love that dedicates to the love of God as the mediator of nothingness-qua-love. At the universal stage of ethics, the crime of self-love that constitutes the rebellion of the particular against the universality of the moral law, once it abandons itself through penitent

confession and turns itself to the love of God, begins to feel the divine love toward the self as the grace and starts to work as a token of his thanks to it."
104 The network of love in Tanabe is supposedly in correspondence with the Buddhist notion of the Pure Land (or the Amida Buddha's Buddha Land as the Nirvana) but since Tanabe's presentation seems to include the Christian (especially Augustinian) notion of the "city of God," I anticipate more interreligious or comparative works on Tanabe's notion of the networks of love.

Conclusion

1 Desmond has observed the same problem of what Tanabe calls "radical evil" in the (post-)modern propensity to privilege the self as the determiner of the between.
2 Tanabe does not talk much about the renewed sense of reason and its universal that is revived through the act of metanoesis, but focuses more on the significance of metanoesis as the condition for the possibility of the activity of noesis. Desmond, in this sense, is much more explicit on the renewed sense of reason or its noesis in its metanoetic relativity to the divine absolute beyond ourselves when he calls it the "intimate universal." But I think it is still possible to develop a similar notion of the resurrected universal if we take a look at Tanabe's logic of species from the metanoetic perspective, which he insinuates in the completing essay, "The Practical Structure of the *Logic of Species*" (1946).
3 DC, 291.
4 PM, 441 (294). See also ELP, 469. Tanabe refers to lotus flower in the same sense.
5 Cf. *Karamazov*, 59.

Bibliography

Primary

Desmond, William. "Are We All Scholastic Now?: On Analytic, Dialectical and Post-dialectical Thinking." *In Yearbook of the Irish Philosophical Society* (2010): 1–24.

Desmond, William. *Art, Origins, Otherness: Between Philosophy and Art*. Albany: State University of New York Press, 2003.

Desmond, William. *Being Between: Conditions of Irish Thought*. Galway: Leabhar Breac, 2008.

Desmond, William. "Being, Determination, and Dialectic: On the Sources of Metaphysical Thinking." *The Review of Metaphysics* 48 (1995): 731–69; *Being and Dialectic: Metaphysics as a Cultural Presence*. Edited by William Desmond and Joseph Grange, 3–36. Albany: State University of New York Press, 2000; *Intimate Strangeness of Being: Metaphysics after Dialectic*, 3–43. Washington, DC: The Catholic University of America, 2012.

Desmond, William. *Beyond Hegel and Dialectic: Speculation, Cult, and Comedy*. Albany: State University of New York Press, 1992.

Desmond, William. *Desire, Dialectic and Otherness: An Essay on Origins*. New Haven, CT: Yale University Press, 1987; Eugene, OR: Wipf and Stock, 2014.

Desmond, William. "Dream Monologues of Autonomy." *Ethical Perspectives* 5, no. 2 (1998): 305–21.

Desmond, William. *Ethics and the Between*. Albany: State University of New York Press, 2001.

Desmond, William. *God and the Between*. Oxford: Blackwell, 2008.

Desmond, William. *Hegel's God: A Counterfeit Double?* Burlington, VT: Ashgate Publishing Co., 2003.

Desmond, William. *The Intimate Universal: The Hidden Porosity among Religion, Art, Philosophy, and Politics*. New York: Colombia University Press, 2016.

Desmond, William. "On the Betrayals of Reverence." In *Beyond Conflict and Reduction: Between Philosophy, Science and Religion*, edited by William Desmond, John Steffen and Koen Decoster, 175–98. Leuven: Leuven University Press, 2001.

Desmond, William. "Responses." *Louvain Studies* 36 (2012): 302–15.

Desmond, William. *The William Desmond Reader*. Edited by Christopher Ben Simpson. Albany: State University of New York Press, 2012.

Tanabe, Hajime. "A Clarification of the Meaning of the Logic of Species." In Vol. 6 of *Tanabe Hajime Zenshū*, edited by Nishitani Keiji, Shimomura Toratarō, Karaki Junzō, Takeuchi Yoshinori and Ōshima Yasumasa, 447–522. Tokyo: Chikuma Shobō, 1963.

Tanabe, Hajime. "The Development of the Concept of Existence." In Vol. 7 of *Tanabe Hajime Zenshū*, edited by Nishitani Keiji, Shimomura Toratarō, Karaki Junzō, Takeuchi Yoshinori and Ōshima Yasumasa, 211–50. Tokyo: Chikuma Shobō, 1963.

Tanabe, Hajime. "Dialectic of the Logic of Species." In Vol. 7 of *Tanabe Hajime Zenshū*, edited by Nishitani et al., 251–372. Tokyo: Chikuma Shobō, 1963.
Tanabe, Hajime. "Eternity, History and Act." In Vol. 7 of *Tanabe Hajime Zenshū*, edited by Nishitani Keiji, Shimomura Toratarō, Karaki Junzō, Takeuchi Yoshinori and Ōshima Yasumasa, 101–70. Tokyo: Chikuma Shobō, 1963.
Tanabe, Hajime. "Ethics and Logic." In Vol. 7 of *Tanabe Hajime Zenshū*, edited by Nishitani Keiji, Shimomura Toratarō, Karaki Junzō, Takeuchi Yoshinori and Ōshima Yasumasa, 171–210. Tokyo: Chikuma Shobō, 1963.
Tanabe, Hajime. *Filosofía Como Metanoética*. Translated by Rebeca Maldonado with Andés Marquina, Sasha Jair Espinosa, and Christina Pérez. Barcelona: Herder Editorial, 2014.
Tanabe, Hajime. *Filosofia Come Metanoetica*. Translated by Tiziano Tosolini. Milan: Mimesis Edizione, 2011.
Tanabe, Hajime. "The General Outline of Philosophy." In Vol. 3 of *Tanabe Hajime Zenshū*, edited by Nishitani Keiji, Shimomura Toratarō, Karaki Junzō, Takeuchi Yoshinori and Ōshima Yasumasa, 371–522. Tokyo: Chikuma Shobō, 1963.
Tanabe, Hajime. "Hegel's Philosophy and Dialectic." In Vol. 3 of *Tanabe Hajime Zenshū*, edited by Nishitani Keiji, Shimomura Toratarō, Karaki Junzō, Takeuchi Yoshinori and Ōshima Yasumasa, 73–369. Tokyo: Chikuma Shobō, 1963.
Tanabe, Hajime. "Historical Reality." In Vol. 8 of *Tanabe Hajime Zenshū*, edited by Nishitani Keiji, Shimomura Toratarō, Karaki Junzō, Takeuchi Yoshinori and Ōshima Yasumasa, 117–70. Tokyo: Chikuma Shobō, 1964.
Tanabe, Hajime. "An Introduction to Philosophy." In Vol. 11 of *Tanabe Hajime Zenshū*, edited by Nishitani Keiji, Shimomura Toratarō, Karaki Junzō, Takeuchi Yoshinori and Ōshima Yasumasa. Tokyo: Chikuma Shobō, 1963.
Tanabe, Hajime. "Kant's Theory of Teleology." In Vol. 3 of *Tanabe Hajime Zenshū*, edited by Nishitani Keiji, Shimomura Toratarō, Karaki Junzō, Takeuchi Yoshinori and Ōshima Yasumasa, 1–72. Tokyo: Chikuma Shobō, 1963.
Tanabe, Hajime. "The Logic of Social Existence." In Vol. 6 of *Tanabe Hajime Zenshū*, edited by Nishitani Keiji, Shimomura Toratarō, Karaki Junzō, Takeuchi Yoshinori and Ōshima Yasumasa, 51–168. Tokyo: Chikuma Shobō, 1963.
Tanabe, Hajime. "The Logic of the Social Ontological Structure." In Vol. 6 of *Tanabe Hajime Zenshū*, edited by Nishitani Keiji, Shimomura Toratarō, Karaki Junzō, Takeuchi Yoshinori and Ōshima Yasumasa, 299–396. Tokyo: Chikuma Shobō, 1963.
Tanabe, Hajime. "The Logic of Species and the World-Scheme." In Vol. 6 of *Tanabe Hajime Zenshū*, edited by Nishitani Keiji, Shimomura Toratarō, Karaki Junzō, Takeuchi Yoshinori and Ōshima Yasumasa, 169–264. Tokyo: Chikuma Shobō, 1963.
Tanabe, Hajime. "The Logic of State Existence." In Vol. 7 of *Tanabe Hajime Zenshū*, edited by Nishitani Keiji, Shimomura Toratarō, Karaki Junzō, Takeuchi Yoshinori and Ōshima Yasumasa, 25–100. Tokyo: Chikuma Shobō, 1963.
Tanabe, Hajime. "Moral Freedom." In Vol. 1 of *Tanabe Hajime Zenshū*, edited by Nishitani Keiji, Shimomura Toratarō, Karaki Junzō, Takeuchi Yoshinori and Ōshima Yasumasa, 119–130. Tokyo: Chikuma Shobō, 1964.
Tanabe, Hajime. "On Moral Freedom Revisited." In Vol. 1 of *Tanabe Hajime Zenshū*, edited by Nishitani Keiji, Shimomura Toratarō, Karaki Junzō, Takeuchi Yoshinori and Ōshima Yasumasa, 131–40. Tokyo: Chikuma Shobō, 1964.
Tanabe, Hajime. *Philosophy as Metanoetics*. Translated by Takeuchi Yoshinori, Valdo Viglielmo, and James W. Heisig. Los Angeles: University of California Press, 1987; Nagoya: Chisokudō Publications, 2016.

Tanabe, Hajime. *Tanabe Hajime Zenshū*. Edited by Nishitani Keiji, Shimomura Toratarō, Karaki Junzō, Takeuchi Yoshinori and Ōshima Yasumasa. 15 vols. Tokyo: Chikuma Shobō, 1963.

Tanabe, Hajime. "Thetic Judgment." In Vol. 1 of *Tanabe Hajime Zenshū*, edited by Nishitani Keiji, Shimomura Toratarō, Karaki Junzō, Takeuchi Yoshinori and Ōshima Yasumasa, 1–10. Tokyo: Chikuma Shobō, 1964.

Secondary

Amane, Nishi (西周). "Hyakuichi-sihnron" (百一新論). In *Nishida Amane Zenshū* (西周全集), ed. Ōkubo Toshiaki (大久保利謙), 232–89. Tokyo: Munetaka Shobō, 1960.

Amstutz, Galen Dean. *Interpreting Amida: History and Orientalism in the Study of Pure Land Buddhism*. Albany: State University of New York Press, 1997.

Anikeeva, Elena. "Orthodox Religious and Philosophical Aspects of Intercultural Communication." In *Communication across Cultures: The Hermeneutics of Cultures and Religions in a Global Age*, edited by Chibueze C. Udeani, Veerachart Nimanong, Zou Shipeng and Mustafa Malik, 239–46. Cardinal Station, Washington, DC: The Council for Research in Values and Philosophy, 2008.

Aquinas, Thomas. *Summa Theologiae (Vol. 2, Ia QQ.2–11), Existence and Nature of God*. Edited and translated by Timothy McDermott. Cambridge: Cambridge University Press, 2006.

Augustine. *The Confessions of Saint Augustine*. Translated by John K. Ryan. New York: Doubleday, 1960.

Augustine. *The Soliloquies*. Translated by John H.S. Burleigh, 23–63. Philadelphia, PA: The Westminster Press, 1953.

Balslev, Anindita N., ed. *Cultural Otherness: Correspondence with Richard Rorty*. Atlanta, GA: Scholar Press, 1991.

Burik, Steven. *The End of Comparative Philosophy and the Task of Comparative Thinking: Heidegger, Derrida and Daoism*. Albany, NY: State University of New York Press, 2010.

Carter, Robert E. *The Kyoto School: An Introduction*. Albany: State University of New York Press, 2013.

Cestari, Matteo. "The Individual and Individualism in Nishida and Tanabe." In *Re-Politicising The Kyoto School as Philosophy*, edited by Christopher Goto-Jones, 49–74. London; New York: Routeledge, 2008.

Chang, Chung-yuan. *Tao: A New Way of Thinking*. New York: Harper Colophon Books, 1975.

Cheng, Chung-Ying. "Preface: Origins and Relations of Philosophy: European and Chinese." In *European And Chinese Philosophy: Origins and Intersections*, edited by Chung-ying Cheng, Eric Nelson and Lyinyu Gu, 1–4. Chichester, West Sussex: John Wiley & Sons, 2013.

Confucius. *The Analects of Confucius: A Philosophical Translation*. Translated by Roger T. Ames. New York: The Random House Publishing, 1998.

Cross, Stephen. *Schopenhauer's Encounter with Indian Thought: Representation and Will and Their Indian Parallels*. Honolulu: University of Hawai'i Press, 2013.

Dante, Alighieri. *The Divine Comedy: The Inferno, The Purgatorio, and the Paradiso*. Translated by John Ciardi. New York: New American Library, 2003.

Dante, Alighieri. *Il Convivio (The Banquet)*. Translated by Elizabeth Price Sayer. London: Routledge, 1887.

Davis, Bret. "The Stimulating Doubleness of the Japanese Philosophy of Religion: Thinking with Nishida and Zen" (日本の宗教哲学における刺激的な両義性：西田と禅を中心に). In *The World-Significance of Japanese Philosophy: Its Receptions and Future Overseas* (日本哲学の国際性：海外における受容と展望), edited by James Heisig, 295–329. Tokyo: Risōsha, 2006.

Derrida, Jacques. *Dissemination*. Translated by Barbara Johnson. London; New York: Routledge, 2004.

Di Giovanni, George. "Faith without Religion, Religion without Faith: Kant and Hegel on Religion." *Journal of the History of Philosophy* 41, no. 3 (2003): 365–83.

Dilworth, David and Taira Sato. "The Logic of Species as Dialectic: Shino ronri no benshoho, by Tanabe Hajime." *Monumenta Nipponica* 24, no. 3 (1969): 273–88.

Dōgen 道元. "Shōbōgenzō" (正法眼蔵). In Vol. 1–2 of *Dōgen Zenshi Zenshū* (道元禅師全集), edited by Kawamura Kōdō (河村孝道). Tokyo: Shunjūsha, 1991–93.

Dostoyevsky, Fyodor. *The Brothers Karamazov*. Translated by Constance Garnett. New York: The Modern Library, 1996.

Dostoyevsky, Fyodor. "The Dream of a Ridiculous Man." In *A Gentle Creature and Other Stories*, translated by Alan Myer, 105–28. Oxford: Oxford University Press, 1999.

Dostoyevsky, Fyodor. *The Idiot*. Translated by David McDuff. London: Penguin Books, 2004.

Dostoyevsky, Fyodor. "Poor Folk." In *Poor Folk and Other Stories*, translated by David McDuff, 1–129. London: Penguin Books, 1988.

Feuerbach, Ludwig. *The Essence of Christianity*. Translated by George Eliot. New York: Harper & Row, 1957.

Feuerbach, Ludwig. "Das Wesen des Christentums." In Vol. 5 of *Gesammelte Werke*, edited by Werner Schuffenhauer and Wolfgang Harich, 47–48. Berlin: Akademie, 1974.

Feuerbach, Ludwig. "Zur Kritik der Hegelschen Philosophie." In *Kleinere Schriften II (1839–1846)*, Vol. 9 of *Gesammelte Werke*, edited by Werner Schuffenhauer and Wolfgang Harich, 16–62. Berlin: Akademie, 1982.

Frank, Joseph. *Dostoevsky: The Years of Ordeal, 1850–1859*. Princeton, NJ: Princeton University Press, 1983.

Fredericks, James. "Philosophy as Metanoetics: An Analysis." In *The Religious Philosophy of Tanabe Hajime*, edited by Taitetsu Unno and James W. Heisig, 43–71. Berkley, CA: Asian Humanities Press, 1990.

Froese, Katrin. *Nietzsche, Heidegger and Daoist Thought: Crossing Paths In-Between*. Albany, NY: State University of New York Press, 2006.

Fujita Masakatsu (藤田正勝), "Tanabe Hajime's Thinking: Through the Concept of 'Absolute Nothingness'." *Shisō* (思想), no. 1053 (2012): 165–83.

Gilkey, Langdon. "Tanabe and the Philosophy of Religion." In *The Religious Philosophy of Tanabe Hajime*, edited by Taitetsu Unno and James W. Heisig, 72–88. Berkley, CA: Asian Humanities Press, 1990.

Godart, Clinton. "'Philosophy' or 'Religion'? The Confrontation with Foreign Categories in Late Nineteenth-Century Japan." *Journal of the History of Ideas* 69, no. 1 (2008): 71–91.

Goto-Jones, Christopher. "The Kyoto School and the History of Political Philosophy: Reconsidering the Methodological Domination of the Cambridge School." In *Re-Politicising The Kyoto School as Philosophy*, edited by Christopher Goto-Jones, 3–25. London; New York: Routledge, 2008.

Goto-Jones, Christopher. "What Is (Comparative) Philosophy?" *Philosophy* 88 (2013): 133–40.
Griffioen, Sander. "Towards a Philosophy of God: A Study in William Desmond's Thought." *Philosophia Reformata* 75 (2010): 1–23.
Hare, John E. "Kant on Recognizing Our Duties as God's Commands." *Faith and Philosophy* 17, no. 4 (October 2000): 459–78.
Harris, H.S. *Hegel's Ladder II: The Odyssey of Spirit*. Indianapolis, IN: Hackett Publishing, Inc., 1997.
Hase Shōtō (長谷正當). "The Structure of Faith: Nothinngess-qua-Love." In *The Religious Philosophy of Tanabe Hajime*, edited by Taitetsu Unno and James W. Heisig, 89–116. Berkeley: Asian Humanities Press, 1990.
Hase Shōtō (長谷正當). *What Is the Original Vow: What Shinran Saw as the Buddhism* (本願とは何か：親鸞の捉えた仏教). Kyoto: Hōzōkan, 2015.
Hegel, G.W.F. *Early Theological Writings*. Translated by T.M. Knox and Richard Kroner. Chicago: University of Chicago Press, 1996.
Hegel, G.W.F. *The Encyclopaedia Logic (1830): Part I of the Encyclopaedia of Philosophical Sciences with the Zusätze*. Translated by T.F. Geraets, W.A. Suchting, and H.S. Harris. Indianapolis, IN: Hackett Publishing company, Inc., 1991.
Hegel, G.W.F. "Enzyklopädie Der Philosophischen Wissenschaften Im Grundrisse (1830)." In Vol. 20 of *Gesammelte Werke*, edited by Wolfgang Bonsiepen and Hans- Christian Lucas. Hamburg: Felix Meiner, 1992.
Hegel, G.W.F. "Grundlinen Der Philosophie Des Rechts." In Vol. 14 of *Gesammelte Werke*, edited by Klaus Grotsch and Elizabeth Weisser-Lohmann. Hamburg: Felix Meiner, 2009–11.
Hegel, G.W.F. *Hegel: Lectures on the Philosophy of World History, Volume 1: Manuscripts of the Introduction and the Lectures of 1822–1823*. Translated and edited by Robert F. Brown and Peter C. Hodgson. Oxford: Oxford University Press, 2011.
Hegel, G.W.F. *Hegel's Philosophy of Right*. Translated by T.M. Knox. London: Oxford University Press, 1952.
Hegel, G.W.F. *Hegels theologische Jugendschriften*. Edited by Herman Nohl. Tübingen: Mohr, 1907.
Hegel, G.W.F. *Lectures on the Philosophy of Religion*. Edited and translated by Peter C. Hodgson et al. Berkeley: University of California Press, 1988.
Hegel, G.W.F. *Lectures on the Philosophy of World History*. Translated by Hugh Barr Nisbet. Cambridge: Cambridge University Press, 1975.
Hegel, G.W.F. "Phänomenologie des Geistes." In Vol. 9 of *Gesammelte Werke*, edited by Wolfgang Bonsiepen and Reinhard Heede. Hamburg: Felix Meiner, 1980.
Hegel, G.W.F. *Phenomenology of Spirit*. Translated by A. V. Miller. Oxford: Oxford University Press, 1977.
Hegel, G.W.F. *Philosophy of Mind: Being Part Three of the Encyclopaedia of the Philosophical Sciences (1830) with the Zusätze*. Edited by M.J. Inwood and translated by William Wallace and A.V. Miller with revisions and commentary by M.J. Inwood. Oxford: Oxford University Press, 2007.
Hegel, G.W.F. *The Science of Logic*. Edited and translated by George di Giovanni. Cambridge: Cambridge University Press, 2010.
Hegel, G.W.F. *Vorlesungen über die Philosophie der Religion*. Edited by Walter Jaeschke. Hamburg: Felix Meiner, 1983–1985.
Hegel, G.W.F. "Vorlesungsmanuskripte II (1816–1)." In Vol. 18 of *Gesammelte Werke*, edited by Walter Jaeschke, 121–207. Hamburg: Felix Meiner, 1995.

Heidegger, Martin. "A Dialogue on Language." In *On the Way to Language*, translated by Peter D. Hertz, 1–56. New York: HarperCollins, 1971.

Heidegger, Martin. "The End of Philosophy and the Task of Thinking." In *Basic Writings: From Being and Time (1927) to The Task of Thinking (1964)*, translated by David Farrell Krell, 373–92. New York: Harper & Row, 1977.

Heidegger, Martin. "Only a God Can Save Us." In *Heidegger: The Man and the Thinker*, edited by Thomas Sheehan and translated by William J. Richardson, 45–67. Chicago: Precedent, 1981.

Heisig, James W. *Philosophers of Nothingness: An Essay on the Kyoto School*. Honolulu: University of Hawai'i Press, 2001.

Heisig, James W. "Philosophy as Spirituality: The Way of the Kyoto School." In *Buddhist Spirituality Volume 2: Later China, Korea, Japan, and the Modern World*, edited by Takeuchi Yoshinori, 367–88. New York: Crossroad, 1999.

Heisig, James W. "Tanabe Hajime and the Hint of A Dharmic Finality." *Comprendre* 13 (2011): 55–69.

Heisig, James W. "Tanabe's Logic of the Specific and the Critique of Global Village." In *Much Ado about Nothingness: Essays on Nishida and Tanabe*, 261–94. Nagoya: Nanzan Institute for Religion and Culture, 2015.

Heisig, James W., Thomas P. Kasulis and John Maraldo, eds. *Japanese Philosophy: A Source Book*. Honolulu: University of Hawai'i Press, 2011.

Henneberg, Peter. "Faith and Grace in the Thought of Tanabe Hajime and Søren Kierkegaard." Ph.D. diss., Université catholique de Louvain, 2010.

Himi, Kiyoshi. *A Study of Tanabe Philosophy: From the Viewpoint of the Philosophy of Religion*. Tokyo: Hokuju Shuppan, 1990.

Himi, Kiyoshi. "Tanabe Hajime's Understanding of Kantian Teleology." *Campana*, no. 11 (2004): 139–46.

Himi, Kiyoshi. "Tanabe's Theory of the State." In *The Religious Philosophy of Tanabe Hajime*, edited by Taitetsu Unno and James W. Heisig, 303–15. Berkley, CA: Asian Humanities Press, 1990.

Hosoya Masashi (細谷昌志). "Preface to the *Shisō* Volume on Tanabe Philosophy: How Does the Absolute Appear in Thinking?" *Shisō* (思想), no. 1053 (2012): 3–6.

Hōnen (法然). *Senchaku Hongan Nembutsushū: Theachings of Hōnen* (選択本願念仏集：法然の教え). Edited by Ama Toshimaro (阿満利麿). Tokyo: Kadokawa Shoten, 2007.

Husserl, Edmund. "The Vienna Lecture." In *The Crisis of European Sciences and Transcendental Phenomenology: An Introduction to Phenomenological Philosophy*, translated by David Carr, 269–299. Evanston, IL: Northwestern University Press, 1970.

Hyde, J. Kieth. *Concepts of Power in Kierkegaard and Nietzsche*. Burlington, VT: Ashgate Publishing Co., 2010.

Ienaga, Saburō (家永三郎). *A Study of Tanabe Hajime from the Perspective of the History of Thought: War and Philosopher* (田辺元の思想史的研究：戦争と哲学者). Tokyo: Hōsei University Press, 1974.

Inoue, Katsuhito (井上克人). "The Philosophical World of Meiji: The Philosophy of Organism and Its Genealogy" (明治の哲学界：有機体の哲学とその系譜). In *Fertile Culture and Philosophy of Meiji Period* (豊饒なる明治), edited by Inoue Katsuhito, 3–22. Suita: Kansai University Press, 2012.

Inoue, Katsuhito (井上克人). "The Philosophical World of Meiji Japan: The Philosophy of Organism and Its Genealogy." Translated by Takeshi Morisato. *European Journal of Japanese Philosophy* 1 (2016): 9–30.

Jaspers, Karl. *The Origin and Goal of History*. Translated by Michael Bullock. New Haven, CT: Yale University Press, 1953.

Jaspers, Karl. *Psychologie der Weltanschauungen*. Berlin: Springer, 1919.

Kaneko Daiei (金子大栄). "The Buddhist Doctrine of Vicarious Suffering." In *Listening to Shin Buddhism: Starting Points of Modern Dialogue*, edited by Michael Pye, 15–26. Sheffield: Equinox Publishing, 2012.

Kaneko Daiei (金子大栄). "Shin Religion as I believe It." In *Listening to Shin Buddhism: Starting Points of Modern Dialogue*, edited by Michael Pye, 47–60. Sheffield: Equinox Publishing, 2012.

Kant, Immanuel. "The Conflict of the Faculties." In *Religion and Rational Theology*, edited by Allen W. Wood and translated by Mary J. Gregor and Robert Anchor, 245–327. Cambridge: Cambridge University Press, 1996.

Kant, Immanuel. "Critique of Practical Reason." In *Practical Philosophy*, edited and translated by Mary J. Gregor, 139–271. Cambridge: Cambridge University Press, 1999.

Kant, Immanuel. *Critique of Pure Reason*. Edited and translated by Paul Guyer and Allen W. Wood. Cambridge: Cambridge University Press, 1998.

Kant, Immanuel. "Groundwork of the Metaphysics of Morals." In *Practical Philosophy*, ed. and trans. Mary J. Gregor, 37–108. Cambridge: Cambridge University Press, 1996.

Kant, Immanuel. *Lectures on Ethics*. Edited by Peter Heath, J.B. Schneewind and translated by Peter Heath. Cambridge: Cambridge University Press, 1997.

Kant, Immanuel. "Lectures on the Philosophical Doctrine of Religion." In *Religion and Rational Theology*, edited by Allen W. Wood, George di Giovanni, and translated by Allen W. Wood, 335–452. Cambridge: Cambridge University Press, 1996.

Kant, Immanuel. "Moral Philosophy: Collins's Lecture Notes (1784–5)." In *Lectures on Ethics*, edited by Peter Heath, J.B. Schneewind, and translated by Peter Heath, 37–222. Cambridge, Cambridge University Press, 1997.

Kant, Immanuel. "On the Common Saying: That May Be Correct in Theory, But It Is of No Use in Practice." In *Practical Philosophy*, edited and translated by Mary J. Gregor, 273–310. Cambridge: Cambridge University Press, 1996.

Kant, Immanuel. "What Does It Mean to Orient Oneself in Thinking?" In *Religion and Rational Theology*, edited by Allen W. Wood, George di Giovanni, and translated by Allen W. Wood, 7–20. Cambridge: Cambridge University Press, 1996.

Karatani, Kōjin (柄谷行人), "Overcoming Modernity." In *Contemporary Japanese Thought*, edited by Richard F. Calichman, 101–118. New York: Columbia University Press, 2005.

Kearney, Richard. "Maybe Not, Maybe: William Desmond on God." In *Between System and Poetics: William Desmond and Philosophy after Dialectic*, edited by Thomas A.F. Kelly, 191–202. Albershot: Ashgate, 2007.

Kierkegaard, Søren. *Eighteen Upbuilding Discourses*. Edited and translated by Howard V. Hong and Edna H. Hong. Princeton, NJ: Princeton University Press, 1990.

Kierkegaard, Søren. *Fear and Trembling*. Edited and Translated by Howard V. Hong and Edna H. Hong. Princeton, NJ: Princeton University Press, 1980.

Kierkegaard, Søren. *For Self-Examination. Judge for Yourself!* Edited and translated by Howard V. Hong and Edna H. Hong. Princeton, NJ: Princeton University Press, 1990.

Kierkegaard, Søren. *The Point of View*. Edited and translated by Howard V. Hong and Edna H. Hong. Princeton, NJ: Princeton University Press, 1998.

Kierkegaard, Søren. *Practice in Christianity*. Edited and translated by Howard V. Hong and Edna H. Hong. Princeton, NJ: Princeton University Press, 1991.

Kierkegaard, Søren. *The Present Age*. Translated and edited by Alexander Dru. New York: Harper & Row, 1962.

Kierkegaard, Søren. *Søren Kierkegaard's Journals and Papers*. Vol. 1–3. Edited and translated by Howard V. Hong and Edna H. Hong. Bloomington: Indiana University Press, 1967–70.

Kierkegaard, Søren. *Three Discourses on Imagined Occasions*. Edited and translated by Howard V. Hong and Edna H. Hong. Princeton, NJ: Princeton University Press, 1993.

Kierkegaard, Søren. *Two Ages*. Translated and edited by Howard V. Hong and Edna H. Hong. Princeton NJ: Princeton University Press, 1978.

Kōsaka, Masaaki (高坂正顕). "Nishida Philosophy and Tanabe Philosophy" (西田哲学と田辺哲学). In Vol. 8 of *The Collected Works of Kōsaka Masaaki* (高坂正顕著作集). Tokyo: Gakujutsu Shuppankai, 2011.

Kuki, Shuzō (九鬼周造). *The Problem of Contingency* (偶然性の問題). Tokyo: Iwanami Shoten, 2012.

Kurata, Hyakuzō (倉田百三). *The Priest and His Disciples: A Play*. Translated by Glenn W. Shaw. Tokyo: Hokuseido, 1969.

Kurata, Hyakuzō (倉田百三). *Shukketo sonodeshi* (出家とその弟子). Tokyo: Iwanami Shoten, 2003.

Kuwaki, Genyoku (桑木厳翼). "Nishi Amane's Philosophy: The Philosophical Tendencies of Early Meiji Era." In *The Philosophies of Miji Era* (明治の哲学界), 71-91. Tokyo: Chūōkōron-sha, 1942.

Lai, Whalen. "Tanabe and the Dialectics of Mediation: A Critique." In *The Religious Philosophy of Tanabe Hajime*, edited by Taitetsu Unno and James W. Heisig, 256–276. Berkley, CA: Asian Humanities Press, 1990.

Laube, Johannes. "The Way of Metanoia and the Way of the Boddhisattva," In *The Religious Philosophy of Tanabe Hajime*, edited by Taitetsu Unno and James W. Heisig, 316–39. Berkley, CA: Asian Humanities Press, 1990.

Lewis, C.S. *The Four Loves*. London: Collins, 1960.

Lewis, C.S. *Surprised by Joy*. New York: Hardcourt, Barce & Co., 1955.

Mall, Ram Adhar. *Intercultural Philosophy*. Lanham, MD: Rowman & Little Field Publishers, Inc., 2000.

Maraldo, John C. "Metanoetics and the Crisis of Reason: Tanabe, Nishida, and Contemporary Philosophy." In *The Religious Philosophy of Tanabe Hajime*, edited by Taitetsu Unno and James W. Heisig, 235–55. Berkley, CA: Asian Humanities Press, 1990.

Mariña, Jacqueline. "The Religious Significance of Kant's Ethics." *American Catholic Philosophical Quarterly* 75, no. 2 (2001): 179–200.

Marra, Michele. "The Development of Mappō Thought in Japan (I)." In *Japanese Journal of Religious Studies* 15 (1988): 25–54.

Marra, Michele. "The Development of Mappō Thought in Japan (II)." In *Japanese Journal of Religious Studies* 15 (1988): 287–305.

May, Reinhard. *Heidegger's Hidden Sources: East Asian Influences on His Work*. Translated by Graham Parkes. London: Routledge, 1996.

Mill, John Stuart. *A System of Logic: Ratiocinative and Inductive*. London: Savill and Edwards, 1842.

Mine, Hideki. *The Confrontation between Nishida Philosophy and Tanabe Philosophy: The Logic of Locus and the Dialectic*. Kyoto: Minerva Shobō, 2012.

Murai, Norio (村井則夫). "Baroque Philosophy of Tanabe Hajime: The Mechanics and Symbolism of the Absolute Dialectic" (田辺元のバロック哲学：絶対媒介の力学性と象徴性). *Shisō* (思想), no. 1053 (2012): 117–43.

Nakayama, Nobuji. *Buddhism, Nishida & Tanabe Philosophy: On Tanabe's Criticisms of Nishida Philosophy and the Teachings of Shinran*. Tokyo: Risōsha, 1956.

Nawata, Yūji (縄田雄二). "Tanabe Hajime's Telegraph to Karl Jaspers" (田辺元のカール・ヤスパース宛電報). In *Shisō* (思想), no. 1053 (2012): 217–18.

Nelson, Eric S. "Heidegger, Misch, and the Origins of Philosophy." In *European and Chinese Philosophy: Origins and Intersections*, edited by Chung-ying Cheng, Eric Nelson and Lyinyu Gu, 10–30. Chichester, West Sussex: John Wiley & Sons, 2013.

Neville, Robert Cummings. "William Desmond's Philosophical Theology." *Louvain Studies* 36 (2012): 239–255.

Nishida, Kitarō. *An Inquiry into the Good*. Translated by Masao Abe and Christopher Ives. New Haven, CT; London: Yale University Press, 1990.

Nishida, Kitarō *Intuition and Reflection in Self-Consciousness*. Translated by Valdo H. Viglielmo, Takeuchi Yoshinori, and Joseph S. O'Leary. Albany: State University of New York Press, 1987.

Nishitani, Keiji. *Nishida Kitarō: His Life and Thought* (西田幾多郎：その人と思想). Tokyo: Chikuma Shobō, 1984.

Nishitani, Keiji. "Reflections on Two Addresses by Martin Heidegger." In *Heidegger and Asian Thought*, edited by Graham Parkes, 145–54. Honolulu: University of Hawai'i Press, 1987.

Nishitani, Keiji *Religion and Nothingness*. Translated by Jan Van Bragt. Berkley; Los Angeles; London: University of California Press, 1982.

O'Regan, Cyril. *Heterodox Hegel*. Albany: State University of New York Press, 1994.

O'Regan, Cyril. "The Impossibility of a Christian Reading of the Phenomenology of Spirit: H.S. Harris on Hegel's Liquidation of Christianity." *The Owl of Minerva* 33, no. 1 (2001-2): 45–95.

O'Regan, Cyril. "Repetition: Desmond's New Science." In *Between System and Poetics: William Desmond and Philosophy after Dialectic*, edited by Thomas A.F. Kelly, 65–94. Aldershot: Ashgate, 2007.

Ozaki, Makoto. *Individuum, Society, Human Kind: The Triadic Logic of Species According to Hajime Tanabe*. Leiden: Brill, 2001.

Parkes, Graham. "The Definite Internationalism of the Kyoto School: Changing Attitudes in the Contemporary Academy." In *Re-Politicising The Kyoto School as Philosophy*, edited by Christopher Goto-Jones, 161–82. London; New York: Routledge, 2008.

Parkes, Graham, ed. *Heidegger and Asian Thought*. Honolulu: University of Hawai'i Press, 1987.

Parkes, Graham. "Rising Sun over Black Forest: Heidegger's Japanese Connections." In *Heidegger's Hidden Sources: East Asian Influences on His Work*. Written by Reinhard May and translated by Graham Parkes, 79–118. London; New York: Routledge, 1996.

Pickstock, Cathrine. "What Shines Between: The Metaxu of Light." In *Between System and Poetics: William Desmond and Philosophy after Dialectic*, edited by Thomas A.F. Kelly, 107–22. Aldershot: Ashgate, 2007.

Plato. *Phaedrus*. Translated by Alexander Nehamas and Paul Woodruff. Indianapolis, IN: Hackett Publishing Company, 1995.

Plato. *Republic*. Translated by Joe Sachs. Newburyport, MA: Focus Publishing, 2007.

Pöggler, Otto. "West-East Dialogue: Heidegger and Lao-tzu." In *Heidegger and Asian Thought*, edited by Graham Parkes, 47–78. Honolulu: University of Hawai'i Press, 1987.

Pye, Michael, ed. *Listening to Shin Buddhism: Starting Points of Modern Dialogue*. Sheffield: Equinox Publishing, 2012.

Pye, Michael, ed. "Shinran's World: A Dialogue of Shin Buddhism and Zen Buddhism: Nishitani Keiji (moderator) with Suzuki Saisetsu, Kaneko Daiei and Soga Ryōjin." In *Listening to Shin Buddhism: Starting Points of Modern Dialogue*, 233–76. Sheffield: Equinox Publishing, 2012.

Rahula, Walpola. *What the Buddha Taught*. London; Bedford: The Gordon Fraser Gallery Ltd., 1959.

Ranke, Leopold von. *The General Outline of the World History: Modern Eras* (世界史概観：近世史の諸時代) Translated by Suzuki Shigetaka and Aihara Shinsaku. Tokyo: Iwanami Shoten, 1941.

Ranke, Leopold von. *Über die Epochen der neueren Geschichte: Vorträge dem Konige Maximilian II. von Bayern im Herbst 1854 zu Berchtesgaden Gehalten*. Leipzig: Duncker & Humblot, 1906.

Rilke, Rainer Maria. "Archaic Torso of Apollo." In *Ahead of All Parting: The Selected Poetry and Prose of Rainer Maria Rilke*, translated by Stephen Mitchell, 67–68. New York; Toronto: Random House, 1995.

Rinaldi, Giacomo. "Metaphysics as a Cultural Presence: Dialectical and Metaxological Thought in the Philosophy of William Desmond." In *Being and Dialectic: Metaphysics as a Cultural Presence*, edited by William Desmond and Joseph Grange, 155–78. Albany: State University of New York Press, 2000.

Sakai, Naoki. "The Kyoto School Philosophy under the Pax Americana" (パックス・アメリカーナの下での京都学派の哲学). In *"Overcoming of Modernity" and the Kyoto School: Modernity, Empire and Universality* (「近代の超克」と京都学派：近代性・帝国・普遍性), edited by Sakai Naoki, Isomae Junichi and translated by Takahashi Hara, 3–28. Tokyo: Ibunsha, 2010.

Sakai, Naoki. "Resistance to Conclusion: The Kyoto School Philosophy under the *Pax Americana*." In *Re-Politicising The Kyoto School as Philosophy*, edited by Christopher Goto-Jones, 183–98. London; New York: Routledge, 2008.

Sasaki, Genjun (佐々木現順). *From Theravada Buddhism to Mahayana Buddhism* (原始仏教から大乗仏教へ). Tokyo: Shimizu Kōbundō, 1978.

Schmidt, Lars-Henrik. "Commonness across Culture." In *Cross-Cultural Conversation: Initiation*, edited by Anindita Niyogi Baslev, 119–32. Atlanta: Scholar Press, 1996.

Shakespeare, William. *Hamlet*. Edited by Joseph Pearce. San Francisco, CA: Ignatius Press, 2008.

Shaw, Christopher David. *On Exceeding Determination and the Idea of Reason: Immanuel Kant, William Desmond, and the Noumenological Principle*. Newcastle: Cambridge Scholar Publishing, 2012.

Shimomura, Toratarō (下村寅太郎). "The Development and the Character of Tanabe Philosophy" (田辺哲学の発展とその性格). In Vol. 12 of *The Collected Works of Shimomura Toratarō* (下村寅太郎著作集), 333–53. Tokyo: Misuzu Shobō, 1990.

Simpson, Christopher Ben. Religion, Metaphysics, and the Postmodern: William Desmond and John D. Caputo. Indianapolis: Indiana University Press, 2009.

Smid, Robert W. *Methodologies of Comparative Philosophy: The Pragmatist and Process Traditions*. Albany: State University of New York Press, 2009.

Solzhenitsyn, Alexander. Mikhail Agursky, A.B., Evgeny Barabanov, Vadim Borisov, F. Korsakov, and Igor Shafarevich. *From under the Rubble*. Translated by Michael Scammel. London: Little, Brown and Co., 1975.

Solzhenitsyn, Alexander I. *The First Circle*. Translated by Thomas P. Whitney. Evanston, IL: Northwestern University Press, 1997.

Solzhenitsyn, Alexander I. *In The First Circle*. Translated by Harry T. Willets. New York: HarperCollins, 2009.

Standaert, Nicolas. "Don't Mind the Gap: Sinology as an Art of In-Betweenness." In *Philosophy Compass* 10 (2015): 91–103.

Stevens, Bernard. *Le Néant Évidé: Ontologie Et Politique Chez Keiji Nishitani*. Louvain; Paris: Peeters, 2003.

Sugimoto, Kōichi. "Tanabe Hajime's Logic of Species and the Philosophy of Nishida Kitarō: A Critical Dialogue within the Kyoto School." In *Japanese and Continental Philosophy: Conversations with the Kyoto School*, edited by Bret W. Davis, Brian Schroeder and Jason M. Wirth, 52–70. Bloomington, IN: Indiana University Press, 2011.

Surber, Jere O'Neill. "Metaxological Metaphysics and Idiotic Sytle: The 'Conceptual Persona' of William Desmond." *Between System and Poetics: William Desmond and Philosophy after Dialectic*, edited by Thomas A. F. Kelly, 53–64. Aldershot: Ashgate, 2007.

Suzuki, Daisetsu Teitarō. *The Japanese Mind: Essentials of Japanese Philosophy and Culture*. Edited by Charles A. Moore. Honolulu: University of Hawai'i Press, 1978.

Suzuki, Noboru. "The System of Knowledge and the Unity of Science in Nishi Amane's Philosophy: In Search of the Sketch toward Synthetization." In *Nishi Amane and Japanese Modernity* (西周と日本の近代), edited by the Nishi Amane Study Group of the Shimane Prefectural University, 282–323. Tokyo: Perikansha, 2005.

Taguchi Shigeru (田口茂). "The Logic of *Tenkan*: The Generation of Tanabean Thinking and 'Logic as Ethics'" (「転換」の論理：田辺的思考の生成と〈倫理としての論理〉). *Shisō* (思想), no. 1053 (2012): 144–64.

Takeuchi Yoshinori (武内義範). *Philosophy of Kyōgyōshinshō* (教行信証の哲学) Kyoto: Hōzōkan, 2002.

Unno, Taitetsu and James W. Heisig, eds. *The Religious Philosophy of Tanabe Hajime*. Berkley, CA: Asian Humanities Press, 1990.

White, Richard. "Schopenhauer and Indian Philosophy: On the Limits of Comparative Thought." In *International Philosophical Quarterly* 50, no. 1 (2010): 57–76.

Wilde, Oscar. *The Picture of Dorian Gray*. Oxford: Oxford University Press, 2006.

Williams, Rowan. *Dostoevsky: Language, Faith, and Fiction*. London: Continuum, 2009.

Yuasa, Yasuo. "The Encounter of Modern Japanese Philosophy with Heidegger." In *Heidegger and Asian Thought*, edited by Graham Parkes, 155–74. Honolulu: University of Hawai'i Press, 1987.

Yuien (唯円). *Tannishō* (歎異抄). Edited by Kaneko Daiei. Tokyo: Iwanami Shoten, 1931.

Zhang, Wei. *Heidegger, Rorty, and the Eastern Thinkers: A Hermeneutics of Cross-Cultural Understanding*. Albany: State University of New York Press, 2006.

Index

Akunin jōbutsu (悪人成仏) 140
Akunin shōki (悪人正機) 140, 173-4, 176, 179-80, 184
Amazon.com 102
Ames, Roger 16
Aristotle 102
Augustine 1, 54, 82, 87, 97, 102, 118, 128
autonomy. *See also* self, self-power
    of reason 8, 82

Becker, Oscar 4
between. See also metaxology
    aida (あいだ) or *ma* (間) 50
Bible 80, 119, 125, 127, 130, 146, 190
bonbu (凡夫) 162, 173, 175-6, 178-9, 190
Buddha 127, 128, 145, 159, 172, 175, 176-7
    Amida 140, 161, 163, 164, 167, 169, 170, 173, 178-9, 182
    Tathāgata 155, 164, 167, 171-2, 175, 177, 178-9, 182
Burik, Steven 23

China
    Chinese philosophy 21, 23, 24, 25
    Ming dynasty 37
    Quing dynasty 37
Christianity 71, 137, 141, 145-7, 172
comparative philosophy vi, viii, xi-xii, 1-3, 6-7, 8-10, 15-17, 21-6, 28-9, 31-2, 35-40, 46, 49, 53, 55-7, 141-2, 146, 188, 191
compassion, viii, xi, 20, 35-6, 51-7, 107, 111, 123, 127-9, 134, 163-6, 168-9, 173-80, 182-7, 189-90
    Great-negation-qua-great- (*daihi-soku daihi*, 大非即大悲) 51, 184
    self-negating 53-4, 56, 166, 174, 178, 185, 189, 190

Davis, Bret W. 8, 25
Decartes, Rene 18, 29, 37, 150

Cartesian Metaphysics 27, 28, 88, 89
deconstructionism 25, 30
Derrida, Jacques 23, 25, 28, 30, 36
Desmond, William
    Being and the Between vi, 4, 93, 98
    Ethics and the Between 4, 68
    God and the Between 4, 115, 190
    Hegel's God 121
    Perplexity and Ultimacy 93
dialectic(al)
    absolute 45, 46-9, 52, 53, 55, 137, 139, 141, 149, 154, 155, 174
    Hegelian 32, 49, 51, 74, 88-9, 105, 139, 149, 152
    and history 33
    instrumentalization/extirpation of the single individual 33, 75-6, 92, 94, 121, 183-4
    self-mediation 18, 27-8, 34, 55, 73, 75-7, 80-1, 165
dialogue
    intercultural 2, 36
    interreligious 36, 113-14, 141, 145, 171
di Giovanni, George 93
Dōgen (道元) 7, 145
Dostoyevsky, Fyodor Mikhailovich 94, 100, 107-8, 118, 126, 128, 190, 191

empiricism 27
emptiness. *See* nothingness
enlightenment 42
equivocity 18, 34
eros
    erotic sovereign 123, 126
    erotics of selving 101, 103, 104, 126
    erotic universal 50
eternity 33, 42-3, 51-2
Eurocentrism 2, 17, 21, 23, 25, 33, 36, 55, 56
European Network of Japanese Philosophy (ENOJP) xii
existentialism 30, 45

Fichte, Johann Gottlieb 37

Gadamer, Hans-Georg 22
gedatsu (解脱) 159–60
generosity. *See* love
gensō (還相) 51, 170, 172, 174, 176, 177
    ekō (還相回向) 51, 169, 175–6
genus 48–51, 53, 138
German idealism 4–5, 41, 46, 151
givenness
    of being 26, 28, 34, 35, 88, 97–9, 106, 109–10, 131
    of self 34, 88, 90, 108, 123–5, 127, 130, 186
God vii, xii, 1, 3–4, 9, 50, 64–8, 71–2, 74–80, 82, 87–9, 97, 99, 113, 115–17, 119–23, 129, 132, 142–3, 147, 171–2, 175, 182, 184, 189–90
Godlessness 9, 87, 89, 97, 189
Greek philosophy 24–5

Hall, David 16
Hegel, Georg Wilhelm Friedrich 37, 41, 45–6, 49, 53, 91, 94, 115, 138, 139, 144, 150, 151, 153, 171. *See also* dialectic(al)
    absolute spirit 74–5, 79, 81, 129, 131, 138
    Lectures on the Philosophy of Religion 71–2, 78
    and non-Western philosophy 21, 32
    Phenomenology of Spirit viii, 15, 76, 77, 93, 151, 153
    and philosophy of history 33, 42, 44, 91
    and philosophy of religion 8, 61–2, 72–4, 79–81, 82–3, 88, 100, 110, 115, 134, 155, 176, 183
    Philosophy of Right 77–8
    self-consciousness 74, 76, 79, 81
    state 77–8, 79
Heidegger, Martin 4, 22, 23, 28, 30, 36, 38, 149, 155, 177
Heisig, James W. 139
Heraclitus 18
Hockings, William Earnest 16
Hōnen (法然) 163
hongan (本願). *See* Original Vow
Hugo, Victor 119, 125, 126, 128, 130, 190
Husserl, Edmund 4, 22, 28, 29, 30, 36

imitatio Dei 124, 170, 189
Indian philosophy 21, 22–3, 25
individual
    single viii, 9–11, 20, 29, 32, 34, 43, 48, 50–1, 53–4, 62–3, 68–70, 75–7, 82–3, 87–96, 98–100, 108, 109–11, 118, 120–1, 125, 127, 129, 130–4, 173–6, 178–80, 185–6, 188
Ireland 93

Japan 108
    Buddhism 38, 51, 145
    philosophy xii, 23, 33, 37–8, 155
    and *sakoku* (鎖国) 37
    and Tokugawa Shogunate 37
    and ultra-nationalism/Japonism 33, 55
Jaspers, Karl 22, 25
jiriki (自力). *See* self, self-power

Kant, Immanuel 37, 41, 45–6, 53, 138, 139, 144, 150, 151, 153
    divine absolute 66–7, 120, 131
    ethics 62–3, 74, 110, 120, 129–30, 140, 171
    philosophy of religion 8, 61–2, 63–4, 71–2, 81–3, 88–9, 91, 100, 110, 115, 134, 155, 176
    and the problems of the philosophy of religion 66–9, 70
    rational faith 64–6, 120, 158, 183
    unity of reason 29, 68, 88, 139, 149
kenosis 118, 119, 132, 147, 163, 164, 166, 167, 174, 179, 182, 184
Kierkegaard, Søren Aabye viii, 9–11, 45, 61, 82, 92, 119, 127, 130, 170, 171
    critique of Kantian and Hegelian philosophy of religion 61–62, 82, 91, 144, 153, 156, 176
    and the parable of mother and child 127, 130, 170–1, 183
Korean philosophy 2, 4, 23
Kōyama Iwao 140
kū-u (空有) *See* nothingness, realization/manifestation of
Kyoto School 3, 37, 41, 144

Larger Sutra 169
Leibniz, Gottfried Wilhelm 18, 29
Lewis, C.S. 99, 118, 123

love
  act of 51, 52, 119, 125, 141, 164, 165, 168–9, 172, 175–6, 177–8, 190
  (net)works of 119, 141, 168, 170, 174, 176, 184, 187
  nothingness-qua- 165, 184
  selflessness/no-self 56, 128, 168

Mahāyāna Buddhism 7, 11, 48, 50, 69, 137, 139, 141–7, 155, 159–61, 177, 180, 182, 189
  Dhammapada 142
  Mahāsaṃipāta Sutra 159, 160
Mall, Ram Adhar 22, 23, 39
Meditation sutra 169
metanoesis 170, 172, 174–5, 178–9. *See also* dialectic, absolute dialectic
  absolute crisis 151, 158
  absolute critique 149, 151, 152, 158, 163, 165, 170, 184
  absolute mediation viii, 49–51, 163, 165–6, 169, 174, 182
  metanoeite vii
  metanoetics vi–vii, ix, 4, 11, 39, 41, 51, 57, 61, 83, 137, 139, 141, 147, 155, 170, 178, 182, 189
  transition/conversation/transformation (*tenkan* 転換) 44–5, 46–7, 51, 52, 53, 54, 55, 56, 128, 168, 172, 173, 176, 181, 184
metaxology
  agapeic astonishment 26, 88, 94, 125
  agapeic mindfulness 34–5, 55–6, 123–4, 134, 181
  agapeic origin 5, 87, 90, 100, 113, 116–17, 121–4, 125, 128, 130, 182, 187–8
  agapeic service 107, 111, 117, 119, 123, 125, 128, 132, 184, 191
  agapeic transcendence/transcending 105–6, 109, 114, 117, 119, 122, 125, 182, 184, 187
  and the between (*metaxu*) 5, 19, 34, 181
  and communivocity 20, 30, 101
  compassio essendi 107, 108–9, 110–11, 129, 132
  conatus essendi 90, 106–7, 108–9, 110–11, 126–7, 129, 132

  and critique of modern philosophy 29
  and critique of post-modern thinkers 28
  and doubleness 20, 34, 87, 101, 104, 106
  fourfold sense of being 5, 18–21, 141
  hyperboles of being 88, 89–91, 99, 103, 113, 121, 133
  idiocy 91–2, 93, 110, 131, 184–5
  intermediation 19, 101, 117
  intimate strangeness 19, 35, 96, 101, 106, 117, 132, 183
  intimate universal 90, 113, 115, 131–2, 189
  inward otherness 34, 96
  overdetermination/ontological surplus 34, 88, 92, 94, 96, 99, 104, 106, 110, 114, 117, 119, 122, 131–2, 184
  passio essendi 90, 96, 98, 106–7, 110, 114, 126, 132
  plurivocity of being 20–21
  porosity 87, 90, 96, 107, 109–10
  posthumous thinking 91, 92, 94, 96, 121, 124, 130–1, 133
  selving 87, 91, 101, 104, 106, 110, 114, 117, 123, 127, 162
  sense of creation 97–8
Miki, Kiyoshi 5
modern philosophy 53
  subject 28, 30, 45–6
mo-fa (*mappō* 末法) 159, 189
  the age of right dharma 159
  the age of semblance dharma 159–60
  the latter age of dharma 159, 160–1, 162, 189
mysticism 155, 156–7, 159, 177

Netherlands 38
  Dutch East India Company 37
Neville, Robert C. 16
Nietzsche, Friedrich Wilhelm 18, 45
  and non-Western philosophy 21
nirvana 143–4, 155, 159, 168, 175, 177, 178
Nishi, Amane (西周) 38
  Hyakuichi Shinron (百一新論) 38
Nishida, Kitarō (西田幾多郎) 4, 8, 137, 138, 145, 155, 177
  An Inquiry into the Good 38

Nishitani, Keiji (西谷啓治) 5
Northrop, Filmer S.C. 16
nothingness 48, 50, 51–3, 54, 56, 118, 133, 139, 141, 152, 154–5, 163–4, 164–5, 167, 170, 173–4, 175–6, 177, 182
    act of 51, 52, 168, 172, 183–4
    realization/manifestation of 52, 164, 165, 168, 170, 172, 175, 176, 177, 179, 183–4

Ōmori, Shōzō (大森荘蔵) 7
orientalism 145, 153
Original Vow (*hongan* 本願) 140, 155, 163
ōsō (往相) 51, 170, 173, 175
    ekō (回向) 51, 169
    -qua-gensō (往相即還相) 168, 170, 172–3, 178, 187
other-power 140, 155, 163, 164, 165, 173, 175, 177, 178

Parmenides 18, 26
Persia 25
phenomenology 30, 151
Plato 25, 93, 95, 149
    Apology 93
    Phaedrus 105
    Republic 144, 190
postmodernity 40–1, 44, 45, 103
prayer 172–3
Pure Land/Shin Buddhism 51, 140, 145, 147, 163, 167, 172, 177–8

Rahula, Walpola 142–3, 157, 176
Ranke, Leopold von 42, 43, 46, 52
rationalism 27, 49, 53
Riehl, Alois 3
Rilke, Rainer Maria 100
Rousseau, Jean-Jacques 37

St. Francis 127
St. Paul 158
Sartre, Jean-Paul 115
Schelling, Friedrich Wilhelm Joseph 37, 152
Schopenhauer, Arthur
    And non-Western philosophy 21
Second World War 4, 138, 141, 161
self. *See also* dialectic, and self-mediation; modern philosophy, subject; love, selflessness/no-self

-power 155, 157, 158, 161, 164, 165, 170, 172, 173, 177, 178
-power-qua-other-power 164, 170
sentient beings 160, 163, 165, 166, 169, 170, 175, 177, 182, 186
Shakespeare, William 102
Shinran (親鸞) 145, 161, 163
    Kyōgyōshinshō (教行信証) 160
    Mappōtōmyōki (末法燈明記) 160
    Tannishō (歎異抄) 140
Smid, Robert W. 16
Socrates 93, 104
Soga, Ryōjin (曽我量深) 145
Solnit, Rebecca x
Solzhenitsyn, Alexander 6, 100, 190
species 48, 50, 53, 57, 138
    logic of 5, 48–9, 138, 139, 141, 174
Steuco, Agostino 22
Śūnyatā. *See* nothingness
Suzuki, D.T. 145

Takeuchi, Yoshinori 145, 160
Tanabe, Hajime vi, 1, 4, 6, 137, 181
    Dialectic of Christianity 138, 141
    Dialectic of the Theory of Relativity 138
    "Either Ontology of Life or Dialectic of Death" 138
    Existence, Love, and Practice 138, 141, 150, 152
    Hegel's Philosophy and Dialectic 46, 138
    The Historical Development of Mathematics 138
    Introduction to Philosophy 138
    Kant's Theory of Teleology 46–7, 138
    Logic of Species 41, 48, 138, 161
    "Memento Mori" 138
    A Memorandum on Mallarmé 138
    Philosophy as Metanoetics vi, 4, 47–8, 138, 141, 157, 161, 190
    Philosophy of Art in Paul Valéry 138
    "Requesting the Teaching of Nishida" 138
    The Urgent Mission of Political Philosophy 138
tariki (他力). *See* other-Power
Tetsugaku (哲学) 37, 38. *See also* Japan, philosophy

Theravada Buddhism 142, 146, 157, 176–7
time 23, 33, 44, 46–8, 51–2, 95, 99, 132, 162
Tosaka, Jun (戸坂潤) 5
transcendence
   divine 9, 10–11, 62, 63, 67, 80, 87–8, 99–101, 107, 109–11, 113, 115–17, 120–2, 129, 131–3, 144, 156, 167–8, 177–8, 182–5, 188–9
   eclipse of divine 9, 87, 131, 144, 178

The United States (U.S.) vi, x, 4, 93, 108
univocity
   mathesis universalis 18
   natural number 18
   unifying intelligibility 28–32, 34
   the univocal sense of being 26
upāya (hōben 方便) 165–6, 173

Weiss, Paul 26, 88
Wilde, Oscar 104
Williams, Rowan 107
will to power 43–4, 51, 90
Wittgenstein, Ludwig 7
world philosophies 53–4, 55

Xiāngyán Zhixián (香嚴智閑) 128

Zange(dō) (懺悔(道)). *See* metanoesis; metanoetics; transition/conversation/transformation (*tenkan* 転換)
Zen x, xi, 8, 145, 155, 157, 159, 177